Critical Issues in Social Theory

Critical Issues
in Social Theory

John K. Rhoads

THE PENNSYLVANIA STATE UNIVERSITY PRESS
University Park, Pennsylvania

Library of Congress Cataloging-in-Publication Data

Rhoads, John K.
Critical issues in social theory / John K. Rhoads:

   p.   cm.
Includes bibliographical references.
ISBN 0-271-00709-5
1. Sociology I. Title.
HM24.R485 1990
301—dc20   90–6873

Copyright © 1991 The Pennsylvania State University
All rights reserved
Printed in the United States of America

It is the policy of the Pennsylvania State University Press to use acid-free paper for the
first printing of all clothbound books. Publications on uncoated stock satisfy the
minimum requirements of American National Standard for Information Sciences—
Permanence of Paper for Printed Library Materials, ANSI Z39.48–1984.

To my wife and to my mother

Contents

Introduction   1

PART ONE: THE SCIENTIFIC CHARACTER OF SOCIAL THEORY

1   Social Theory According to Positivism   7

    Comte Lays the Foundations   9
    Durkheim's Positivism   13
    Weber on Causality and Ethical Neutrality   19
    Law and System According to Parsons   22
    Homans on the Nature of Science   26
    Merton on the Nature of Social Theory   32
    Positivist Social Theory   35

2   Social Theory According to Antipositivism   39

    The Antipositivist Methodology of Max Weber   40
    Ideal-Type and Analytical Concept: Weber and Parsons   48
    Concept Formation According to Schutz   50
    The Indexical Expression in Ethnomethodology   56

viii   Contents

Habermas's Critique of Positivism	60
The Hermeneutical Circle Reexamined	67
The Issue Reconsidered: Type Versus Class	69

PART TWO: THE BASIC UNITS OF SOCIAL THEORY

3	Methodological Structuralism	75

The Structuralism of the Social Fact	76
Suicide	80
Methodological Structuralism in Marx	84
Revolution in Paris, 1848	89
Organism, Personality, Society, and Culture in Parsons's Action System	91
The Functions of the Social System	94
Modern Medical Practice	99
Merton on Anomie	102
Capitalism as System	106
Crisis Tendencies in Advanced Capitalism	109
Methodological Structuralism	112

4	Methodological Individualism	117

Tarde Disputes Durkheim	118
The Forms According to Simmel	122
Individuality	125
The Development of Individuality	128
Weber the Individualist	132
Homans Brings Men Back In	135
The Phenomenology of the Integrative Function	139
The Issue Reconsidered: The Reification of Structure	145

PART THREE: RULES AND SOCIAL ORDER

5	The Normative Order	155

Comte on Morality and Religion	156
Durkheim Defines Morality	160
The Legitimate Order According to Weber	166
Norms and Values in the Social System	173

Habermas on the Legitimation of Norms	178
Theory of the Normative Order	182

6 The Construction of Order — 185

Mead's Reconstruction of the Act	186
The Ethnomethodological Conception of Rules	190
Bentham's Theory of Order	196
Spencer's Law of Equal Freedom	201
Functionalist Critiques of the Utilitarian Theory of Order	204
Utilitarianism in Homans's Exchange Theory	207
The Issue Reconsidered: Duty and Interest	214

PART FOUR: THE DUALITY OF CONSENSUS AND CONFLICT

7 Consensus — 221

Collective Conscience and Representation in Durkheim	222
Consensus in the Social System	228
The Dyad	228
Instrumental Activism in America	230
Religion in the Social System	232
Equilibrium	233
Power and Polity	235
The Societal Community	240
Social Evolution	245
Concluding Remarks on Parsons	247
Consensus and Symbol According to Mead	247
Intersubjectivity in Schutz's Phenomenology	249
The Role of Consensus	254

8 Conflict — 257

The Hobbesian State of Nature	258
Marx and Conflict	263
Conflict in the Division of Labor	263
Social Class	265
The State	268
Ideology	270
Revolution	272

x   Contents

Marxism and Functionalism	274
Status Groups as Conflict Units	277
Dahrendorf's Critique of Parsons	280
Dahrendorf's Theory of Class Conflict	282
Legitimation as Domination	288
Collins's Conflict Sociology	292
Functions of Conflict	298
The Issue Reconsidered: Power and Authority	300

9	The Limits of Rationality	307
	The Limits of Positivism Again	308
	Rationality and the Reification of Social Structure	311
	Rationality and Consensus	314
	Novelty and Rationality	317
	Legitimacy and the Limits of Rationality	321

Notes	323
Index	367

Introduction

Some years ago I set out to compare the various groups of ideas that sociologists recognize as general theories in their discipline. The objective was suggested by Thomas S. Kuhn's tantalizing conjecture in his influential book *The Structure of Scientific Revolutions* that scientific paradigms might well be emerging in parts of the social sciences.[1] Kuhn held that normal, puzzle-solving science relating to a given part of nature is conducted by a community of scientists within the framework of a paradigm—a set of beliefs that define the essential characteristics of the domain of investigation. Could a single paradigm be found in sociology through an analysis of the concepts, definitions, and generalizations within the relatively small number of social theories?

It soon became apparent, however, that the task of finding such a paradigm was foundering on the presence of contradictions. These tend to fall into two classes. First, some of them simply reflect opposing notions about such matters as the nature of societies and how they relate to individuals. Such contradictions arise simply from a conflict of scientific opinion. Second, others stem from contradictory dimensions of the social domain, which become manifest in theoretical contrasts as the result of the selectivity exercised by social theorists. It is conceivable that these contradictions are logically reconcilable, but those falling into the first category are not.

The recognition of such contradictions gave birth to the idea of a

2 Introduction

critical issue in social theory. In ordinary discourse the word *issue* means a controversy consisting of two opposing sides that offer the possibility of choice. In the context of this work this definition is broadened to include some closely related possibilities. Consequently, the issues in social theory fall into three categories. The first includes arguments between parties who are aware of each other, as illustrated by the debate between Tarde and Durkheim. The second includes "one-way" arguments, in which one thinker criticizes the ideas of another and opposes his own ideas to them. The criticisms Durkheim leveled at Spencer's utilitarianism are an example. The third category includes ideas whose contrasts in the works of social theorists are recognized and explicated by an observer, who thereby contributes to the constitution of an issue. Parsons's formulation of the Hobbesian problem of order illustrates this type. As the following analysis will show, all three kinds of issues can be found in social theories.

The word *critical* denotes that which is important, crucial, or decisive. Something is crucial in the sense that it is a juncture or turning point. Hence, an issue critical to social theory denotes a controversy whose opposing sides form important junctures that divide various theories. In this context, the term *important* is given meaning by the recurrence of the issues in the reasoning of thinkers whom sociologists consider important—thinkers like Comte, Marx, Spencer, Durkheim, Weber, and Parsons, whose ideas are believed to have contributed substantially to the sociological tradition. It follows, therefore, that the importance of a critical issue in social theory is measured by the attention given to it by important thinkers and by the manner in which it sets them in opposition to one another.

These broad criteria in the definition of *critical issue* have led me to distinguish four critical issues. The first is the controversy over whether the construction of social theory is amenable to the model of the natural sciences. To what extent can social theory be scientific in a strict sense? The second is the question of whether societies have an existence that is not totally reducible to the characteristics of individuals or whether they are merely abstractions from the latter. What is the nature of the fundamental units upon which social theories are built? The third is whether social order is the consequence of rules or the product of ongoing constructions. What is the ultimate ground of social order? The fourth is whether consensus or conflict dominates human relationships.

Which is more important? The first of these issues is methodological, the second is conceptual, and the last two are substantive.

The significance of these issues becomes clearer when one considers the specific dimensions they involve. The practicality of the positivist model for social theory, for example, involves the question of whether a different logical system and constructs with different logical properties than the class logic of natural science are appropriate for the understanding of subjective meanings, or does the unity of science, as Comte insisted, entail a unity of methods, only slightly amended to take into account the greater complexity of social factors? The vexing problem of the relationship between individuals and society is reflected in the problem of the relationship between microsocial and macrosocial theories. Can we make valid inferences from one level to the other, or do ontological differences place severe restrictions on knowledge about social structures based on knowledge about individuals, as Durkheim claimed? With regard to the relation of rules to social order, we find Durkheim and Parsons defending the role of morality in opposition to the utilitarians, who advocate the integrating role of self-interest rationally sought. Overlapping this issue is the controversy over the roles of consensus and conflict. Which is of greater import, for example, agreement about rules and the values they reflect or conflicts over them?

I do not claim to have exhausted the set of critical issues in social theory. It is obvious that different analyses would reveal others. Indeed, the literature abounds in analyses of theoretical controversies. Nonetheless, I contend that these are important in the sense already defined and long-standing as well, reaching far back into the history of social thought and appearing in presociological as well as sociological contexts.

The materials upon which the following analysis is based are mostly the relevant notions of influential sociologists and a few social philosophers (for example, Thomas Hobbes), most of the latter having written before the rise of academic sociology. I will attempt to explicate the influences that particular positions on controversial issues had for the thinkers' overall approaches and on the manner in which they approached certain problems. Their theoretical expressions, consequently, are not treated in their totality, but only as they relate to the issues under consideration.

It is conceivable that the positions set forth in this book could have been constructed in terms of a slightly different selection of thinkers. Those considered, however, were chosen on the basis that their ideas,

4   Introduction

when combined into a synthesis, provide the sharpest and most complete delineation. I have expressed the issues as ideal-types—synthetic constructs which the formulations of different writers merely approximate, for the diversity of these formulations defies rigid, classlike categorization.

When I referred at the outset to general theories, I had in mind functionalism, conflict, symbolic interactionism, phenomenology, ethnomethodology, exchange, and critical theory. Although the facts on which my analyses are based are the relevant notions of individual writers, they can be thought of as representatives of these theories. And although the protagonists have come forth with different versions of the same theory and in some cases one thinker can be identified with more than one theory, wide consensus exists concerning which theories the writers are primarily identified with. Talcott Parsons, for example, is almost the personification of functionalism; George H. Mead's ideas are recognized as a foundation of symbolic interactionism; and Alfred Schutz is generally acknowledged as a key figure in phenomenological social theory.

Despite the fact that this is a book about social theory, I believe theory is a means rather than an end in itself. Therefore, I have presented in the light of each controversy my own conclusions, the aim being to say something both true and interesting not only about the theoretical enterprise itself but also about society, which, after all, is the object of social theorizing. These conclusions are not precise, unambiguous solutions to the problems entailed in the issues; nevertheless, a clear juxtaposition of the contradictory stands has led me to certain insights. The thinker I have relied on most in these attempts at understanding is Max Weber, whose work has exerted so great an influence on the sociological enterprise. The concluding chapter explicates various strands of thought running through the issues that reveal a startling convergence—the tension between rational thinking and factors that restrict it. This theme reveals that faith in the rule of reason must be qualified by recognition of irrationality as an unavoidable counterpoise.

PART ONE

The Scientific Character of Social Theory

Social Theory According to Positivism

In 1651 the English philosopher Thomas Hobbes wrote the following:

> *Science* is the knowledge of consequences, and dependence of one fact upon another; by which . . . we know how to do something else when we will, or the like another time; because when we see how anything comes about, upon what causes, and by what manner; when the like causes come into our power, we see how to make it produce the like effects.[1]

A little further on he outlined the sciences of his time and included politics, which he defined as the consequences of the commonwealth for the rights and duties of the sovereign.[2] Two important observations can be made about the foregoing: First, science appealed to Hobbes because it states the causes and consequences of things, a knowledge of which enables human beings to intervene in the conditions of their existence. Second, he thought of politics as a science along with mathematics, astronomy, geography, and meteorology.

Hobbes was one of a long line of thinkers who believed in the possibility of a science of the social according to the model of the science of the material. As is well known, mathematics and mechanics cast a spell over the minds of literate people of the seventeenth century and were held up as models for the sciences of human nature.

8   The Scientific Character of Social Theory

In line with these developments, the relationship of sociology to the natural sciences was on the minds of the discipline's founders; and the vision of a science of society acted as a powerful impulse to bring the new field into existence. As the science of society, sociology was to be defined in terms of the logical criteria of the science of the physical, and the spirit of Newton still influences sociological texts on how to study social phenomena scientifically and how to build scientific social theories. Many sociologists believe either that a truly scientific sociology is possible or that it has been achieved, but still requires a great deal of refinement.

The scientific or *positivist* conception as a practical ideal for all those disciplines dealing with human beings has not gone unchallenged, however. Kant laid the basis for a distinction between natural and spiritual events and asserted that human beings participate in both. According to him, persons as material beings can be studied according to the canons of natural sciences; but as creatures of ideas they can be studied only by the methods of speculative philosophy. The study of what is distinctive to human beings cannot follow a natural-science model. Consequently, for want of a better term, an *antipositivist* conception of social science was developed in the post-Kantian era.[3] Therein lies the basis of the critical issue analyzed in this and the following chapter.

Sociology in America has been generally more sympathetic to the positivist than to the antipositivist side of the controversy.[4] The dominance of positivism has even hindered debate. But within the last two decades or so, some long-held views have come under scrutiny, and the controversy has been rekindled.

This chapter fashions a conception of scientific social theory in its purely formal dimensions through a synthesis of the relevant ideas in the discussions of a small number of prominent social theorists. Although four of the six, namely, Comte, Durkheim, Parsons, and Merton, are identified with functionalism, this theory cannot claim a monopoly on the positivist approach; for positivism has influenced nearly all of the other general theories considered in this work. The choice of the theorists whose ideas are analyzed in this chapter is dictated by two considerations. First, their methodological discussions are detailed. Second, they actually attempted to apply their methodological principles to their theoretical constructions.

The complexity of the overall positivist conception accounts for the fact that different writers have focused on different logical dimensions of

Social Theory According to Positivism   9

it, giving greater emphasis and more detailed treatment to some aspects while ignoring others. Yet, overall, there is a great deal of shared content in their discussions and proposals. Because they elucidated criteria of a positivist theory in the context of actual attempts to build such a theory, their discussions were not limited to the propaedeutic. However, inasmuch as the following analysis is concerned with the form of theory, the substantive ideas of these sociologists will be brought in only to illustrate formal characteristics, for what follows is concerned with what theory should be rather than what various theories actually are.[5]

Comte Lays the Foundations

It is to Auguste Comte (1798–1857) that we are indebted for the term *positivism*. For him positivism was at once a method of scientific investigation and a stage in the development of the human mind. The mind passes through the theological, metaphysical, and positivist stages, distinguished primarily by their methods of explanation. Since these states of mental development are also methods of inquiry, each reflexively reveals its own laws of logic through its investigations. In the theological stage, phenomena are explained in terms of supernatural entities such as spirits and gods. In the metaphysical stage, explanations are couched in terms of abstract, personified forces within nature such as the moral law. Finally, in the positivist stage, explanations are expressed in terms of the laws that connect each fact with others. Positivist logic explains any single phenomenon by the law of which it is an instance.[6]

Comte contrasted the positivist with the theological and metaphysical approaches it displaces. All explanations in terms of unobservable entities like spirits, gods, and unseen natural causes must be expunged from positivism; for such explanations belong to obsolete stages. Comte was so convinced that each method follows its predecessor with predictable regularity that he saw in this progress a "law of the three stages." Hence, all of humanity evolves toward a single final end—positivist thinking.

These methods of investigating the world (Comte called them philosophies) are applied in succession to the various phenomena that make up the subject matter of the familiar sciences. Therefore the "law of three stages" manifests, not only within the development of humanity as a whole, but also within the development of each of the sciences. It follows

10   The Scientific Character of Social Theory

that each science originates with theological explanations, which yield in succession to metaphysical and positivist ones. Only when a science enters its positivist stage does it attain maturity by giving accounts of its subject in terms of universal laws, said Comte. Moreover, scientific knowledge experiences a twofold progression: Not only is there detectable progress within any single science, but progress in one science engenders progress in another. Progress in astronomy makes possible the development of physics, which in turn makes possible progress in chemistry. It follows that each science at any given time is at a different stage in its movement toward positivism,[7] astronomy having more *positivity* than chemistry and chemistry more than biology. Progress both within and among sciences can, therefore, be measured by a single standard.

This progress of the human mind is determined, according to Comte, by a gradation in complexity of the objects of each science, which establishes a corresponding hierarchy of sciences—mathematics, astronomy, physics, chemistry, biology, and sociology. Scientific development thus follows nature's progression. General and simple facts lay the foundation for those of greater particularity and complexity, complex events depending on combinations of simpler ones. This dependence in nature explains why the stages of scientific progress are interdependent.[8] Because the laws of astronomy affect terrestrial events, astronomical principles must be incorporated in the laws of terrestrial physics. The laws of physics must be incorporated within chemistry, and so forth. At the same time, no science can be reduced to those lower in the hierarchy; for each must discover laws based on observations peculiar to itself.[9] Nature displays discontinuity as well as continuity, and the complex originates from combinations of simpler elements, yet is not reducible to them. From all this Comte drew the conclusion that sociology studies the least general, most complex facts and is consequently the least advanced science. In fact, sociology has not yet entered its positivist stage.

The unity of the sciences extends to their methods as well as their logical structures, according to Comte. As each science enters its positive stage, it employs the methods common to all, although it also adopts procedures specific to its own facts.[10] So convinced was he of science's unitary character both in method and logic that Comte called for a revision of the education of scientists. A biologist, for example, ought to be trained in all the physical sciences, which should all be studied in their proper order.[11]

Sociology will become positivist when sociologists begin to discover the static and dynamic laws of social life. Social statics will reveal the manner in which social facts coexist at any given time, while social dynamics will reveal how events succeed one another in time.[12] Statics will explain social order; dynamics will explain human progress, order and progress being the stuff of human history. In order to discover social laws, Comte continued, sociologists must be guided by theory as they make direct observations of facts. Science cannot be based on lay observation, for facts isolated from social laws are "idle."[13]

Because of the laws governing the hierarchy of sciences, sociology cannot be launched until its relationships with the other sciences have been worked out. The new discipline will be especially dependent on biology. Indeed, one reason for the absence of a scientific sociology is the undeveloped state of biology.[14] The connection is so close, speculated Comte, that biology will furnish the ideas that will guide sociological research.[15] Biology is the starting point for all social speculation. The entire social evolution of humanity proceeds in accordance with biological laws; all social phenomena are founded on the invariance of the human organism, whose physical, intellectual, and moral characteristics are always the same. Sociological laws, for instance, cannot contradict the biological fact that human intellect is subordinate to man's affective faculties.[16] Sociology will also be linked to the inorganic sciences. Take the law of inertia as an example. At the organic level inertia is manifest as habit and at the social level as the tendency of political systems to perpetuate themselves.[17] Comte was convinced that all the sciences are different branches from one trunk.

At the same time, sociology, resting as it must on purely social observations, can never be a mere appendage of another science. It not only has autonomy; but once it becomes a positivist discipline, sociology will react upon the other sciences. By discovering laws of human evolution, upon which scientific progress depends, sociology as the latest science will foresee the future of all sciences in broad terms and supply them with ideas to be investigated. This reciprocity between sociology and the other sciences completes the unity of science as Comte saw it.

In defining the logical properties of scientific laws, Comte distinguished between two types. We find in nature, he said, both abstract and concrete laws. Abstract laws govern the attributes (he spoke here of phenomena) that are induced from concrete objects and follow the Law of Three Stages. These attributes are abstracted from the concrete objects

12   The Scientific Character of Social Theory

that contain them and are expressed in terms of laws that state their relationships. Concrete laws, on the other hand, are combinations of the abstract laws that govern *all* the attributes of concrete objects. On the one hand, the reference is to modes of activity, on the other, to systems of existence. When all the abstract laws that govern all the attributes of an object are properly combined to form the concrete law of that object, its behavior can be understood and explained.[18] The implication is that every aspect of an object is potentially lawful. From this model it follows that to explain social life one must combine the physical and chemical laws of society's physical environment and the biological laws of its organic environment with the laws of sociology.[19] Thus, the unity of science reflects the unity of the world.

With the right combinations of abstract laws, it will be possible, according to Comte's vision, to intervene in human history. By decreasing deviations, delays, and inconsistencies, human intervention can aid social evolution but cannot change its course.[20] The possibility of intervention varies directly with the complexity of phenomena. Consequently, social phenomena offer the greatest possibility, although, as noted above, only in their "secondary relations." Despite the possibility of intervention, nature's order is the subject of our thought and determines the course of our lives.[21] Comte attempted to reconcile a lawful human history with the goal of modifying its course.

The distinction between abstract and concrete law paved the way for how Comte understood the relationship between theory and practice. Simply put, the distinction between theory and practice is reducible to that between abstract and concrete law.[22] Abstract laws state invariant generalizations abstracted from the exceptions in events precipitated by individual circumstances and peculiarities. Concrete laws, by contrast, are specialized in their reference to individual objects. The greatest difficulty in applying the truths of science is in the transition from the abstract to the concrete.[23] Comte called for a strict division of scientific labor between abstract and concrete sciences such as geology and meteorology, positivist philosophers building the former and engineers the latter. Moreover, the only concrete research the leaders of a reconstructed society will allow is that which deals with practical problems,[24] for the pursuit of truth as end in itself is a form of egoism.[25] Comte would have terminated some concrete sciences and would have encouraged the discovery of only those concrete laws necessary to solve practical prob-

Social Theory According to Positivism 13

lems, for the end of all scientific synthesis is to serve humanity's practical and moral needs.

In the corpus of Comte's writing we thus find recurring essentials of a positivist sociology. In addition to inventing the terms *positivism* and *sociology*, Comte rejected all metaphysical notions as incompatible with science, interpreting the decline of theological and metaphysical explanation as a universal trend. His indomitable conviction of the existence of invariant social laws from which explanations of social phenomena can be deduced came later to be identified as the *deductive-nomological* model—a cornerstone of positivism. The laws of society are comparable in their nomological possibilities to the laws of nature, and social observation can be as effective in discovering the former as physical observation is in discovering the latter. Indirect experimentation and comparison are merely variations of direct social observation, which, of course, rules out all metaphysical factors.

Although Comte never discovered any social laws that commanded the assent of sociologists, perhaps his most significant contribution to positivist sociology was the idea that all sciences are similar in their logical structures and methods. The similarity of the sciences is manifest in his belief that those lower in the hierarchy furnish hypotheses to those higher. Although he rejected the possibility that all scientific knowledge would eventually be reduced to a single formula,[26] the interconnectedness of sciences promises the unification of knowledge under ever-fewer principles. His postulated unity of science lent the prestige of the natural sciences to sociology—a prestige given the force of an evolutionary law according to which all human thinking follows a positivist path. The immaturity of social explanation results from the enormous complexity of social phenomena, but such complexity is bound to yield to the scientific method in the long run.

Finally, Comte believed that the development of sociology along the lines as he conceived them will place in the hands of humankind the ability to control its destiny. Whereas scientific knowledge of physical laws enables control over nature, scientific knowledge of social laws will inevitably yield control over society.

Durkheim's Positivism

Comte influenced Emile Durkheim (1858–1917) directly; the latter admitted his debt to the former. Durkheim agreed with Comte that there

14   The Scientific Character of Social Theory

are discoverable social laws comparable to those governing the rest of nature,[27] and he approved of Comte's view that *social facts* are also facts of nature. Nevertheless, Comte failed to conceptualize social facts properly and tried to create a sociology whose objects of study were ideas.[28] For Durkheim, the social fact provides the definition of sociology: Sociology is the scientific study of social facts.[29] The key to his sociological positivism is to be found in how he conceived of social facts.

Under the term Durkheim included phenomena as diverse as laws, moral rules, religious beliefs and practices, money, and institutions such as the family. These he believed are possessed of an existence as real as the physical facts of nature. Although dependent upon individuals for their existence, social facts transcend the individual and possess unique properties.[30] In order to discover the laws that connect one social fact with another, the sociologist, Durkheim emphasized, must study them objectively, i.e., as they really are and not as they appear. How is this to be done?

His answer came in the form of both prohibitions and positive injunctions. From a negative point of view, if the science of society (every society is composed of social facts) is to follow the path of the natural sciences, it cannot rely on concepts of social facts held by ordinary men. Like the concepts of physics, the concepts of sociology must be far removed from commonsense experience. Does not common sense tell us that the elimination of crime would be desirable? Yet a truly scientific analysis demonstrates its usefulness, for it turns out that a certain level of crime is a normal phenomenon in every society.[31] Common sense leads us astray where matters of science are involved.

Durkheim put forth other reasons to justify his skepticism about the scientific possibilities of lay conceptions of social facts. First, even though we create institutions, each of us makes only a small contribution to the collective product. By examining our experience of an institution, we cannot really grasp it in its entirety. We can never discover its origins because every institution has been handed down to us already formed. Second, we often are mistaken about our experiences. We believe we are acting unselfishly when we are really acting egoistically. We think we are under the passion of hatred when we are really dominated by love.[32] Durkheim shared Comte's distrust of commonsense opinion.

Concepts of social facts, therefore, must be formed objectively. For the purposes of science, they therefore must be conceptualized as things. By this methodological postulate Durkheim did not mean that social

Social Theory According to Positivism   15

facts are literally things, but that their treatment as such attests to their external and independent reality. But the mind cannot understand a thing from the inside. Therefore, a sociologist must approach a social fact as an object of external observation and experimentation in a way similar to the approach a physicist takes toward a physical object. Like a material thing, a social fact proves recalcitrant to the will. A religious dogma, for instance, cannot be changed by merely thinking about it. Social facts are resistant, impose themselves on individuals, and are formed outside of individual consciousness.[33] Such reasons justify the conceptualization of social facts as things for the purpose of observation. What can a scientist do with a thing? He can see it, measure it, weigh it, and analyze it into its essential properties.

Thus, Durkheim's first rule of scientific observation is that social facts should be treated as things. Another rule of observation calls upon the sociologist to look at social facts as detached from their purely individual manifestations and see them as collective entities. Separated from any single individual, a written law, for instance, can be observed objectively. It is what it is, said Durkheim, and there is only one way of perceiving it.[34] To understand the import of this rule, one ought to take into account the distinction he drew between a social fact as a collective being and its expressions in the experience and actions of individuals.

The sociologist must define as well as observe social facts, and there are rules for their definition. It is unnecessary to observe all the facts that one can subsume under a given definition, for that would defeat the economy of effort, which is one of science's purposes. It is not necessary to observe every single instance of suicide in order to define it. Neither is it necessary to observe every single aspect of a phenomenon that fits under a definition, for an infinity of attributes makes this impossible. Instead, the sociologist should arrive at those characteristics essential to his purpose, use these as his definition, and by observation determine which particular instances share the defining characteristics. These, and only these, fall into the class of particulars so defined.[35] Durkheim pointed to crime as an illustration. All actions that evoke punishment by society fall into a class. Hence, punishment is the definition of crime, all crimes sharing this attribute.[36] All actions that fail to elicit this collective reaction do not belong to the class and therefore do not fit the definition.

This method of defining social facts is that of *genus proximum* and *differentia specifica*. When a particular social fact has been defined, the

16   The Scientific Character of Social Theory

definition provides a basis for discovering other characteristics that can enlarge the definition.[37] Durkheim's rule for definitions thus entails the process of induction: Definitions are based on inductions from a number of particulars and extended to as yet unobserved instances.

Scientific observation and definition were for Durkheim necessary preliminaries to fulfilling Comte's vision of explaining concrete social phenomena. In devising a model of scientific explanation, Durkheim, however, introduced a factor avoided by Comte as metaphysical, namely, the principle of causality. Accordingly, the explanation of a social fact is to be found in its causes. But what in general are the causes of social facts? Durkheim's answer formulated another rule of the sociological method: The determining causes of social facts must be sought among antecedent social facts.[38]

What is a causal relationship? John Stuart Mill was wrong, concluded Durkheim, when he said that the same effect can be produced by several different causes. It is not true that at one time a consequent can be the effect of one antecedent and at another time the effect of a different one. Durkheim's arguments for rejecting a plurality of causes expressed a positivist view. In the first place, if the same effect could be produced by different causes it would be difficult to derive a consequent from an antecedent. Such indeterminacy limits logical deduction. In the second place, a plurality of causes contradicts the proportionality between cause and effect. The law of proportionality, which states a cause must be proportional to its effect, assumes an inherent connection between cause and effect. The latter flows from the essential nature of the former.[39] Hence, for every social fact there is only one other social fact that is its cause. The cause of a social fact thus turns out to be both its necessary and sufficient condition.

It was this concept of causality that Durkheim applied in his classic study of suicide. He found suicide to be statistically associated with a range of social facts—Protestantism, men, the liberal professions, the single, and the educated.[40] On the surface the associations appear to indicate many different causes of the social fact of suicide. Durkheim, nevertheless, thought he discovered a single factor, i.e., a relative lack of integration, shared by these diverse facts, which is the sole cause of the egoistic type of suicide. Thus, he interpreted the data to reveal the one-to-one causal formula. In conformity with this formula, he also identified three types of suicide—the *egoistic*, *altruistic*, and *anomic*—each being the effect of a single cause.

Social Theory According to Positivism   17

In giving causal explanations, Durkheim used what Comte called the *comparative* method, which John Stuart Mill elaborated upon in devising a theory of causality. Again Durkheim disagreed with Mill. In his opinion, Mill's methods of *agreement* and *difference* are inadequate for sociology because of the complexity of its subject matter. The method of agreement calls for the attribution of a causal relation between two facts that invariably co-occur among constellations of facts that are otherwise different in all other instances. But we will never find, Durkheim argued, a society that differs from another in every fact but one. The method of difference as formulated by Mill calls for the attribution of a causal relation between two facts that regularly coexist among constellations of facts that are otherwise identical in all instances. Durkheim criticized this with the observation that we will never find a society that is like another in every respect but one.[41]

Mill, however, formulated another method that Durkheim thought to be adequate for sociology. The method of *concomitant variations* warrants a causal inference between two facts whose quantitative values regularly coexist. A certain quantity of one regularly associates with a given quantity of the other. When a phenomenon develops according to some mode, its development expresses its essential nature. Quantitative increments of it is a manner of such expression. Therefore, when two variables associate in a quantitative, continuous fashion their mutual development expresses a correspondence between their natures. And for a relation of cause and effect to obtain, the cause and effect must be inherently linked. Concomitant variations meets this criterion, and that is why the method is proof of causality. Durkheim went on to say that causality obtains even if one finds an instance of one without the other, for the anomaly could be explained by a third factor either preventing the cause from producing the effect or masking its causal influence.[42] He optimistically concluded that concomitant variation is the primary method of sociological proof. Once again, his research on suicide illustrates applications of his abstractly stated methodological postulates. He demonstrated with statistical indicators, for example, that the integration of groups varies inversely with the suicide rates of their members.[43]

In proving causal relationships, we are often compelled to rely on observable indices. It is easier, according to Durkheim, to study internal facts, which tend to escape us, in terms of external indicators that symbolize them. In explaining organic solidarity as an effect of the division of labor and mechanical solidarity as an effect of common

18   The Scientific Character of Social Theory

beliefs, he found it necessary to study and classify these two types of solidarity through various types of law. Law is something visible, tangible, and external and can truly be regarded as a thing. In its written form it is detached from individuals. Juridical rules are closely bound up with social relationships; and, therefore, types of law should reveal types of solidarity. Thus, types of solidarity can be analyzed through study of types of law, which are their indices.[44]

If sociology is to be a science, then what more reasonable way is there to make it so than to find social analogies to the facts of nature? After all, Comte had believed that despite discontinuities in nature's hierarchy the science of society would borrow suitable hypotheses from the other sciences. Accordingly, in his research Durkheim resorted to concepts reminiscent of physical and biological science. Modern divisions of labor, whose organic solidarities reflect a unity of differentiated but functionally articulated activities, evolved out of primitive societies, whose mechanical solidarities reflect a unity of similar beliefs and sentiments. Durkheim found this social evolution analogous to biological development, according to which higher organisms composed of differentiated organs evolved out of lower forms composed of unspecialized body-segments. He saw an analogy between the class of primitive societies and the rings of earthworms and an analogy between complex divisions of labor and the organization of vertebrates.[45] In these biological analogies the origins of contemporary functional social theory can be found. Although such analogies, said Durkheim, are metaphorical, biological terminology is useful.[46] Other naturalistic concepts that he found useful for sociological purposes were *social species, social morphology, social equilibrium*, and *dynamic density*.

Having faith that sociology could be a science, Durkheim conceived of social facts in accordance with this faith. Neither organic nor psychological, social facts constitute another level of reality that is, nevertheless, equally receptive to the methods of science. Having the attributes of exteriority, autonomy, and generality and capable of exerting constraint over individuals, the social fact should be considered for scientific purposes as a thing. Like things, social facts can be investigated, defined, and classified and their relationships of cause and effect discovered through the use of objective indices and clearly defined criteria of proof. When the causes and functions of social facts are known, it will be possible to reduce human behavior to cause-and-effect relationships, which can then be transformed into rules of action.[47] Causal knowledge will facilitate control over the human environment analogous to scientific control over the natural environment. Removed from common sense, sociology is indeed the preserve of specialists. Although with considerable modification and elaboration of Comte's ideas, Durkheim preserved the latter's overall scientific vision.

Weber on Causality and Ethical Neutrality

It is easy to find in the complexities of Max Weber's (1864–1920) methodology both positivist and antipositivist notions, and contradictory emphases can even be found in his analysis of single topics. This section, however, focuses on those of his notions more consistent with a positivist approach to social science.

Causality for Weber was to play a central role in the social sciences and history.[48] What is causality? In its most complete sense it possesses two characteristics. First, it consists of an actual dynamic bond between two qualitatively different facts, the effect and its cause, that is more than a category of the mind. The bond, however, is not a necessary one, as Durkheim held; for a social cause merely establishes a sufficient ground for its effect. The implication follows that an effect could have been brought about by some other cause. Second, causality is defined in terms of subordination of a particular cause to a rule or generalization.[49] Consequently, the bond between cause and effect recurs, at least part of the time; when a cause occurs, its effect materializes.

The definition suggests two tasks for social science in general and sociology in particular. The first is to formulate causal generalizations through induction, to establish which effects are "effected" by which causes. In the absence of empirical rules one cannot impute specific causes to effects. The second, which is more important than the first, is to explain individual events in terms of their concrete causes. The importance of generalizations is demonstrated by the fact that, as already noted, in their absence causal imputation is impossible. To determine whether a given fact was caused by another, one must assess the matter with reference to what we generally expect from the latter.[50] Although methods of verification are different, the logic of causal explanation is the same for social and material events, even in the case of social events with an intentional meaning.[51] The only logical exception is the principle

20   The Scientific Character of Social Theory

of causal equivalence of natural phenomena,[52] as illustrated by a mass exerting on another mass a force equivalent to its own. This principle does not apply to social causation, involving, as it does, qualitatively different facts.

Where do the causal generalizations relevant to social science come from? Weber identified two sources. First, there is the scientist's commonsense experience sharpened by his scientific training. These rules derived from personal experience are seldom formulated explicitly. Because of their triviality and imprecision, this would be a waste of time. Rather they form the implicit basis of causal imputation.[53] Second, there are the generalizations developed by the specialized sciences like economics. The more comprehensive the nomological applicability of such generalizations, the more certain the causal imputations based on them.[54]

Weber devised logical concepts and methods to facilitate the imputation of causes. In this context he spoke of *objective possibility* and *adequate causation*. In estimating whether an event was causally relevant, i.e., produced an effect in a sequence of outcomes, the historian imagines whether the latter would have been different by imagining one of two things about the former. Engaging in an "imaginary experiment," he imagines either that the event whose causal status is at issue had not occurred at all or that it had occurred differently. If under either imagined condition, the sequence of succeeding events, selected of course from an infinite array of facts, could be expected to be different, then the event in question would be considered a cause of the former. Could a theoretically expected difference be objectively possible? If so, the event in question was an adequate cause in the sequence.

Weber illustrated this method of ascertaining cause and effect with the wars between Greece and Persia. He performed the logical operation in the context of analyzing and evaluating certain methodological notions of the historian Eduard Meyer. Meyer posed the question of whether European values were affected by the outcome of the Persian wars. Let us imagine, said Weber, that the battle of Marathon had been won by Persia. In that case one can conceive on the basis of a generalization about Persian policy established through historical research that Persia would have imposed on the city-states a theocratic regime that would have stifled the development of Greek philosophy and drama, which became a part of Western culture. Such an outcome was objectively possible. Thus, an imaginary experiment allows the inference that the

Social Theory According to Positivism   21

Greek victories were an adequate cause in the development of Western culture.[55] Weber's example incorporates the notions of objective possibility, adequate causation, and empirical generalization. It is also evident that the logic in the example approximates John Stuart Mill's method of difference.

Thus, both Weber and Durkheim were of the opinion that the discovery of causes with the use of purely empirical methods is essential. They both agreed that relationships of cause and effect recur, making possible nomological knowledge that is indispensable for explanations. They also agreed that the logic of causal explanation of social facts is identical with the logic of causal explanation of natural events and the discovery of social causation proceeds squarely within the framework of science.

Aided by empirical rules in the search for causes, Weber went on to logically separate the latter from the process of evaluation. Placing a judgment of value on a cause is very different than ascertaining its existence. Since an unambiguous logical distinction obtains between judgments of value and judgments of act, he enunciated the position that social scientists and historians ought to remain ethically neutral. Value-judgments are "practical evaluations of the unsatisfactory or satisfactory character of phenomena,"[56] whereas judgments of facts are empirically verifiable. Ethical neutrality, Weber insisted, calls upon the scientist to refrain from practical evaluation as a part of his investigations; for science should content itself with the establishment of facts and their causal explanations.[57] "[T]he validity of a practical evaluation as a norm and the truth-value of an empirical proposition are absolutely heterogeneous in character."[58]

A value-free approach to sociology does not rule out scientific inquiry into evaluations made by the individuals and groups that are objects of investigation, for their values affect their actions. In addition, Weber pointed out that the logical disjunction of facts and evaluations is not erased by the fact that a large degree of agreement exists upon a particular evaluation. For instance, that there is unanimous agreement that a given individual is a scoundrel does not endow the judgment with the authority of science. A "science of ethics" in the sense that one can objectively ascertain the influence that certain ethical judgments have cannot establish what *should* happen. Neither does a value-free science sanction purely formal ethical rules. One cannot, for example, unambiguously

22   The Scientific Character of Social Theory

determine that justice requires rewarding superior contribution or that it requires those with outstanding ability to contribute more.[59]

Ethical neutrality raises the question: What, if anything, can a purely empirical social science tell us about social policy? Weber's answer marked out a more limited practical role than that envisaged by Comte and Durkheim. The ethically neutral scientist can accomplish several things concerning social policy. First, he can, within the limits of available knowledge, ascertain which means are adequate to the achievement of a given end. Second, he can determine what consequences will follow the application of the appropriate means other than the end itself, namely, repercussions and side effects. Third, he can ascertain the implications of the policy for values. He can, for example, determine what ideals are implied by the choice of one end rather than another and what values are implied by the employment of one given means rather than another. What ethically neutral social scientists can never do, however, is tell someone what *should* be done.[60]

In advocating a value-free science, Weber implied a cardinal tenet of positivism, i.e., that all notions that cannot be derived from sensory experience are scientifically irrelevant. For it is apparent that the value attributed to an object cannot be found within the object itself.

Law and System According to Parsons

Talcott Parsons's (1902–1979) positivism[61] is grounded in the concept of *analytical realism*. The term *realism* indicates the existence of an objective world of nonrandom events, external to the sociological observer. Its exteriority and objectivity are reminiscent of Durkheim's social facts. Its order is one of recurring events. Furthermore, the order of the world is congruent with the order of human logic; and that is why it is possible for the human mind to know the world. The term *analytical* refers to the type of concepts, if formulated correctly, Parsons believed can adequately represent the external world. Analytical concepts can never represent the world completely, however, because its complexity exceeds the limitations of the human mind. They can only abstract and represent aspects of it.[62]

The number of selective viewpoints from which a social reality can be examined is inherently unlimited. Consequently, the more concepts that

Social Theory According to Positivism   23

represent given events, the more we know about them. If each concept abstracts an aspect, then the more concepts that are applied to a phenomenon, the more of its dimensions are brought to light. This parallels the relationship that Comte saw between abstract and concrete laws. More encompassing theoretical schemes subsume previous ones, which leave valid precipitates of knowledge that are absorbed into the former. Scientific progress and the cumulation of scientific knowledge are thereby possible, and the totality of humanly possible knowledge can be asymptotically approached.[63]

If the *analytical concept* is the proper scientific representation of things, the question arises: What does this term mean? Parsons recognized that every concrete entity is composed of elements or properties that cannot exist in isolation. Analytical concepts indicate or point out such elements, which are abstracted from others with which they are intertwined. Thus, an *analytical element* of a physical particle is its mass, which cannot be physically detached from the particle itself. Velocity is another. Classical mechanics captures these quantifiable elements through analytical concepts.[64] Separation is accomplished by mental abstraction.

But Parsons did not end the analysis of scientific concepts and their relation to reality at this point. Analytical elements indicated by analytical concepts stand in fixed relationships to one another. For example, the force of a body is related to its mass and velocity. These relationships, which from the standpoint of science are ideally quantifiable, are, said Parsons, *analytical laws*. Such laws can be expressed as relationships among the numerical values of the elements.[65]

Parsons attempted to delineate the analytical elements of human action. The most fundamental action that can exist as a concrete entity Parsons called the *unit act*, which he broke down into four analytical elements. The first is the actor's *end*—a future state of affairs to be brought about by the action. The second is the *means* available to him to achieve the end. The third is the *conditions* over which the actor has no control and are therefore obstacles.[66] Means and conditions are elements of a situation. The fourth element of the unit act is the *normative*. This consists of the actor's ideas, often shared with others, upon which he draws to select his end and the means to attain it. The normative element is a selective factor.[67] When these elements are considered to be concepts in the action frame of reference, they are analytical concepts. When they refer to elements of a real action, they

24   The Scientific Character of Social Theory

are analytical elements. Theory, Parsons cautioned again and again, must not be confused with those aspects of the world to which it refers. An idea of a thing must not be confused with the thing itself.

The identification of the elements of concrete unit acts sets the stage for the formulation of analytical laws comparable in their logical form to the laws of mechanics. The analytical laws of unit acts take the form of interrelationships among variable values of ends, means, conditions, and norms. *The Structure of Social Action* does not go very far in this direction, but Parsons gave as an example of a law of action an idea from Weber. Human action, stated Parsons, tends to increase in rationality. More specifically, whatever ends are selected in accordance with norms, they tend to become more effectively and efficiently achieved through the selection of better means. In this example, the relationship between the elements of means and ends forms an analytical law. Parsons compared this law of rationality with the second law of thermodynamics.[68]

To be sure, Parsons admitted, the laws of social action will probably not be very precise in purely quantitative terms because the values of the analytical elements are not expressed as numbers with metric properties. Alternative means put at the service of a given end, for example, cannot be stated as variations of a unidimensional order of magnitude. Yet, it is a question of coming as close as possible to a scientific ideal, and future progress in quantitative measurement is possible. What can be accomplished at present is that all observations of facts can be made with reference to one theory, namely, the general theory of action.[69] John Stuart Mill's method of concomitant variations as adopted by Durkheim became for Parsons, at least as an ideal, applicable to analytical laws.

All scientific knowledge strives toward the logical structure of an *empirical-theoretical* system—a system of analytical laws stating quantitative relationships among enough analytical elements to make possible precise predictions outside of experimental situations. Prediction requires that most, if not all, of the relevant elements be identified and the laws connecting them worked out. Furthermore, all these laws must be logically interrelated, which justifies the term *system* as descriptive of scientific knowledge. If achieved, Parsons's call for logical interdependence among laws would make possible the logical deduction of predictions of empirical events. Although social theory has not yet achieved this form, an empirical-theoretical system, according to Parsons, is the ultimate goal of all scientific endeavor.[70]

Social Theory According to Positivism   25

Since the general theory of action, composed of four analytical concepts, abstracts from real events, it is possible for other theories to abstract different elements of the same events and explain them in terms of different laws. Thus, a physicist and a sociologist make different abstractions from an act of suicide by a person jumping from a bridge. The former abstracts the height of the bridge as a relevant feature of the situation and takes as an unproblematic given the fact that the person jumped. He subsumes the action under the law of falling bodies. The sociologist, on the other hand, takes the height of the bridge and the physical destruction as givens and focuses on the motive for jumping.[71] The point of this example is Parsons's conclusion that the same reality comprehended by more scientific theories becomes progressively explained. And insofar as they are logically interrelated, each explanation reinforces and verifies the others.[72] Explanations from diverse theoretical perspectives can be integrated to yield cumulative knowledge logically unified.

Parsons strove toward the theoretical unity of sociology with other sciences through the concept of *system*. System is the conceptual foundation of all generalizing disciplines.[73] It makes sense, said Parsons, to divide the world into *physico-chemical*, *biological*, and *action* systems, the last term applying specifically to the social sciences.

What is a system? In defining the concept Parsons drew upon the other sciences, especially biology, for the concept of the *living system*.[74] Three conditions define the living system. First, it is composed of interdependent, differentiated parts that distinguish it from its environment. Clear boundaries, such as the skin, divide the organism from its environment. The parts are uniformly interdependent, showing constancy. Second, the living system is self-regulatory, maintaining its structure in the face of environmental changes. Compensating processes fulfill indispensable functions for the living system, as in the example of warm-blooded organisms preventing loss of heat in the face of dropping temperatures in the environment. Third, the living system takes in substances such as food and oxygen, processes them, and returns to the environment products such as carbon dioxide.[75] These characteristics are common to organisms and species at the organic and personalities and societies at the human level.

Parsons saw other analogies between organic and human levels.[76] Biological species and social systems adapt to their environments. Organisms, personalities, and social systems all strive to attain goals. The

26   The Scientific Character of Social Theory

cultural symbol is analogous to the biological gene. The gene in the DNA gives "directions" to the cell; and the symbol, such as a religious creed, guides the social system. The relationship between genotype and phenotype is analogous to that between norm and society. Whereas natural selection winnows out genetic developments, cultural competition prevents the institutionalization of certain values.[77] Such extensions of biology into sociology are consistent with Comte's idea of the relation between the two disciplines.[78]

Parsons's drive toward the unification of scientific knowledge did not end with the reduction of various types of system to a single formula. In one of his last publications he mapped the entire universe into *physico-chemical, human-organic, action,* and *telic* systems, all of which fulfill the same four functions. Each type of system interacts with the others through interchanges of materials and influence.[79]

If the ultimate goal of science is the logical interrelationships of propositions, ideally so interconnected that they can all be derived from primary definitions and postulates,[80] i.e., a *system* of theory, such a goal is more likely achieved if indeed the reality to which such a theory refers consists of interdependent factors. In other words, a theoretical system is more likely if it reflects an empirical system. In that case, the functional interdependence of such factors, in which changes in one are causally related to changes in others, is represented as logical interrelations among propositions. Theory is congruent with reality. In his desire to make social theory into a system of theory, Parsons conceptualized the phenomena sociologists study—societies, personalities, and cultures—as systems. At the same time, he tried to corroborate the validity of these conceptualizations by drawing analogies with the organic and inorganic worlds. Furthermore, if all levels of empirical facts do indeed form systems, it is likely that logical unification of all sciences is possible. Parsons's positivist commitments led him to conceptualize sociology's subject matter as systemlike just as Durkheim's belief in the possibility of a scientific sociology led him to conceptualize social facts as things. Positivism not only furnished a method of approaching facts, but also shaped the facts to suit its own demands.

Homans on the Nature of Science

Influenced by logical positivism, George C. Homans (1910–) believed there is a logical unity of the sciences, similarities in logical structure obtaining between natural and social sciences. The differences between them, said Homans, are matters of degree rather than kind.[81] The fact that the social sciences in general and sociology in particular have a long way to go to realize their scientific potential does not alter this fact. In delineating the logical ideals of social science, Homans explored in greater detail some aspects of science that Parsons merely touched upon.

Two goals of any science are discovery and explanation. Discovery consists of finding out how the properties of things are related, and those sentences that state such relationships are called *propositions*. Others might call them empirical generalizations. Homans gave as an example Boyle's law drawn from physics: Within a sealed container, the volume of a gas varies inversely with the pressure upon it. This proposition has two characteristics relevant to the logic of science. First, it indicates two properties (Parsons would have called them analytical elements) of something, in this case a gas, which are its volume and pressure. Second, it states a quantitative relationship between them: As pressure rises, volume decreases. Pressure and volume stated as an equation take on continuous quantitative values, but legitimate scientific propositions may state relationships between purely qualitative factors. An example is humans without functioning kidneys are dead.[82] Propositions vary in the extent of their generality, i.e., the range of phenomena to which they are relevant. Highly general, Boyle's law, for instance, applies to all gases.

The propositions of science are accompanied by auxiliary information called *texts*. The text of Boyle's law includes the definitions of *gas*, *pressure*, and *volume* and how they are measured. These, said Homans, are *operating definitions*. Unlike *nonoperating definitions* in sociology such as *role* (more and less of a role are never associated with more and less of something else), operating definitions actually enter into propositions.[83] Just as nonoperating definitions in social science are to be distinguished from operating ones, so *orienting statements* in social science are to be distinguished from authentic scientific propositions. Orienting statements are pseudopropositions, which do not really indicate what will change in a given direction with a change in a given direction of something else. An orienting statement is illustrated as follows: When two persons interact, each will sanction the behavior of the other.[84] The trouble with this statement, Homans complained, is that it doesn't state what will happen in detail.

28   The Scientific Character of Social Theory

A second goal of science is explanation. What constitutes a scientific explanation? A fact is scientifically explained, according to Homans, when it is deduced as a logical conclusion from general propositions whose truth has been established. Logical deduction is essential to scientific explanation. Explanatory propositions must be taken in conjunction with other given conditions that must be specified. These conditions are the circumstances of the occurrence of the fact to be explained and are sometimes referred to as initial conditions. In technical language, the general propositions are *explananda* and the fact to be explained the *explicandum*. An explicandum can be either a single event or another scientific proposition. The explananda, the explanatory propositions, must have greater generality than the explicandum. The deduction should proceed only in one direction in order to avoid circular reasoning.[85] In sum, for Homans the standard of a scientific explanation is logical positivism's deductive-nomological model.[86]

To illustrate such explanations he presented another example from physics. Why is it that when the wind blows toward shore the water near the shore is warmer than away from it? Well-known scientific propositions tell us that surface water is warmer than deep water and that wind affects surface water more than deep water. The wind blowing toward shore at a particular time is a given. The two propositions in conjunction with this condition explain why the water adjacent to the shore is relatively warm. Its relative temperature, the explicandum, is a deductive implication of the former. Moreover, these explanatory propositions themselves are subject to explanation by other, more general propositions to the effect that warm water rises and all water seeks its own level.[87] Depending on how far explanation is carried, chains of deduction are possible.

The deductive-nomological model provides Homans with a definition of theory. A theory consists of the explanations, not just of one, but of a number of related facts having some of their explanatory propositions in common. In the above example, for instance, if not only variations in the temperature of water were explained by those propositions but also other facts relevant to thermodynamics, then the entire deductive system would form a theory. Homans's definition incorporates the logical interrelationships of laws that Parsons identified as science's ultimate objective. The connection of a variety of facts through common explanatory generalizations is a strict definition of theory. A less restrictive definition, according to Homans, is simply a deductive explanation of a single fact.

Social Theory According to Positivism   29

In this sense the theory of something is its explanation in terms of its logical deduction from explanatory propositions. [88]

Homans illustrated deductive explanation with a revision of a part of Durkheim's theory of suicide:

1. In any social grouping, the suicide rate varies directly with the degree of individualism (egoism).
2. The degree of individualism varies with the incidence of Protestantism.
3. Therefore, the suicide rate varies with the incidence of Protestantism.
4. The incidence of Protestantism in Spain is low.
5. Therefore, the suicide rate in Spain is low. [89]

Here are, said Homans, propositions expressing relationships in which more of something varies with more of others. Revealing logical interdependence, number 3 is deduced from 1 and 2 taken together and 5 from 3 and 4 taken together. Numbers 3 and 5 are explained through logical implication, the former a proposition and the latter a statement expressing a single fact. The truth of the propositions in this theory is contingent, i.e., based on empirical evidence. Thus, the variation of suicide with individualism is given by relevant facts. The propositions in the example vary in generality, numbers 5 and 2 being less general than number 1. This theory is incomplete because the higher-order propositions are themselves explainable by others of even greater generality that are unstated. Why, for example, does suicide increase with individualism? Homans chose this example to illustrate the feasibility of the deductive-nomological model for social science.

Homans continued his analysis of the nature of social science by defining two other types of concepts that cut across the previous distinction between operating and nonoperating terms. First, some concepts are explicitly defined in terms of the way valid instances are observed and measured. These concepts are real definitions, illustrated in the preceding example by suicide rates and Protestantism. The suicide rate, for instance, is defined by the criteria according to which deaths are classified as suicides. Second, some concepts within a theory may be implicitly defined, that is, defined solely in terms of other concepts in the theory. Reverting to physics, Homans selected as an illustration of an implicitly defined concept force, which is defined in terms of the real definitions of

30   The Scientific Character of Social Theory

mass and acceleration: $f = ma$. A sociological example is the concept of value in the proposition: The greater the value of a reward going to an individual, the more often he will engage in the activity that brings him the reward. When a theory defines the relative importance of values in terms of the selection among them, choice becomes the implicit definition of value.[90]

Homans briefly discussed the mathematical expression of theories. In the light of deductive explanation, the great advantage of expressing a theory in terms of mathematical symbols is that it makes possible deductions not ordinarily apparent when its propositions are stated in verbal form.[91] The positivist ideal once again leads down the road to quantification.

As noted at the outset, Homans identified the two major goals of science as discovery and explanation. But he believed the latter to be far more important than the former in social sciences.[92] The social sciences, according to Homans, have already made many discoveries and have come forth with all sorts of empirical propositions. That all societies are stratified, that the amount of intergenerational mobility is similar in industrial societies, and that family instability is high in the lower class are examples of generalizations with supporting evidence.[93] One problem, however, is that these propositions are not very general and hold up only under certain conditions not usually specified. The result is that it is difficult to explain using such propositions. And it is not simply the case, Homans concluded, that a different set of circumstances merely marks the influence of an explanatory proposition, but rather that these circumstances require different propositions, even contradictory ones, for their explanation.[94]

The reason for this difficulty is the historical character of human life. The way a person acts in a given situation is explained by his historical experiences derived from past circumstances in combination with psychological tendencies expressed by few basic psychological propositions.[95] Although these apply to everyone, the conditions in which individuals find themselves vary and consequently affect the impact of the propositions, which are operative at any given time but are modified in their effects by past circumstances of the individual. In fact, as these propositions have been formulated by Homans, they have built into them the historical factor. Natural sciences are not so much bothered by this difficulty. A physicist, for example, can explain what a lever does by the laws of mechanics without having to know how it came to be in the

Social Theory According to Positivism 31

condition it is in at present. He need not, in other words, reconstruct the lever's history.[96]

What is to be done? Homans concluded that because most sociological propositions are about aggregates—classes, groups, and organizations—explanation would be immeasurably advanced if these propositions were themselves explained by few propositions about the behavior of individuals. But this is only a part of the solution. The conditions or circumstances in which individuals find themselves also need to be explained by these same psychological propositions. We must know how these circumstances came to be what they are. For example, Durkheim's theory explains why the suicide rate in Spain is low but merely takes for granted that there are few Protestants there without explaining that fact.[97] Homans's proposal assumes that if such conditions were deductively explained with psychological propositions, which would result in genetic chains of events linked together in which the givens of one deductive system become the explicanda of others,[98] sociological knowledge would have greater explanatory power.

In sum, sociological explanation requires explaining the large number of generalizations about social aggregates through deductive genetic chains in terms of a small number of propositions about the behavior of individuals.[99] In other words, sociology needs genuine theories. Homans's proposal will be realized with the achievement of explanations that are both necessary and sufficient to characterize the relationships Durkheim believed to obtain between social facts. For if unique circumstances prevent the explanation of an event in terms of a relevant proposition, but those circumstances and the relevant proposition are susceptible to explanation in terms of a small set of propositions, it follows that there really are no exceptions. In the final analysis, everything, including empirical propositions and the exceptions to them, can ideally be explained as logical deductions from psychological propositions. Although Homans does not expect such an ideal ever to be completely fulfilled (it is a matter of degree), his approach implies the task of ascertaining relations of necessity and sufficiency between explananda and explicanda.

Explaining lower-level generalizations about social aggregates in terms of a small number of propositions about individuals reflects the goal, so characteristic of the positivist tradition, of the reduction of complexity through the unification of knowledge. Explanation takes the form of ever-fewer deductive systems of ever-greater power. Although Comte

32   The Scientific Character of Social Theory

denied the possibility of expressing all knowledge in one all-encompassing formula, he clung to the ideal of "pursuing the philosophical aim of all science, the lessening of the number of general laws requisite for the explanation of natural phenomena."[100] With this sentiment Homans would have to agree.

Merton on the Nature of Social Theory

In identifying the products of various scientific activities that contemporary sociologists refer to as theory, Robert K. Merton (1910–) believes the term should be reserved for a system of logically related propositions that Homans indicated as the model of scientific explanation. When an empirical generalization is logically deduced from higher-order generalizations, it is, said Merton, a social law, and the higher-order generalizations are a theory. Consequently, there are empirical generalizations (Homans called them *propositions*) that state relationships between variable factors and generalizations that are logically derived from theory. The former, as illustrated by Halbwach's finding that laborers spend more money per unit of food than white-collar workers of the same income category, are isolated, standing apart from some more encompassing theory. In short, they are not social laws.[101]

Having distinguished these types of generalizations, Merton, like Homans, went to Durkheim's study of suicide to find an example of what he meant by a social theory. He modified Durkheim's presentation as follows:

1. Social cohesion provides psychic support to group members subjected to acute stresses and anxieties.
2. Suicide rates are functions of *unrelieved* anxieties and stresses to which persons are subjected.
3. Catholics have greater social cohesion than Protestants.
4. Therefore, lower suicide rates should be anticipated among Catholics than among Protestants.[102]

Theories have advantages over isolated generalizations, Merton emphasized. In the first place, a theory extends the scope of a generalization deduced from it. In the above example, a relationship between two religious groups with respect to self-destruction is set within the more general context of cohesion, which in varying degrees characterizes all groups. Furthermore, other uniform differences among groups with regard to suicide, such as those between the single and married, can be brought under the theory's jurisdiction. In the second place, theory adds to the verification of the laws deduced from it. For instance, the discovery of higher rates of suicide in other groups with little cohesion adds support to the generalization about differences in suicide rates between Catholics and Protestants. In the third place, the above example of theory makes it possible to connect other areas of life with suicide. Merton cited research that ties other maladaptive behavior such as obsessions to inadequate social cohesion. In the fourth place, theory provides a sounder basis for prediction than simple extrapolation from past trends. With the above theory, for instance, a sociologist (if the theory is true) can predict that if cohesion declines among Catholics, suicide rates will rise. He need not rely on extrapolation from past suicide rates. In the fifth place, a prediction logically deduced from a theory is more likely to be correctly explained by it than by some alternative hypothesis. With all the data supporting an inverse relation between suicide and cohesion, the observation of the relationship in a new group is likely to be explained by cohesion rather than some other factor associated with it.[103] The foregoing are logical advantages of the deductive-nomological model.

Consistent with his emphasis on the logical integration of sociological knowledge, Merton emphasized the procedure of codification. This scientific activity is closely related to the deductive model of social theory. The social theorist discovers that generalizations derived from unconnected investigations into different areas are explicable by some common factor that serves to systematize or codify them. For example, studies repeatedly turn up some practice or recurring action that appears to be irrational or nonsensical on the surface, such as a primitive ritual whose manifest goal is to produce rain. Some latent or hidden benefit, called a *latent function* by Merton, that is no one's intended purpose is determined to account for the continuation of the practice.[104] The concept of latent function achieves a codification of knowledge. In order to facilitate codification, Merton constructed several well-known conceptual schemes (he called them *paradigms*), one purpose of which is to enable different investigators to classify relevant facts in diverse areas of research so that they fall into the same system of classes. The paradigm determines what the relevant facts are. A paradigm can also be used after

34   The Scientific Character of Social Theory

the fact, so to speak. It can be used as a guideline for the critical analysis of existing studies in order to codify them.[105] In either case, the purpose of a paradigm is to introduce some order into scientific knowledge by integrating it.

Merton cautioned against confusing *post factum* sociological interpretations with social theory. A *post factum* interpretation is a hypothesis constructed to explain a set of facts after they are given. Devising such an interpretation is very different than testing an *a priori* generalization in the light of facts relevant to its truth. It is the *a priori* generalization, not the *post factum* explanation, upon which social theories are properly built. The trouble with a *post factum*, Merton went on to say, is that it *must* correspond to the facts it purports to explain because it was chosen to do precisely that. A number of different explanations serve equally well with no criterion to choose among them. Suppose, for example, a generalization turns up that the unemployed read fewer books than they previously read. A *post factum* interpretation explains the change as caused by anxiety. But then a revised finding shows that the unemployed read more, not less, than previously. A new explanation readily comes forth that they now have more time. Such generalizations, Merton concluded, do not meet the test of falsifiability. What should be done is to consider them in the light of new evidence.[106] In any case, they should not be confused with social theory.

Merton also discussed the formation of concepts. Although concept formation is not identical with theory, it is indispensable to it. A theory must incorporate concepts because generalizations express relationships among concepts. If concepts are formed, however, in such a fashion that no relationships can be found among them, there are no generalizations, no theory, and no scientific knowledge. That is why concepts must be formed with great care. They cannot be formed correctly by trial and error because there are an infinite number of variables in the social world that are not connected. Neither should concepts be defined in such a way that they include facts that are antinomies, for they may mask the relationships among concepts.

As an example of how concept formation affects generalization, Merton cited Sutherland's work on white-collar crime. By clarifying the concept of crime to include all violations of criminal law in the legal sense, Sutherland brought white-collar crime into the class defined by the concept. That upset previous generalizations about the relation of poverty, social class, and other factors to crime conceived strictly in terms of official statistics. We should recognize that concepts shape the investigator's perceptions; they tell him what to look for. But in order to know what to look for, he must know what they mean. That is why they must be clear.[107]

The formation of concepts raises the question of the role of *indices*, for some sociological concepts do not refer to observables. How, for example, does one go about establishing criteria for observing cohesion? This is a problem, it will be recalled, that Durkheim addressed in his study of the division of labor. The sociologist should, Merton observed, develop objective indices in the form of observable facts. The ideal index is an observable fact or set of facts that stands in a one-to-one relationship to the unobservable facts indicated by the concept. These facts are then studied through the index. The index operationalizes the concept.[108] This is precisely the conclusion Durkheim arrived at when he considered types of law as indices of types of solidarity. Consequently, a scientific sociology often arrives at empirical generalizations expressed as relationships among indices of concepts.

Positivist Social Theory

We can distill from the preceding rather detailed discussion general notions that express the sense of the positivist model of social theory as an ideal-type. This model assumes that a social order consisting of recurrences and interrelationships of social facts exists independently of a scientific observer. It can therefore be objectively investigated and scientifically understood, and the ways in which it is investigated leave it untouched. The scientist neither creates nor alters it. Subject and object remain separate.

The positivist view places the social sciences in the context of all the sciences. Although the subject matter of the sciences varies, similarities among them obtain in logic and method. Notwithstanding these likenesses, the natural sciences, especially physics, are considered the ideal for the social sciences to emulate. Positivism assumes a unity of the sciences.

The immediate goal of a scientific sociology is the discovery of the recurrences and interrelationships among the facts of societies expressed in generalizations. In the ideal case, generalizations are universals that

36   The Scientific Character of Social Theory

hold without exception under specified conditions and state causal relations in terms of necessary and sufficient conditions or in terms of universal associations without reference to causality. The nomological ideal is, however, considerably relaxed in actual practice to admit generalizations of a statistical character. Nevertheless, the social order is lawful.

The nomological ideal reaches its apex in the logical integration of generalizations, in which the lower are derived according to logical rules from higher-order, more general ones. This deductive-nomological (sometimes known as the *hypothetico-deductive* and sometimes as the *axiomatic*) conception of theory is the basis for explanation and prediction. Being logically symmetrical, explanations and predictions of social phenomena consist of deriving them as logical implications from theory. The deductive approach is definitely superior to *ad hoc* explanations.

Precision demands that the general propositions of theory be expressed in quantitative form, but here again scientific practice compromises and discovers relationships among purely qualitative facts. The idealized goal of theory is to explain the entire social order in terms of the logical derivation of lower-order generalizations from decreasing numbers of more general ones. Movement toward more general explanation requires increasing logical integration of more encompassing theory, which provides the best measure of scientific progress.

All sciences reveal a unity of method as well as logic. Accordingly, social facts must be observed, measured, and classified in unambiguous categories in conformity to the law of the excluded middle. As subjects and predicates of propositions, concepts must be clearly and precisely defined. That human behavior involves subjective factors like motives and beliefs complicates methods of data collection and measurement but poses no intrinsically insuperable barriers to scientific classification. Inasmuch as the truth of propositions and the validity of concepts depend on a correspondence with reality, they must be tested in the light of relevant facts. Possessed of special methods and formal theory, social science must be carried out by specialists and set apart from lay conceptions.

The unity of sociology with natural science is also manifest in analogies between the facts of society and the facts of nature. In its zeal to adhere to an idealized unity of science, positivist social theory tends to erase some of the distinctions between the natural and the social, proceeding in the direction of conceptualizing the latter in terms of properties of the former. The history of sociology in its positivist phase shows an especially pronounced influence from biology.

Consistent with an emphasis on empirical facts and a rejection of metaphysics as outside the purview of science, positivism draws an unbridgeable distinction between empirical facts and judgments of value. The value of an object is not an inherent quality, but rather something attributed to it by a subject. At the same time, a social theory constructed according to the aforementioned logical principles and method makes possible intervention into the social order on behalf of nonscientifically selected values.

This overly brief delineation of a positivist social theory takes on meaning when it is considered in the context of actual discussions and theoretical inquiries of sociologists. The positivist model is held as an ideal by many sociologists and influences profoundly the way they formulate problems and conduct research. The fact that sociological practice deviates from this ideal, in some cases very far indeed, does not deny its influence. It is so ingrained in sociological thinking that it is mostly taken for granted, being formulated explicitly primarily for polemical or pedagogical purposes. It has been created largely as an adaptation of what natural scientists are believed to do in the course of their disciplines to the realm of the social. Behind the positivist conception of social theory lies the understandable desire to extend the success of the physical sciences into the domain of the social—a desire so apparent in the writings of sociology's acknowledged founder, Auguste Comte. A science of society, in turn, is defined as a potential instrument to improve the human condition by making it yield to scientific control.

Despite fairly wide agreement on the validity of the positivist conception, there have always, as noted at the outset of this chapter, been challenges. Arising, at least in part, from the recalcitrance of social theory to be squeezed neatly into the positivist mold, these criticisms can be synthesized into an antipositivist model of social theory.

2

Social Theory According to Antipositivism

Criticisms of the positivist ideal for the social sciences were soon forthcoming, especially in Germany with its idealistic tradition. The debate over methods (the *Methodenstreit* of the 1870s and 1880s), the controversy over the role of values (the *Werturteilsstreit* immediately preceding World War I), and the positivist dispute in sociology in the 1960s raised important methodological as well as substantive questions. Challenges to positivist pronouncements were enunciated in several broad areas.

First, the strict dualism of the social scientist and his object-domain, according to which the observer using the right methods can arrive at objective results, gave way to the notion that an observer's concepts and values constitute rather than only reflect external objects. Is an observer completely independent of what he investigates? Also, is the distinction between fact and value as clear-cut as Weber made it out to be? Second, positivist inclinations to minimize the differences between physical and social facts were replaced by an emphasis on the qualitative character of meanings, which have to be grasped in some way other than through observation. Third, the deductive-nomological model was replaced by a more realistic concern with the concrete and unique. Fourth, the belief in a clear distinction between scientific knowledge and common sense yielded to the recognition of an obscuring overlap between them.

The term *antipositivist* as used here should not be interpreted to mean

40   The Scientific Character of Social Theory

that the social sciences in general and sociology in particular lack all scientific dimension. On the contrary, everyone believes that sociologists solve problems, form hypotheses, obtain relevant facts, make controlled inferences, and explain social phenomena. The term *antipositivist* refers to differences in logical and methodological perspectives stated as antitheses to positivist conceptions and exaggerated somewhat for the purposes of emphasis and clarity.

Antipositivism is thus defined negatively in terms of its opposition to positivism as it relates to social theory. As in the discussion of positivism, the following attempts to separate matters of logic from matters of substance, bringing in the latter only to illustrate the former. At the same time it should be recognized that insofar as logical considerations have sometimes shaped definitions of subject matter this separation is to some extent artificial. Social theories especially influenced by antipositivist conceptions are critical theory, phenomenology, and ethnomethodology. In addition, some of the methodological conceptions of Max Weber, despite being interwoven with positivist notions, are especially important to the foundation of antipositivism.

The Antipositivist Methodology of Max Weber

Weber put forth methodological analyses of the sociocultural sciences in the context of controversies occurring within economics, history, psychology, law, and other disciplines concerned with human beings. The arguments centered on the logical character of these sciences and their methods considered in relation to the sciences of nature. The antipositivist notions in Weber's discussions were developed largely within the framework of these debates. The sweep of Weber's thought includes many of the essentials of an antipositivist approach to social science.[1]

In the beginning of his first methodological essay, Weber briefly outlined the positivist model of science, which the natural sciences approximate, although not exclusively. Natural scientists arrange their data under generic concepts that indicate common features of natural objects. Observable, contingent facts are stripped away by such concepts, leaving quantitative, measurable factors such as mass and motion. Common to a large number of objects, these properties of material objects are subsumed under universal laws that relate their quantitative features in terms of causal relationships. Generic concepts are subsumed under others still more general and of increasing quantitative precision. The qualitative aspects of natural phenomena given to ordinary sense experience are progressively lost, deemed to be scientifically irrelevant in the face of what is worth knowing, i.e., the general. Scientific concepts suppress the qualitatively unique in favor of ever-greater extension. The science of mechanics carries this logic to an extreme.[2]

Discovery of universal causal laws depends upon the subsumption of facts under generic concepts; natural science copes with the multitude of facts by classifying them. Interest coincides with the general. In contrast, the sociocultural sciences, said Weber, come to grips with the multitude of facts by selecting those that distinguish one social phenomenon from others. These sciences focus upon those characteristics that make a social phenomenon unique. For instance, a social scientist is interested in what constellation of factors makes an organization bureaucratic rather than the fact that all its members speak. This it shares with other organizations. What are of concern are its qualitative distinguishing characteristics. Yet even those features selected by the concepts of social science, which like bureaucracy are "individual" concepts, are only a tiny fraction of the total, namely, those that the scientist regards as essential. The essential, however, is not the generic. Hence, the natural and social sciences (Weber sometimes referred to the latter as sciences of concrete reality) adopt two logically distinct methods to overcome, as far as this is possible, the infinite number of facts within their spheres.[3]

Selection of the unique as the focus of interest is correlated with other differences between natural and social scientific concepts. In their aim of covering as many phenomena as possible, natural science concepts indicate highly abstract characteristics that are relatively empty of content and tend to reduce qualitative to quantitative differences expressible as mathematical equations. Motion is an example. On the other hand, concepts of social science indicate configurations of qualitative, substantive factors that are relatively rich in content. A rational-legal bureaucracy, for instance, implies rational thinking, official duties, separation of the incumbent from the office, etc.[4] Remaining close to concrete reality, such concepts, in contrast to the concepts of natural science, are intensional rather than extensional.[5]

Weber qualified these distinctions, which do not coincide exactly with the difference between natural and sociohistorical sciences, as being matters of degree of emphasis. Mechanics approximates very closely the

42   The Scientific Character of Social Theory

search for the generic;[6] a natural scientist, however, may find of interest the unique features of an erupting volcano. A social scientist, on the other hand, may want to specify a characteristic shared by all groups.

If the concepts of social science tend toward the qualitative aspects of historical individuals, the question arises: What is the standard the scientist uses to distinguish one constellation of facts out of an infinity as an object of investigation? Since even a single act of exchange presents a multitude of dimensions,[7] e.g., the manifold of biographical experiences of the partners and all the physical aspects of the object exchanged, a selective principle is required to describe it. Weber identified this principle as *value-relevance.*

Value-relevance is the selection of those facts that are relevant to the investigator's values.[8] It is assumed that these values are shared by those within a given culture, a fact that homogenizes scientific interests. Shared values lend the relevant facts a cultural significance.[9] Ideas of what is important in the light of shared values have the effect of defining the problems for investigation and, indirectly, the entire field of a social science. It is not, however, necessary, Weber cautioned, that each scientist share precisely the same negative or positive evaluation of a significant social object, but only the broad significance it has for culture.[10]

As a logical way of coming to terms with the inexhaustibility of reality, the criterion of value-relevance further differentiates cultural from natural sciences. As already noted, the natural scientist attempts to capture, insofar as possible, the infinity of nature in a net of generic concepts and natural laws, logically arranged and hierarchically ordered. From these he deduces concrete events. But even if a corresponding set of social laws existed, no matter how encompassing, it could never be the basis for a logical deduction of the culturally significant. This is so because we are neither interested in every social event nor in every single cause that brought it into being.[11] The source and direction of scientific interest in things social are derived from value-relevance—a principle logically distinct from the generalizing interest typical of natural science. Moreover, in light of their intensionality, the more general the social scientific concept, the less its meaning and cultural significance. What is of interest about a historical individual is not what it shares with every other, but wherein it is different. The general properties of exchange are now as they were in antiquity, but what we are interested in is how a money economy acquired the importance it has in the modern world.[12]

Consequently, for Weber, the criterion of value-relevance subordinated the search for analytical laws to the end of investigating culturally significant facts of concrete reality.

In contrast to a system of unchanging class concepts, the concepts of social science and history change with changes in perceived significance of events. "The stream of immeasurable events flows unendingly towards eternity."[13] Changing evaluations of the significant are accompanied by shifting intellectual and scientific contexts within which events are viewed. Thus, the knowledge of social science does not remain static, encased in scientific laws. Value-relevance generates a changing social science, one not evolving toward a system of hierarchically ordered laws in relationships of cumulative dependence.

Nomological knowledge derives from universal laws based on class concepts that omit the individualities of particular objects.[14] Yet it is precisely the latter that are of interest to social scientist and historian. But what is absent in a premise cannot appear in a conclusion derived from it. Take, for example, Parsons's law of rationality, which, ironically, he drew from Weber. It is impossible to deduce from it *which* means in the service of *which* ends become more effective and efficient, yet it is precisely such concrete content that is of interest.

Weber put forth the following supposition: Assume that economists know every single cause of an economic phenomenon. In that case an exhaustive knowledge of economic "laws" from which it could be deduced as a conclusion from premises would be superfluous.[15] It would be cognitively worthless precisely because the end of cultural knowledge is a knowledge of concrete phenomena and their concrete causes, and so-called economic laws are only means to that end. What is the point of acquiring means if one already has the end?

Nevertheless, the question of the relationship of "social laws" to concrete reality is more complicated. As noted in the discussion of Weber in the preceding chapter, in order to discover concrete causes of particular historical individuals the social scientist must employ generalizations, under which he subsumes the hypothesized causes. These empirical rules, however, lack the logical characteristics of natural laws; and that is the reason why concrete causes cannot be deduced as conclusions from premises. It was Weber's conclusion that their peculiar logical status is related to the character of social scientific concepts. Let us therefore consider the ideal-type, which, according to Weber, is the concept indispensable to social investigations.

44   The Scientific Character of Social Theory

Well-known examples of types Weber used as heuristic devices in his investigations were bureaucracy, feudalism, capitalism, Christianity, individualism, and handicraft economy. A close connection obtains between the criterion of value-relevance and the ideal-type insofar as the scientist selects culturally significant aspects of reality to be included in a specific type. It follows, argued Weber, that there is no such thing as a type formed without presupposition. [16]

The constellation of characteristics that define an ideal-type, however, are not those that are common to all phenomena to which it refers. If that were the case, the ideal-type would have the logical structure of a class—the generic concept of natural science. An instance of an ideal-type may lack certain of the characteristics stated in the type or possess them only to a degree. For example, we define capitalist economy as an economy of exchange, free competition, and rigorously rational action. [17] Nevertheless, no given capitalist economy ever incorporates perfect rationality of economic conduct; actual capitalist economies only approximate this type of thinking. Consequently, every empirical instance that is relevant to a given type deviates in a certain way from it. The approximation of reality to it makes the ideal-type a utopian concept, [18] which can never be a reproduction of social reality, only a limiting case. [19] Lacking the character of a class, the ideal-type poses a challenge to theorists like Durkheim whose vision of social laws expressed uniform relations among classes of social facts.

The irreality of this concept stems from the way it is constructed. The scientist accentuates a characteristic of reality and idealizes it, not in the sense of establishing it as an ideal to be striven for, [20] but of exaggerating it in order to render it clear and unambiguous. The various characteristics that define a type are synthesized into a unity, a systematized whole with interrelated parts. Therefore, in its conceptual purity and coherence an ideal-type cannot copy the realities to which it refers. [21] Those are admixed with other elements and deviate from the scientific imagination. It is logically incorrect, therefore, to consider an object as an instance of a type in the manner in which a dog is an instance of a mammal.

Weber pointed out that value-relevance opens up the possibility that a number of types can be worked out with reference to any set of facts. Capitalist culture could be defined in different ways depending upon the scientific interest, each type having the appearance of a self-contained entity. [22] Consequently, there is no essence or essential trait of a social

Social Theory According to Antipositivism   45

fact apart from an investigator's interest. There is no "true" type in an absolute sense.

This conceptual picture, however, is complicated by the fact that some constructions in social science do have the character of logical classes. These turn out to be concepts of purely observable phenomena. An example is relations of exchange when the subjective intentions of the partners are neglected. Barter and the exchange of commodities for money occurred again and again throughout history with essentially the same elements. However, when the idea of *marginal utility* is built into the concept of exchange, which is the subjective calculation of relative amounts of value, then the concept becomes an ideal-type. According to Weber, the more the focus of the scientist is on mass phenomena, especially of a statistical character, the more the mode of conceptualization becomes a classification system.[23]

Weber's qualification of the conceptual picture with variation between conceptual poles has important implications. The principal mode of social scientific concept formation turns out to apply to subjectively intended meanings. Take, for example, the idea of medieval Christianity. The meaning of Christianity to so many indefinite and changing individuals was so variable in content and clarity that it is impossible to capture it in concepts defined in terms of *genus proximum* and *differentia specifica*. The portrayal of every individual's idea would, even if possible, result in a chaos of often contradictory meanings despite the fact that the Church enforced uniformity to a high degree.[24] Consequently, the exposition must take on an ideal-typical form.

Weber went on to emphasize that ideal-types are indispensable to make clear investigation and exposition. Unless the scientist explicitly forms types, neither he nor others are certain of what he means, given the chaos and contradictions among relevant facts. Without clear concepts, everyone remains in the "realm of the vaguely 'felt.' "[25] But when ambiguities are eliminated and the type appears as an internally coherent unity, it inevitably diverges from reality.[26] That explains why concrete events and historical individuals cannot be logically deduced as conclusions from laws. The empirical generalizations under which facts to be explained are subsumed are not laws that can substitute for premises, but rather are ideal-typical in their relation to reality.

Despite this limitation Weber was convinced that ideal-types are indispensable. An ideal-type furnishes the means for talking about a historical individual and describing it. It is not itself a description, but an

46   The Scientific Character of Social Theory

instrument for that purpose.[27] The scientist compares a given reality and describes the relevant facts in the light of the type as theoretical guide. Does this particular religious group reveal the characteristics of the ideally described sect and to what degree? Which sectarian features does it lack and why? In raising such questions, an ideal-type, although not a hypothesis, suggests hypotheses for exploration.

Weber gave the example of handicraft economy, characterized by ground rent as the only source of capital accumulation. It is possible to construct an idealized picture of the development of a capitalistic organization out of handicraft economy, a shift conditioned by limited land, population growth, influx of precious metals, and growth in rationality. If comparison of the actual course of events shows that history did not correspond to the ideal sequence and if the handicraft type were properly constructed, the hypothesis that medieval society contained other than purely handicraft principles would be proved.[28]

As the example of medieval Christianity shows, intentional meanings give the social world a complex, multiform character, which requires the use of types. Let us, therefore, examine the role of subjective elements according to Weber's methodology.

The reader will recall that the goal of the sciences of concrete reality is to come to grips with the unique qualities of those aspects of social reality that satisfy the criterion of value-relevance. They are to be studied with reference to their qualitative differentiations, which are their essential features as determined by cultural criteria of significance, and investigated with reference to relevant ideal-types. Furthermore, consistent with his emphasis on concrete reality, Weber also defined a goal of these sciences as the imputation of concrete causes and effects to those aspects of reality.[29] But causes and effects, according to Weber, are also subject to the criterion of value-relevance. The causal nexus of a historical individual and the causal claims are infinitely large; so again it is an axiological relation, a relationship to culturally significant values, that determines which causes become foci of scientific interest.[30] Value-relevant selection of particular causes and consequences constitutes another departure from the nomothetic ideal of the sciences of nature. Rather than discover laws that explain all causes and effects, the socio-cultural scientist selects only the few that interest him.

There is also a difference between the two types of science in causal imputation. The most significant causal factors in history are to be found in the subjective states of individuals, in their intentional meanings and motives, the understanding of which provides causal explanations of their actions.[31] Although, as we have seen, the purely logical principles of causal explanation are similar in the natural and sociocultural sciences inasmuch as concrete causes must reflect some more general regularity,[32] the social scientist has an opportunity to do what the natural scientist cannot do; he can understand and interpret the subjective meanings inherent in his subject matter.[33] Hence, causal imputation in social science and history involves both generalizations and the understanding of meaning. Without understanding, causal explanation accomplishes no more than the explanations put forth in the natural sciences.

Let us explore a little further the relationships among interpretive understanding, causal imputation, and nomological knowledge according to Weber. Despite the logical necessity of general knowledge for explaining purposes, causal explanation in the sociocultural disciplines calls also for understanding. We are not satisfied, said Weber, with only empirical generalizations. Suppose we have explained a given social phenomenon by understanding it. To make it the basis of the formulation of a generalization would add nothing, even if the latter had the status of a universal law admitting of no exceptions. Again the general and abstract are subordinated to the concrete and particular. On the other hand, suppose that a statistical demonstration shows that everyone in a given situation reacts the same way without exception. Such a demonstration involving no interpretation of motive would on that ground fail to satisfy the kind of causal interest specific to social science.[34] Likewise, any statistical generalization not susceptible to interpretation, such as a possible correlation between rationality and the cephalic index, is merely a given that does not satisfy the interest in subjectively intended meaning. It does not constitute uniquely sociological knowledge.[35]

For Weber, then, the overall concern of history and social science is with the understanding of the particular and qualitatively different rather than the general. Their concrete objective is to describe selected aspects of concrete reality and to impute causes and consequences to them. In accomplishing these, the ideal-type and the understanding of meaning are indispensable. Before culturally significant causes of some aspect of reality can be determined, reality must be described with reference to a relevant type. At this point, the type and interpretive understanding converge; types conceptualize in a pure form subjective meanings.

Take, for example, the concept of purposive rationality (*Zweckrationalität*). This type of action consists of the selection of those means that

48   The Scientific Character of Social Theory

are adequate to the attainment of a clearly defined end. In selecting means and end the actor also takes into account the desirability or undesirability of consequences other than the end itself. In determining the relationships among means, end, and consequences, he relies on established generalizations as guidelines. As a means of description and explanation, this construct is brought to bear on a particular action. For example, according to the means used by the actor and in the light of their established relationships to an end, we can, said Weber, hypothesize that he was motivated by a given end. Or if we know his end, we can explain why a different result materialized in the light of the objective inappropriateness of the means chosen in the light of established generalizations.[36]

This simple example illustrates essentials of Weber's method—the use of empirical generalizations, the ideal-type, and explanatory understanding to satisfy a scientific interest in a selected aspect of concrete reality. This leading interest in the concrete is the central theme of Weber's antipositivism. Other antipositivist conceptions in his methodology can be derived from it. Thus, general knowledge and constructs are not ends as in the sciences of nature, but means. The emphasis on the general is reversed. It is not the task of sciences of human beings to subsume all the facts under generic terms and organize the latter into universal laws, which when combined in the correct manner will provide the basis for deducing reality. The deductive-nomological model is neither an attainable nor desirable ideal. The concepts of social science are typical rather than generic. Explanation in terms of cause and effect cannot therefore assume a purely deductive form leading to unambiguous conclusions. Nor can knowledge reach a high degree of logical integration.

In addition, the interest in the qualitatively unique necessitates the selective function of value-relevance in forming concepts. Culturally determined notions of what is important drive the formation of concepts. The searchlight of knowledge sweeps over and illuminates only a small section of human history.

Ideal-Type and Analytical Concept: Weber and Parsons

Fertile in antipositivist conceptions, Weber's methodology provides a frame of reference for the analysis of relevant ideas of other social theorists

Social Theory According to Antipositivism   49

who have treated the issue of positivism in social theory. To begin with, let us reexamine some of Parsons's positivist ideas discussed in the preceding chapter in the light of Weber and consider his criticisms of Weber's conceptions.

It can be shown that the analytical concept as defined by Parsons possesses the logical characteristics of a class. It is a generic concept. Although the analytical concept is an abstraction that does not exhaustively describe reality, it nevertheless conceptualizes aspects of reality in the form of what Parsons called analytical elements. The reader will recall that this selective "capturing" of reality is why Parsons called his methodological position *analytical realism*. Despite the fact that analytical elements are not self-existing units, but rather aspects of such units, they nevertheless fall into appropriate classes. The analytical concept, therefore, lacks the logical characteristics of the ideal-type, for it conceptualizes the common features of things according to the way Parsons defined it. Parsons himself recognized the distinction between the two constructs and criticized Weber's treatment of the ideal-type:

> A fourth attitude toward scientific concepts and their relation to reality which has been encountered in this study is that they are not reflections of reality, but "useful fictions." The principal example was Weber's own formulation of the status of his ideal-type concepts. . . . There is . . . an element of truth in this view . . . but when applied, as Weber was inclined to apply it, to all general concepts of social or any other science, it also is untenable. [37]

Parsons conceived of concrete analytical elements as variable values of their appropriate classes. A particular means used by an actor, for example, is one value of all those cases that form the class of means. With concepts that define classes of elements Parsons hoped to cover, as far as this is possible, the theoretically significant features of the entire social world. Analytical concepts were to facilitate the discovery of analytical laws that specify the uniform relationships among them. The deductive and predictive power of such laws were to be enhanced through the working out of their logical interrelationships and arrangement in a hierarchical order. Parsons believed he had made progress in this direction through the concept of the elements of action and the mechanisms

50   The Scientific Character of Social Theory

of systems of action.[38] This deductive approach did not accord with Weber's view of the social sciences.

Parsons's commitment to positivist ideals for social theory also led him to take issue with Weber's picture of a nonprogressive, noncumulative social science derived from the belief that there are as many concepts as points of view from which the world can be observed. This picture in turn is derived from the role of value-relevance in concept formation and contrasts with the idea prevailing in the natural sciences that the significant coincides with the general.

In order to bridge the gap between the two models of concept formation, Parsons argued that when concepts are constructed in light of their value-relevance, the resulting theory itself will generate a secondary interest in the relevant facts. The facts take on a purely theoretical interest in addition to the interest elicited by their cultural significance. The value-relevance thus becomes integrated with the theoretical interest,[39] and the concepts formed are not lost to science. In other words, if a sociologist studies red tape as an aspect of bureaucracy, for example, primarily because of a prevailing interest in this troublesome factor, the theoretical apparatus of the study can, if valid, be translated into a more general one. Thus, if a succeeding generation has lost interest in this particular problem, the research will still have contributed to theoretical progress.[40] The more general theoretical scheme that Parsons had in mind as the vehicle of progress was, of course, his general theory of action. In that way Parsons attempted to avoid what he thought were relativisitic implications in Weber's approach.[41]

Grafting a secondary, theoretical interest onto the value-relevance redirects the course of investigation away from Weber's goal of explaining the individuality of events and cultural configurations and reverses the subordination of the general to the particular. It is evident that these contrasting priorities and the logically heterogeneous concepts upon which they depend go to the heart of the positivist controversy.

Concept Formation According to Schutz

Alfred Schutz (1899–1959) believed that certain assumptions that social scientists take for granted can be analyzed with reference to the phenomenological baseline provided by Edmund Husserl. In studying Weber's

Social Theory According to Antipositivism   51

analysis of method, Schutz became aware that these phenomenological presuppositions also informed Weber's interpretive sociology. A good place to accomplish a phenomenological inquiry into them was in relation to the latter's social action theory. In attempting to clarify Weber's ideas in the light of phenomenological philosophy, Schutz reinforced and drew implications from the antipositivism in Weber's methodology.

At the same time, Schutz's contributions to social scientific method flatly contradicted Durkheim's positivist conceptions. As brought out in Chapter 1, Durkheim was firmly convinced that commonsense ideas of ordinary persons about law, morality, state, family, and society are inadequate to provide a scientific foundation for sociology. Commonsense thinking develops ideas about institutions to achieve strictly practical ends but mistakenly concludes that family, state, and society are simple developments of such ideas. The ordinary mind, said Durkheim, confuses its ideas with social reality. And in order to build a science of society on firm ground, Durkheim told sociologists to regard social facts as if they were things and observe them objectively, apart from commonsense notions.

Schutz's conclusions about the concepts of social science and the way they ought to be formed provide a stark contrast to Durkheim's injunctions. These differ, he said, from the concepts formed by the natural scientist, who is obliged to conceptualize the facts relevant to his discipline only in terms of the rules of science. Because the physical world holds no meaning for atoms, electrons, and molecules, the facts and events that compose his observational field are neither pre-selected nor pre-interpreted.[42] The natural scientist need not take nonexistent meanings into account.

On the other hand, the goal of social science is organized knowledge about social reality, which consists of the objects and events within the social world as experienced by commonsense thinking. In contrast to Durkheim, this definition builds into social reality what individuals think about it. The ideas individuals have of one another determine their behavior. Therefore, these commonsense thought-objects must be conceptualized by the concepts of social science in order to yield knowledge of social reality. It follows that the proper concepts of social science must be constructs of constructs, i.e., scientific constructs of commonsense constructs. The fact that the thought-objects of social science conceptualize the thought-objects of common sense, said Schutz, makes them

52   The Scientific Character of Social Theory

into second-order constructs. In contrast, the concepts of natural science are first-order constructs.[43] In both cases scientific concepts supersede commonsense concepts but in different ways.

Durkheim's rules for observing social facts make sociological concepts into what Schutz would have called first-order constructs. True to his positivism, Durkheim envisioned sociology as a science that was to follow the rules of concept formation prevailing in the natural sciences. He thereby avoided the problem implicit in second-order constructs that plagued Schutz: How it is possible to form objective concepts of subjective structures of meaning? In other words, how is it possible for a sociologist to form concepts of commonsense constructs in accordance with the rules of science? This question, Schutz averred, is the most serious problem that the methodology of the social sciences must grapple with.[44]

In order to find an answer he tried to clarify Weber's analysis of the ideal-type, for he agreed with Weber that it is the paramount social-scientific concept in terms of logic. The materials from which the social scientist constructs ideal-types are the actions of individuals in everyday life; and consequently the types, which are secondary constructs, should conceptualize the concepts of common sense. These actions are aimed at achieving practical ends, and the practical actor defines his situations according to criteria relevant to his practical ends. With himself at the center of the universe, he forms commonsense constructs of objects. His "here" and "now" are decisive for his interpretations. In constructing ideal-types of practical actions, the social scientist, however, substitutes for these practical goals and criteria of relevance those that stem purely from his scientific problem. In observing an action the scientist has no biographically determined "here" and "now." His interpretations derive from a stock of knowledge acquired from his discipline and should not contradict it. As a disinterested observer he makes interpretations guided by a system of relevance different from that of a practical actor.[45] Two persons in a dispute over money, for example, define their interaction differently and have an interest in its outcome different from that of the scientific observer who is studying conflict.

In order to clarify further than Weber did the methods of ideal-type construction, Schutz formulated three general postulates. The first he called the *postulate of logical consistency*. This sets forth two criteria that enable the ideal-type to supersede common sense. The first is absolute clarity of content—a notion Schutz borrowed from Weber, who held that the ideal-type should gain in clarity and precision what it loses in the

Social Theory According to Antipositivism   53

reduction of content. The second is the compatibility of the type with the principles of formal logic.[46] Commonsense thinking, which often lacks clarity and adopts inconsistent views, violates this methodological postulate.

Schutz also borrowed the other two postulates from Weber, which he called the *postulate of subjective interpretation* and the *postulate of adequacy*. Subjective interpretation requires the social scientist to construct ideal-types of the minds of individuals, whose subjective processes explain the course of their actions. It is obvious that this postulate is the heart of Weber's interpretive sociology.[47]

In clarifying the methodological postulate of subjective interpretation, Schutz found it essential to distinguish between subjective and objective meaning—a distinction he said Weber did not sufficiently take into account. The subjective meaning of an action is what it means to the actor; that, according to Weber, is what the sociologist must understand. The objective meaning of an action is what it means to an observer.[48] In this context observation need not be limited to an actual perception of what someone does, as in the case of one who sees another chopping wood, but can also refer to the awareness derived from any other sources that an action has occurred. For example, one can infer that an unknown postman delivers letters. Schutz called this experience of a postman whom a person thinks about an indirect observation or an indirect relationship.[49] In thinking about a living, anonymous person, we experience him merely as a contemporary and form an indirect relationship with him.

Now it is evident that an objective meaning of an action may not correspond to its subjective meaning, for the observer may situate it in an entirely different meaning-context than does the actor. In fact, Schutz defended the proposition that in observing a contemporary indirectly the observer can never experience the former's subjective meaning with the vividness and concreteness that is possible in a direct, face-to-face relationship. In such a relationship the two can talk to each other and "live" within each other's stream of consciousness. Here it is possible to grasp the other's subjective meaning.[50] In an indirect relationship, however, the observer is able to grasp the other only as an ideal-type. If he is a commonsense observer, the type is a commonsense construct; if the observer is a social scientist who follows the methodological postulates of concept construction, then the type is a scientific ideal-type.[51]

An ideal-type describes a contemporary's subjective meaning-context

54   The Scientific Character of Social Theory

as a typical subjective state of an anonymous individual. Knowledge of contemporaries given in ideal-types is anonymized. Thus, we think of a typical, anonymous mailman, who performs typical actions with typical motives in the course of an occupation. Reflecting the meaning-contexts of observers, however, such anonymous types are objective meaning-contexts of subjective meaning-contexts. [52] Therefore, the problem for social science, already raised by Schutz in a more general way, is how to form ideal-types of indirectly experienced contemporaries in accord with the rules of science.

The postulates of logical consistency and subjective interpretation give only a partial answer. The postulate of adequacy, which Schutz also borrowed from Weber's interpretive sociology, provides additional guidelines.

According to this methodological postulate, the scientist is required to formulate a type in such a fashion that if an individual performed the action indicated, the type would make sense to him and his fellow men. In other words, the type should be consistent with commonsense constructs and understandable to whom it applies. [53] Suppose an observer comes upon a scholar counting the frequency of certain words in Plato's dialogues. The observer finds out about a rule that in different periods of persons' lives they prefer certain words. He constructs a type of classical scholar whose motive is to establish the chronology of literary works and fits it to the action. Insofar as it is understandable to classical scholars, the type has adequacy. [54] In establishing this rule Schutz adapted Weber's criterion of adequacy on the level of meaning to his own scheme. [55]

An ideal-type is an objective-meaning construct of the subjective meaning of a hypothetical actor endowed with consciousness. The construction provides a yardstick with which real persons can be compared. At the same time, the subjective meaning stated in the type, which conforms to the above postulates, is an objective-meaning context created by a scientist lacking at the time he formed it access to the subjective states of real contemporaries to whom the type refers. The observer's constitution of the actor's subjective states, therefore, derives from his interpretations of his own direct and indirect experiences and from his science. Since an observer experiences a contemporary indirectly, the scientist imagines an anonymous actor with typical meanings. Lacking the individuality of a real person, the actor is endowed with typical ends obtained through typical means and given no more content than necessary for the scientist's purposes. [56] Acting the way the scientist

Social Theory According to Antipositivism   55

has designed him, the actor should not be confused with any particular individual. Schutz called the person in a type a puppet.[57]

The foregoing postulates are relevant to the formation of types. Although principally concerned in his methodology with their construction, Schutz also touched on their uses. First, an ideal-type can be used to explain a recurring or repeatable act. The scientist formulates a course-of-action type and connects it to an ideal-typical subjective meaning in accordance with logical consistency, subjective interpretation, and adequacy. Schutz called the postulated actor a *personal ideal-type,* whose subjective processes include typical means applied to typical ends.[58] The personal ideal-type functions as the explanation of the recurring action. Here the scientist uses the type in order to explain an action in the manner of Weber. An example of this type of explanatory use is the previously given example of Weber's purposive rationality.

Second, the social scientist has at hand a personal ideal-type and constructs a repeatable course of action that corresponds to its structure of meaning. He knows, for instance, the typical bureaucrat and derives actions correlated with the meaning that will probably occur. In this context we can speak of Weber's objective possibility. This use of the type is scientific prediction and corresponds to Weber's criterion of causal adequacy. The explanatory and predictive uses of the ideal-type complement one other. In explanation the scientist has an action as datum and fits the appropriate personal type to it; whereas in prediction he begins with a personal type and fits a corresponding action to it.[59]

In general, Schutz's methodological analysis of social science sustains Weber's approach and at the same time provides phenomenological clarifications and supplementations of some of Weber's antipositivist conceptions. Like Weber, Schutz believed the ideal-type to be social science's principal concept. If, however, the only way a scientist can understand contemporaries is as types, then scientific knowledge of contemporaries is organized strictly in terms of objective constructs. Although an ideal-type is defined in terms of subjective meaning, as anonymous idealizations these are only approximations of the meaning-contexts of concrete persons; and the greater the generality of a type with reference to the scope of its predication, the greater its objectivity and the less its meaning. This was Weber's view, which Schutz developed in fine phenomenological detail. But Schutz also made the case, again from a phenomenological baseline, that only in a simultaneous, face-to-face relationship can one grasp the subjective meanings of another, and

56   The Scientific Character of Social Theory

even that understanding remains incomplete. Consequently, if a scientist uses a type to explain or predict some particular action or actions, it follows from Schutz's analyses that he ought to use techniques that get as close as possible to establishing a direct relationship between himself and the actors.

Here again we encounter a dialectic between the general and particular, which Weber saw so clearly. If the task of sociology as a social science is to interpret subjective meanings in order to explain and predict concrete events, then a strictly ideal-typical form of knowledge is incomplete. Weber took the position that such knowledge is only of heuristic value. What is of greater worth is the understanding and causal explanation of particulars. Although his phenomenological analysis implies the existence of the issue, Schutz never really faced it.[60] Is the abstract, anonymous knowledge given in scientifically constructed types an end or a means?

The Indexical Expression in Ethnomethodology

As a leading architect of ethnomethodology, Harold Garfinkel (1920–) drew heavily on Alfred Schutz's work. Whereas Schutz distinguished clearly between the logical characteristics of the constructs of common sense and the constructs fashioned by sociologists for scientific purposes, Garfinkel concluded that the boundaries between them are blurred.

If, as Schutz held, social science proceeds in terms of second-order constructs, the characteristics of the first-order constructs of everyday thinking will shape them. One such characteristic is that commonsense meanings are shaped by their contexts. Contextual factors that influence commonsense constructs (Garfinkel called them *accounts*) include the individual's unique biography, his immediate purpose in putting forth an account, the circumstances in which he developed it, and his particular relationship to another at the time. Following Bar-Hillel, Garfinkel labeled context-dependent accounts *indexical expressions*. Insofar as actions are oriented to these contents, the quality of indexicality extends also to overt actions. The centrality of indexicality in the practical actions and practical accounts of everyday life is implied in Garfinkel's definition of ethnomethodology as the investigation of the rational

Social Theory According to Antipositivism   57

features of indexical expressions and other actions as accomplishments in everyday life.[61]

Now if all actions and their subjective states are context-dependent, what happens when a sociologist tries to generalize about them? Does the indexical character of accounts limit the ability to explain an action by logically deducing it from a relevant generalization? Garfinkel answered that their indexicality does constitute a logical obstacle to rigorous generalization and to the treatment of accounts according to formal rules of logic. The trouble is, he went on to emphasize, that sociologists almost unanimously agree that indexical expressions, the accounts individuals articulate, i.e., their interpretations and definitions of situations, can be converted into objective, context-free meanings for the purposes of science. This assumption has the convenient effect of placing the social sciences on a par with the natural sciences. The meaning, for example, of the statement "Ice floats on water" does not depend on who says it or under what circumstances. In contrast to majority opinion, Garfinkel denies the possibility of transforming indexical expressions of commonsense thinking into objective contents through scientific procedures.[62] This conclusion supports an antipositivist interpretation of social theory.

In order to define the characteristics of commonsense thinking more precisely, Garfinkel and Egon Bittner conducted a study of an outpatient psychiatric clinic. Their specific problem was to discover what criteria the personnel of the clinic utilized to admit patients. The data to answer this question came from the application forms filled out by prospective patients and the contents of the patients' case folders maintained by the personnel of the clinic.[63] Information relevant to the problem of selection had to be extracted from the documents.

Garfinkel and Bittner soon discovered that apart from data such as the sex, age, occupation, and marital status of patients it was difficult to obtain the kind of information needed to determine the admission criteria. They finally concluded that the records could not be read the way one reads a bank statement. Any competent reader of the latter can follow the transactions and easily discover imbalances and omissions. A bank statement is an example of what Garfinkel and Bittner called an *actuarial record.*

Instead, it makes more sense to interpret the patients' files as contracts between patients and clinic. According to a therapeutic contract the patient places himself in the hands of medical professionals and suspends

58   The Scientific Character of Social Theory

his own judgment about what is best for himself. The clinic in turn assumes a legal and moral obligation to make decisions in his interests. Although any contract specifies the terms of an agreement, it does not specify all the details of how they are to be fulfilled. It regulates rather than describes a relationship. Consequently, the documents of the clinic should be read by investigators as decisions made in the course of the fulfillment of contracts rather than as actuarial accounts. The overarching criteria of relevance for clinic personnel who wrote and read the folders was whether the record could in its totality stand up as having met the terms of the contract.[64]

But this criterion still did not allow the investigators to obtain the information relevant to their problem. It did, however, enable them to understand the inadequacies of the documents. The remarks in the folders, for example, were consistently elliptical because the personnel who wrote them assumed that the personnel who read them would understand them because writers and readers knew one another's jobs. The writers, furthermore, knew the readers knew something about their biographies, their purposes in making entries, the circumstances in which they wrote the entries, and the relationships between writers and readers. Therefore, the compilers of the files could afford to be elliptical. Garfinkel and Bittner concluded that the contents of the folders presupposed an understanding of the social order of the clinic rather than revealed it[65]—an irony inasmuch as the goal of their study depended for its accomplishment on precisely the opposite assumption.

Interpretations of a folder also depended upon what uses a reader wanted to make of it. Changes in use changed interpretations of content. It was not the case that a use depended upon what a document revealed, but rather the revealed content was interpreted to fit the use a reader already had in mind. Also, a use evolved in the reader's mind as he went through the file; and insofar as a reader's goal lay at the basis of his interpretation, inconsistencies, omissions, and repetitions were irrelevant. Purposes served by its content were fashioned by previous interactions of clinician and patient. Garfinkel and Bittner consequently concluded that not only were the meanings of documents dependent upon the specific occasions of their use, but also upon the operation of the clinic as a total context.[66]

The way a clinician consulted a record is an example of documentary interpretation. A record exhibited an underlying pattern of meaning arrived at through an interpretation of its individual items. The items

Social Theory According to Antipositivism   59

documented the pattern, but this whole pattern in turn functioned as a context for the reader to interpret a given item. Parts and whole interacted.[67] Consequently, each item was not approached as a self-contained datum without presupposition; but rather the pattern, which formed a more or less consistent unity, functioned as a presupposition, a context, for the grasp of a single item. The fact that an item was construed in relation to an *a priori* context contributed reflexively to the latter's consistency.

In sum, it follows that most of the facts relevant to a real solution of the problem of the investigation had to be considered as indexical expressions. When approached as actuarial records, the patients' files were useless, filled with inconsistencies and gaps. But when approached with reference to the appropriate contextual factors, they made sense. For the most part, the records of the clinic consisted of indexical rather than objective expressions and had to be read as documentary texts. Had the same items of information appeared in the documents of another clinic, their meanings would have been different.

It is apparent that the generalization defended by ethnomethodologists, that commonsense thinking and actions are indexical, furnishes a logical basis for Weber's view that the indispensable social scientific concept is the ideal-type. For the dependence of commonsense interpretations on various contexts makes it difficult to formulate transsituational generalizations about them. Insofar as they are context-dependent, interpretations do not readily fall into well-defined classes. And, indeed, this is what ethnomethodologists contend.[68] If, for example, the criterion of selecting patients varies with every clinic because each is a different context for decision making, the only thing an ethnomethodologist can do is to form an ideal-type of such a criterion. Although Garfinkel did not explicitly discuss this logical construct, it is evident that his and Bittner's strategy of conceptualizing the patients' records as contracts illustrates Schutz's ideal-type as an objective meaning-context. The subjective meanings of the readers and writers of the files are deviations.

Nevertheless, Garfinkel arrived at more radical methodological conclusions than Weber and Schutz. Characteristics of commonsense thinking can be found in sociological formulations. What sociologists come forth with as substantive theories and methods are also context-bound. Research designs, the selection of problems and data, and the interpretation of findings are dependent on particular research situations.[69]

This contention can be illustrated by Garfinkel's study of the graduate

60   The Scientific Character of Social Theory

students who coded information from the patients' files in the aforementioned study. This project amounts to a study by Garfinkel of aspects of his own study. He found a high amount of agreement among the coders in the way they coded the items. The conventional sociological explanation of high reliability is that the coders correctly identified and described facts about the clinic. Garfinkel, however, had a different explanation. He found that they made *ad hoc* decisions as to what coding categories to allocate items to. Examples of such decisions were "et cetera," "unless," "let it pass," and *factum valet* (an action otherwise prohibited by a rule is accepted once it is done).[70] In sum, the coding was based on arbitrary decisions.

Garfinkel discovered that in making these decisions the student coders were trying to apply their prior knowledge about the clinic. They tried to interpret the folders the way the clinicians did. They resorted to documentary interpretation, for instance. The inference Garfinkel drew was that the coding instructions, which, after all, were scientific rules, were inadequate by themselves to furnish criteria for coding decisions. No matter how precisely formulated, they had to be interpreted in a context. Instead of the instructions being used to interpret the files, the files were used to interpret the instructions. The actual social order of the clinic, Garfinkel concluded, was not discovered.[71] Thus, scientific constructs, like commonsense constructs, are indexical. And social theory suffers from a lack of objectivity, for the meaning of the same terms used in different studies varies with context. Such skepticism was not shared by Weber and Schutz, who believed that ideal-types formed adequately for scientific purposes take on characteristics that distinguish them from everyday thinking.

Habermas's Critique of Positivism

In a critique of positivism Jürgen Habermas (1929–) identified antipositivist elements in science concealed by dominant positivist interpretations. According to a tripartite scheme, he classified sciences into the *empirical-analytical*, the *historical-hermeneutic*, and the *critical*.[72] Facilitated by this classification, his critique reveals antipositivist aspects of the social sciences and social theory.

The scientific method, according to Habermas, incorporates dimen-

Social Theory According to Antipositivism   61

sions often neglected by practicing scientists and those who attempt to define it. All sciences accomplish three things. They constitute the objects that are relevant, they study those objects according to methodological rules, and they apply the resulting knowledge.[73] The first and third of these activities are in a sense external to a given science, whereas the second, which involves concepts, propositions, the relationship of theory to facts, and verification, compose its internal structure. Empirical-analytical, historical-hermeneutic, and critical modes of inquiry differ with regard to each of these activities.

Let us consider the constitution of the objects of science. *Object-constitution* is the selection of those aspects of reality that become objects of investigation. A part of the world becomes objectified through selection. The constituting criteria are transcendental insofar as they are prior to science and organize the scientist's experience.[74] Before a scientist is able to study something, he must identify it, bring it into focus, and experience it. Take, for example, the hardness of a diamond. Although this property exists independently of its being perceived, when a scientist rubs a sharp object against a diamond he "constitutes" the diamond's quality. He makes it into an objective property. The hardness preexists the operation, yet the operation constitutes it by providing a perspective on reality.[75] Although the constituting criteria are not, strictly speaking, part of science, they make science possible. They are "quasi transcendental," said Habermas. Generalized as types, these constitutive criteria turn out to be very general interests, each type of interest making possible the objects relevant to one of the three aforementioned types of science.

The interest that constitutes objects relevant to the empirical-analytical sciences is technical control.[76] This *knowledge-constitutive* interest is expressible as a means-ends relationship. Accordingly, the goal of controlling objects is accomplished through the constitution of objects as a means. The objectification of nature is, therefore, a means of controlling it, of subordinating it to human needs. Empirical-analytical knowledge depends in the final analysis on this nonscientific interest. The hardness of a diamond is useful in the production of goods and gives human beings control.

Whereas the empirical-analytical sciences constitute physical objects in order to control them, the historical-hermeneutic sciences, Habermas goes on to say, constitute meanings in order to understand them. In other words, the general interest that lays the foundation of the historical-hermeneutic sciences by objectifying meanings is satisfied by mutual

62   The Scientific Character of Social Theory

understanding.[77] Insofar as they employ the hermeneutic mode, history, sociology, and political science have as their goal understanding semantic content. They investigate, for instance, cultural traditions. Habermas calls this interest the practical interest.[78]

The rule of these general interests contributes to an antipositivist conception of science. Their constitutive role denies that a scientist approaches his subject without presuppositions and repudiates the notion that facts are independent of scientific cognitions. It is not the case that facts simply confirm or falsify theory. Habermas called the independence of facts and theory an "objectivist illusion." On the contrary, knowledge-constitutive interests contribute to scientific objectivity.[79]

Another neglected aspect of science, one hidden by a positivist self-understanding of science, is the application of scientific knowledge as part of the verification process. Habermas located the sphere of life in which empirical-analytical knowledge is applied as the world of work or instrumental action. In this sphere human beings subject nature to their control. By contrast, the sphere of application of historical-hermeneutic knowledge is the world of human communication. In this sphere of life individuals talk to one another, understand one another, and arrive at consensus.[80] This is the sphere of communicative interaction.

The application of knowledge raises the problem of the relation between theory and praxis (practice) in these spheres. The empirical-analytical and historical-hermeneutic sciences reveal different relationships between theory and practice. Insofar as social scientists follow the empirical-analytical model, they attempt to control individuals by the application of nomological knowledge. Individuals are manipulated as passive objects just as natural objects are manipulated by natural scientists.[81] An administrative system, for example, implements a policy derived from a social theory in order to produce certain effects in the lives of individuals under its jurisdiction. If the policy produces the intended consequences, the theory is verified. In contrast, the historical-hermeneutic approach instructs individuals in the meaning of the policy and enlists their cooperation to make it work. The underlying theory is corroborated through understanding. Here the relationship of theory to practice is consistent with the interest in mutual understanding. In general, scientific theory is verified by the kind of action it takes toward the world. The action in turn reflects its general interest.

Habermas's conclusion that *a priori* interests weaken the independence of scientist and object also has consequences for the logic of the

Social Theory According to Antipositivism   63

investigation itself. That the world is not independent of the knower has a bearing on scientific method and especially on hermeneutic inquiry as a form of it. Let us examine Habermas's discussion of this type of inquiry, which attempts to demonstrate that the positivist conception of the independence of subject and object is further compromised by the nature of understanding.

Originating in the interpretation of historical texts like the Bible, the methods devised by hermeneutics were generalized to the understanding of any meanings, including the intentions of contemporary actors. The broadening of hermeneutics thus converged with the understanding (Verstehen) of meanings, which plays an essential role in the social sciences. These, as already noted, are oriented to both historical-hermeneutic and empirical-analytical modes of investigation.

Understanding has always posed a problem for measurement in social sciences insofar as they are oriented to empirical-analytical procedures. A tension prevails between them and the hermeneutical mode of social sciences, the latter limiting their positivist possibilities. Borrowing from ethnomethodologists like Cicourel and phenomenologists like Schutz, Habermas concluded that measurement of meaning falls prey to the same troubles that plague ordinary communication. We cannot assume that the categories employed by the sociologist correspond to those of his subjects. Does the category "strongly agree" with a statement on a questionnaire have the same meaning to both? Despite the fact that it is impossible to verify, correspondence is assumed, and the mental contents of the subject are measured by fiat. Then the investigator performs operations, such as combining categories and measuring the extent of their association, on subjects' responses transformed by categories into data. Such operations, argued Habermas, do not, however, rectify any lack of correspondence. Rather, these operations impose characteristics on the data while failing to measure the characteristics of meaning.

Furthermore, definitions of concepts are often replaced by indicators assumed to relate to underlying meanings. Sociological concepts designed to measure subjective states are not rigorously defined in terms of a theoretical language, but retain instead the semantics of common sense. Scientist and subject use the same language. Consequently, definitions of categories reflect the notions derived from their biographically determined situations. Precise measurement, concludes Habermas, can occur only when the problem of commonsense meanings is solved.[82]

64   The Scientific Character of Social Theory

These are a few of the problems arising from understanding that stand in the way of an empirical-analytical approach.

The idea that definitions by social scientists are results of their life experience can be subsumed under more general notions put forth by Habermas in his critique of positivism. *Meaning-complexes,* which are the objects of hermeneutical inquiry, can be understood only through a process called the hermeneutical circle. The interpreter always has some preconceived notion about a meaning-complex that provides a frame of reference for his understanding of the parts. The meanings of the parts are contained in the whole, which in turn presupposes them. The parts react upon the holistic preconception, effecting a reinterpretation of it. The interaction between whole and parts repeats. Thus, a hermeneutic circle is an ongoing dialectic between the understanding of parts and whole, similar to Garfinkel's documentary interpretation. Borrowing from Gadamer, Habermas presented an example from jurisprudence. In the process of adjudication, the jurist interprets a law in order to determine how to apply evidence in a given situation. The interpretation then becomes incorporated into the meaning of the law. Moreover, the law is reinterpreted with every subsequent application.[83] The relation between law and interpretation is not a deductive relationship like that between premise and conclusion but rather a relation of judicial determination.

Where do preconceived understandings originate? Continuing to follow hermeneutic theory, Habermas traced them to the social scientist's sociocultural situation. His prior understandings are shaped by his total society,[84] whose influence he cannot escape. If, for instance, his task is to understand democratic ideology, his membership in a democratic society provides presuppositions concerning the relevant facts obviously not derived from scientific theory. Originating in life experience, these preconceptions (one might even call them prejudices) influence his interpretations. An interpreter can thematize his pre-understandings and revise them in the light of interpretations, but the modifications merely function as new pre-understandings.[85] The basis of hermeneutical inquiry is thus atheoretical. In this context Habermas criticized Schutz's concept of the scientist's theoretical attitude,[86] for his "natural attitude," i.e., his common sense, penetrates the theoretical stance.

Consequently, Habermas's idea of the objectivist illusion takes on another nuance. It is not only the case that general interests of sciences constitute their objects; science and its object-domain are not entirely

Social Theory According to Antipositivism   65

separate. But in addition, the scientific objects relevant to the hermeneutical mode are understood in the light of pretheoretical presuppositions. The failure to take cognizance of object-constitutive interests and the failure to recognize preconceptions regarding meaning are both, according to Habermas, forms of objectivism.[87]

Insofar as the hermeneutical circle operates during the course of inquiry, it violates certain positivist conceptions. The circularity involved violates the strict implication of conclusions by premises. Although premises may be logically deduced from more general ones, they cannot, according to the deductive-nomological model, depend on their conclusions. Yet the hermeneutic circle results in interpretations consistent with the meanings of the whole reacting upon the parts. Furthermore, the understanding of complexes of meaning in light of preconceived notions is bound to result in a correspondence between them, interfering with objective tests of hypotheses.

Habermas's analysis of the process of understanding involves other antipositivist elements. A scientist who generalizes about meanings on the basis of individual cases can test the generalization's validity only by determining whether the relevant subjective states are actually reproduced in the experiences of those to whom the generalization applies. This, however, can be known only through communication, in which the scientist is a participant along with the subject. Here Habermas adopts as model the relationship between psychoanalyst and patient.[88] If a patient denies that an experience stated in a general interpretation applies to him, the interpretive scheme does not apply to him. His case cannot serve as a test of the scheme. The cooperation between scientist and subject, who is at the same time an object of investigation, is not a criterion that empirical-analytical inquiry must meet.

In the context of a theory of communicative action, Habermas explored another dimension of the process of understanding, which has the logical consequence of repealing the dualism between factual assertions and value judgments. In order to understand the meaning of a speaker or writer, an interpreter is obliged to judge the validity claims that can be raised about what he said or wrote. If a speaker makes what purports to be a factual assertion, an interpreter needs not only to know on what grounds the speaker asserted it to be true; he must also assess for himself the validity of those grounds, asking himself, "Am I convinced that the grounds on which he stated something are sufficient to warrant its truth?" Only in judging the validity of the claim to truth, either by explicitly

66   The Scientific Character of Social Theory

questioning it or implicitly accepting it can the interpreter grasp the meaning of what was said or written.

Habermas identified two other validity claims that must be satisfied as conditions for understanding. One is the basis on which a speaker or writer claims that his statements about his actions or intentions are right. On what grounds are they justified as being appropriate? Are the norms to which his actions are oriented good ones? The other claim to validity is that raised by a speaker's sincerity. What basis is there to conclude that he really believes what he says? In sum, adequate understanding depends upon a rational assessment of how an interpreter relates himself to the three worlds indicated by these areas of validity: nature, society, and subjectivity.[89]

If understanding in general goes beyond a literal interpretation and requires the settlement of these validity claims, then the interpretations made by social scientists must be subject to the same conditions. Habermas therefore concluded that these conditions apply to the hermeneutical mode of scientific inquiry. Social science, said Habermas, cannot separate the question of meaning from the question of its validity.[90] In arriving at this position he equated the social scientist with a layman. The former has no other access to the meanings he attempts to understand than the latter. The social scientist has no special instruments like those of the physical scientist. He must belong to the same world (Habermas called the world of shared subjective meanings the *lifeworld*) that he interprets; for to understand it he must be able to participate in its production. And such participation presupposes that he is a member. Hence, a social scientist cannot understand an individual in a neutral fashion because his understanding depends upon the pretheoretical knowledge he acquired as a member of the same world. These are the reasons why meaning and its validity are not logically separate.[91]

There is more to the argument. According to Habermas's theory of the ideal-speech situation, the goal of communication is to achieve mutual understanding through arrival at a consensus, which in turn is a necessary condition for cooperation. It is reached either through a resolution of conflicts over the aforementioned validity questions or through an implicit acceptance of the validity claims. Unless a consensus is obtained on these matters, there is no mutual understanding. The goal, Habermas went on to say, is to develop freely formed agreement in a rational way about the definition of a situation and the goals to adopt as a basis for

Social Theory According to Antipositivism   67

action. To reach consensus individuals raise validity claims, discuss them, rebut them, and come to rational agreement.

Now the scientist who attempts to understand these "communicative actions" must also become a participant in the dialogue. Involved in the speech situation, the social scientist is a participant-observer. He too joins the conversation, influences it, and discusses the types of validity that any conversation implicitly raises. His status in the discussion is that of a layman. His scientific status gives him no position of methodological privilege, for understanding arises within a relationship rather than from the perspective of an outsider.[92] Thus, Habermas assimilated scientific interpretation to the understanding occurring in everyday life.

A social scientist's involvement in practical discourse as a condition of understanding breaches the ideal of ethical neutrality. By including the determination of political goals and ethical rules according to rational criteria as within the scope of critical sociology, Habermas proposes that science do what Weber said it cannot, namely, tell individuals what they ought to do. The implicit rejection of a value-free social science stands alongside his analysis of the role of knowledge-constituting interests, his attack on objectivism, and his discussion of pretheoretical presuppositions as a challenge to a positivist social theory. Habermas's critique of positivism attempts to overcome the dualisms of subject and object, theory and practice, and fact and value.

The Hermeneutical Circle Reexamined

It is evident that Habermas's interpretation of the hermeneutical circle sustains the notion that objectivity is an illusion. If prior conceptions reflecting an interpreter's sociocultural position form a whole within which he construes the units of meaning to be understood, the whole of the circle is the interpreter's meaning-context rather than that of the other's objectified meanings. Consequently, the circle is not constituted solely out of the coherent elements created in the mind of the other.

Accordingly, it is instructive to draw the obvious distinction between the actor's context (or that of the producer of a document) within which he placed the meaning to be understood and the interpreter's context of meaning. A knowledge of the actor's context facilitates the interpreter's understanding of the actor's intentional meaning; whereas, the interpreter's context is an addition of meaning by the interpreting subject. If the interpreter, however, permits elements of his meaning-context to infuse into the object to be understood, the distinction between subject and object is obscured with a corresponding loss of objectivity. There is a subtle shift of meaning from the object to the interpreting subject.

Reconsider Garfinkel's study of coders in the light of the preceding distinction between meaning-contexts. Recall that he found that coders relied more on their prior knowledge of the clinic to make decisions than on the coding instructions. Their knowledge of the clinic functioned as a context of interpretation. Garfinkel concluded, therefore, that the research assumed a knowledge of what the research was aimed at achieving. It constructed what it was looking for in the process of looking for it.

It is evident that this view of the investigation is consistent with Habermas's explication of the role of the hermeneutical circle. Prior understandings of the coders functioned as a whole according to which the items of information in the records were interpreted. The implication of Garfinkel's explanation is that interaction between whole and parts did not represent a circle derived strictly from the documents. The interpretive scheme of the coders contributed to the inconclusiveness of the study. As Garfinkel put it, the true social order of the clinic remained to be discovered.

His report of the research, however, also lends itself to another interpretation. Meaningful categories applied to the patients' files such as "motivation for therapy" and "psychological mindedness,"[93] unlike age, sex, and marital status, are susceptible to understanding. Had the creators of the files developed these categories into systematic accounts of coherent meaning-structures, the coders could have followed the instructions more exactly and with less arbitrary improvisation. In view of the fact that events and routines in the clinic as experienced by personnel must have shaped their entries, a more detailed knowledge of the clinic could have facilitated a better interpretation of the files—one reflecting the intentions of their creators. But in the absence of the ideas that functioned as meaning-contexts for the writers of the files, Garfinkel's coders were compelled to substitute their own meaning-contexts.

This reanalysis suggests a hypothesis different from the conclusion arrived at by Garfinkel: An interpreter is likely to utilize his presuppositions when there are gaps in the meaning-context to be understood. The demand for clarity creates a circle that is not contained within the object itself. It is in frequently occurring situations of ambiguity that the reflexivity emphasized by ethnomethodologists is likely, and the act of understanding imputes meaning in the process of grasping it.

Experience reveals barriers to understanding as, for example, a strong personal interest in interpreting a complex of meaning differently than was intended. In social research one such interest is the desire to sustain a hypothesis. But experience also shows that we often become aware of our previous misunderstandings as new facts come to our attention. The universal experience of correcting misunderstandings is proof that a degree of objectivity is possible and that there can be limits to the reflexivity of accounts in social investigations. Furthermore, the hypothesis of the determinative impact of society as a totality on distortive presuppositions is useless for explanatory purposes in view of the fact that incompatible understandings occur among both laymen and social scientists who live in the same society.

The Issue Reconsidered: Type Versus Class

The inescapable fact at the basis of the issue is, of course, the meaningful character of human life. All the differences between the positivist and antipositivist models of social theory are related to the understandability of meanings created by individuals. What is less obvious is that the role played by subjective states requires a somewhat different logical system. We agree with Weber that the ideal-type is the only construct appropriate to conceptualize this dimension and that attempts to classify mental contents the way physical objects can be classified will fail. However, ideal-type generalizations have limited explanatory power.

Beliefs, values, and other subjective states are, nevertheless, interwoven with physical objects and processes. Human life has a dual nature, which consists of observables and meanings. Observables relevant to social investigation—age, sex, income, years of education, births, deaths, and migrations—lend themselves to classification systems and statistical generalization. Cost and practical difficulties aside, it is in principle possible to determine with precision what proportion of persons with one observable characteristic fall into another category defined in terms of another observable characteristic. A kind of nomological knowledge is possible with observables.

70   The Scientific Character of Social Theory

The problem is that the classification of such observables through sense observation fails to reveal causal relationships directly. The causes in which we are interested are to be found in the sphere of subjective meanings, which cannot be observed but must be inferred from the relationships found to obtain among observable factors. But when we try to generalize about subjective experiences and their effects, the statements depart from the concrete. As Weber noted, they do not refer to commonalities among particulars, but are rather idealizations of reality. The social scientist is forced to navigate among the facts with types— synthetic constructs of idealized meanings. That is why no social scientist can know in advance how rational a large organization is. He is not like a geologist who need not study a particular drop of water to discover at what temperature it freezes. An ideal-type indicates what to look for rather than what is seen.

The explanation of an action in terms of its subjectively intended meaning is vulnerable to two sources of ambiguity. First, it is not always clear which generalization or rule applies. Social science is not in a position to deduce a given action from a rule because experience shows that it is often the case that different and sometimes incompatible rules are all consistent with the action. Hence, it is a matter of choosing through informed guesswork the most likely rule in view of the known facts. Second, since the explanatory rules are ideal-typical, the subjective meaning of the action deviates from the rule even when it is the correct one. The deviations are exaggerated by the meaning-contexts in which individuals locate their intentions. These sources of ambiguity and lack of precision have nothing to do with the fact that generalizations are often stated statistically according to the formula: A given percent of A's are B's.

Little recognition, however, is accorded the distinction between classes and types; and the assumption is widely shared among sociologists that all data relevant to research can be allocated to their appropriate categories. It is generally believed that, despite technical difficulties, opinions, beliefs, and values can be classified, quantitative variations can be measured, and generalizations can be formulated. It is assumed that the only difference between such generalizations and laws is that the former are expressed statistically, but more knowledge about the conditions under which they hold will strengthen the relationships and make them more lawlike. Comte's view—that the ideal of explaining everything in terms of nomological knowledge although in practice unrealizable is a

Social Theory According to Antipositivism   71

worthy goal and that progress is slow only because of complexity stemming from a large number of variables—has prevailed.

These commitments are encouraged by the dualism of the social; and the investigator finds observables relevant to his research, which, as already noted, lend themselves to treatment according to positivist criteria. There is an understandable tendency to apply to one area what proves successful in another. That explains why there is a positivist conception of social science to begin with. Accordingly, there is a tendency for the logic of observables to encroach upon the logic appropriate to subjective meanings. Consistent with this tendency, Durkheim advised sociologists to conceptualize social facts as things; and Parsons analyzed Weber's type-rational action into analytical concepts. Both were reaching for social laws. This tendency also explains, at least to some extent, why so much effort is devoted to amassing statistical data on observables.

For the sake of clarity, the social theories that dominate the contemporary sociological scene—functionalism, symbolic interactionism, conflict, etc.—ought to be recognized as ideal-typical in their formulations. Their value is as guides to the investigation of particulars. The value of conflict theory, for example, is the help it gives a sociologist in explaining particular conflicts rather than what it states about conflict in general. For, as Weber so insightfully noted, the more general a social concept, the less meaning it has. What individuals are interested in are specific conflicts rather than conflict in the abstract. Interest in such abstractions is nourished only by their ongoing comparisons with the concrete. They must be continually illuminated by the particular. The reason why rational thinking as a type has proven its mettle is that it has been brought to bear on so many past and present concrete occurrences.

If the scientific value of social theory is heuristic and if theory is a means rather than end, social theories and their relationships are frequently evaluated by logically inappropriate standards. None is in a position to demonstrate superiority in the way Newton's theory of gravity is superior to Kepler's laws. None can substantiate the claim of greater predictive power than another. None can demonstrate greater explanatory potential because of greater generality than another. To judge social theories by such criteria is in the language of Habermas a "scientistic self-misunderstanding." Yet at the level of formal argument such criteria are often employed and the assumption made that the real aim of social theory is to formulate empirically true generalizations about classes of large numbers of instances. The argument, for example, has often been stated that Parsons's theory of the social system is faulty because of the proposition that societies are organized on the foundations of a value-consensus and a stable equilibrium. But the pervasiveness of conflict, so the argument goes, demonstrates the empirical error of this claim; therefore, the social system ought to be replaced by a better theory. If, however, the social system is thought of as an ideal-type despite Parsons's positivist pretensions, the indication of exceptions is not necessarily a valid counterargument.

If the value of a theory is to be found in its heuristic, one suspects that beneath the formal argument lies another reason why any given theory is chosen, which is that it is relevant to the sociologist's interests. Those who are interested in conflict, for example, defend conflict theory as a general perspective, whereas those interested in the myriad transitions of the content of the self are drawn toward symbolic interactionism. Such a criterion of selection is logically appropriate.

Strong commitments to a positivist sociology have concealed the realities of its subject matter and the limitations of what can be achieved. At this point, accuracy demands that I qualify this observation, for the very fact that positivism is an issue proves there is a range of opinion. Indeed, it would seem that the weight of sociological opinion is with positivist social theory as a viable ideal. Whichever view prevails, however, a discipline must have a clear conception of itself and its subject matter.

PART TWO

The Basic Units of Social Theory

Methodological Structuralism

The seventeenth century, the "century of genius" according to Whitehead, created the science that dominated Europe's intellectual life down to the present. Galileo, Descartes, Pascal, Huyghens, Boyle, and Newton dominated the science of the future because they defined units of investigation that engaged the attention of scientists and guided their research in productive directions. Configurations of matter with simple locations in space and time were the basic units of the cosmography of scientific materialism.[1] From them physicists readily derived motion, mass, force, and acceleration, the mathematically expressed relationships among which became the laws that disclosed nature's order. The price paid, according to Whitehead, for exclusive focus on these particular units by subsequent generations of scientists was, of course, the fallacy of misplaced concreteness.[2] Yet any area of scientific inquiry must abstract what it deems important and omit what it believes irrelevant.

As sociology emerged as a distinct discipline, what was problematic was not so much what sociologists ought to study, but rather the ontological nature of their object domain. Most accepted the idea that societies in their totalities and the social relationships that constitute them are legitimate objects of investigation. In addition, of course, there were customs, norms, groups, collectivities of all sorts, and institutions to be studied. But for some a fundamental question remained unanswered: What is the relationship between individuals and the societies

76   The Basic Units of Social Theory

and collectivities they form? This question implies the problem of the mode of being of social structures. Do they have an existence even partially independent of their members?

Two contradictory answers to the latter question were put forth and are still being argued. One line of thought takes the position that social structures have an independent existence that is not reducible to the characteristics of individuals. Consequently, societies and their structures are to be studied on their own terms. Another line of thought holds that collectivities are constituted solely by individuals and their relationships. Consequently, the study of societies can be reduced to the study of their members. The problem of the ontological status of the units of sociological investigation represented by these alternatives is a critical issue for social theory. In the following analysis, I call the first view *methodological structuralism* and the second, *methodological individualism.* [3]

Accordingly, the issue of the status of the elements that define the field separates social theories into structuralist and individualist theories. Yet it is again necessary to proceed in terms of the logic of the ideal-type; for individualist theories incorporate notions of structuralist thinking, and structuralist theories incorporate aspects of individualism. In analyzing the issue in its complex ramifications, one must judge the extent of approximation to a model. It should also be noted that not every theory that gives an account of social structures or refers to them exemplifies methodological structuralism. What is decisive is whether or not a theory assumes that structures have a certain mode of existence. However, those social theories, such as functionalism and conflict, that are macrosocial in scope have a special affinity for the structuralist approach. This chapter and the one that follows not only attempt to delineate the issue, but also to demonstrate that how the issue is answered affects the kind of explanations a theory adopts.

Again, I must emphasize that the formulations of those thinkers who exemplify a given theory, such as functionalism, for example, are analyzed not in their entirety, but selectively to delineate the issue under consideration. Although structuralist thinking can be detected in a number of writers, as will be seen, it is especially pronounced in the approaches of Durkheim and Parsons.

The Structuralism of the Social Fact

Methodological structuralism of an extreme form pervades Durkheim's functional theory and markedly influenced his approach to specific topics. We have already seen that the social fact lies at the center of his positivism. As the unit of investigation, the social fact, however, is also a reality *sui generis*, to be explored on its own terms.

To substantiate his conviction that the social fact represents a unique reality, Durkheim resorted to analogies. Throughout nature one can find the principle that whenever elements of a kind combine, their combination yields new phenomena that are not within the elements themselves but obtain rather in their union. Thus, the hardness of bronze lies in neither the copper nor the tin that were united to form it. The liquidity of water is to be found not in its component gases but rather in their combination. Likewise, the properties of life cannot be discovered in the nonliving carbon, hydrogen, nitrogen, and oxygen that make up the living cell.[4]

The analogy that Durkheim developed most extensively, however, was that between the individual representation and its collective counterpart. Collective representations are a type of social fact and include moral rules, religious beliefs, legends, and legal codes. As collective ideas of society, their characteristics cannot be reduced to the representations (ideas) of individuals. Like the levels just mentioned, they are a *sui generis* reality. What Durkheim meant by this can be explicated by the relationship of individual ideas to the neural cells in the brain. Again he resorted to analogy.

An entity in its own right, the mind cannot be regarded as a mere epiphenomenon of the brain's neural elements. If ideas are identical with the excitations of nerve cells, then how does one explain memory? If an idea is merely a vibration of nerve cells, how is it that when these cells are stimulated a second time so as to produce the same idea the individual recognizes it as a previous experience? How could it be recognized as a previous experience if the idea vanishes when the cells are no longer stimulated? The answers to these interrelated questions must be, Durkheim concluded, that the idea did not vanish when the cells ceased to be stimulated.[5]

Memories not only exist independently of cerebral cells; but inasmuch as they direct the individual's attention and behavior, they also have independent effects.[6] Moreover, they associate with one another according to their own laws. Were that not so, every idea would associate with another only in correspondence with contiguous neural paths whose excitations caused the ideas to come into being.[7] Consequently, the mind is able to bring forth a diversity of ideas in relation to one now

78   The Basic Units of Social Theory

being formed through a physical stimulus. That mind produces ideas in a succession that does not reproduce the order in which their organic antecedents were originally stimulated was proof for Durkheim that mind is a real entity[8] whose elements associate according to their own laws. For example, according to the law of resemblance, two ideas will associate if they resemble each other.[9]

Durkheim assumed point–for–point correspondences between the relationships of neural cells with individual representations and those of individual representations with collective ones. Accordingly, collective representations are not epiphenomena but realities in their own right. Formed through the interaction of individual minds, they are partly exterior and lead a partially autonomous existence. As wholes, they cannot be distributed among the individuals from whom they arose. A collective representation can be disseminated to different individuals from those whose interactions brought it into being. Collective representations combine according to their own laws to form other collective representations. Finally, they exert independent effects.[10]

Since collective representations are types of social facts, what characterizes them also characterizes the social facts. Let us, therefore, further explore the social fact in general, which, as chapter 1 explained, is—for Durkheim—the proper unit of sociological investigation.

In the first place, inasmuch as a social fact is not reducible to the minds of individuals, it cannot be explained by states of individual consciousness.[11] If it cannot be explained in terms of the properties of the level from which it emerged, the only logical conclusion for Durkheim was that the cause of a social fact is always some other social fact. Since a conscious desire for the utility of a social fact is a characteristic of an individual, it follows that such a desire cannot explain any given social fact. For instance, the desire for the renewal of family solidarity because of its advantages for individuals cannot be the cause of family solidarity. Nevertheless, said Durkheim, such desire can set the real cause, which must be some other social fact, in motion. The other side of this proposition is that a social fact can come into being without serving any intended individual purpose at all. The inability of an individual fact to yield a causal account of a purely social fact supported Durkheim's contention that sociology is a science distinct from psychology.[12]

In the second place, although the cause of a social fact is not the desire for its utility, it must have such utility to survive. But in this context

Durkheim avoided a contradiction with the preceding by distinguishing the utility of something for individuals and its utility for society. The utility of a social fact for society is its function. Again, there is the notion of distinct levels of reality. Therefore, in addition to the methodological precept that a sociologist is to locate the causes of social facts in social facts themselves, Durkheim legislated a second: The sociologist is to explain the functions of social facts with respect to how they relate to society's ends.[13]

That causes and functions occur on a plane distinct from individual consciousness explains why he distrusted explanations put forth by the actors themselves.[14] If a social fact cannot be brought into existence by the intended goals of social actors, then how can they give a causal account of it? Operating on a social level, social causes and functions are concealed from individual participants.

In the third place, social facts must be treated by the social theorist as if they were things. Durkheim made it clear that the intention behind this methodological principle is that social facts must be accorded a reality equal to that of physical things. Although they are not really physical things, social facts are as real as physical things. And just as in the case of the physical fact, the social fact must be explored from the outside and its features comprehended through observation and experimentation until its innermost core is laid bare. It must be regarded as a datum comparable to the data passing before the eye of a physicist. Exterior to its participants, and possessing a certain autonomy, a social fact cannot be understood by looking within. Again, that is why the opinions of actors regarding the nature of the social fact cannot be taken seriously.[15] The notion that a collective representation can be comprehended by grasping how it appears in an individual's mind in effect reduces it to the level of an individual representation.

In the fourth place, social facts, although created through combinations and syntheses of individual minds, exert influence over the latter. Collective beliefs, unlike habits which dominate individuals from within, act upon them from without. Unlike physical objects that exert physical constraint, collective beliefs impose themselves because of their moral authority, but they also make their impact felt in other ways. Laws, said Durkheim, act to prevent him who is inclined to violate them from doing so; and if he does, they punish his deviance. Public opinion is ever-watchful over those who offend the common conscience, and he who violates customary procedures encounters difficulties in achieving his

80   The Basic Units of Social Theory

most routine objectives. From these examples we can see that the social fact is experienced as an external force by those whom it affects.[16]

In Durkheim's discussion of the social fact, we can find several "directions" of causal influence. Interactions among individuals create a new level of reality, a social one "higher" than individual minds. Within the social sphere, a causality occurs in a "horizontal" direction from one social fact to another. The social level in turn reacts "downward" upon individuals in a variety of modes. Durkheim's famous definition of the social fact expresses its reality and its relation to individuals.

> *A social fact is any way of acting, whether fixed or not, capable of exerting over the individual an external constraint;*

or

> *which is general over the whole of a given society whilst having an existence of its own, independent of its individual manifestations.*[17]

Durkheim's analysis of the ontological status of the social fact and the methods he devised as appropriate for its investigation reveal notions long central to methodological structuralism. Individual and society are distinct levels of reality, each guided by its own principles. Society and its structures have a partially autonomous existence. Although the two interact, the social cannot be explained by the individual even though it is brought into being by the latter. Consequently, sociological cannot be derived from psychological generalizations.

SUICIDE

It can be shown that these methodological principles, which reflect structuralist premises, determined the direction of Durkheim's investigations and the conclusions he reached. Let us, therefore, examine his theory of suicide in light of them.

In view of the principle that a social phenomenon cannot be explained by facts about individuals, it is impossible to explain variations in suicide on the basis of the motives of those who kill themselves. We cannot, said Durkheim, place credence in the revelations in notes by the suicide of

Methodological Structuralism   81

his own condition; for individuals are prone to make mistakes about themselves, even to the point of believing that they are calm when in fact they are excited.[18] This skepticism about the reliability of motives was reflected in his analysis of the shortcomings in those official statistics that listed motives as the presumptive causes of suicide.

That poverty, family problems, physical pain, and disappointments in love as listed in official records cannot account for this type of death is established by the fact that although the suicide rate in a given society rises, the relative proportions of cases attributed to the various motives remain constant. On the assumption that these motives were really the causes, if the suicide rate doubles over a period of time, then the contribution of each type of motive would also double. But, Durkheim argued, this constancy of proportion reflected in the statistics is highly unlikely and could occur only by chance. The real cause of this apparent proportional constancy must be found in the constancy of the states of society that the motives reflect. As another example, take the cases of suicides among agricultural workers and among members of the liberal professions. Here again the statistics indicate similar proportions of various types of motives as causes. But because these occupations are so different, suicides among their practitioners must have different causes, which, of course, cannot be the motives as listed.[19] With arguments like these, Durkheim concluded the official attributions of motives as causes are suspect.

His definition of suicide also reflected the disqualification of motives. Suicide is death resulting from a positive or negative act by the victim that he knows will have his death as an outcome. This definition has the effect of classifying as suicide some actions not ordinarily thought of as such. For instance, the person who risks his life for another does not want to die, yet his awareness of the probability of death classifies his heroic act as very close to suicide. His motive, however, is vastly different from that of one who willingly seeks his own death. The diversity of motives is too great to account for actions that fall into a single class.[20] Again, motives are suspect.

The basic reason, of course, for our inability to explain suicide by motives is that the several tendencies to suicide are social facts, which can only be explained by other social facts.[21] As a *sui generis* reality, suicide must be understood on its own terms.[22]

Having defined the problem in sociological terms, Durkheim focused on the variations among suicide rates. Such rates are objective indicators

82   The Basic Units of Social Theory

of social facts that are the real causes. Why is it, for example, that under all sorts of conditions Protestants take their lives more often than Catholics and Jews, the single more often than the married, and that suicide declines during political crises such as wars and revolutions?

The answer is to be found in the fact that men acquire their beliefs, their goals, and their values from societies that exist in and through them. Religious beliefs are derived from a religious society that needs them for its own existence. Religious society superimposes itself upon its members, indoctrinating them with its dogmas. For although society is a reality transcending its members, it still needs them for its own existence. Moreover, it is the moral codes of the group, such as the obligation to treat others as ends in themselves, that attach religious man to life. The existences of individual and group are thus inextricably bound together. Consequently, when a group becomes less cohesive, its capacity to impose its beliefs is lessened. And because individuals derive the goals for which they live from the group, their reason for existence weakens as the latter weakens. Escaping the moral domination of collective beliefs, they become individualistic; and as a result the suicide rate rises. In this relative loss of group cohesion, Durkheim found the explanation of variations in the suicide rates disclosed by official statistics. Protestant groups are less integrated than the Catholic Church and Jewish communities, the single do not belong to a cohesive family, and political society grows more cohesive during political crises. That is why the rates are higher among Protestants and the single and lower during wars, revolutions, and election crises.

From these statistical comparisons and explanations, Durkheim inferred the following social law: *Egoistic* suicide rates vary inversely with the degree of integration of groups.[23] Reformulated, this causal law fits his methodological formula of sociological explanation: Declining group integration, one social fact, is the cause of egoistic suicide, a second social fact.

On the other hand, when a group is overintegrated, its collective beliefs impose an extreme hold over its members, subjecting them to an excessive moral domination. In that case, a type of suicide opposite from the egoistic becomes probable. Valuing society so highly, the individual sets little value upon himself. Valuing himself so little, he renounces life under compelling circumstances. Whereas in egoistic suicide the victim escapes society's faltering influence, in this type the individual remains too closely under its control. Therefore, when society expects him to end

Methodological Structuralism   83

his life, he willingly does its bidding. A person too old or sick takes his life to serve social ends. The willingness to sacrifice himself gives the name *altruistic* suicide to such an act, which, Durkheim thought, is most typical of primitives and the modern military.[24]

The rate of a third type of self-destruction, *anomic* suicide,[25] rises during periods of rapid economic change and among the divorced. What is happiness, Durkheim asked, but an equilibrium between human needs and the means to satisfy them? The contented person has the means to obtain the ends that gratify his needs. When this balance, however, is upset, i.e., when desires exceed resources, contentment turns to discontent; and the individual becomes vulnerable to suicide. A beneficent equilibrium of means and ends can be readily transmuted into a disequilibrium in two ways. First, a sudden loss of wealth reduces the means to satisfy desire. Second, desires increase and needs multiply faster than the means to satisfy them. In both cases the resulting unhappiness increases the chances of suicide.

What causes both rapid loss of wealth and expansion of need? Here Durkheim identified crises in economic life. During stock market crashes and bankruptcies, rapid economic change causes some to lose large amounts of wealth in short periods of time. On the other hand, economic crises can be of a positive sort, such as rapid growths in production. As an example, Durkheim pointed to the political unification of Italy, which was followed by increases in industrial output, trade, communication, and transportation.[26] But growing prosperity expands desire. Prosperity creates the needs it fulfills, and the means to satisfy them always lag behind. Therefore, both rapid economic decline and growth, by upsetting the equilibrium of means and ends, increase tendencies to self-destruction.

These economic changes, however, are objective indicators of disturbances of society. In a disturbed state, society loses its ability to subject appetites to moral restraint. Only society can set limits to what people want, for the person is too small to restrain himself. A well-ordered society places individuals into categories and defines how much each can legitimately expect. But during economic crises, it loses its power to impose the appropriate moral limits. This loss of regulatory power of norms is a condition of *anomie*. Then it happens that rapid loss of wealth reclassifies individuals, but society cannot immediately readjust them to a lower rank. In a state of crisis, it cannot recommend them to a set of reduced wants. On the other hand, the crisis of rapid increments of

84   The Basic Units of Social Theory

wealth stimulates expectations so that desires exceed their gratifications. The individual suffers the frustration of walking toward an infinitely receding goal. The divorced male is in a similar state—a sexual anomie in which the rules of marriage no longer limit his sexual desire.[27] In both cases anomic suicide grows out of a disequilibrium between means and desire created by a weakening of society's regulatory authority. The collapse of moral authority is a social fact that causes anomic suicide, another social fact.

Individual facts, however, do make their effects felt within the system of social effects. Leading a double life, the individual is torn between his purely individual inclinations and society's collective representations. Because of variations in individual tendencies, some offer stronger resistance to society's collective representations. Variations in egoism explain why some Protestants kill themselves while others escape egoism's destructive impaet. Collective representations, however, always seek out those persons most vulnerable to their influence.[28]

At the basis of these explanations is society as a collective actor. A thinking and acting substance, an entity in its own right, it seeks its own religious, scientific, political, moral, and artistic goals. But in order to achieve these goals, society must press its members into its service. When, however, it becomes weak, it loses its capacity to bend individuals to its will, and those individuals are left without beliefs to live by and ends to achieve. They are thrown back upon their egoistic impulses. In a weakened state, society also loses its power to subject wants to moral restraint. As a result, its members lose their commitments to its norms. On the other hand, when society grows excessively strong, its grip, being too firm, deprives its members of the freedom necessary for life.

This theory is predicated on the assumption that society is an actor oriented to its own goals, guided by its own principles. In the process of carrying out its activities, it exerts a causal force upon its members, transmitting to them either its normal state or its pathological condition. Without the postulate of a collective being, a social structure with unique imperatives, Durkheim's explanations of the variations in suicide among different groups would have taken a different turn. They depend upon that postulate.[29]

Methodological Structuralism in Marx

Although it is easy to find contrary tendencies in Marx's thinking,[30] one can detect in his formulations structuralist elements that shaped his

Methodological Structuralism   85

explanations of specific historical events. Although Marx's thought diverges in many respects from that of Durkheim, structuralist ideas inform both. Structuralist premises, therefore, are not limited to functionalism.

It is well known that, unlike Durkheim, Marx (1818–1883) did not describe societies (communism is a possible exception) as integrated wholes, but rather as permeated by contradictions. The parts of any society are structures in states of contradiction relentlessly passing into overt conflict. According to the materialist interpretation of history, the dominant structure, the one that shapes the others, is the economy. The other structures—social classes, state, law, and ideology—form what Marx and Engels referred to as the superstructure. Thus, society consists of *economic base* and *superstructure*, whose interrelationships must be grasped in order to explain its dynamics. Two sets of factors compose the economic base. First, the social forces of production consist of material factors like the raw materials used in production, tools, and technology. Second, the social relations of production consist of the social relationships that form an economic division of labor.

What is the ontological status of these social relations of production? A series of quotations from Marx reveals them as structural realities:

> But in the course of historical evolution, and precisely through the inevitable fact that within the division of labor social relationships *take on an independent existence*, there appears a division within the life of each individual, insofar as it is personal and insofar as it is determined by some branch of labour and the condition pertaining to it (my italics).[31]

In the following Marx expressed his belief that the social relations of production are independent of the will of individuals:

> In the social production of their life, men enter into definite relations that are indispensable and independent of their will, relations of production which correspond to a definite stage of development of their material productive forces.[32]

Again, a dichotomy obtains between social relationships and the individual will:

> The social structure and the State are continually evolving out of the life process of definite individuals, but of individuals not as

86   The Basic Units of Social Theory

they appear in their own or other people's imagination, but as they *really* are; i.e., as they operate, produce materially, and hence as they work under definite material limits, presuppositions and conditions independent of their will. [33]

Accordingly, men create a division of labor out of their relationships, which they are bound to do if they are to live. Economic structures having therefore been formed, they attain an autonomous existence, independent of the wills of their creators. The social relations of production in turn exert effects. [34] Marx emphasized again and again that the social relations of production become an objective power beyond human control:

This fixation of social activity, this consolidation of what we ourselves produce into an objective power above us, growing out of our control, thwarting our expectations, bringing to naught our calculations, is one of the chief factors in historical development up till now. [35]

In the same vein he wrote:

But individuals are dealt with here only in so far as they are the personifications of economic categories, the bearers *(Träger)* of particular class-relations and interests. My standpoint, from which the development of the economic formation of society is viewed as a process of natural history, can less than any other make the individual responsible for relations whose creature he remains, socially speaking, however much he may subjectively raise himself above them. [36]

As a kind of collective actor, an economic structure is imbued with its own characteristics. One such characteristic that plays a paramount role in revolutions, according to Marx, is the factor of objective interest. As a structural characteristic, it is not reducible to the subjective interests of individuals:

Further, the division of labour implies a contradiction between the interest of the separate individual or family and the communal interest of all individuals who interact. This communal interest does not exist merely in the imagination as the general interest but first of all in reality . . .[37]

The generalizations in these quotations cover some of the conceptual territory of methodological structuralism. The social relationships in a division of labor form a transcendent structural reality, a collective entity acting independently of the wills of individuals and against their interests. Social relations constitute a lawlike supraindividual entity that cannot be identified with the motives, beliefs, and perceptions of individuals.

Marx's materialist conception of history, the guiding thread of his research, has the effect of generalizing the *sui generis* nature of the social relations in the economic base also to the institutions in the superstructure. Let us, therefore, have a closer look at this famous conception.[38]

As noted above, the economic division of labor, the "modes of production," consists of both material factors and social relationships. The latter are shaped by and correspond to the stage of development of the former. Accordingly, the social organization of production adapts to the given raw materials, tools, machines, and technology. The institutions of the superstructure, which include the state, law, and religion, arise out of this twofold economic base. Embodying "definite forms of consciousness," they correspond to the latter. Hence, the modes of production condition the politics, law, and religion in the superstructure and the way individuals think about them. It is within this context, which states a kind of ideological determinism, that the well-known phrase appears: "It is not the consciousness of men that determines their being, but, on the contrary, their social being that determines their consciousness."[39]

At a certain stage of development, however, the social relations and material factors come into conflict; the former act as restraints on the further development of the latter. Accordingly, contradictions develop within the economic base. These contradictions eventually result in a type of revolution in which the base rapidly changes and effects a rapid transformation of the superstructure. Legal, political, religious, and philosophical changes in the superstructure are the forms of thought in which individuals become conscious of economic conflicts. Marx drew an analogy between the consciousness an individual has of himself and the consciousness of society: Just as we cannot explain a person by what he thinks of himself, so we cannot explain the transformation of society in terms of the ideological forms in the superstructure. Rather, all social

88   The Basic Units of Social Theory

transformations must be explained in terms of the contradictions and conflicts in the base. Thus, the materialist interpretation makes changes in structure precede changes in thinking. Here Marx evinces a Durkheim-like skepticism regarding beliefs of individuals as explanations of histori-cal events.

Inasmuch as legal, political, and religious structures arise from the social relations of production, the implication follows that, like the latter, the former are also *sui generis* realities. Transcending individuals, their dynamics are determined by the economic base. Furthermore, the thinking of individuals depends upon these structures, which are neither explicable in terms of the thinking of individuals nor merely shorthand ways of referring to them. Rather, they are independent determinants subject to their own historical laws.

The existential nature of social structures carries over into Marx's theory of social classes. Modes of production generate within the division of labor objective interests that are in conflict. Such interests are ulti-mately determined by the ownership of the material instruments of production, the tools and raw materials. Those who own and control these are under the compulsion of one set of objective interests, while those excluded from such control labor under the compulsion of another. Economic interests, said Marx, include the conditions of work, such as dignity and subordination, as well as the material interests in money and sustenance.[40] Thus, Marx spoke about objective class situations shared by those who find themselves similarly situated with reference to the modes of production. Those in a similar situation constitute what he called a *class in itself*. Hence, just as the superstructure grows out of the base, so do classes grow out of it.[41]

A class in itself, however, has only the potential to affect the dynamics of social transformations. For such a potential to become actualized, a class in itself must become a *class for itself*.[42] The latter consists of those who become united through attaining a recognition of their common interests, the awareness of which leads them to organize a class for itself.[43] Marx called this awareness of common interests *class consciousness*.

Because of the contradictions between class interests, fully organized classes, namely, those having acquired class consciousness, engage in all forms of conflict. The oppressed class eventually overthrows society and realizes its interests. Oversimplified, Marx's scheme boils down to a sequence of events: Changes in the modes of production create constel-lations of objective interests. Class consciousness eventually converts them into subjective interests, which become the basis for organization. Classes in the full sense, i.e., classes for themselves, are thus created and engage in overt conflict leading to revolution.[44]

This analysis leads to the implication that objective class interests preexist their subjective recognition by those whose psychological realities they become. Classes exist in themselves before they exist for themselves. Objective interests obtain as characteristics of social structure before the thinking of individuals corresponds to them.[45]

REVOLUTION IN PARIS, 1848

It can be shown that structuralist thinking in Marx's theory of class, class consciousness, and revolution affected his explanations of particular historical events. As an example, let us analyze in this context his account of the revolution that occurred in France in 1848. In view of the fact that the great revolution in 1789 and the revolution of 1830 benefited primarily the bourgeoisie, the question for Marx was why the February revolution in 1848 did not result in the ultimate proletarian victory. The question is raised by the materialist interpretation of history, which, as noted above, makes of social classes decisive revolutionary actors.

Historical facts also lend plausibility to the question. Manning the barricades, the Parisian workers in February played a major role in forcing the resignation of King Louis Philippe. When the provisional government that replaced the monarchy stalled in proclaiming a republic with universal suffrage, the workers stormed the Hotel de Ville and forced the proclamation.[46] Although in a meager way, the proletariat was also represented in the provisional government. As concessions to their demands, the government established a commission to explore how to improve the living standards of workers[47] and employed 100,000 workers in national workshops as a means of reducing unemployment.[48] Such historical facts indicate that as a consequence of the February revolution the proletariat increased its influence in the state. Nevertheless, in June, only four months after the downfall of the monarchy, the Paris proletariat again took to the streets and was crushed.[49] This bloody defeat removed the working class from the center of the political stage.

How did Marx explain a failure of the proletarian revolution?[50] His answer was that the workers lacked the revolutionary consciousness necessary to get a clear understanding of their situation. Unaware of their

90   The Basic Units of Social Theory

true interests, they were incapable of accomplishing the revolution to destroy capitalism. The reason for their theoretical immaturity goes directly to the state of the modes of production in France, for as a class the French proletariat was insufficiently developed because the French industrialist class was insufficiently developed. French industry was subordinate in power to finance capital. It was the bankers, speculators, money lenders, and stockbrokers who dominated Louis Philippe's government and who composed the upper bourgeoisie. French industry, in contrast to industry in England, was dependent on protective tariffs and was not linked closely to the international market. Thus, the industrial mode of production was not developed sufficiently to create a class-conscious proletariat. The "finance aristocracy" usurped the position of the industrialists as the principal opponent of both the lower bourgeoisie and the working class.[51]

Furthermore, since the workers thought they had beaten the bourgeoisie after the provisional government proclaimed the republic, they inadvertently handed the bourgeoisie weapons that were shortly thereafter used against them.[52] Again Marx implied that they lacked a true class consciousness. Then in December of 1848 the working class voted for the presidency of Louis Napoléon,[53] who in 1851 replaced the republic with the Second Empire.

Marx's explanation can be summarized in the proposition that the objective conditions for revolution were not yet present in 1848. The communist revolution must occur only when exploitation has proceeded to the point where all the injustices of society have come to focus on the proletariat. Unlike previous revolutions, which merely substituted one minority rule for another, the communist upheaval will concentrate in itself the interests of the entire society. But how could this identity of interests occur if capitalist exploitation had not reached that extreme? Writing in 1895, Engels located the proof of this proposition in the fact that big industry took root in France and other parts of Europe after 1848,[54] with the consequence that there was much room for expansion of the capitalist modes of production. What he was really saying, in agreement with Marx, was that objective class interests were not developed enough to be consciously perceived. Yet, Engels went on to write, the latter "must soon enough become clear in the course of giving practical effect to them, by their convincing obviousness."[55]

This air of inevitability was shared by Marx, who emphasized the historical event that in February of 1849 workers and petty bourgeoisie joined forces to form the Social Democratic Party.[56] He construed this development as an indication of the class polarization that is one necessary condition for a communist revolt.[57]

These explanations and predictions depend on Marx and Engels's assumption of historical laws that define interrelationships among *sui generis* social structures. Changes in modes of production intensify contradictions among real class interests. Eventually grasped by class consciousness, these become realities in the minds of social actors; and as psychological realities, they motivate them to engage in practical actions both in defense of and in the overthrow of capitalism. It is evident that Marx's equation for the final revolution combines both supraindividual factors and the subjective experience of individuals. His theory of the inevitable march of history incorporates elements of methodological structuralism, for the whole of history is more than the sum of its individual parts.

Organism, Personality, Society, and Culture in Parsons's Action System

From the physical to the organic to the level of human action, a series of transformations occurs that constitutes the basis of Talcott Parsons's version of methodological structuralism. The emergence of unique properties begins in the organism and continues to manifest itself through the personality, social, and cultural levels. Although consonant with Durkheim's idea of society as a reality, Parsons's theory of action is a more complex version of structuralist thought. Nevertheless, his conceptions find their parallels in the former.

Parsons called attention to the fact that action cannot occur without a human organism as a supplier of energy. It is patently obvious that no one can act without expending energy. Organic energy is created by the combustion of oxygen with compounds of carbon and represents a higher level of organization. Organic energy, a "transformation" of matter, constitutes therefore a new level of reality.[58] Durkheim also believed that a new level of reality comes into being with the emergence of the organic from the physical.

Borrowing from Freud, Parsons noted that in the form of stimulation

92   The Basic Units of Social Theory

energy flows into various parts of the body. With regard to its effect, it is
the erogenous zones—mouth, anus, breast, and reproductive organs—
that captured Parsons's interests. The child's mouth, stimulated by energy
from his organism, comes into contact with the breast of the mother.
The child experiences this contact (or that with another food object) as
pleasurable. While being fed, he also experiences as pleasurable being
held; the pleasure of being fed generalizes to being held. These physical
contacts obviously come through the senses of taste and touch. The
internal flow of stimulation to the mouth combines with the external
stimulus of the breast to produce in the child's psyche the meaning of
his mother as a source of nurturant care. This symbolic constitution of
the mother indicates, said Parsons, that the child has "internalized the
object." The meaning of mother forms the starting point for his personality development, according to which new meanings are differentiated
from the original through recurrent processes of binary fission.[59] In sum,
organic energy, itself the product of a transformation of matter, becomes
qualitatively transformed into meaning, which cannot be reduced to the
biochemistry of the brain.[60] In other words, meaning is an emergent
reality.

Thus, meaning emerges on the level of personality; and specific
meanings link needs of the organism with the external objects that satisfy
them. Needs, such as the need for food are really *need-dispositions*, the
second half of the term denoting the tendency of personality to gratify its
needs through obtaining the relevant things from its environment.[61] The
personality system, according to Parsons, is guided by the tendency to
optimize the gratification and minimize the deprivation of its needs
through establishing the appropriate relationships with external objects.
The latter acquire meanings that define how they satisfy its needs. It is
obvious that in the course of time a personality develops new needs and
internalizes new meanings.

Personality, therefore, can be conceptualized as a system of action
organized to satisfy its needs, some organic, but most of them learned,
through establishing meaningful relationships with objects. Interaction
among individuals, however, creates another level of organization, one
with dimensions not present in a person's orientation toward a physical
object. This level, of course, is the social system, whose constitutive unit,
according to Parsons, is the *role-expectation*.[62] In order for an ego and an
alter to interact, they must either develop within or bring to the situation
mutually held expectations of how each should act and the attitudes each

should hold. Accordingly, the role-expectation emerges with the social system formed through interaction. Although constituted by meaning, like Durkheim's collective representation, it has more than purely individualized meaning. It is a kind of synthesis of individual representations.

Role-expectations, mutually held, are only one type of element of a social system. The actual conformity of ego's and alter's actions to these expectations converts them into *roles*. Thus, the role—action oriented to an expectation—is a second element of a social system. Nevertheless, although a unit of a social system, a role is also the action of a personality. It thereby links personality and social systems, enabling them to "interpenetrate." Despite the interpenetration of these systems through a common element, each is a system in its own right and follows its own imperatives—a conclusion dictated by Parsons's belief that they form distinct levels of organization.

Although the role-expectation is a social system unit, it is also an element of a cultural system. Penetrating the social system, it links cultural and social systems. And like the role, it enters the personality through internalization. Despite the interpenetration with the other two systems, Parsons conceived of culture as another level of reality. The cultural system is constituted by shared ideas of how individuals are expected to conceive what objects are, how objects relate to their needs, and how individuals ought to act toward them.[63] Put this way, role-expectations are really norms.

Consequently, organic energy, meaning, personality, society, and culture form distinct levels roughly comparable to the types of emergence Durkheim saw throughout nature and society. Each is an outcome of interactions of units at lower levels, and consequently the higher depend on the lower. Although levels overlap through shared elements, each operates according to principles peculiar to itself. Although cultural norms are institutionalized within social systems and internalized within personalities,[64] organisms, personalities, societies, and culture are, nevertheless, discrete systems.

It was Parsons's contention that these four systems, each with its own imperatives, make up a total system of action that provides an adequate theoretical scheme to explain any course of interaction among any number of individuals. Whenever two or more individuals take one another into account, the action system can be analytically broken down into their organisms, personalities, a social system, and a cultural system. Elements that unite systems have different functions in each. Each

94   The Basic Units of Social Theory

depends on another for its existence, but cannot be reduced to the other. Hence, knowledge of the culture and personalities of the actors falls short of knowledge of the social system formed by their interaction. Nor can the facts of the social system and its culture yield a knowledge of the personalities. And neither is it possible for a knowledge of social and personality systems to yield a comprehension of culture.[65] Each must be understood on its own terms.

At the same time, the functioning of each system depends on the resources supplied by the others, the mutual contributions of which form, according to Parsons, a system of interchanges.[66] The social system gets from the personalities of its members the performance of its roles, which depends upon motivations "manufactured" in personality systems.[67] In return, the social system gratifies its members with rewards such as approval and the means to achieve their goals.[68] Culture supplies the social system with broad patterns of meaning, which Parsons referred to as *codes*. From these are derived definitions of situations, which when applied to particular situations are role-expectations.[69] The social system reciprocates by "validating" these cultural codes through putting them into effect.[70] The social system tests them by acting on them.

Finally, these systems are rank ordered in influence that roughly parallels in principle the relations Durkheim found among levels. Parsons called this hierarchy of influence the "cybernetic hierarchy of control." Accordingly, cultural codes control the social system, which controls personalities, which in turn control organisms. The influence reaches its completion with the control that personalities through their organisms exercise over the physical environment. In the cybernetic hierarchy, systems higher in information but lower in energy control systems lower in information but higher in energy.[71] Culture's symbolic content, which is pure information, lacks energy, while at the other end of the hierarchy the organism abounds in energy and relies upon higher-level systems for its meanings.

THE FUNCTIONS OF THE SOCIAL SYSTEM

What are the imperatives that distinguish the social from the other subsystems? A brief summary of its functions ought to yield a clearer notion of society as a real structure and collective actor. These are the activities it engages in that differentiate it from other systems and make it a unique reality.[72]

Methodological Structuralism   95

For Parsons, a society is a fairly autonomous social system, one capable of surviving pretty much on its own for longer than a generation through biological reproduction. Since societies are a subclass of social systems, they fulfill the functions that any social system must fulfill. Parsons identified four such universal functions: *adaptation* (A), *goal-attainment* (G), *integration* (I), *pattern-maintenance* and *tension-management* (L).[73] The first two relate a social system to its environments; the last two maintain its structural integrity. Hence, one pair of functions is "external," the other internal. Functions are problems that the social system must continually solve in order to survive.

Goal-attainment consists basically of three interrelated activities. First, it involves the selection of the system's collective goals. Second, it involves the mobilization of the means to achieve them. Third, it involves establishing priorities among the selected goals, arranging them in a scale of urgency. The G function rests on the simple assumption that a system cannot act, it cannot "go anywhere," unless it has goals toward which it moves. Social systems are teleological. Parsons drew a distinction between the collective goals of a social system and the individual goals of its members, the G function relating only to the former. In the fullest sense, a collective goal is one that can only be achieved through the cooperation of members of the system and whose achievement gratifies them in various ways. Parsons cited as an example the goal of America after World War II to motivate its citizens to counter the spread of international communism.[74] Setting priorities is required by the fact that a system rarely strives for only one goal.

Goals establish relationships between the system and its various environments, reducing the discrepancy among them. A system's environments include other social systems, the personalities of its members, its culture, and its physical environment.[75] Consequently, the other subsystems of action turn out to be environments of the social system. Regarding personalities, Parsons again distinguished between those elements of a member's personality that enter the social system as roles and those elements that remain outside it. Only the latter constitute an environment.

Goal-attainment is a political function. Inasmuch as every social system attempts to achieve collective goals, every such system engages in politics. Thus, it is logical to speak of the politics of a family as well as the politics of a society. For society as a whole, it is the polity that specializes in goal-attainment, selects society's goals, and mobilizes the

96   The Basic Units of Social Theory

means for their achievement. To carry out its functions, the polity, of course, must have the power to claim the necessary resources. Every polity, said Parsons, is evaluated with regard to its effectiveness, i.e., how well it achieves the collective goals of the society of which it is a part.[76]

For any theory that focuses on ends it is logical to focus also on means. The adaptation function, therefore, consists of all those processes involved in producing or acquiring in some other way the means required to achieve the social system's goals.[77] Parsons emphasized the generalized character of the means, which can be allocated to the service of a variety of alternative goals. As a generalized resource, for example, a truck can transport bricks or soldiers. Much of a social system's production is not immediately designated for a specific end, for how a resource will ultimately be utilized cannot always be foreseen. The most important types of means are control over physical objects, access to human services, and the knowledge of how to do things. Although a means can also be an end and the end a means to some other end, Parsons contended that the G and A functions are analytically distinguishable. In this regard, it is the goal-attainment function as noted above, not adaptation, that allocates a resource to a collective end.

Like goal-attainment, adaptation is an external function, also essential to establishing satisfactory relationships between a system and its environments. An obvious example is society extracting food and other materials from its physical environment. In general, adaptation ranges from a passive coming to terms with some environment to an active mastery over it. A system can let a resource "come its way" or exert active mastery by intervening to change an environment.

There are economic processes at work in adaptation. Just as every social system involves politics, every system, no matter how small, involves economics. Through its breadwinner, for instance, a family acquires the income that it allocates to its goals. In society at large it is the economy that carries the major burden of adaptation, producing enormous quantities and varieties of resources that the polity, mostly through taxation, claims for collective goals.

Parsons identified the integrative function as the "central core of the concerns of sociological theory."[78] Integration refers to those processes in a social system that establish the proper relationships among individuals. Put another way, this function effects their mutual adjustments with respect to their capacity to contribute to system functioning. How, for example, must its members be organized so that the social system can attain its G and A functions? These specific relationships give to a social system an identity that distinguishes it from its environments. Consequently, the I function also maintains the system's boundaries.[79]

In delineating integration, Parsons presented some specific details about how it is accomplished. The adjustments among individuals involve their respective rights and duties, namely, what they can expect and what they owe to one another. The distribution of rights and duties is brought about by the social system's norms, which, as noted above, are its structural elements. It follows, therefore, that at the level of a total society one structure contributing to integration is its legal order. The functioning of the legal order involves activities such as making laws internally consistent, interpreting them in the light of specific contexts, and enforcing them. These are integrating processes.

Other such processes maintain individuals in their roles so that they perform their duties. They include two types of distribution: (1) rewards and punishments, which are mechanisms of social control, and (2) resources individuals must have to play their roles. The allocation of rewards such as money and prestige to those who fulfill their duties and the imposition of negative sanctions upon those who fail to do so act as motivations for compliance. Insofar as they are effective, rewards and punishments maintain social relationships. It is also obvious that the provision of resources such as authority to those who need them to play their roles also contribute to social integration. Moreover, insofar as they are unequal, these allocations stratify a system.[80] As a result, along with the legal system, for Parsons stratification turns out to be an integrative mechanism.

Solidarity also contributes to integration. By solidarity Parsons meant the attachment individuals feel toward one another and the recognition that they are sources of mutual gratification.[81] In solidary relationships individuals are willing to subordinate their individual interests to the collective goals of the system.[82] Solidarity thereby contributes to system integration. It is produced by minimizing conflict and settling disputes.[83] For Parsons, integration and conflict are inversely related.

The phrase pattern-maintenance and tension-management directs attention to two previously discussed interrelationships. Pattern-maintenance relates to the institutionalization of cultural elements within a social system and tension-management to their internalization within personalities. The L function, therefore, maintains both the institutionalization and internalization of culture.[84]

98   The Basic Units of Social Theory

If the cultural codes were no longer maintained, the social system would either collapse or undergo a change in its identity; for pattern-maintenance cooperates with integration to define a society, whose patterns of norms and values differentiate it from others.[85] The L function thus refers to processes that perpetuate a social system's culture. Parsons identified the various processes of socialization as having a primacy of pattern-maintenance function; and the family, education, and religion are structures centrally involved in socializing activities. Religion also contributes to the L function by furnishing rituals and beliefs that legitimate the normative order.[86] These beliefs furnish justifications for obedience to society's values and norms.

As noted above, the integrity of cultural codes also depends upon their internalization within personalities. Parsons observed that as individuals play their roles and fulfill their obligations tensions often arise, which if not reduced (managed) destroy their motivations for continued role-performance. And it is through the latter that society's values and norms are realized. One easily recognized source of tension is the suppression of personality needs in favor of the fulfillment of social obligations.[87] This is the classic conflict between self-interest and the collective good. Tensions are released through safety-valve mechanisms or are channeled in directions that do not undermine normative commitments.[88] Thus, the continual renewal of motivation contributes to the L function.[89]

The social structures specializing in the social system's functions form, according to Parsons, another cybernetic hierarchy. The control, how-ever, is not totally determinative, for the lower-level structures condition the higher-level ones; and some degree of autonomy and reciprocity obtains within all levels. The hierarchy is formed by the functions in the order of LIGA. Pattern-maintenance controls integration, which in turn controls goal-attainment, which in turn controls adaptation. The acqui-sition of facilities (means) is controlled by the goals they are intended to serve. Yet goals must be selected such that the integration of society and its internal arrangement of parts are preserved. Cultural codes impreg-nated with information exert preponderant control over the societal community and, indirectly, over the polity and economy. These codes also set the general direction followed by the course of society's develop-ment.[90]

Parsons believed that this hierarchy of functions articulates with the cybernetic hierarchy of the subsystems of action. Thus, symbolic control originates in the cultural system, flows into the social system through the *fiduciary* (pattern-maintenance) system, then into the societal community, polity, and economy in that order, then out of the social system into the personality, and finally from the latter into the organism.[91] At the same time, these subsystems in reverse order set constraints within which cultural controls operate. Although the higher levels of reality develop out of the lower, once a higher order comes into being, it exerts control over that from which it emerged.

In the preceding, rather complicated analyses of ontological levels within the overall action system and the unique functions of the social system, we find a complex version of what I have called methodological structuralism. Different structural features occur at the organic, psychological, social, and cultural levels, all of which are interrelated in various hierarchies of superordinating and subordinating functions. Although Parsons made it clear that culture by itself is unable to act, it is the factor of predominant control over society as a collective actor. And, although society controls its members, this great actor acts through the personalities and organisms of its members. It is obvious that Parsons's theory of action is a complex elaboration of Durkheim's emergent view of nature and his theory of society as a *sui generis* reality.

MODERN MEDICAL PRACTICE

In line with the contention that structuralist thinking profoundly affects the ways in which social theorists explain facts and approach problems, it can be shown that Parsons's structuralism shaped his explanations. As an illustration, let us examine his discussion of modern medical practice in the light of social-system functions.

The practice of medicine takes place largely within the relationship between patient and physician. The roles they play constitute a social system, which, however, must be thought of as a structure within a more inclusive structure, a subsystem of society as a whole. What is the role of a patient? Parsons delineated four norms that define the sick role. First, everyone expects that the sick individual be exempt from routine social obligations such as work. In some cases the person who is certified as being sick refuses to admit it and must be pressured to acknowledge his condition. Second, he is expected to recognize that he cannot cure himself by an act of will. Third, everyone expects him to want to get well so that he can return to his obligations. Fourth, he must seek professional

100   The Basic Units of Social Theory

advice from a physician. These norms make it clear, argued Parsons, that being sick is a social role and not merely a condition that just happens to a person. In fact, being ill can be conceived of as a form of deviance.[92]

Parsons raised the question of how a person comes to be in this role. There is no doubt that much illness is unmotivated; falling ill just happens. Yet, more and more motivational factors are coming to light. In addition to the vast area of mental illness, there are psychosomatic conditions and psychological proneness to accidents. Some illness can be explained as a response to social pressures and as a way of avoiding social duties.[93] That proportion of illness that is consciously or unconsciously motivated justifies the label of deviance.

But Parsons went further. Those motivations that make a person sick could have expressed themselves in alternative actions of greater destruction. Insofar as these actions are channeled into illness, the sick role limits the destruction to society. In the first place, the role thrusts the individual into a relationship with physicians, other therapists, and his family rather than into the company of other deviants with whom it would be possible to form a deviant subculture. In the second place, the person who is ill is expected to get out of this undesirable state as fast as possible.[94] Parsons interpreted the prevention of greater damage as a latent function for the social system.

The doctor's role is also normatively defined. The physician is required to apply universalistic norms of medicine to specific cases. His role is also characterized by specificity, which is to say that his interest in a patient is strictly limited to the latter's condition that falls within his competence. The doctor is collectivity-oriented; he is expected to put the interest of the patient ahead of his own. He is also expected to play his role with neutrality, which means that his likes and dislikes of patients are not to affect his treatments. The norm of neutrality also prevents him from exploiting the relationship for his personal gratification.[95] These are well-known attributes of the physician's role that Parsons expressed in the language of the pattern-variables.

Parsons analyzed obstacles a physician must overcome in medical practice. Medical practice is more than a rational application of techniques. It involves all sorts of nonrational and irrational dimensions. Because of fears regarding his illness, a patient will sometimes attempt to broaden his relationship with a physician. He wants to become the doctor's friend or develop some other kind of intimacy. Some of this

Methodological Structuralism   101

search for intimacy stems from revealing intimate knowledge to his physician. In the language of pattern-variables, there is a tendency to introduce affective, diffuse, and particularistic orientations into the therapeutic relationship. In order to guard against these tendencies, the doctor supports the patient but only up to a point; there are limits to his permissiveness. He cannot drive the patient away, but on the other hand he cannot "let him get away with it." Parsons concluded that all physicians, not only psychiatrists, practice psychotherapy whether they are aware of it or not.[96]

Indeed, the psychotherapy practiced in ordinary medicine did not originate in the science of psychotherapy, for it preceded the latter. Rather it was the result of an unplanned, spontaneous development of social structure, which the later science of psychotherapy capitalized upon. Nevertheless, this ordinary psychotherapy reintegrates deviants into routine life.[97] It is a latent function. Furthermore, variations of it can be found in other areas of social life such as faith healing. In all these relationships permissiveness inhibits the aggravation of alienative tendencies, but at the same time deviance is not reciprocated.[98]

Illness and psychotherapy, therefore, turn out to be mechanisms of control that limit deviance and reintegrate the deviant. They are, according to Parsons, processes that contribute to society's integrative function by maintaining people in their roles.[99] In this context Parsons spoke of "the motivational balance of the social system."[100] A good deal of his analysis of the doctor–patient relationship points to the rational choice of means by particular individuals to attain deliberately chosen goals. But over and above this analysis from the perspectives of the actors, Parsons identified unplanned aspects of the relationship. Hence, unrecognized motivations behind illness, even physical illness, and psychotherapy turn out to be latent functions on behalf of society. The conclusion of latent functions presupposes the assumption of society as a collective actor apart from its members that fulfills integrative functions for the sake of itself.

A logical similarity obtains between Parsons's explanation of integrative latent functions and Durkheim's explanation of suicide. In order to achieve its purposes, society works through individuals, pressing them into its service and bending them to its will. Of course, in the case of suicide, it doesn't mobilize individuals very well; and since the effects come from society, individuals are not aware of what is happening. The causes of suicide are shifted, according to theory, from the motives of individuals to the motives of society. Within the functionalist tradition

102   The Basic Units of Social Theory

in general, the identification of latent functions employs the assumption that society is a reality.

Merton on Anomie

Robert Merton's considerable contributions to functional theory reveal a theoretical continuity with the functionalism of Durkheim and Parsons. According to Merton, the right-thinking functionalist carefully identifies a social or cultural structure such as a role, norm, or institution and then calculates the net balance of manifest and latent functions and dysfunctions it contributes to other structures in the sociocultural system. The functional theorist then carefully delineates those structures whose survival is facilitated by functions and structures whose survival is jeopardized by dysfunctions. In identifying such structures and functions, the sociologist describes the specific mechanisms through which one structure fulfills a function for another. Merton's paradigm also requires the functionalist to take account of alternative structures that are capable of providing the same functions as structures already identified as operative. Accordingly, the determination of function-fulfilling mechanisms and functional equivalents also enter into the logic of functional explanations. At the same time, Merton makes it clear that, in addition to social and cultural structures, individuals can also be both beneficiaries of functions and victims of dysfunctions.[101]

This last observation points the way toward the distinction his paradigm draws between psychological, group, societal, and cultural functions. Structures, in other words, can be functional for individuals, groups, societies, and cultures.[102] This array of functions reflects a dualism of individual and structure, a dualism paralleled in Merton's writings by the distinction he makes between psychology and sociology.[103] This dualism imposes the methodological requirement that the sociologist examine the actions of individuals in the light of their personalities, social structure, and culture, the latter two forming a sociocultural environment of the former on a distinctive sociological plane of reality.[104] The dualism is an indication of structuralist thinking.

Are there universal elements of a cultural structure? Merton's answer is twofold. First, there are culturally defined goals that are held out as ends all members of society are expected to work toward. These ends are

Methodological Structuralism   103

more or less integrated into a hierarchy of values. The latter in effect
turn out to be equivalent to the values identified by Parsons as elements
of the cultural system. Second, there are cultural norms that prescribe
the legitimate means individuals may apply to obtain prescribed goals.
These norms limit the range of expedients to be used and generally rule
out force and fraud.[105] Accordingly, means and ends are cultural universals.

Means and ends, however, are not independent of each other, and the
functionalist can objectively detect variation along a continuum in the
way they are related. At one end of the continuum, Merton notes,
culture accords greater importance to its goals than to the means it
prescribes. At the other, culture de-emphasizes the achievement of goals
and concentrates disproportionately on compliance with norms. These
two extremes constitute two types of cultural malintegration in which
means and ends are not in balance. There is, however, a third possibility,
in which the cultural emphasis on achieving the ends equals the
emphasis on employing the prescribed means. Such a balance between
means and ends makes for a stable society, one in which individuals
derive as much satisfaction from employing means as they do from
achieving ends. This cultural structure results in a high degree of
conformity within society. Merton identifies this balance with society's
equilibrium.[106]

In a society in that state of disequilibrium resulting from the cultural
malintegration in which the culture gives greater emphasis to its ends,
individuals feel pressured to achieve those ends at the cost of violating
the normatively defined means. They are prone toward achievement
through means that are effective but illegitimate. Consequently, the
legitimacy of the norms is eroded to the point of collapse, which
condition Merton identified as *anomie*.[107] His analysis at this point tacitly
agrees with Parsons; culture is the driving force of the social system.
Consistent with the dualistic conception of individuals and society as
existing on different levels of reality, Merton cautions that anomie is a
state of society and should not be thought of as a psychological state of
individuals. Hence, in measuring it, the sociologist must be careful to
develop sociological rather than psychological indicators. By distinguishing between anomie as a property of social structure and the perception
of it by its members, Merton rightly sees himself following in Durkheim's
footsteps.[108]

There is, in addition, another type of malintegration that generates

104   The Basic Units of Social Theory

the anomie of the erosion of norms. This malintegration is a lack of fit between culture and social structure. Culture and society are malintegrated when the latter fails to provide some of its members with the means prescribed by cultural norms to attain cultural goals. Then those individuals who lack legitimate opportunities to achieve are again pressured to resort to illegitimate means.[109] Again the regulatory authority of norms has been eroded.

As structural elements, means and ends and anomie as a structural property all have a sociological existence apart from individuals. Merton attempted to explain various types of deviance in America in light of these structuralist concepts. What, he asks, is one very important goal that American culture holds out for all Americans to achieve? The answer is clearly success measured in terms of money. All Americans are bombarded by family, school, and press to become rich by applying the normatively ordained means of education, hard work, and occupational mobility. The problem is, however, that these means are unavailable to the lower classes, who lack money for education and have jobs with no upward mobility. This malintegration explains why the greatest amount of crime is found among the lower classes. They resort to crime to obtain success. Merton called this type of deviance *innovation*.[110] Nevertheless, crime as an avenue to wealth also occurs among the middle and upper classes, who do have access to legitimate opportunities. But the greater cultural emphasis on success than on the sanctioned means to attain it accounts for innovation in these classes.[111] This innovation, therefore, is explained by another type of malintegration, a cultural malintegration.

Merton proceeded to identify other types of deviant adaptations to the anomie of America that is related to the goal of monetary success. In one type of adaptation the individual relinquishes the goal of getting rich, but still employs the means in a somewhat compulsive way. Despairing of getting rich, he still works hard to fulfill his duties but without trying to get ahead. Despite the fact that American culture forbids anyone to give up, the person who adapts in this way to structurally induced stress has done just that. Merton called this type of deviance, which he expects will turn out to be typical of the lower-middle class, *ritualism*.[112]

On the other hand, the *retreatist* relinquishes both the goal of success and the legitimate means to attain it. Having culturally approved opportunities, he becomes demoralized because the application of legitimate means does not make him successful. At the same time, the retreatist has been too thoroughly socialized into the norms to resort to illegitimate

Methodological Structuralism   105

means. The conflict between his commitment to the norms and his failure to succeed with conventional means results in his relinquishing the goal. The retreatist "drops out" of society. The ranks of vagabonds, psychotics, alcoholics, and drug addicts, said Merton, are filled with retreatists.[113]

Finally, the *rebel*, as Merton describes him, blames the sociocultural order for his failure and renounces his allegiance to it. He, however, does not retreat from the race to success, but embraces alternative goals as part of a new social order. He becomes part of a social movement that seeks radical cultural and social change. Rejecting the cultural belief that failure is the result of personal inadequacy, the rebel instead rejects the legitimacy of the prevailing social order.[114]

Even though a product of it, innovation that achieves monetary success also increases the amount of anomie. Those who witness innovation being rewarded by success but who did not respond to the original amount of anomie now turn to crime. This in turn creates more anomie and ever more deviance as those less vulnerable to anomie to begin with become vulnerable to its intensification. Deviance and the sociocultural system react upon each other until mechanisms of social control intervene.[115]

Merton's explanations of deviance explicitly incorporate Durkheim's concept of anomie and implicitly incorporate his notion of the reality of the social fact, but in an attenuated form. Society and culture are structures exerting effects upon individuals. They are independent variables in the production of deviance, although, to be sure, individuals differ in their psychological vulnerability to structural pressures. As a property of malintegrated structures, anomie cannot be reduced to the characteristics of individuals. Measures of it, therefore, should not be confused with measures of individual awareness of it. Because the existence of anomie does not depend on its being recognized by its victims, an ontological differentiation between the objective and subjective has methodological consequences. Furthermore, a Durkheimian-like, structurally induced disjunction between means and ends forms a matrix of individual discontent. Nevertheless, the innovative responses of individuals in turn affect these structures to which they are reactions and can be assessed with reference to their functional and dysfunctional contributions. Like Durkheim's and Parsons's explanations, Merton's account of crime in America assumes causally effective structures that have a degree of autonomy.

106   The Basic Units of Social Theory

Capitalism as System

Although every society is a system, it is the system of advanced capitalism
that Jürgen Habermas, in the tradition of critical theory, is most concerned with. His analysis of advanced capitalist societies reveals both
continuities and discontinuities with Marx and both similarities to and
differences from Parsons's theory of the social system. The continuities
and similarities, however, carry with them structuralist assumptions that
have left an impact on some of Habermas's theoretical formulations.

Every society, according to Habermas, establishes relationships with
three environments. First, it must exploit its material, nonhuman environment. In adapting to it, society develops an economic system that
employs *purposive* or *instrumental rationality*. Drawn from Weber's
Zweckrationalität, this type of thinking arrives at verifiable conclusions
regarding the means necessary to achieve ends. Second, a society must
obviously come to terms with other societies. Third, it must conquer the
organic substrata of its members. Like Parsons, Habermas regards the
personalities of its members as one of society's environments; the inner
nature of individuals is both system environment and system element.[116]
That is to say that parts of a personality enter into a social system while
parts remain beyond it. In order to adapt the personalities of its members
to its purpose, society develops a sociocultural system that socializes them
to its norms through communicative action.[117]

The foregoing indicates two types of action, each of which predominates within a different social structure. Purposive rationality dominates
the economic system and formulates technical rules of work capable of
being judged according to scientific criteria. Technical rules either do or
do not work. *Communicative action*, on the other hand, dominates the
sociocultural system and produces a consensus about the rights and
obligations of individuals. People understand one another through language and come to agree upon norms and values. When a technical
work norm is violated, nature punishes the infraction with failure. When
someone violates a sociocultural norm, however, it is society that inflicts
punishment. As noted above, instrumental action predominates in the
economy and communicative action in the sociocultural system. It is
apparent that these two structures, with some modifications, parallel
Marx's division of society into economic base and institutional superstructure.

In contrast to the economy, the sociocultural system consists of the world views, values, and norms of society; and Habermas's concept of it overlaps Parsons's concept of a society's normative culture composed of values, norms (role-expectations), and constitutive symbolism (religion). When regarded from the perspective of individuals, these world views, values, and norms constitute a society's "lifeworld."[118] The lifeworld is really the psychological side of the sociocultural system, constituted by intersubjective symbolic structures formed through communicative action. Through it, individuals develop common interpretive frameworks, share definitions of situations, and solidarity. As lifeworld, society must be understood by the sociologist from the perspective of its members. An understanding of their orientations to the lifeworld enables the observer, in principle, to ascertain the extent to which a given society is socially integrated. Social integration stems from the normative consensus of its members and their feelings of solidarity. Habermas equated this type of integration with the L and I functions of Parsons's social system.[119]

In societies beyond the primitive level of development, the state is a third structure that becomes differentiated from the other two. Especially in advanced capitalist societies, this political-administrative system functions as a "steering mechanism" of the economy and as a control center of society as a whole.[120] It steers the economy by regulating the business cycle and by intervening to rectify the deficiencies of an imperfectly functioning capitalism.[121] Providing benefits such as unemployment compensation and social security, the modern capitalist state is a welfare state. Like the economy, it is oriented to purposive rationality.

Whereas the sociocultural system achieves society's social integration, economy and state together achieve its *system integration*. By the latter Habermas means the extent to which actions are coordinated into functionally interconnected sequences to cope with the exigencies of the physical environment.[122] Economy and state form a complex division of labor whereby goods and services are produced and exchanged. When considered in terms of functional interdependence, society is a self-maintaining, self-regulating system.[123] In contrast to the social integration of the lifeworld, the ascertainment of system integration depends strictly on the objective, external perspective of a sociological observer.[124] The criteria are system and function that do not include the subjective definitions of actors. Habermas further translated his own theory into Parsons's by identifying the system-integrative function of economy and state with Parsons's A and G functions.[125]

108   The Basic Units of Social Theory

In an analysis resembling Parsons's input-output scheme, Habermas identified the interchanges among these three systems in advanced capitalist societies. The scheme reveals the dynamics of self-maintaining systems.

From the economy the political-administrative system receives resources, primarily in the form of taxes, that it needs to steer the economy. Habermas calls them "fiscal skim-off," which is both output from the economy and input to the state. In return, the state gives "steering performances" to the economy, which take the form of subsidies, loans, government contracts, and an infrastructure of roads, housing, etc.[126] The outputs of the state are at the same time inputs to the economy. On the other side, the state exchanges inputs with the sociocultural system, giving to it inputs of social welfare performances in the form of transfer payments to the elderly, sick, and unemployed.[127] In return, the state receives inputs of mass loyalty. This is really the equivalent of an output of legitimation of the sociocultural system.[128] Oriented to social integration, this system draws on world views to legitimate the state. Dominated by communicative interaction, it socializes individuals into its world views, values, and norms. In addition, the sociocultural system exchanges inputs with the economy. It furnishes the latter with motivation for role-performances (work) and is "repaid" with goods and services (use-values).[129]

This theory, which conceptualizes society as constituted by subsystems exchanging inputs and outputs, implicitly assumes the subsystems to have the status of collective actors. The *system-integrative* function of economy and state takes place according to objective principles not reflected in the subjective orientations of social actors. They are structures with their own imperatives. Accordingly, every social system, says Habermas, has at any given time a goal-state defined by the values of its four functions (*AGIL*), which it tends to maintain in the face of both internal and external change.[130] In other words, it tends toward equilibrium. Economy, state, and sociocultural system are, thus, subjects that exchange resources in order to maintain themselves and fulfill their functions.

Societies, like their members, according to Habermas, possess identities[131] and appropriate their members' inner nature. Even after being integrated into the social system, the individual's inner nature constitutes an inner environment of the latter; individuals resist being absorbed.[132] The idea of society with an identity separate from the

Methodological Structuralism   109

identities of its members and standing in a relationship of conquest over the latter implies a Durkheimian-like dualism between individual and society.[133]

CRISIS TENDENCIES IN ADVANCED CAPITALISM

This system model provides Habermas with conceptual machinery for locating and explaining tendencies toward crises faced by advanced capitalist societies. The theory of the functionally articulated system shaped his conclusions about the possible fate of advanced capitalism.

Advanced capitalist societies are vulnerable to four crises. The first consists basically of the same tendencies Marx analyzed in the liberal capitalisms of his day. These are the vicissitudes of the business cycle marked by periodic depressions. Productions slows. The public is not provisioned with the goods and services it had come to expect. Here Habermas adopts Marx's laws of value and the falling rate of profit. Constant capital (machinery, etc.) displaces variable capital (labor) in order to maximize surplus value (profit). Unemployment, however, follows as a result; and a consequent fall in consumption culminates in production slowdowns. The market, says Habermas, fails as a steering mechanism of economic activity.[134]

Such crises associated with the business cycle occur in the economic system. Two other types of crisis, however, manifest in the political-administrative system. The first of these is a rationality crisis. On the one hand, an economic crisis is at the same time a crisis of rationality inasmuch as it is the function of the state to prevent it. Therefore, the appearance of a depression, let us say, is a measure of the failure of rationality. On the other hand, if the state succeeds in defusing a potential economic crisis, it may do so only at the expense of adverse by-products such as budgetary deficits and inflation. Although production is maintained, an economic crisis has been transformed into a political crisis. One crisis has been substituted for another.[135]

Habermas adduces structural reasons for rationality deficits. One is that the political-administrative system depends for its information upon the very economic enterprises it tries to regulate. It, therefore, makes faulty decisions. Another source of deficit is the contradictory interests among capitalists that result in conflicting demands on the state. Consequently, a decision facilitates production in one area while blocking it in

110   The Basic Units of Social Theory

others. Also, Habermas puts forth the conclusion held by Marx that the collective demands of capital as a whole contradict the general interests of citizens.[136] For such reasons the state has difficulty making rational allocations of taxes (fiscal skim-off). It is easy to see that a crisis of rationality can be conceptualized as a failure of the political-administrative system to hold up its end of the bargain in the interchange system; it fails in its output of steering performances.

A second potential crisis in the political system is what Habermas calls a legitimation crisis. If the state fails to carry out its steering function satisfactorily, if it fails to raise taxes appropriately and spend them wisely, then a decline in mass loyalty is likely to occur. What the state does and how it does it are not approved by the mass public. If the state fails to prevent economic crises because of irrational decisions, it has endangered its legitimacy. Whereas rationality crises are output deficits of the state, legitimation crises are input deficits to the state.[137]

Several factors aggravate the difficulties of the state in its quest for legitimation. First, its appetite grows as its steering function requires increasing intervention into the capitalist economy. Second, an extension of political intervention into hitherto unpoliticized cultural areas accompanies increasing economic intervention. For example, the state involves itself in planning educational curricula and in family planning. Such involvements transform traditional activities into subjects of political discourse with a resulting weakening of tradition. The effectiveness of political policies in these areas now becomes subject to mass scrutiny.[138] The state is compelled to meet more tests of its legitimacy.

These economically relevant activities of the state have blunted class conflicts. By supplementing the market through subsidies, by replacing it with noncompetitive armaments contracts, and by indirectly raising wages, the state blunts the conflicts between capital and labor, rendering them latent, or else transfers the conflicts to the political system.

Habermas argued that the only source of political legitimacy is the sociocultural system. The state cannot legitimate itself. It cannot, says Habermas, produce meaning.[139] Guided by purposive rationality rather than communicative interaction, it does not deal with values, norms, and world views. On the other hand, these are precisely the object-domain of the sociocultural system, which, as we have seen, supplies motivations usable by the other systems.

Motivations required for system functioning are grounded in cultural values and world views. Take, for example, the cultural pattern of familial vocational privatism, which generates the achievement motive. This consists of the value of hard work that yields income, leisure, and security for the individual and his family, which rewards ought to be distributed on the basis of individual achievement.[140] Of obvious benefit to the economy, the motivation for hard work developed out of such traditions as possessive individualism, Benthamite utilitarianism, and the Protestant ethic. The problem, however, is, according to Habermas, that familial-vocational privatism is being destroyed. It and other cultural patterns relevant to the production of motivation are undermined by the expanding rationalization of life as analyzed by Weber.[141] The demands of economy and state are "colonizing the lifeworld."[142] Consequently, a crisis of motivation originating in the sociocultural system but affecting the economy and state may develop.

Overall, socioculturally generated motivational complexes functionally required by economy and state are being destroyed because their cultural matrices are being eroded. Furthermore, there are no functional equivalents for these spent traditions, for cultural traditions such as scientism that are dominant today have followed their own internal and irreversible logic.[143] They are incapable of functioning as substitutes for the achievement motive and familial-vocational privatism.

In sum, advanced capitalist societies are vulnerable to types of crises made possible by the dynamics of their structures. Although Habermas refuses to make an unequivocal prediction, each crisis is a possibility inherent in one of the three structures composing society as a totality.[144]

Since it is the sociocultural system that engages in communicative action, it is the sole source of political legitimation and motivations for work. Oriented to purposive rationality, state and economy must acquire these inputs from the sociocultural system. As systems with different functions, they are limited in their ability to develop their own legitimacy and motivation. So long as the exchanges balance, crises are kept under control. But when imbalances (deficits) occur, crises may appear. Crises of legitimacy and motivation in advanced capitalism are especially likely to occur because the rationality of the "base" pushes "up" more than the sociocultural "superstructure" pushes "down." The powerful upward thrust of purposive rationality impoverishes the sociocultural system's capacity to meet the terms of exchange equivalence. The sociocultural system has trouble supplying the required amounts of legitimation and motivation. Like Marx, Habermas holds that the economy exerts preponderant influence. But unlike Marx, he also groups the state with the

112   The Basic Units of Social Theory

economy in regard to this influence. Translating these relationships into the language of Parsons's theory, one can say that the *I* and *L* functions are not being addressed satisfactorily because of the ways the A and G functions are being carried out.

The structuralist assumptions that inform Habermas's theory of advanced capitalism carry over into his analysis of its tendencies to crisis. For, as already noted, these tendencies are possibilities of social structures as collective actors. The penetration of his theory by structuralist notions from Marx and Parsons has also been noted. Moreover, in applying Weber's concept of purposive rationality, he did not give it the logical status of an ideal-type but brought it into line with structuralist thinking. Economy and state are structures oriented to a rational adaptation of means to ends. The sociocultural system is a structure oriented to communicative action that establishes agreement about ends. Both these elements, the rational choice of means and the rational choice of ends, are dimensions of Weber's concept *(Zweckrationalität)*. In adapting this concept, however, Habermas abstracted both dimensions and attributed each to a different structure of advanced capitalist societies. Thus, state and economy are collective actors guided by one analytic aspect, namely, the rational selection of means; the sociocultural system is another collective actor guided by another aspect, namely, the rational selection of ends.[145] Weber's ideal-type is shattered and its fragments allocated as principles of different collective actors in a specialization of function compatible with systems theory, whose conceptual units are systems and subsystems rather than individuals.

Methodological Structuralism

The preceding ideas can be synthesized into one answer to the question posed at the beginning of the chapter: What is the ontological status of social structures? The reader will recall that this question arises within the context of queries into the nature of the units out of which sociologists construct theories. Methodological structuralism's answer is that social theories are theories about *sui generis* social structures.

A social structure is a kind of whole, a substance, a collective actor that is more than individuals. It cannot be reduced to them nor to their characteristics. It combines with other structures to form societies, which also take on an autonomous existence even though ultimately traceable to individuals. Thus, society itself is conceived of as a sociocultural structure consisting of interrelated structures such as statuses, roles, norms, values, and institutions. When structures combine, they often acquire characteristics that have counterparts, such as conflict and exchange, in the relationships among individuals.

Societies are unities rather than aggregates and comply with unique imperatives in order to maintain themselves. As functioning systems they do certain things in order to survive as recognizable entities. Their internal structures are differentiated and articulated to perform specified functions on their behalf. Nevertheless, one can readily discover structural contradictions and dysfunctions leading to social transformations. These contradictions are not random, but reveal explainable regularities and patterns.

Methodological structuralists have a tendency to be aware of the *sui generis* principle manifest in a series of ontological levels extending from the inorganic to the organic, the psychological, and finally the sociocultural. Relationships between individual and society are analyzed within this cosmic context, which provides relevent analogies. Each level is organized differently than the others while at the same time arising from and depending on those below it. As the *sui generis* concept denotes, each level is a class in itself. The world thus presents to the methodological structuralist a hierarchy of levels of organization that originates below the individual and extends beyond him. In this hierarchical context, concepts such as system integration, social equilibrium, social relations of production, and anomie acquire definitions that cannot be applied to individuals without some revision of meaning.

Despite their distinctiveness, the levels are connected by the postulates of reciprocal causality and the interpenetration of elements. Insofar as a higher level of reality arises from interactions of elements on the lower, it absorbs them into its own organization. Elements on one level penetrate other levels. Accordingly, individuals have beliefs and goals that are also collective beliefs and goals of society transformed according to the *sui generis* postulate by the interactions of the former. It follows that social structures are both internal and external to individuals and take on independent existence. Therefore, societies maintain a continuity despite changes in their members. This simultaneous location of social structures internal and external to individuals yields the conceptualization of the inner lives of individuals as a boundary condition of society.

114   The Basic Units of Social Theory

Reciprocity of causation holds that societies are both causally effective in relation to their members and subject to their influence. The arrangements of the structures of society organize the lives of its members, forming a sociocultural environment. One's life chances, for instance, are determined by one's position in the structure of stratification. Working through individuals, societies bend them to their will to achieve social ends. The effects of society discovered by structural inquiries form a continuum ranging between the extremes of the good and bad in the perspectives of its members. Society is subjectively experienced as either furthering their material and ideal interests, or depriving them of advantages. On the one hand, it sustains them and fulfills their needs; on the other, it imposes upon them its pathologies. The precise effects depend upon an individual's structural location. These diverse impacts are explained, according to methodological structuralism, by the successes or failures of society to meet its imperatives or to achieve its goals. The fate of the individual is determined by the dynamics of society. The idea of social determinism lurks in methodological structuralism.

Despite a causal priority of the social over the individual, individuals make a difference—a conclusion representing the other side of the postulate of reciprocal causation. Individuals make society possible; and without their efforts, society could not achieve its goals. Its stability depends upon individual conformity to its codes. Furthermore, social change comes about through individual discontent that responds to structural imbalances and malintegrations. In case of either stability or change, the lives of individuals and the existence of society are mutually dependent. At the same time this mutual dependence occurs within an overarching dualism.

The *sui generis* postulate nevertheless inhibits explanation of the social solely in terms of the individual, for the former cannot be reduced to the latter. Avoidance of reductionism drives methodological structuralists toward a clear-cut distinction between psychology and sociology. Consequently, an understanding of subjective states or an analysis of individual dispositions cannot adequately explain the dynamics of societies; explanations of social phenomena are rather to be sought in lawlike, sometimes unconscious tendencies of structural factors. The impact of social forces is also often concealed from those being affected. For these reasons, methodological structuralists take a skeptical attitude toward the accounts of individuals as revelatory of social causes. Social causes and structures must be studied from an objective stance, and a clear distinction must be drawn between individual and social indicators. The methodological necessity of an objective stance is especially evident in the discovery of latent functions.

This pattern of ideas outlines one side of an issue critical for social theory and has made a difference in the way social theorists influenced by it have answered particular questions. It should be pointed out, nevertheless, that the pattern is an ideal-type of sociological thinking, not reproduced completely in the works of any single writer. In some it is replicated more fully, more of its dimensions apparent, than in others. This pattern has been shaped by the desire of sociologists to delineate an autonomous subject matter for the field of sociology that sets it apart from other disciplines that study human beings. Theories that are concerned with societies as totalities have the greatest affinity for it. In the following chapter, which analyzes the individualist side of the controversy, I will attempt to explain why this is so.

Methodological Individualism

Chapter 3 identified the problem of the units of social theories with the following question: Do societies and other social structures have a mode of being different from their members? Answering in the affirmative, methodological structuralism was challenged immediately by a contrasting set of notions that I refer to as *methodological individualism*.

Methodological individualism is defined primarily by the belief that society consists solely of its members. They alone are real. It follows that society and other social structures lack an independent, or partially independent, status with unique characteristics and dynamics, rather being reducible to characteristics abstracted from individuals. The abstractions turn out to be elements of individuals' subjective experience, such as norms, that form cultural patterns or interactions that form networks of social relationships. Social relationships consist of the ways individuals think about and treat one another. They lack an existence external to those who form them. However, a distinction is drawn between the point of view of social theory and that of subjects who think of groups and other social structures as real entities—a conception that must be taken into account by individualist theories insofar as it affects courses of action.

Individualism rules out social structures as supraindividual causes and traces causal influences to particular individuals or to individuals in general. Social causation does not operate in the sphere of Durkheimian

118   The Basic Units of Social Theory

social facts, for, in contrast to the French thinker's views, social facts are definable in terms of facts about individuals. Conformity to rules, for instance, is explained in terms of the commitments of actors rather than as the effect of a *sui generis* normative order. Thus, individualism does not eliminate social structures from its vocabulary, but insists that scientific explanations translate them into individual terms. And, as argued in the conclusion of chapter 2, when the facts indicated are meaning-contents, the concepts have the logical properties of the ideal-type. With causal factors expressed in such concepts, methodological individualism holds that individuals are free to form themselves out of the materials they present to one another and, possessing freedom of choice, are active agents rather than passive recipients of the unmediated impact of transcendent structures.

The following discussion illustrates this ideal-typical formulation with concrete detail from arguments and explanations of writers who self-consciously adopted the individualist perspective. Again we are interested not only in questions abstractly stated but also in how they influenced particular explanations in ways that contrast with structuralist approaches. The contrasts considered—between Simmel and Durkheim, Weber and Marx, and Homans and Parsons, for example—illustrate how differing conclusions result from differing presuppositions concerning specific topics of long-standing theoretical interest. With their focus on face-to-face relationships, microsocial theories, such as exchange, phenomenology, and symbolic interactionism, lend themself to the individualist approach.

Tarde Disputes Durkheim

Durkheim's concept of the social fact as a reality was criticized by a number of his contemporaries,[1] most severely by Gabriel Tarde (1843–1904). Armed with a psychological conception of society, Tarde in his criticisms expressed some of the tenets of methodological individualism.

It is fashionable, said Tarde, for cultivated minds to embrace the theory of *sui generis* levels of reality, which holds that the combination of several beings can itself become a new being different from its elements and superior to them. Among others, chemists and biologists have contributed to this "prejudice." No one really knows, however, what is really

Methodological Individualism   119

within the inmost recesses of a chemical molecule or a living cell. It is ignorance, therefore, that leads to the postulation of an *ex nihilo* creation of something that was not present before. On the other hand, observed Tarde, the sociologist is uniquely privileged to possess an intimate, direct knowledge of society's element, namely, individual consciousness. This knowledge leads to the certainty that if the conscious experiences of individuals of both the past and present were subtracted, then nothing of the social would remain.[2] Tarde dismissed the idea of a social sphere distinct from the psychological as a form of mysticism.

To Durkheim's postulate that individual representations are not social facts because the latter belong to society and are therefore quite different than their refractions in individuals, Tarde asked how is it that a social fact can be refracted within individuals before it exists? How is it possible for a social fact to obtain an existence outside all individuals? To these questions he replied, in contrast to Durkheim, that the sole reality of a social fact *is* the totality of its refractions within the consciousness of individuals. Inasmuch as any social fact cannot be transmitted from society to its members, but only from one individual to another, Durkheim's definition of the social fact is an "ontological illusion."[3] When no one conforms to a moral rule and no one repeats it to someone else, then that rule lacks an objective existence. Durkheim's theory that a social fact transcends its individual manifestations constitutes a revival of Plato's doctrine of Ideas.[4]

In similar fashion, Tarde criticized Durkheim's notion of the constraint exerted by the social fact. According to Durkheim the social fact is general because it is collective, not that it is collective because it is general. A property of society, the social fact as a manner of collective thinking or acting subjects individuals to externally imposed restraint. But, said Tarde, even if one concedes the exteriority of the social fact, that does not prove it possesses coercive power. Food is external to the cell that absorbs it, yet one cannot characterize the relation between cell and its nourishment as one of coercion. To define the social fact as coercive is to reduce all social relationships to the level of that between master and slave or victor and vanquished.[5]

With regard to the social fact's exteriority, it should be noted, Tarde argued, that the proposition that it has an existence apart from all individuals is vastly different from the proposition that it is external to each. Yet it is quite clear from his writings, Tarde contended, that Durkheim meant the former. Nevertheless, it is evident that a social fact

120   The Basic Units of Social Theory

can exist outside any particular person, but get inside him, who then makes it his own.[6] In the latter event, the social fact loses its coercive power. In the language of American sociologists, it has been internalized.

Finally, we must reject Durkheim's methodological conclusion drawn from the above premises that the cause of a social fact must always be sought in another social fact and not in an individual characteristic. According to Durkheim, explanations of social facts must proceed on a strictly social level, for sociology cannot be reduced to psychology. Tarde asserted, however, that this clear-cut distinction between sociology and psychology cannot be sustained; for the social is no more than the consciousness of individuals. Therefore, a social fact can be explained only in terms of the psychology of individuals both living and dead. Durkheim's social environment in reality consists only of everything contained in the minds of individuals, such as ideas, memories, habits, and aptitudes. If Durkheim were correct, then the sociologist would explain the railroads of France as caused by the preexisting networks of roads rather than by the conscious states of inventors like Papin, Watts, and Stephenson.[7]

In the light of such criticisms, Tarde presented his own definition of the social fact and thereby developed an individualist theory of society. The two elementary social facts are belief and desire, both of which are states of individual consciousness. What gives them a factual status is their real existence in consciousness, and what makes them social is that they are established by imitation. According to Tarde, every belief and desire is established in the individual mind through the process of copying from some model. Thus Tarde described society as vast networks of the diffusion of beliefs and desires. When a new belief or desire is acquired, it modifies the individual's state of consciousness. And Tarde called such a modification of consciousness a social act. Of course, at some time or other every belief and desire had to be invented by someone; but it is imitation that is society's master process, and it is imitation that most intrigued Tarde. Familiar social acts that result from imitation are praying to an idol, wearing a garment, cutting down a tree, knifing an enemy, and sculpting a stone.[8]

Accordingly, the conceptual foundations of Tarde's theory come down to belief and desire as units of consciousness and the process of imitation, which establishes social relations through acts that alter consciousness. Once beliefs and desires are reproduced in consciousness, they eventuate in imitative actions. Every social act, therefore, implies an imitative

Methodological Individualism 121

relationship among individuals, some of whom are models, others copiers.[9] Imitation is what gives different minds whatever unity they have. And without such beliefs and desires, minds could not be compared; nor could persons form groups. Imitation consists of, for example, a reproduction within one mind of the words spoken by another, of a religious ceremony, or of an industrial process, all of which are models. As mental imprints, these reproductions are relevant to psychology; but imitation exteriorizes the models, transforming them into sociological factors.[10] Imitation rather than emergence bridges the gap between psychology and sociology.

Thus, sociology's subject matter consists of psychological events. Although the repetitions of beliefs and desires are variations around an original model, all social resemblances, all social similarities, said Tarde, are brought about by imitation.[11] Even when two persons independently invent the same object or idea, that is because each has drawn on the same common fund of instruction.[12] So important is imitation that Tarde built it into his definition of society as a "group of beings who are apt to imitate one another, or who without actual imitation, are alike in their possession of common traits which are ancient copies of the same model."[13] Elsewhere Tarde defined a group as consisting of individuals interrelated through imitative bonds.[14]

Tarde found a place for statistics in such resemblances. Statistics record the frequencies of the repetitions of resemblances in the form of such things as fashions, dress, wants, housing, and ideas. Were nothing copied or repeated, the universe would lack quantity; and the science of mathematics would not exist.[15] Tarde pointed to population changes, growths and declines of speakers of a language, and the number of commodities consumed as examples of statistics. They are social statistics by virtue of the fact that they are the sums of mental entities ultimately traceable to beliefs and desires established through imitation.[16]

This abbreviated account reveals several consequences of the type of theory that rejects the reality of society as existing separately from its members. Without the notion of the *sui generis* nature of the group, Tarde had to find another way of accounting for social unity than by a theory that society is subject to its own laws. He could not postulate the *conscience collective* or the social system's integrative function. Rather, he was forced to explain the similarities among individuals with reference to rises and declines in repetitions through imitation. Minds achieve unity through psychological processes. For Tarde, society becomes exteriorized through words and actions that reproduce themselves in other states of consciousness.

Statistics function as an auxiliary to sociology differently than Durkheim thought. In contrast to his use of statistics to indicate variations in group properties, statistics for Tarde were aggregations of individual characteristics. For Durkheim, statistics were quantitative indices of society's ability to use its members to achieve its ends, whereas for Tarde statistics measure how far the unifying tendencies of beliefs and desires have proceeded at any given time. It is no accident, therefore, that Durkheim was interested in how many Protestants commit suicide rather than which ones—a scientific task properly reserved for the psychologist. Neither was it an accident that Tarde tried to explain all sorts of crime by how far they had diffused,[17] whereas Durkheim was preoccupied with levels of deviance that are normal for each society.

In its focus on the laws of imitation, Tarde's methodological individualism made a hesitant step toward enlisting the elements and processes of conscious experience to explain problems of interest to sociologists. His definition of the social in terms of the psychological was carried further and in more complex ways by subsequent theorists in the individualist tradition.

The Forms According to Simmel

Although all sociologically relevant processes are ultimately situated in human minds, Georg Simmel (1858–1918) denied that sociology therefore is reducible to psychology. This, nevertheless, does not classify his work as representative of methodological structuralism. Rather, Simmel developed an individualist theory of society.

As Kant posed the question of how nature is possible, Simmel posed the question of how society is possible. For Kant, nature is made possible by the power of the mind to transform sense impressions into the picture of nature that we experience. The forms of the human intellect—causality, space, time, etc.—impose themselves upon sense impressions and convert them into natural objects and laws. As resultant of both what is objective and subjective, nature depends therefore upon an external observer to synthesize sense materials into a unity. Society also comes into being through a synthesis, but it differs from nature in that its own

Methodological Individualism   123

elements synthesize themselves into a unity. These elements are of course individuals. While connections between sense impressions of the material world are established by the mind's cognitive properties, it is the individual who in his conscious experience creates a unity between himself and others. In other words, when individuals think about how they are related to one another, their experiences constitute society. The unity of society thus resides strictly within the minds of its members. Consequently, for its existence society requires no outside observer.[18] Its own elements bring it into being.

By a synthesis of society Simmel did not necessarily mean harmony, but rather a combination performed in each mind whereby each person conceives of how he is related to others. The individual arranges one concrete content alongside another, yet few are capable of explaining abstractly what they are doing. Thus, processes of association (Simmel called them processes of *sociation*) occur as conscious experiences and eventuate in associated actions. Within these conscious processes society is formed.[19]

The question now becomes: What are the forms of thought that make sociation possible? In other words, what are the latter's *a priori* conditions? These originate in consciousness when one becomes aware of sociating or being sociated. Simmel regarded these forms as the sociological counterparts of the forms that make nature possible according to Kant. He set forth three relevant to the context of this discussion.

When we interact with another, we do so on the basis of a generalized conception or picture of the other. However, our picture is always a distortion based on fragmentary knowledge composed of bits and pieces of information that we juxtapose to form a type. The fundamental reason, said Simmel, for this distortion is that we cannot completely picture an individuality that differs from our own. Similarity to oneself is a condition for the construction of another; and since no one can be totally like another, no one can completely grasp another. On the other hand, distortion also stems from other, very familiar sources such as incomplete information, defective understanding, and positive and negative prejudices.[20]

The typical conception a person has of another blends his singularity with general categories such as good, bad, moral, lordly, etc. The other's individuality is "raised" or "lowered" in relation to the type. The type, moreover, remains unverbalized. The picture of another delineates how he would act if he truly conformed to the type, which does not fully

124   The Basic Units of Social Theory

cover him. Furthermore, types are shared by members of a group, who mutually impose them upon one another. Every member of a church, a party, or an occupation perceives the others as members of "my group." The general conceptions we build up of others based on our personal knowledge and the conceptions we obtain from society always add to and detract from them and conceal their individuality.[21] These distortive, incomplete, unverbalized characterizations, however, function as *a priori* conditions that make sociation possible; for we interact with others on the basis of them and we cannot do otherwise. Thus the first form that is an *a priori* condition of society is a type.

The second consists of the fact that when an individual sees himself in relation to others he is at the same time both part of society and outside it. As an outsider he confronts at the same time that of which he is only a part. An implication is that the parts of society are also parts of individuals. Put another way, the individual enters into sociation with only a part of his personality, the remainder being left outside. Thus, the bureaucrat is not only a bureaucrat, the officer not only an officer. However, the part of the individual that is absorbed into a social relationship is affected by the part that is withheld. Everyone knows, for example, that the nonbureaucratic life of the bureaucrat—his temperament and interests—affects the way he plays his bureaucratic role. And the picture formed by those who meet him includes these nonsocial elements. Individuals' relationships would be vastly different if everyone believed that anyone is nothing more than what his role expects of him. That in some respects the person is not a part of sociation constitutes the condition for the fact that in other respects he is. The sociated aspect of the person is subject to a twofold determination: First, the nonsocial elements of his personality affect those elements that participate in a social relation. Second, the latter elements are affected by the sociated elements of the other participants.[22] The personality elements entering into society are shaped by those exterior to it and by those of others which participate in it.

Simmel pointed out that social roles form a continuum with respect to how much personality content they include. At one extreme are love and friendship, which minimize the nonsocial elements. What remains after the lover attends to his beloved is almost nothing, for the process of sociation is so inclusive as to encompass one life lived from two sides. The same is true of the Catholic priest, whose religious personality, absorbing his existence, is never dropped. At the other extreme is the role of the buyer, whose nonsocial elements are excluded from the transaction.[23] There is a kind of "sliding scale" in the absorptive power of sociation.

In this frequently quoted chapter, Simmel identified a third *a priori* condition for society's existence—individuality. Every individual, said Simmel, differs from every other, even under socialism; for the contents of experience and life destinies vary. There is a place in the social division of labor for everyone—a preexisting niche that facilitates both the individual's self-development and the accomplishment of social functions. The unique qualities of every person drive him into those positions in the division of labor that suit him. Yet society is not a perfect harmony; for dissonances and conflicts produce deviations from the conceptually perfect society, where the uniqueness of every individual complements that of every other.[24]

It is evident that these apriorities force the inevitable conclusion that society is a psychical phenomenon. In this regard Simmel observed that all processes of sociation are located in minds. Thoughts, feelings, and needs are both bearers of social relations and their essence; the causes of social events are deducible from psychological propositions. Events of sociocultural life are concatenations of psychological events that the sociologist reconstructs in understandable sequences. Nevertheless, sociology is not identical with psychological laws, for here Simmel drew a distinction between those lawlike processes of mind that produce psychic contents and the contents themselves, such as motives, interests, and needs. What is relevant to the sociologist is the configuration formed by contents and the forms of sociation abstracted from them.[25] Although sociological theories are constructed out of elements of individuals' minds, it does not follow that sociology is reducible to psychology.

INDIVIDUALITY

As we have seen, individuality, according to Simmel, is a form that makes society possible. It is also a central theme in his wide-ranging studies of social evolution and is cast in a different light than in Durkheim's studies. It can be demonstrated that their differing conclusions are linked to contrasts between methodological structuralism and individualism.

What is individuality according to Simmel? Although historical think-

126   The Basic Units of Social Theory

ing evolved several conceptions,[26] the one that claimed his interest as an object of historical explanation was what he called the *individualism of uniqueness*. Coming out of nineteenth-century Romanticism, this ideal represents the individual as driven by the desire to be different from, indeed, better than others. The individualism of uniqueness compels him to realize his own significance by contrasting himself to and measuring himself against others. Not social resemblance, but personal peculiarity is what preoccupies the person guided by this ideal. A person's character differentiations take the form of acquiring power, status, or wealth or result in his need to reciprocally complement his differences within a division of labor in which he plays an irreplaceable role. Production and fulfillment of the unique aspects of his character become his moral ideal.[27] It is evident that the need to play this role in a division of labor corresponds to individuality as a sociological apriority: Society is produced out of the incomparability of character differences. The desire to be different makes society possible.

So defined, individuality is an ideal antithetical to similarity, which if carried to an extreme leads to an absolute equality among individuals. The decision of a person to adopt one or the other of these ideals stems from the "very depth of his being," said Simmel; for differentiation and equality are not means to the achievement of some other end such as personal happiness, but constitute the grounds of all other decisions. How a person answers the question "Do I want to be similar or different?" shapes his overall relations with others.[28]

The will to be different is expressed in numerous ways. A person can devote his energies to the cultivation of courage, strength, beauty, nobility of character, and intellect as well as to the fulfillment of narrow material interest. Hence, the pursuit of some ideal of self-perfection need not be egoism; nor need it be an altruistic effort on behalf of others. Yet, whatever the ideal, wrote Simmel, it can involve the individual in conflicts with groups to which he belongs and which seek to enlist his energies on behalf of the roles they expect him to play. Such conflicts between society, which seeks to impose a one-sided function upon the individual in order to create a social unity, and the individual, who seeks to unify his personality around an ideal, are insoluble dilemmas.[29] Here it is evident that another form making society possible comes into play. The individual's capacity to participate in sociation with only a sector of his personality makes it possible to avoid conflict between group and individual ideals.

Methodological Individualism   127

The individual, Simmel continued, is able to "decompose himself into parts and to feel any one of them as his proper self."[30] He is able to select some of his tendencies and goals as those which have the highest value and which form the core of his self. These need not be those subsumed under the role expected by a group; the core of his individuality may not enter into his social being. It is apparent, for example, that the possibility of moral perfection in terms of individuality may not enter into his social being.

The conviction that moral perfection in terms of individually chosen ideals is possible clashes with Durkheim's conclusion that the individual is incapable of fashioning on his own beliefs worth living for.[31] As we have seen, for Durkheim the beliefs that sustain interest in life are collective beliefs, *sui generis* realities of religious, domestic, and political societies. When such beliefs lose their authority, the will to live declines. The individual's insufficiency in the face of society's moral authority is also evident in the face of anomie, a condition under which he is too impotent to impose restraint on himself. For Durkheim, morality is a social rather than individual phenomenon.

Simmel's observations about individuality contradict the correlations Durkheim saw between individuality and egoism and between similarity and altruism. The quest for an ideal that makes one different need not, as noted above, serve a narrow material interest. Nor need it be in the service of others, for it can be sought as an end in itself. Yet society's conquest of the individual to serve its ends is itself a form of egoism that often does violence to him for the benefit of the many.[32] Hence, for Simmel separation from the group can be altruistic and integration into the group egoistic.

In contrast to Durkheim's theorem that society imposes itself on the individual through the constraint of the social fact, Simmel observed that everyone creates the elements of his personality out of the elements of society. On the one hand, each person weaves in a unique fashion the traits and tendencies of his character out of the elements of his groups. On the other hand, the elements of sociation consist of elements of diverse personalities. There is, consequently, a reciprocal relationship between person and group. When he joins a group, a person surrenders his personality to it. In participating in a unique way, however, he regains his individuality;[33] for his creative role makes possible an individualism of uniqueness. This outline of the formation of personality out of social elements once again sustains Simmel's image of individualism. Forms

128   The Basic Units of Social Theory

existing within the individual not only make society possible but also produce his individuality. Conflicts between individual and group and the separation of the former from the latter need not express an egoism that reflects personal and social pathology.

THE DEVELOPMENT OF INDIVIDUALITY

Having defined individuality, Simmel proceeded to identify factors in its historical development. His conclusions once again contradict Durkheim. He found a subtle interplay between external factors pertaining to interrelationships among groups and factors internal to the mind.

In contrast to a concentric pattern of group relationships typical of the Middle Ages, the modern pattern is one in which an individual has the chance of belonging to several single-purpose groups. He enters one group with a slice of his personality while in other groups he pursues different interests encompassed by other sectors of his being. He may well belong to an occupational group, a scientific society, and at the same time sit on the board of a corporation. These groups "intersect" in his personality. A proliferation of groups makes it unlikely that two individuals belong to precisely the same combination. Multiple-group memberships therefore not only differentiate segments of the personality, but they also differentiate individuals.[34] Once again Simmel emphasized that a person complements his irreplaceable uniqueness by assuming diverse roles. The converse, of course, is that membership within a single group (employing geometric analogies, Simmel referred to groups as *social circles*) restricts character development and makes its members similar to one another.

Simmel supplemented this synchronic analysis of the relation between individuation and patterns of groups with a diachronic approach. In doing so his thinking was channeled in directions that led him to draw conclusions at variance with Durkheim's pessimism concerning economic anomie.

Simmel found a correlation occurring again and again: "Individuality in being and action generally increases to the degree that the social circle encompassing the individual expands."[35] As a group grows larger, its members become more individualized in thoughts and actions. Quantitative growth occurs internally or by inclusion from without. When expansion occurs, increasing competition for existence brings in its wake greater specialization of means. As people become specialized, they act differently from others. Increase in number thus differentiates the group. At the same time, each acquires a heightened awareness of self because he is compelled to compare and unify diverse experiences. The individual finds existence of his ego on the basis of these diversities and contrasts.[36]

Simmel illustrated the correlation between group size and individuality with the medieval guilds. Originally the guilds imposed equality upon their members, who were obliged to conform to determined quantities and qualities of production, power, and markets. In the long run this lack of differentiation could not be maintained. Some masters became rich by developing new markets, expanding their line of products, and acquiring more apprentices. Differentiation of rich from poor, capitalist from laborer, and merchant from producer occurred with an expansion of contacts beyond the previously narrow confines of the social circle. The expansion of the guild came in the form not only of more outside contacts and greater memberships, but also expansion to cover larger territories.[37]

The correlation between expansion and individuality is accompanied by another, namely, that between freedom and inequality—a correlation implied by the former. Expansion accords greater freedom of thought and action, which contributes to differences that make individuals unequal. In his encyclopedic study of the sociological significance of money, Simmel demonstrated how money fosters freedom. Thus, from his study of money emerges another correlational pattern, which articulates with the former. The expanded formula is that money contributes to freedom, which in turn contributes to individuality.

In order to draw the contrasts with Durkheim more sharply, let us examine this pattern more closely. First, money promotes individuality by facilitating the economic expansion of the group. An economy of barter is restricted because of the difficulty of coordinating possessors who want to exchange a specific commodity with potential acquirers. Money lessens this restriction on the process of exchange, making it possible, for example, for the master of the guild to expand the territorial extent of the transactions and the range of his contacts.[38]

Second, money enhances an individual's freedom with respect to his obligations. It lightens the burden of obligations. Simmel identified three methods of meeting one's obligations. In the first place, if the obligation consists of some service to be performed directly to another, the amount

130 The Basic Units of Social Theory

of freedom involved is minimal. The individual who discharges the obligation is dependent totally upon the other's will, who can demand any method of performance and any level of energy. This form of obligation is illustrated by slavery. In the second place, if the obligation consists of the provision of a commodity by his own labor, the person has greater freedom in how he produces it. Thus, the serf, who had to hand over a fixed portion of his yield from the soil, had greater leeway in determining his methods of production. In the third place, if the obligation consists of a money payment the person who owes it has even greater freedom of choice as to how he acquires the money.[39] With the transmutation of payments in kind into payments in money, serfs gained greater personal freedom.

The freedom acquired through money is evident in the modern economy. Today we are dependent for the satisfaction of our needs upon a vast number of individuals organized in complex networks. Yet we are hardly dependent on any specific individual, for we are at liberty to choose from a variety of different producers for a service. Each producer is interchangeable with another, and we are not interested in the unique personality of any. An aspect of freedom is the ability to change at will those upon whom we depend. His personality traits recede from the person's objective function. In contrast, primitive man depended upon fewer persons, but entered into a personal relationship with each.[40]

Freedom in relationships of dependence is both connected to and parallel with an internal freedom, which freedom provides a third explication by Simmel of the correlation among money, freedom, and individuality. An individual is internally free when the various sectors of his personality are allowed to develop along their own lines and pursue their own goals without hindrance from one another. The individual whose energies develop on behalf of their own purposes and interests is free. The amount of internal freedom depends therefore on the limits of the number of points of connection between psychic sequences. Of course, Simmel noted, internal freedom can never be total, just as total independence of others can never be total. This type of freedom is expressed in the old saying that freedom means living according to one's own nature.[41] Simmel thought of internal freedom as a counterpart of the freedom given by the aforementioned relationships among individuals.

Interferences with partly separated lines of psychic development come from both inner and external sources. An inner source of interference is

Methodological Individualism   131

illustrated by a relation between intellect and sensual desires. Philosophers, said Simmel, speak of the moral freedom of a person insofar as his sensual appetites do not impede the development of his reason and direct it into channels alien to it.[42]

It is, however, the external constraints on inner freedom that is of interest here. Simmel illustrated this relationship with that between intellectual and economic interests. He who has a desire to develop his intellect and build his real self around it is free to practice this ideal to the extent that the intellectual and economic sectors of his psychic experience are generally rather than specifically related. The two mental series must be broadly rather than narrowly interwoven. A generality of interconnection between psychic sectors is a counterpart to the generality of the ways a person can fulfill an obligation to another. The more possibilities open to him the freer he is. For example, intellectuals for a long time derived their economic sustenance from land ownership because its management intruded to a lesser extent than other forms of economic dependence. However, the differentiation between intellectual pursuit and economic fulfillment is intensified by money, which is so far removed from any economic specificity that it intrudes less on the intellect. Simmel cited examples from Italy to support this point. Intellectual production in Florence exceeded that of Venice and Genoa, even though the latter were as wealthy as the former. However, their wealth depended on commerce whereas the Florentines became rich as bankers. Banking ties one less specifically than trade to concrete objects.[43] Insofar as it promotes internal differentiation of the sectors of inner life, money contributes to individuality; and it does so through the intermediary of freedom.

The liberating power of money and the commercial and industrial expansion it makes possible contrast starkly with Durkheim's emphasis on the pervasive anomie within the modern economy. For Durkheim, economic anomie, being pathological, dooms the individual to the frustration of unfilled desire. Having lost the capacity to regulate appetites, industrial and commercial society lets individuals slip out from under its moral control just as in the case of egoism it lets them elude its intellectual control. Whereas Simmel concluded that the modern web of group-affiliations makes people free, Durkheim arrived at the conclusion that escape from society's moral authority weakens the will to live.

These conflicting conclusions are traceable, in part at least, to their contrasting theories of modes of thinking. According to Durkheim, a

132   The Basic Units of Social Theory

collective belief is always a collective product. It does not arise from individual minds, but from the association of minds. Although each may contribute a part, in the process of forming such a belief a fusion occurs that makes individual thoughts into something else. A collective representation is a reality *sui generis*, a whole found in no one. It thinks, feels, and wishes although it can do none of these except through individuals.[44]

On the other hand, without the *sui generis* postulate Simmel was open to the alternative that an individual is capable of fashioning a belief that organizes his life. Neither is he doomed to search for the infinite, for he can limit himself. A synthesis of social elements occurs within a single mind instead of a transforming fusion among many minds.[45] This conclusion then opens the way for the model of the individual mind as segmented into either loosely or tightly connected sectors of experience, some of which are subsumed under social roles while others are more or less independent. A psychic division of labor parallel to a social division of labor is grounded theoretically in the apriorities that make society possible. It is immediately apparent that these contrasting analyses by Durkheim and Simmel of the relationship between individual thinking and society are implications of contrasts between methodological structuralism and methodological individualism.

Weber the Individualist

Max Weber's conception of sociology is a consummate expression of methodological individualism. As such, it yields conclusions that oppose some of those of Marx.[46] According to Weber, the sociologist ought to devote himself to rendering causal accounts of the course and consequences of social actions. A social action is one that takes into account another individual and is oriented to the latter throughout its course. To the implied question of what an action is, Weber's immediate answer was any behavior that has a meaning to the actor. The definition of action thus yields a clue to where the social scientist is to discover the cause of social action. In order to arrive at an explanation of its cause and effects, he must understand what the action means to the actor;[47] for it is the meaning as it appears to the actor that is its predominant cause.

Although located in an individual mind, subjective meaning can roughly be categorized as deriving from two sources. It finds its first

Methodological Individualism   133

source in the immediate situation in which the action occurs. Here, for example, are located the means which the actor uses to achieve an end in a rational fashion. In chopping wood a person must define the wood, the axe, and the conditions in the situation. In solving a mathematical problem, he must know the rules of mathematics and the meaning of numbers. Such rational actions are readily understandable to an observer having grown up in that culture.[48] A second source of meaning is the context within the actor's mind not immediately derivable from the situation itself.[49] Included in the meaning-context may be ultimate values he holds,[50] emotions such as rage, and his motive for performing the action.[51] It is also possible for an actor to be unconscious of elements such as motives within his meaning-context.[52]

What is the relationship of social actions to groups and collectivities? In briefly taking up this matter, Weber left no doubt about his individualist assumptions. There is, said Weber, no understandable action except the action of individuals. Collectivities like the state, business corporations, and religious associations must be treated solely as constituted by the particular actions of concrete individuals. They are not collective actors with their own realities and cannot be understood on their own terms. To be sure, collective terms are convenient ways of expressing the social actions of many persons. The state, for instance, is a shorthand way of referring to actions of persons in their political roles. Also, insofar as collective concepts are interpreted by an actor to have a real existence, *his* conception of a collectivity affects the course of his action and must therefore be understood as such by an observer.[53]

Insofar as two or more individuals are oriented to one another, their actions form a social relationship.[54] Weber went on to contrast two types of relationship. An *associative relationship* exists when individuals mutually take each other into account in order to rationally achieve some end. They may mutually adjust their interests, or band together to achieve their interests, or cooperate in a voluntary association because they share some absolute value like salvation. The prototype of an associative relationship is a market transaction.[55] A *communal relationship*, on the other hand, exists when persons join together because they believe they belong together because of tradition or emotional attachments to one another. Where genuine solidarity exists, Weber observed that every long-term relationship that involves more than the attainment of immediate goals, even though shared, takes on to some degree communal dimensions.

134   The Basic Units of Social Theory

On the basis of these types, Weber set forth a generalization contra-
dicting Marx's conclusions about social classes, revolutions, and the
course of history. The mere existence of common characteristics among
persons, such as race, sex, or wealth, their performance of similar
actions, or finding themselves in a common situation does not necessarily
lead to either an associative or communal relationship. Should they act
in similar ways in a common situation, they may not take one another
into account, let alone develop the solidarity characteristic of a communal relationship.[56] Weber applied this generalization to his analysis of
social classes and directly challenged Marx.

What is a social class? Weber's answer was that a class is composed of
all those who share a similar class situation. Here the similarity with
Marx's definition of a class in itself is evident. However, Weber then
diverged from Marx. A class situation is not solely determined by the
individual's relationship to the modes of production (although property
ownership is a basic dividing line between classes), but rather by his
relation to the markets for goods and labor. A common class situation is
shared by those who have similar commodities or types of labor to sell in
markets that are free to operate according to supply and demand. Those
who own land they can sell, for example, compose a class and those with
unskilled labor to sell compose another class. Without commodity and
labor markets, there are no social classes.[57]

It is by no means certain, however, that either associative or communal
relationships will arise out of a class situation. Either outcome is only
probable. It should be remembered that actions that are similar but are
not mutually oriented, such as workers' grumbling, are neither an
associative nor a communal relationship. The ways that workers, as an
example, strive to fulfill their market-determined interests are highly
variable; and there are factors that affect the avenues in which they
channel their economic interests. One such factor is the transparency of
the causal connection between a class situation and the consequences
experienced by those within it. If they come to perceive the cause of their
plight to stem from the way the property of society is distributed or from
the way the economic order is organized, they may organize as an
association or a community. On the other hand, if they do not draw
such connections, they may assume their class situation to be an absolute
given and do nothing. Accordingly, a class struggle arising out of a class
situation, concluded Weber, is only a probability.[58]

Weber cited examples of the transparency of the cause of a class

Methodological Individualism   135

situation to those who find themselves within it. An interesting one is the conflict between proletariat and industrialists in modern capitalism—a conflict which of course is central to Marxism. The greatest bitterness, observed Weber, obtains between these two classes because they face each other as enemies in conflicts over wages. Yet, it is not the managers but the shareholders and bankers who are the recipients of the profits of these struggles. Those who actually receive the unearned income are not generally the targets of the workers' hostility,[59] for the struggles are shaped by the causal connections established in the minds of workers.

Weber's reluctance to admit the inevitability of class consciousness and the formation of "classes for themselves" is logically related to his methodological individualism. Lacking a theory of class interests as structural realities inevitably pressing upon consciousness, he was logically compelled to locate the source of class consciousness within the orientations of individuals in class situations. The sphere of social causation resides within individuals, whose choices of method to pursue self-interest are not homogenized by transcendent social structures.

Indeed, Weber went on to criticize in its entirety Marx's formula of historical materialism. He did so partly on the ground that the "laws" of history involved in historical materialism are really ideal-types and should be considered as such. When given the status of real forces or tendencies, they become "truly metaphysical" and "pernicious."[60] Weber's individualist presuppositions precluded the postulation of developmental laws of social structures as realities.

Homans Brings Men Back In

The intellectual parents of functionalism, said Homans, were Durkheim and Radcliffe-Brown. They stood at the head of an approach eagerly embraced by American sociologists, the most influential of whom is Talcott Parsons. Functional theorists in America took very seriously indeed Durkheim's precept that sociologists should study the power of social facts to impress themselves upon individual consciousness. Accordingly, they defined institutions as clusters of roles oriented to norms and studied how they are interrelated. They were fond, Homans continued, of demonstrating how the existence of one institution imposes limits on

136   The Basic Units of Social Theory

the variations of others. They concluded, for instance, that the nuclear family is the kinship structure most compatible with industrialism.[61]

The trouble is, Homans charged, that functionalists never explained *why* a given configuration of institutions exists. They never really discovered the causes of social phenomena. The reason for their failure is that they never developed deductively related propositions that state the behavior of individuals, for in the final analysis one must explain social phenomena strictly in terms of the characteristics of people. Durkheim was wrong, Homans concluded: Sociology *is* reducible to psychology.[62]

To avoid these errors, Homans developed a system of general propositions stating psychological relationships.[63] With them he tried to explain a range of facts of interest to sociologists, among which is social status. Let us, therefore, examine his explanation of status in terms of the assumption that social facts must be explained by individual behavior and contrast it with Parsons's functional explanation of this factor.

According to Homans, the distribution of status in a small group is determined by the dynamics of the exchange relationships among its members. Those who are accorded high rank give a large amount of some good in scarce supply relative to the demand for it. In return they receive something whose supply is plentiful. For example, if expert advice on how to do a job in an office is scarce, then the individual with expertise who exchanges it for another's approval will have high status. An experienced worker gives advice to his inexperienced colleagues in exchange for their approval. It is assumed, of course, that approval is in plentiful supply and there is a high demand for advice. Thus, the general formula for the distribution of status, said Homans, is that high status is the product of giving what is scarce and getting what is plentiful; whereas low status is the product of receiving what is scarce and giving what is plentiful. The rank order of members of a group is not determined by one exchange, but by a consistent pattern of transactions over time.[64] Consistent with his exchange theory, Homans explained this aspect of stratification in terms of a series of such exchanges.

However, for a status system to exist, a consensus must form, if not totally then to a large degree, among members with regard to who is of high and low rank and with regard to the dimensions upon which rank is based. How does consensus on these matters come about? Insofar as the many want what the few are able to withhold and fear that they might do just that, the many want the same things because they are in similar situations. In the office, for example, the novices find themselves in need of help to do their jobs. Consensus, therefore, arises out of common wants and situations. Even the few who do not need advice and therefore need not exchange approval for it will talk as if those with high status actually do have it in order to make themselves understood by all the rest.[65] They want to be included as full members of the group.

Homans applied this theory to explain the status structure of a particular group. The group he looked at consisted of sixteen workers in a federal agency, whose jobs were to enforce certain federal laws that applied to business. Government agents collected information from business firms and wrote reports stating whether federal laws had been violated. The quality of the reports was for the most part the basis for their efficiency ratings. Although the reports were individual products, the social scientist who observed the agency found a good deal of cooperation among the workers that gave rise to differences of status.[66]

The observer found very high agreement among the agents about the distribution of competence. They and their supervisor concurred in who had the greatest skill in finding which laws were relevant to the information obtained. He also kept records of who consulted whom about difficult cases and who ate lunch together. Thus he was able to figure out a set of relationships between competence and giving advice, between competence and eating together, and between consultation and eating together.[67]

In reviewing this research, Homans found that his formula for the allocation of status held up in this setting; for in general those agents of greatest competence were consulted most frequently and earned the highest status. These consultations occurred "behind the supervisor's back." The experts gave a scarce service and received in return an abundant reward, namely, approval. But the costs of repeated requests for advice in the form of social subordination drove those of lesser competence to form consulting partnerships with those of similar status and competence. By that method they were able to acquire help "more cheaply" and at the same time avoid the risk of being rebuffed.[68] Consequently, a status structure emerged in the group as a consequence of a recurrent pattern of social exchanges conditioned by tendencies to minimize costs.

Homans also noted from the research reports a tendency for the less competent workers to seek out the experts for lunch. Their motive was to acquire, to "borrow" the status of the experts. Some experts rejected these advances, which contributed to an inverse relationship between compe-

138   The Basic Units of Social Theory

tence and luncheon engagements. Also contributing to this inverse relation was the fact that those of lesser competence sought one another for these informal relationships. These lunches thus entered into the overall stratification of the group.[69] They helped to determine the status of individuals.

In this explanation of stratification Homans did not rely on a theory of the social system that fulfills functions as his point of departure. Instead, he gave an account strictly in terms of the inclination of each member to maximize his gratification and minimize his costs. The rank order of members is an individual phenomenon, the result of the pursuit of individual goals rather than the collective goals of a social system. The desire of inferiors, for example, to associate informally with those of high rank in order to enhance their standing has nothing to do with the achievement of collective goals. And in giving and seeking advice, the members of the group calculated the costs to themselves. For example, experts became tired of diverting time from their own work; and those of lesser skill avoided too much degradation by forming consulting partnerships with their equals. Such calculations of purely personal advantage render the exchange of values as the real, manifest foundation of the distribution of status.

Homans's individualist approach also informed his explanation of anomalies. He pointed out that two experts refused to help others and discouraged their advances. Despite their contribution to the goals of the group, not only did they lack high status; they were also generally disliked. Homans also compared this agency to another in which the knowledgeable workers were neither consulted nor esteemed because the members placed a negative value on expertise. In this case other values than contribution to system goals must have determined the stratification of the group.[70] These facts contradict the explanation that status is allocated on the basis of relative contribution to the realization of those values that are the highest organizing elements of the system.[71] One can also point to the consulting partnerships turned up by the original research, which were formed to reduce excessive subordination but which did not yield the best advice. The agents, calculating balances between their own rewards and costs, were more concerned about their own standing than the agency's collective goals.

Parsons believed stratification to be a mechanism that helps to achieve a social system's integrative function. The system allocates its money and prestige to those members and structural units that stand in the closest

Methodological Individualism   139

relation to its values. It does this in order to maintain people in their roles. In contrast to a system achieving functions, Homans rejected the assumption that societies have needs.[72] Instead of explaining the dynamics of a group with reference to social needs, which are the equivalents of the group's social functions, he produced an account in terms of the needs of individuals.

Homans also argued that it is possible to generalize about stratification in societies on the basis of the same factors that stratify small groups. The same factors that stratify the latter stratify the former.[73] These are outcomes of decisions made by individuals who rationally pursue their material and ideal interests according to the principles of economics and behavioral psychology. These principles—propositions that express relationships among characteristics of individuals—are expressions of methodological individualism.

The Phenomenology of the Integrative Function

The phenomenologist Alfred Schutz accepted Weber's individualist presuppositions,[74] but concluded that his analysis of action, although undoubtedly a pioneering step, left many relevant problems unclarified. Schutz therefore set out to produce a more complex analysis of the multiform dimensions of social action. Armed with a more complete account of social action and an understanding of the relationship between the viewpoints of observer and actor, he hoped to construct a more complete model of the social world than Weber's, one devoid of the uncritical assumptions of commonsense thinking.[75] In accomplishing the ambitious task to build on Weber's foundations, he found himself at variance with some of Parsons's formulations.

There is, for example, an ambiguity in Parsons's concept of the normative.[76] On the one hand, Parsons conceived of the normative as an autonomous, teleological element in the actor's subjective state of mind. In this sense, norms, which reflect values, select the goals of action that are compatible with the actor's overall system of goals and values. Through voluntary reflection, an actor chooses what future state he wants to achieve as a result of his action. In their selective function, norms integrate the actor's personality. They also select means available to the actor that are capable of achieving his ends. This use of the term, Schutz

140   The Basic Units of Social Theory

argued, makes of the normative a subjective, teleological factor within the actor's control and part of a plan. On the other hand, Parsons also conceived of a norm as society's heteronomous command that decrees that an action oriented to a given goal through acceptable means *should* occur.[77] This usage makes of the norm a moral obligation.

The trouble is, said Schutz, that these two senses of the term are inconsistent; for the second limits the actor's choices whereas the first does not impose any such socially derived limitations. Only the first definition, the teleological one, is really adequate; for every individual is compelled to choose whether he will or will not follow norms in the light of their desirable and undesirable consequences. Therefore, an actor must decide whether he wants to accept the sanctions likely to follow his violation of a norm. Consequently, the normative really reduces to an actor's motivation, which is a conclusion compatible with Parsons's teleological definition. However, Parsons did not, said Schutz, give sufficient importance in his social action theory to motivation, which the teleological conception of the normative requires.[78]

There is another difficulty with the heteronomous conception. By assuming that moral norms actually do guide actions, Parsons substituted the objective point of view of a sociological observer for the subjective view of the actor. He assumed, Schutz contended, that norms actually determine action without requiring the observer to grasp the actor's actual motivation.[79]

On the assumption that Schutz was not guilty of assuming an objective point of view for which he criticized Parsons, it is worthwhile to examine relevant aspects of his analysis of action to discover where they conflict with Parsons's theory. Such an examination should reveal the implicit contradiction between structuralist and individualist notions.

Since he believed motives to be important in action, the question arises of what Schutz meant by the term. He distinguished two types of motives. First, there is the actor's *in-order-to* motive, which is the future state of affairs that he intends to bring about. It is the end he has in view as he acts and corresponds in all its essentials to the goal of action in Parsons's theory. Second, there is the actor's *because* motive, which is the factor or factors sedimented in his past experience that led him to choose the action. The because motive is obviously a cause of the in-order-to motive. As an example, a murderer's in-order-to motive is to obtain his victim's money. It is the goal of the act of murder. His because motive, let us say, could consist of those experiences related to his having

Methodological Individualism   141

grown up within an environment that condoned violence, or it could also be some repressed experience uncoverable by psychoanalysis.[80]

Schutz went on to analyze interaction as founded on a relationship between these two types of motives. Take, for example, a simple question and answer. When one person asks a question of another, his in-order-to motive is to elicit information. If the other comes forth with an answer, the in-order-to motive of the questioner was his because motive. What led him to reply was the experience of having been asked. And the in-order-to motive of his reply was to convey information. Hence, interaction is fashioned out of the interlocking of motives, in which the in-order-to motive of the first person becomes the because motive of the second.[81] It comes down to the simple fact that one did something because another wanted him to do it.

More, however, is involved than interlocking motives. In order for individuals to interact, they must possess certain kinds of knowledge of one another. Schutz believed this knowledge belongs to those common-sense beliefs that make everyday life possible. For example, if someone asks another "Where is the ink?" he assumes the latter knows English, that he knows where the ink is located, and that he will disclose its location. He assumes that his own in-order-to motive will actually become the other's because motive. Schutz called this assumption the idealization of the reciprocity of motives, which is a construct of commonsense thinking in everyday life.[82] Had the questioner not assumed the reciprocity of motives, he would not have asked the question.

The knowledge upon which interaction is based is never complete, nor is the interlocking of motives ever perfect. The person who replied to the question by telling where the ink was located did not know that the other wanted it to complete an application for a research grant that would change the course of his life. He did not know that the application was an event in a sequence that fit into a life-plan. Neither did he know the other's because motive.[83] Also, the interaction might not have turned out as anticipated by the questioner because the person might not have answered.[84] The completeness, precision, and detail of the knowledge possessed by both individuals about motives, means, personalities, and situation increase the rationality of a project that requires cooperation.[85] The more extensive the project the more each must know about the other's motives, life-plans, and knowledge if the project is to succeed.

Hence, shared knowledge and mutual understanding are necessary conditions of interaction. According to Schutz, the *form* of knowledge

142   The Basic Units of Social Theory

also has a direct bearing on social action. Our knowledge always comes in the form of *typifications* of objects, which are constructed out of our past experiences of particulars. A typification is a general context, selected by our thinking as relevant to the object that is compared to it. When we see a dog, we recognize it as conforming to our previously established typification of dog and therefore expect it to possess certain characteristics and act in certain ways. The same is true of motives. During the course of interaction, each grasps the other's because and in-order-to motives as typical. Each interprets the other's motives in the light of his typifications, grasping them not in all their uniqueness and singularity but only in regard to the features essential to the purpose at hand. In the face-to-face relationship, typifications, insofar as they are understood, have, relatively speaking, a low degree of anonymity and high degree of fullness. There, where each experiences the other directly and is in tune with his stream of thought as it unfolds, the chances of accurate understanding increase.[86]

The knowledge a person has of a contemporary with whom he is not directly interacting is, however, much more problematical. Let us take as an example an employee of the post office whom I have never met. My knowledge of his motives is highly anonymous and hypothetical, and I construct him and his actions as ideal-types. Thus I conceive of him as a *personal type* and a *course-of-action type*. I typify his in-order-to motive as delivering my letter and his because motive as my posting of it. I assume that he typifies me as a customer and typifies my motives. I can never be certain, however, that my letter will actually be delivered until after the fact; for I have no way of verifying the validity of my typifications in this particular case, as I do in a face-to-face relationship. I do not really know that he typifies me such that my in-order-to motive is his because motive. The subjective probability of my typifying scheme being objectively probable in such a relationship is less than in a face-to-face relationship. Schutz described the contemporary relationship as *"the subjective chance that the reciprocally ascribed typifying schemes will be used congruently by the parties."*[87] The objective probability of the reciprocity of motives is unknown.

With regard to interaction among contemporaries, Schutz drew the further conclusion that the greater the institutionalization of anonymous typifications the greater is the probability that the reciprocity of motives will be fulfilled. As examples of institutionalized typifications he cited law and traditions.[88]

Methodological Individualism 143

It is evident that typifications of individuals correspond closely to one of Simmel's forms as an *a priori* condition for society's existence. The reader will recall that a form for the synthesis that is society is the construction by one individual of a generalized conception of another—one that omits his total uniqueness. In other words, an individual always conceives of another as a type. And no matter how individualized the concept, it can never capture the person in his total individuality. Members of groups define one another in terms of types, such as military officer and professional man, which become the foundation of their relationships. Thus, both in definition and function Simmel's form corresponds to Schutz's concept of the typification of the other. The convergence of these concepts derives from their individualist presuppositions concerning society.

Schutz identified other commonsense assumptions in addition to the reciprocity of motives that make interaction possible, assumptions that are part of everyone's stock of knowledge. Everyone knows that two individuals who face each other have different locations in space and consequently see the same object differently. Lapsing into the first person singular, Schutz stated that I who am here typify that object differently than you who are there. I see different aspects of it in different spatial contexts than you. Yet we both realize that if I were in your place I would experience the object pretty much the way you do. And if you changed places with me, you would experience it the way I do now. Schutz called this assumption the *idealization of the interchangeability of standpoints*.[89]

Furthermore, we both realize that a mutually experienced object has different relevance to each of our purposes. Because of our unique biographical histories, each of us has a different interest in the object. It fits into different life-plans and goals. Yet we both assume that we are able to disregard our private systems of relevance and talk about it, interpret it in a nearly identical manner, and cooperate with respect to it. We can coordinate our responses sufficiently "for all practical purposes." Schutz called this assumption the *idealization of the congruency of the system of relevances*. This assumption and the interchangeability of standpoints combine into what Schutz called the *general thesis of the reciprocity of perspectives*.[90] Like the reciprocity of motives, the reciprocity of perspectives is a necessary condition for interaction; if individuals were not to assume it, there would be no point to the attempt to coordinate their efforts.

The two assumptions are related. Reflection shows, Schutz said, that

144   The Basic Units of Social Theory

the idealization of the reciprocity of motives depends upon the reciprocity of perspectives. Although the motives of each partner in an interaction are interpreted within different biographical contexts, nevertheless, each assumes that for all practical purposes the typical motives he imputes to the other are the same as his own. Therefore, cooperation is possible since the because motive of one is the in-order-to motive of the other.[91]

Schutz's analyses of direct and indirect relationships focus on what in the context of Parsons's theory is the social system's integrative function. It is evident that the reciprocities of motives and perspectives bring about the adjustment of individuals with respect to the roles they play. Thus, although he did not refer to integration, Schutz's treatment of social interaction really addresses this factor.

As the preceding chapter shows, Parsons laid a heavy burden on norms as the elements that integrate social relationships. The reader will also recall that Schutz pointed out the ambiguity in his conceptualization of the normative and concluded that Parsons's identification of it with the teleological is defensible but at the same time rejected his identification of the normative with a heteronomous command. Schutz himself then identified the normative with the actor's motives, which, however, can only be grasped typically. For interactions to occur so that the ends of the actors are achieved, each individual must typify the other's motives. How this is done depends on the relevant typifications as elements of stocks of knowledge. It is quite clear that in Schutz's account, integration is accomplished by personalities. It is strictly a personality function, not a social system function as Parsons held.

Because the reciprocity of motives can never be complete, the implication of Schutz's analysis is that integration can never be achieved totally. Even within the direct relationship, one individual is unable to locate the other's motives within the total organization of his life-plans and goals. Only the subject can do that. Therefore, a complete sharing of the elements necessary for interaction is impossible, with the result that interaction has a somewhat different meaning to each. This "gap" in interpretive schemes is bridged by commonsense fictions such as the reciprocities of motives and perspectives. I know that your relevances differ from mine, and your typifications therefore will differ from mine; but we can link our motives anyway for practical purposes. These assumptions, according to Schutz, are the way individuals come to terms with the fact that everyone's stock of knowledge is unique.

With the collapse of the normative into shared typifications, norms are deprived of the ontological status of objective moral imperatives that Parsons gave them. They are not structural elements of a social system, whose function is to maintain it by integrating it. Nor can the unity of such a system be preserved by solving the motivational problem of order. In contrast, for Schutz, integration is accomplished strictly according to the dynamics of individuals' experience and ever-changing stocks of knowledge. That is why in analyzing social interaction he did not focus on such integrating factors that Parsons identified as reward and punishment, social control, clarification of the legal order, and stratification.

Accordingly, for social system function Schutz substituted a phenomenology of the integrative function—a theoretical shift dictated by a logical transition from methodological structuralism to methodological individualism. It is not the social system that integrates individuals but individuals themselves. With this Georg Simmel would have agreed.

The Issue Reconsidered: The Reification of Structure

In constructing social theories individualists have always located the sources of their explanations in the characteristics of individuals. As a result, all social structures are identified with what individuals do and the conscious experience that lies behind their actions. A role, e.g., refers only to that which certain individuals repeatedly do in certain situations. Since they are the fundamental units of theory construction, all social theories must be about individuals. In conceiving of societies and social structures this way, individualists have avoided a fallacy that underlies all theories based on methodological structuralism. This is the fallacy of the reification of social structure.

Ordinary experience reveals to us that the only substantives are human beings, their creations embodied in material form, and natural objects. In contrast, social structures such as norms and institutions are really characteristics abstracted from individuals. The self-evident nature of these propositions suggests the following question: Why did social theorists like Durkheim and Parsons lose sight of the fact that social structures are abstractions and come to conceive of them as having an independent existence?[92] The answer to this question will uncover some of the conceptual damage inflicted on social theory by the reification of structure and also ought to help resolve the issue. To address the question, let

146   The Basic Units of Social Theory

us briefly reexamine in the light of individualism ideas of some of the aforementioned theorists whose work reveals structuralist notions.

In laying the foundation of social action theory,[93] Parsons distinguished a unit act from a system of action. The latter consists either of a number of unit acts of the same actor or the interrelated acts of several actors. Parsons argued that properties emerge within a system that cannot be found within a unit act. The examples he gave were *economic rationality* and *value integration*. It is impossible, said Parsons, to ascertain how much economic rationality there is in a unit act; for this type of rationality can only be discovered by comparing acts, either of the same individual or those of different individuals. Comparison is required by the very definition of economic rationality, which is the application of those means to achieve an end that are the least costly so as to minimize the sacrifice of other ends. Parsons cited the specific example of generating electricity with either water power or coal; whichever is cheaper is more rational.[94]

The second example, value integration,[95] comes down either to the sharing of values among individuals or a consistency of values reflected in the acts of a single individual. It is obvious from both these cases, said Parsons, that value integration, like economic rationality, cannot be found as a characteristic of a unit act. If the sociologist were to break down a system into single, isolated acts, he concluded, economic rationality and value integration would disappear.

These examples reveal the logical starting point for Parsons's structuralism. They imply that the relationships he perceived among actions are as substantive as the actions themselves. He then proceeded to emphasize that the two systems of action delineated above must themselves be differentiated. On the one hand, the action system of a single person must not be confused with the action system of a plurality of persons. They must be distinguished because they give rise to different emergent properties. The former, of course, turns out to be the personality system and the latter the social system[96]—two of Parsons's four subsystems of action.

At this point a clue to the origin of the reification of the social system comes to light.[97] By analyzing the relations among the actions of one individual, the sociological observer can find their emergent properties strictly according to individualist presuppositions. He can explain the actor's system in terms of a personality theory, which identifies as relevant his ends, means, and commitments to norms and values. On the other hand, in denying that the emergent properties of a social system can be discovered in the unit acts of its members, Parsons implicitly abandoned the subjective view of the actor; for if the observer relates their actions in a different way than do the actors, then these properties are not explicable in terms of the actors' experiences. They do not experience their relationships the way the observer, i.e., Parsons, does. This made it possible for him to impute his idea of their relationship as a property of a social system, which is irreducible to their orientations. If, for example, they are not aware that their relationship is subject to equilibrium tendencies, Parsons can still discover equilibrium in a social system.

We do not contend here that an objective perspective of an observer must necessarily result in the reification of social structures, but only that it makes that possible. It is possible, for example, for an observer to discover factors within an actor or in his situation (which obviously includes other individuals) that influence him of which he is unaware. Facts influence individuals in ways unknown to them all the time. The temptation, however, is present for the imputation of such influences to autonomous social structures.

Let us, however, assume in Parsons's example of value integration that both individuals *are* aware that they share values. Indeed, their actions are integrated by these values. But there is no relationship external to them. Instead, there are two ideas in two minds, each idea being a comparison between values. The relationship therefore "dissolves" into the ideas within the thought streams of two individuals, each of whom recognizes the similarity of his own values to those of the other. If an observer were present to grasp the fact that each is aware of the identity of values, there would be a third idea of the relationship, namely, that in the observer's mind. Thus, the relationship is strictly an internal phenomenon.[98] Parsons, however, attributed value integration to an emergent social system. It cannot be discovered in unit acts.

Hence, Parsons's reification of the social system can be traced to a double source: a shift in perspective from that of an actor to that of an observer and the projection of internal meaning-contents onto an entity at least partially outside of individual minds. The latter converges with Durkheim's definition of the social fact, and the former substitutes what Schutz called second-order for first-order constructs.

Similar logic provides the explanation of the reification evident in the ideas of other thinkers. Take Durkheim, for instance. Persuaded by the authority of Comte's classification of the sciences,[99] Durkheim agreed

148   The Basic Units of Social Theory

that each level of reality ought to be studied by its appropriate science. Sociology, therefore, is destined to have its own subject matter, one different from that of biology and psychology. Consequently, the sociologist can discover the explanations of social facts neither in the subjective orientations nor in the biological qualities of individuals. Sociological explanations in terms of motives are ruled out. Moreover, the sociologist is obliged to "see things in a different way from the ordinary man."[100] Durkheim thus corroborated the Comtean assumption of levels of being and sciences to match with the use of analogies drawn from nature. His acceptance of Comte's theory led him to the conclusion that the path for the sociologist to follow involves an objective method. For the experiences of social actors, the sociologist, therefore, should substitute an objective view of the social fact. Unknown to actors, the social fact must have an existence apart from them.

As in the case of Parsons, therefore, Durkheim's reification and the perspective of the observer are bound together. Moreover, their theories are parallel in other respects. A collective representation is formed through the association of individual minds. But although each contributes a part to the whole, the whole is different from all of its parts. As individuals combine their individual representations, *sui generis* synthesizing forces produce something else. All the individual contributions, said Durkheim, are transformed.[101] In the synthesizing process a collective representation comes into being that is external, or at least partially so, to the minds of particular individuals. Again we find not only what individuals think about one another, but also a collective view that Durkheim attributed to society. A similarity obtains between this analysis and the relation Parsons discovered between unit acts and social system. The observer projects his own conception of the relationship among individuals onto a real social structure, thus transfiguring his scientific constructs into collective entities.

The foundation of Marx's reifications is to be found in the concept of objective class interests. As we have seen, properties of the modes of production have an existence prior to their internalization as conscious experiences of those in a class situation. The class interest of greatest concern to Marx was, of course, the proletariat's interest in the destruction of capitalism. Aware, however, that many workers had no such interest, he sustained his faith in socialism's inevitability by postulating the existence of economic structures with class interests as their properties. With laws of structural transformation making for trends toward a communist goal in history, the actual subjective orientations of proletarians could be dismissed as temporary aberrations—as a false consciousness.

Marx's theory of class interests, therefore, represents an abandonment of a subjective for an objective frame of reference. What he thought to be true interests, Marx attributed to reified social structures. From this comes the expectation that the individuals who find themselves in common class situations will become aware of independently existing interests and will act upon them.

Other propositions of Marx's materialist interpretation of history lend themselves to similar interpretation. For example, ideological elements in the superstructure are reflexive distortions that hinder an accurate understanding of class interests. As a result, social structures not only generate structural interests, but also produce mechanisms that conceal, at least in the short run, those very interests. The dynamics of those structures evolve in predetermined directions unintended by anyone.

Marx's treatment of social structures, at least in some contexts of his thought, follows a logic similar to that followed by Parsons and Durkheim. His historical analysis from his own perspective led him to ascertain certain interests not, or at least not yet, within the perspectives of historical actors. These he attributed as real interests to social structures that are more than abstractions.

As we have seen, the individualist model of social theory does not eliminate social structures, but gives them a different definition and ontological status than they have in methodological structuralism. Let us, therefore, reformulate some parts of Parsons's theory in accordance with an individualist approach.

We postulate two hypothetical individuals who have an enduring relationship. Whereas one defines his relationship with the other as giving him satisfaction, the latter defines it as unsatisfactory but maintains it for want of a better alternative. This example involves two different concepts of a relationship. A sociological observer compares these conceptions and concludes they are asymmetrical. The concept of asymmetry is a second-order scientific construct describing the relationship between ideas in the minds of two individuals rather than the property of a malintegrated social system. Moreover, the boundaries of the relationship are constituted by the subjective experiences of each. Those elements of his personality that each actor does not use as a context of meaning to define his relation to the other stand outside of it. Thus, the

150   The Basic Units of Social Theory

boundaries of their relationship are solely determined by processes of personality systems rather than by a relationship between a social system and two personality systems.

Furthermore, the four functions *(AGIL)* turn out to be activities of two personalities and are thereby transformed in meaning. For example, on the assumption that the asymmetry reflects different values, these must be maintained by subjective definitions within their experience if the interaction is to continue as it has. Accordingly, two pattern-maintenance mechanisms within personality systems function to maintain the relationship in contrast to a pattern-maintenance function of a social system. The other functions of Parsons's social system could be similarly reconceptualized as personality processes.[102]

Reconceptualizing Parsons's theory strictly in terms of personalities results in other changes. In the absence of an independent social system, there is no institutionalization, but only an internalization of values and norms. The cybernetic hierarchy, according to which culture exerts preponderant control, is reconceptualized as similar values in a number of individuals exerting a broad influence over other elements of their consciousness. The dominance of the social system over personality is transmuted into the influence of others on the individual's choices of ends and means. In general, recognizing the social system as an abstraction reduces the confusion in Parsons's theory that arises from the attempt to determine which system is responsible for which effect.

The thesis of the relation between the objective stance and the reification of structure also has a bearing on the problem of microsocial and macrosocial levels of reality. Contemporary discussions equate the former with face-to-face relationships and the latter with transcendent structures. Macrosocial structures emerge from the microsocial level with unique properties, and the problem then becomes how to explain these emergent characteristics. Sometimes the idea is presented that intermediate structures emerge between the microsocial and the most encompassing macrosocial level, i.e., society as a whole.[103] Accordingly, the macrosocial level is itself differentiated into levels. These intermediate levels are analogous to Durkheim's theory that collective representations associate according to *sui generis* principles to form other collective representations of a still higher form.[104]

The conclusion is also sometimes drawn that the microsocial and macrosocial levels require different methods of study by different fields of inquiry, such as social psychology and institutional sociology, in order to

Methodological Individualism   151

explain the different things that go on at each level. This strategy is compatible with Comte's classification of the sciences and his idea that the complexity of the social facts increases at higher levels.

From an individualist perspective, these levels turn out to be conceptual levels distinguished by the scientific observer rather than ontological levels of reality. Consequently, the principal difference between microsociology and macrosociology reduces to a difference in the numbers of individuals indicated by the concepts. Sociological concepts whose reference is to small numbers of individuals who are all able to engage in face-to-face interaction are microsocial concepts; macrosocial concepts refer to larger numbers.

The conclusion of the last chapter observed that theories about total societies and theories of historical change have a greater affinity for structuralism than theories of a more restricted scope. One reason for this is that in thinking about large numbers it is easier to lose sight of them as individuals and to replace them with anonymous abstractions in the form of social structures. Replacing a large number of individuals with a small number of social structures is one way to reduce an uncomfortable complexity with which the mind has to deal. On the other hand, in studying a small number of individuals, either as real persons or analyzing them as hypothetical actors, it is easier to think of them as individuals. Structuralist theories, therefore, have resorted to the reification of social structures as one method to overcome the limitations of the human mind, which seeks to reduce a perplexing complexity to a comprehensible simplicity.

PART THREE

Rules and Social Order

The Normative Order

In the *Laws* Plato set forth a conception of the city-state in which every aspect of life, every relationship, is regulated by law. Property, material interests, birth, marriage, death, and every passion and belief are defined by law, the goal of which was a perfect moral harmony. The laws of the good state, according to Plato, were reflections of absolute virtues and embodiments of the principle of reason. Yet this extensive regulation was not, in his conception, to be an external imposition but rather was to be rendered incarnate in the very fiber of the soul through education.[1]

In this state we find a conception of social order that was to be expressed again and again throughout the history of social theory: Order is the result of rules internalized. Although enforced by rewards and punishments, rules are principally maintained by a sense of moral duty based on the idea that they are intrinsically good. There is a tendency, according to this theory of order, to portray all facets of human existence as governed by normative models. These are standards regarded as "oughts," which either prohibit or prescribe and whose "oughtness" is conveyed in the idea of sanctions. Authority is vested in those whose function it is to enforce the norms. With regard to the notion of order itself, it has often remained implicit and somewhat vague; but broadly conceived it refers to the state of affairs in which individuals come together to get things done, to regularly achieve certain ends that reflect

156   Rules and Social Order

certain values. This theory of order is reflected in the commonsense slogan "law and order."

Plato's conception of order, however, was challenged by some of a group of philosophers called Sophists, who believed that the nature of man is to seek as much pleasure and gratification as he can get. The desire for pleasure has given rise to laws that are instituted by the weak, who really believe it is right to take advantage of others but lack the power to escape harm from retaliation. Their weakness forces the conclusion that the middle course is best, namely, that no one is to derive pleasure from taking advantage of others and that everyone is to escape the pain of being victimized by the strong.[2] Laws and the political order, consequently, are the effects of a social contract dictated by self-interest. The motivation to comply with a rule, according to these Sophists, is not a sense of moral obligation, but rather self-preservation and the desire to avoid punishment.

These contrasting theories reappeared in subsequent thought in diverse contexts. On the one hand, social order is identified with norms; on the other, order is the product of a more or less spontaneous compromise between self-interest and fear. These theories functioned like polar types, specific accounts tending toward the one extreme of no order apart from rules or toward the other in which the role of norms is minimized. The two types of explanation, however, have not remained separate; for the idea of the ongoing construction of order has been articulated with the concept of normative order and has influenced the investigation of rules.

Although not limited to this theory, the proposition that social order is a function of rules has often been identified with functional social theory. Furthermore, this theory has followed Plato in conceptualizing rules within a moral context; and the connections between rules, order, and morality were strongly emphasized by Comte, Durkheim, and Parsons, whose analyses of the normative order will be considered in this chapter. And, as we shall see, the issue also sweeps into its scope other social factors such as religion, values, and legitimacy—factors that have also played prominent roles in social theory.

Comte on Morality and Religion

Comte envisioned sociology as devoted to the discovery of the laws of social order and progress, which are respectively the conceptual foci of

The Normative Order   157

the study of social statics and dynamics. Thus, social dynamics is to explain progress, the law of which Comte believed he stated in the Law of Three Stages. Correlated with the progress of human thinking through the theological, metaphysical, and positivist stages is the progress of the whole of mankind toward a final moral condition. Moral evolution is one aspect of human evolution in general.

What is morality? As noted previously, Comte believed sociology must be consistent with the laws discovered by all the other sciences. It thus follows that a scientific concept of morality must be compatible with what biology has discovered about life. Biology tells us, said Comte, that our self-regarding instincts are of greater strength and steadiness than our social instincts. Self-interest occurs more often and with greater intensity than concern for others. Egoism preponderates over altruism. The problem is, however, that if our selfish instincts were given free play, then human relationships would shortly become impossible. Here was a good functionalist argument. Accordingly, Comte defined morality as the subordination of our selfish to our sympathetic instincts.[3] For example, temperance is moral not because it is advantageous to one who remains temperate, but because it better enables the individual to fulfill his social duties.[4] The moral person practices temperance out of a sense of altruism.

Thus, a struggle goes on within all individuals between two antithetical types of feelings. Moral progress is measurable in terms of the triumph of one over the other, of altruism over egoism, of love of mankind over love of self. The moral problem for a positivist sociology, according to Comte, is to strengthen sympathy at the expense of the regard for ourselves. Humanity's progress toward moral perfection is measurable by these inverse tendencies, which will be encouraged by a reformist sociology.[5]

What does sociology tell us in this regard? Comte's inquiries led him to believe that the vehicle of such progress is religion, for religion and morality are inextricably bound together. How does religion foster moral progress? It does so by bringing about a twofold unity. First, it unifies each individual within himself; and, second, it brings about a unity among individuals. These two functions are correlative; for in unifying individuals within themselves religion at the same time combines them into a social unity.[6] In the process of molding the person, religion molds society.

Precisely how does religion achieve these unifying functions? According to Comte, religion unifies the individual by intervening in the internal conflicts between his egoistic and altruistic feelings and taking the side of the latter. Religion helps to subordinate egoism to altruism by unifying them into a hierarchy of control; and by regulating internal conflicts in this manner, religion fashions individuals into moral beings. Moreover, in working toward altruism's victory, it combines individuals into a unity; for in a state of altruism each considers the welfare of others and translates this into harmonious action. Comte thus saw the unity of the person and the unity of society as two sides of the same coin.

Religious doctrine plays a decisive role in these unifying functions. Doctrine defines the various orders of reality upon which our existence depends; for just as the organism depends upon its environment, the human being depends upon an external power. Once dogma has defined this superior power, the instinct of veneration comes to focus upon it. The person under the influence of religion wants to submit to a power for which he has affection, respect, and gratitude. He becomes attached to it. And all those who stand in the same relationship with such a power experience feelings of benevolence—the highest of the altruistic instincts.[7] Comte thus explained altruism by a psychology of submission. Religious doctrines define a power infinitely superior to the human being. A sense of dependence results in a willingness to submit, which engages the altruistic feelings and brings them to focus on the power. These altruistic emotions generalize to others in the form of a universalized benevolence. And as a result of these psychological processes, the egoistic inclinations of the individual are subordinated to the altruistic.

It is obvious that no one can experience submission, gratitude, and respect toward an object unless he can conceive it. Therefore, human intellect forms religious doctrines that define the nature of the awesome power that evokes these feelings. In this respect, feelings follow intellect. The subordination of egoism to altruism, which is a consequence of the submission to a superior power defined by religious doctrine, requires moral discipline, however. Comte here spoke of moral force, which he analyzed into the elements of command and discipline.[8] The superior power is the source of moral command, which imposes disciplined obedience upon an individual acting morally.

This analysis of how religion accomplishes the function of unifying individuals singly and socially suggests the elements of which it is composed. The intellectual aspect of the human being fashions doctrine which, as already noted, explains the external order and this power superior to the individual. The moral aspect of the human being includes both feelings and actions, the former resulting in worship (ritual) and the latter in religious government.[9] Hence, the three elements that constitute any religion are doctrine, ritual, and government. Ritual has a profound influence on feelings and government on actions. Of the two, ritual is especially significant in nourishing altruism.

What is this superior power? Comte came to the startling conclusion that the power that is the object of all this veneration, attachment, and love, is humanity. Man's realization of his dependence on humanity will be the source of his forthcoming moral perfection. It is humanity that makes life possible, that is the source of thought, and that controls feelings. Humanity is the "Great Being,"[10] which individuals experience as a superior power. The trouble is that past religions failed to recognize humanity as the supreme power and incorrectly explained man's dependence as a dependence upon supernatural beings. Deities of all sorts have been thought to be the cause of existence and source of morality, but past religions, even Catholicism, are merely way stations on the road to Comte's Religion of Humanity, which is derived from positivist philosophy. Humanity will eventually replace God as the object of devotion. Although its details need not concern us here, Comte prescribed a ritual for this religion, replete with saints, calendar, rituals, and priests.

Comte believed the anarchy plaguing Europe brought on by the events leading up to the French Revolution was ultimately caused by the decline of religion. The revolutionary doctrine most destructive of social order stated that either no spiritual power (religion) on earth ought to exist or if it does exist that it ought to be subordinated to the state. Comte vehemently disagreed. The orders of both society and mind depend on religion. Furthermore, this institution flourishes best under the separation of the spiritual and temporal powers.[11] His concern over the contemporary crisis led him to develop the outline of the Religion of Humanity, which, devoid of the mystical elements of Christianity and earlier religions, he saw as the solution to the disorder of his time.

Comte's ideas provided a matrix for further theoretical development. The conclusion that order depends upon morality, the destructive impact of self-interest, and the glimmer of a normative order in the guise of religious codes were absorbed by succeeding thinkers who wove them into a functional theory of society. The notion that the conditions regulating individuals coincide with those that combine them into a unity shows up later on in Parsons's theory as the idea that normative

160   Rules and Social Order

regulation fulfills an integrative social function. Comte's analysis of the individual's attachment to society through religion shows up in Durkheim's work as the attachment of the individual to society by complying with its rules through moral discipline. The opposition of self-interest and social order is a recurring theme in the theories of normative order.

Durkheim Defines Morality

The line of influence from Comte to Durkheim was direct, and the latter admitted his debt to the former. Durkheim gave to Comte's notion of altruism a more specific meaning in terms of moral rules and the ends they serve. A moral act is one that conforms to a moral rule. Examples Durkheim had in mind are rules prohibiting murder, theft, incest and those requiring the positive fulfillment of duty such as the civic duty to serve in the army and the professional obligations of physicians to patients. Some rules are customs and others laws. Hence, the morality of a society is the sum total of its moral rules, which cannot be expressed in a single formula like utilitarianism.[12] Nevertheless, the attitudes of individuals who comply with such rules and certain consequences that ensue are also encompassed by Durkheim's conception of the morality of a society.

Durkheim distinguished between moral and utilitarian rules, the difference being the type of sanction that follows from their violation. Anyone who violates a utilitarian rule is punished by the intrinsic consequences of his act. One who violates the rules of hygiene is punished by the resulting disease, just as one who fails to follow a work rule is punished by the failure of the project. In contrast, the consequence of the violation of a moral rule cannot be predicted from the intrinsic nature of the violation. A murderer, for example, is punished by society solely because he failed to comply with a moral rule. The absence of an intrinsic connection between crime and punishment is proved by the fact that homicide is approved in one context and condemned in another. Positive sanctions, on the other hand, take the form of praise and honor that reward compliance.[13] Hence, the consequence of violating a moral norm is painful and the consequence of compliance pleasurable.

There is more to morality, however, than the sanctions suitable to

The Normative Order   161

morally relevant actions. A moral rule elicits within us the idea of duty because, said Durkheim, it possesses authority. It imposes itself upon us from outside, it constrains us, and we are not free to choose. We perform the duties of life out of respect for rules that we ourselves did not create. We perform moral actions in the spirit of discipline, and the person who performs his duty does so because it is right, not because it is useful to him. To the extent that he hesitates and calculates the advantages and disadvantages of the action to himself or to the extent that he complies to escape punishment, to that extent the action ceases to be moral.[14] For Durkheim, authority, duty, and discipline were all bound together; one simply yields to a moral norm. Compliance is neither a matter of taste nor preference. Comte's influence here is apparent.

Submission to a rule results in regularity of conduct, for the situations relevant to the rule recur. A rule thus has an "again-and-again" character, and by its very nature prevents the production of novelty or at least confines it within limits. Individuals are thereby relieved of the necessity of always devising behavior anew. Moral actions become habits, and duties are fulfilled daily. With its homogenizing effect, a rule thus promotes constancy, regularity, and repeatability.

Durkheim went on to point out that moral rules are oriented to ends. They are designed to achieve certain goals. But the question arises of whose ends moral actions are aimed at. He narrowed the logical possibilities to two. An action can be a means toward some end of the actor himself or a means toward an end for other beings. Durkheim categorically denied the morality of any action aimed at exclusively accomplishing some benefit to the actor, even if the benefit consists of his self-improvement. No one ever regarded the pursuit of self-interest as the essence of morality, Durkheim concluded.

But what about the morality of an action whose end is the benefit of someone else? With regard to this question Durkheim argued that if a person cannot make the pursuit of some benefit to himself into a moral action, neither can someone else make the same action aimed at the same end into a moral act. For it would be an absurdity for someone to devote himself to my preservation and for me to devote myself to his preservation merely so that each of us could consider ourselves to be moral. A corollary is that neither is my act devoted to the benefit of several individuals moral because actions lacking morality when added together add up to zero. If an action that benefits one person cannot be

162   Rules and Social Order

moral, then neither can it be moral if it benefits more than one person. Morality cannot be the sum of all self-interest.[15]

If the interests of all individuals cannot be the goal of morality, the only remaining possibility is that the end of a moral action is the benefit of society, which, as we have seen, is for Durkheim a reality *sui generis*. Therefore, if an individual complies with a rule whose beneficiary is society, he has then performed a moral action. Obeying the rules of hygiene in order to carry out one's duties so the family is preserved is therefore a moral action. However, the fact that all members of a given society are bound to it as a collective reality explains why in common-sense thinking altruistic feelings and actions toward others are *thought* to be moral. Although individuals are not morality's true objects, they are morally interconnected through being society's instruments. That explains, concluded Durkheim, why one who loves his country wants to help his countrymen.[16] Although not intrinsically moral, altruism develops the habit of morality because acting for the good of others inclines individuals to act for the good of society.[17] Thus, actions of benefit to family, corporation, or state are moral.

Now when a person acts morally, the action attaches him to society. Comte too had identified the attachment of the moral actor to humanity as an aspect of altruism. In attaching him to society, the action also, as already noted, indirectly attaches him to its members. At the same time, individuals act morally *because* they are attached to society. But why are they so attached? Durkheim's answer was again reminiscent of Comte. Society is so vast, so much greater than we who depend on it for our very being that it alone is capable of inspiring the awe, reverence, and respect that lend it authority. Since society exists within us and shapes us, we cannot cut ourselves off from it without destroying ourselves. Consequently, the elements of discipline and attachment are related; for we bow to the authority of that to which we are attached. Rules like "thou shall not kill" are compelling by virtue of the authority of the society from which they originate. They acquire the sacredness possessed of society itself. However, ordinary consciousness confuses society with a supernatural being and believes that a god established rules. It is therefore up to sociology to penetrate the reality hidden behind the mythical veil. Not God, but society is morality's source.[18] Here again Comte's influence is evident.

Nevertheless, discipline and attachment are separate dimensions, both necessary conditions of morality. Duty is essential; but Kant was wrong, said Durkheim, in reducing morality to duty. For every moral act is also believed to be good. Its goodness is to be found in the social end that is its goal. Whereas duty is related to discipline, goodness is related to the benefit a moral act confers on society. Kant, Durkheim charged, neglected the element of goodness in morality. No one performs a moral action because of duty alone, for he is also convinced of its social advantages. Neither duty nor goodness is subordinate to the other. They are also experienced differently, discipline as a constraint, goodness as a pleasure. However, the individual also derives pleasure from acting in a morally disciplined way. Thus, Durkheim combined asceticism and eudaemonism in this concept of morality.[19]

Autonomy is a third moral dimension and one of growing importance in the modern world. It is not enough that when we act morally we fulfill obligations that attach us to society, but also that we understand the nature and necessity of morality in general. A general knowledge of why we act morally transcends our knowledge of the goodness of a specific act and its social end. A deeper level of understanding consists of a knowledge that society is the source of both moral authority and the functional necessity of moral rules. When an individual has grasped these ideas, he obeys rules by giving his enlightened assent. He obeys because he has good reasons. Moral discipline still remains, but the individual gains autonomy due to knowledge. He is willing to submit because he understands its necessity. Hence, discipline and autonomy are reconcilable. This general knowledge, which is the science of morality, is only now in its beginning stages.[20] Durkheim, of course, had in mind his own theory, which was an attempt to fulfill Comte's ideal of a science of morality built on the foundation of sociology.

Discipline, attachment, and autonomy, therefore, are three aspects of a moral orientation. Forces acting from without, they impress themselves upon individuals, constraining them to fulfill their social duties and making them into a cohesive group.

What else does an emerging science of morality tell us? It makes us aware of the benefits, hitherto only hinted at, that rules confer upon individuals in addition to those conferred on society. When a person has an unlimited desire, Durkheim observed, he cannot satisfy it. The desire for unlimited wealth, for instance, is bound to lead to frustration and unhappiness. And the acquisition of some wealth always stimulates the desire for more. Unrestricted desire is like walking toward a destination that continually recedes. Durkheim believed the same psychology oper-

164   Rules and Social Order

ates with regard to sentiments. Even love for others if it exceeds certain limits results in pathology and derangement. Because ends are interconnected, the frustration of a single unfulfilled goal leads to the frustration of others; and the man who devotes himself relentlessly to wealth has little time or energy to devote to his other needs. When any single desire receives more than its due, the others suffer. The equilibrium of mental elements is upset. Consequently, the person can experience contentment only through a measure of denial, which makes possible the achievement of goals confined within their proper bounds. [21]

Now the only force capable of containing desire is the moral restraint of rules. When rules defining duties of spouses, for instance, weaken, sexual passion escapes restraint; and the elusive search for unrealizable gratification is set in motion. In the final analysis, the only forces capable of regulating desire are the moral forces that stem from the authority of rules. [22] Again it is evident that morality involves contradictory elements. Moral inhibition ironically makes possible self-expansion, for he who binds himself to rules gains freedom.

Rules have other functions according to Durkheim. As already noted, adherence produces regularity and stability; for a rule is a formula that fixes behavior. The availability of an *a priori* formula frees the person from the necessity of constructing conduct appropriate to the situation relevent to a rule. By telling him what to do, the rule saves him the trouble of having to figure it out. If we had to constitute all our relationships *de novo*, we could not benefit from the time saved by past experiences incorporated in rules. [23] The regularity proceeding from rules is a method by which the past determines the present.

Rules also have a more general social function. Each group, said Durkheim, is a whole consisting of all who belong to it. For it to survive, each must act as if he were the whole, i.e., as if the interests of the group were also his own. But the interests of the individual are not always identical with the collective interests and may even be antagonistic. One result of divergence is that the individual does not always know the interests of the group; or if he does he may only dimly perceive them. Therefore, rules are necessary to tell him what to do. By following them in a disciplined way, he need not ascertain the collective interests on his own. The general idea behind this defense of the informative function was Durkheim's conviction that private interests lead ultimately to chaos—a proposition axiomatic to functional theory. In light of the informative function of rules, Durkheim went on to explain that norms are more necessary in large than small societies because in the former each person is able to see only a small part of the social scene, whereas in the latter it is easier to see the whole.[24] In large societies rules are more necessary to inform individuals of their moral duties.

As a society grows larger and its division of labor more complex, customs and laws decline into what Durkheim called *formalism*. At the primitive level a custom prescribes behavior down to the finest detail, prescribing how one should eat and dress, the gestures he should make, and the formulae he is obliged to repeat. With progress in the division of labor, rules lose their sharpness and specificity, prescribing what should be done rather than how to do it. The greater generality of expression is tied to the need to cover more situations. Custom and law now refer to categories rather than particular concrete objects and persons. Increase in generality and abstractness is accompanied by an increase in rationality, but at the same time norms permit greater variation in conduct. Losing some determinative power, rules require greater reflection and discretion in their application. A consequence is that variations in action elude moral influence. Moreover, rationality makes norms more susceptible to criticism; for individuals demand reasons, and examination diminishes their moral force.[25] The implication is that progress in the division of labor is accompanied by a decline in morality.

To reverse this decline and foster progress, Durkheim, like Comte before him, foresaw the further development of a science of morality grounded in a proper sociological analysis. Such a science tells us that each society has a moral system more or less compatible with its structure. The latter is therefore capable of promoting an objective standard for the assessment of the former. For example, such a science could very well indicate whether or not a particular moral maxim is obsolete by virtue of its compatibility with a social structure now in decline. Or it could tell us whether a new rule struggling to be born is compatible with a social structure also in process of emerging. For example, the principle of individual rights is closely bound to the structure of contemporary European societies. We are thus in a position to correct trends where such rights are being violated and thereby bring morality and social structure into alignment. Durkheim drew another example from history. Socrates's moral ideals were more suited to his society than those of his judges. It is easy to demonstrate, said Durkheim, that a decline of kinship disturbed the old religion—a trend that necessi-

166   Rules and Social Order

tated a new morality. Socrates and the Sophists enunciated this new moral code.[26]

Comte and Durkheim identified the essential element of morality as submission to a superior authority. Submission is based on the belief in the individual's total dependence. Through submitting to a superior will, the person attaches himself to the power that guarantees his well-being. Where religion is dominant, this superior power is identified with some supernatural entity, whether an impersonal force as in animism or an anthropomorphic deity as in Christianity. Sociological analysis, however, discovers in supernatural authority a society transfigured. And where religious commitment gives way to secular thinking, the idea of society as the supreme moral authority achieves conscious recognition. Moral duty consequently arises from a matrix of intense sentiments focused on society either directly or indirectly in transfigured form.

The existence of society and individual are functionally interdependent; the welfare of each is bound to that of the other. Moral feeling is maintained and strengthened through acts of devotion to society in the form of ritual. The worshiper advances his well-being by aspiring to society's ideals. Whereas Comte held that submission results in altruism, Durkheim saw submission resulting in compliance with norms. And since these norms serve society's ends, compliance guarantees its survival. Morality is inseparable from rules. As religion declines, the goodness of rules is increasingly evaluated rationally with reference to the criterion: How well does this particular rule benefit society? Rules thus form a normative order of moral determinism, functionally required for the continuity of society and the survival of the individual. The science of morality confronts the problems of how to make a moral order consistent with society's structure and how to guarantee its continued sacredness.

The Legitimate Order According to Weber

Max Weber's wide-ranging investigations of law resulted in some of the same conclusions Durkheim arrived at in regard to moral rules. Nevertheless, Weber's expert legal knowledge revealed dimensions and opened up theoretical avenues not apparent to the French sociologist. In addition, since Weber did not consider society a reality *sui generis*, he also reached conclusions that diverged from Durkheim's.

The Normative Order 167

What we have in mind as the normative order is largely encompassed in Weber's discussions of convention and law, although these do not exhaust the empirical uniformities of action.[27] Convention and law constitute what Weber called a *legitimate order*—rules regarded as valid or legitimate by actors. The test of their legitimacy is whether an actor actually complies because he perceives them to be obligatory. Would his failure to comply offend his sense of duty? Since it is apparent that individuals comply with laws and conventions because of a sense of obligation only some of the time, the *empirical* validity of a rule, Weber concluded, is the actual probability that it will be complied with for that reason.[28] A rule's empirical validity is strictly a function of subjective orientation, and a rule adhered to because of duty only a small part of the time has low validity. Weber's concept of validity is analogous to Durkheim's concept of moral duty.

It is not only a question, however, of the frequency with which a rule is complied with because individuals regard it as binding; for reflection shows that conformity arises from a diversity of motives. An individual may comply because he sees it in accord with his self-interest. He may want also to avoid punishment. Or he may follow the rule with little reflection simply out of habit. An individual may also comply because he believes his action will further some ultimate value such as justice. Consequently, a rule may be upheld for reasons having little to do with a belief in its validity, but the latter increases the probability of conformity.[29]

As an "ought," a legitimate order is enforced by sanctions. Since the members of a group regard law and convention as obligatory, there is a probability of punishment for violations. The criterion of distinction between law and convention is to be found in those who administer sanctions. He who defies a convention is the object of disapproval by anyone who is part of his environment, i.e., anyone in a position to make his disapproval known. His action is punishable by such measures as disapproval, exclusion from the group, or boycott. Familiar examples of convention given by Weber are forms of greeting, modes of dress, and standards of honor. A law, in contrast, is enforced by a staff specially designated for that purpose, such as police, judges, and attorneys. At primitive levels of organization those who punish infractions of legal codes are members of kinship groups seeking blood revenge. It is not always the case, Weber reminded us, that punishment for violation of law is more severe than that inflicted on someone who flouts a conven-

168   Rules and Social Order

tion. The person excluded from a group, for example, suffers more than he who spends a night in jail.[30]

A staff consists of one person at the minimum, but the more typical case is a larger number. Its members are specifically designated to hold themselves ready to secure compliance and punish noncompliance, their motives consisting of the belief in the law's validity. In upholding law they are permitted to resort to physical and psychological violence as techniques of coercion. Extending the concept of empirical validity to the process of law enforcement, Weber pointed out that a staff has varying probabilities of taking action, enforcing some laws to a greater extent than others, just as there are variations in conformity as a result of duty. According to Weber's concept, law includes other rules as well as those promulgated by the state;[31] consequently, it is proper to speak of laws of business firms, religious organizations, and universities. The staff of such organizations resort to exclusion (firing is an example), remonstrance, and threats of divine punishment to enforce their laws. In this context, Weber reiterated the well-known fact that conflicts often obtain between the laws of organizations and those of the state.[32] In sum, a legitimate order in Weber's sense consists of empirically valid rules differentiated by their modes of enforcement into either conventions or laws.[33]

Weber saw empirical transitions between *custom, convention,* and *law.* A custom is a long-standing practice confined to the realm of the "is," and individuals unreflectingly act according to custom through habituation. Although it may be inconvenient to violate a custom, such as eating breakfast at noon, no sanctions are imposed for deviating from a custom. However, a custom may become an "ought," acquiring the characteristics of either convention or law. If it comes to be guaranteed by a staff, custom becomes law; and here Weber spoke of *customary law.*[34] Unless a custom becomes convention or law, however, it lacks empirical validity.

Since law is a most significant element of legitimate orders, let us further consider Weber's analysis of law. Legal rules involve the processes of *lawmaking* and *lawfinding,* the former being the creation of law and the latter its application to concrete facts, better known as law enforcement. The most familiar example of law enforcement is the adjudication of a case by a judge, and the most familiar example of lawmaking is the enactment of a statute by a legislature.

Weber went on to distinguish two aspects of each of these activities, one being the content and the end a law is designed to achieve and the other the procedures that guide the activities. Content and purpose relate to the *substantive* aspect of law, while the procedures relate to the *formal* aspects of law. He then identified another dichotomous dimension—*rationality* and *irrationality*—that cuts across the substance and form of lawmaking and lawfinding. The resulting classification yields eight logical possibilities: lawmaking or lawfinding rational or irrational in form or substance.[35]

Since the rationalization of law is a most significant historical trend in legitimate orders, let us look at these various types. Irrationality in making and applying laws, as defined by Weber, consists of the use by legal functionaries of means that cannot be controlled by their intellects. Examples of irrational procedures in the determination of what a law is and how it is to be applied are ordeals, oracles, and supernatural revelations.[36] In resorting to such procedures individuals who deal with law let the outcome be determined by factors they do not control. The procedures are *formally irrational*.

Law enforcement is *substantively irrational* when the judge does not decide a case by applying general norms to the facts but instead arrives at decisions on the basis of some ethical, political, or expediential criterion dictated by his emotions. He selects concrete facts of each case for evaluation with reference to his substantive interest rather than existing legal principles. The result is that cases that would be decided similarly if existing laws were used as standards are judged in contradictory ways. At the extreme, this type of "lawfinding" becomes personal whim and arbitrary judgment. Here no law in the literal sense is involved, only a series of unconnected decisions. At this point, noted Weber, the distinction between lawmaking and lawfinding evaporates.[37] In general, one can say that lawfinding is substantively irrational when legal rules are either minimized or nonexistent.

Legal enactment, on the other hand, is substantively rational when a law is deliberately devised to achieve some preconceived goal, and it is obvious that entire systems of law approximate the rational model. An example of law created deliberately to foster some specific interest was the freedom of individuals to make wills disposing of their property (freedom of testation). The Church, which benefited from this freedom, worked for this legal right.[38] *Substantive rationality* in Weber's sense, therefore, is the creation of law specifically adapted as a means to some well-defined end. Lawmaking is *formally rational* when it adheres to deliberately created procedures that define the processes of legal enactment. Procedural norms, examples of which can be found in the United

170   Rules and Social Order

States Constitution, are also deliberately formed as means to certain ends. They provide an obvious contrast with oracles and ordeals.

In contrast to substantive irrationality, the application of law is substantively rational insofar as general legal rules are applied so that political, ethical, or utilitarian ends are accomplished. What makes the difference is the use of rules. Again rationality consists of an adaptation of means to ends. For example, judges gradually defined the repayment of a loan of money from a member of one kin group to a member of another as an enforceable contractual obligation, failure to repay being considered a tort. Weber traced the widening concept of freedom of contract to the substantive interests stimulated by the extension of markets.[39]

Finally, formally rational lawfinding is rational in its procedures, which are designed to best reveal the relevant facts of a case and establish their truth. The most important rational method is, of course, the testimony and examination of witnesses.[40] Weber discovered two types of formal rationality in the application of law. The first includes "external" criteria, such as a signature on a legal document, the utterance of certain words ("I promise"),[41] and the issuance of a summons served at a legally required place. These criteria are given to the senses. The second type of legal formalism, referred to by Weber as *logical rationality*, consists of the logical analysis of the meaning of terms appearing in legal propositions established by statute and enunciated by judges.[42] Laws are clarified, made more abstract, and the bases for decisions based on them reduced to principles. Out of this type of reflection and analysis grow purely legal interests over and above the substantive political and ethical goals that laws were designed to achieve. Here we see the possibility of conflict between formal and substantive rationality,[43] which Weber detected in other areas. Logical rationality, said Weber, appeared only in the law of occidental societies.[44]

Legal formalism culminates in the systematization of law—a logical integration of all the legal propositions derived from a logical analysis of meanings. Conceived of as an ideal-type, a system of law is gapless, inasmuch as every concrete fact is potentially capable of being subsumed under the relevant terms and propositions. Weber specified five postulates that define such a system. First, every legal decision is the application of an abstract legal norm to a concrete situation. Second, every case is to be decided according to legal logic. Third, the law is a gapless system in the aforementioned sense. Fourth, any fact incapable of interpretation in terms of legal concepts is legally irrelevant. Fifth, every social action must be conceptualized either as an application or infraction of a legal proposition.[45] Carried to this extreme, formal rationality becomes a total legal determinism.

As noted above, legal formalism is bound, according to Weber, to come in conflict with substantive goals, which is to say that formal rationality conflicts with substantive rationality. The layman, who sees the law solely as means to substantive goals like justice, does not understand, said Weber, the legal formalism of lawyers. For example, the German Supreme Court ruled that stealing electric power is not a larceny because the Criminal Code defines larceny as the unlawful taking of a chattel. But electric power is not a chattel; therefore it cannot be the subject of larceny.[46] The attempt to fit concrete facts under categories to achieve substantive ends sometimes contradicts the subsumption of those facts under formally legal terms. Herein lies the conflict between formal and substantive rationality of law.

Consisting of laws and conventions experienced as valid, Weber's conception of the legitimate order suggests the following question: On what grounds are conventions and laws subjectively experienced as legitimate? Weber traced the legitimacy of rules to three types of beliefs.

The first is that an order is subjectively believed to be legitimate because it is defined as both rational and legal. A law, as we have just seen, is substantively rational insofar as it was deliberately and intentionally established (enacted) to achieve some end specified in the legitimate order of a group and presumably approved by a significant number of its members or at least not disapproved by them. The legality of a law is to be traced to the fact that it was enacted in a procedurally correct way and is applied in such a manner as to advance the legitimate interests of the group. Hence, a rational-legal order is legitimate insofar as it is formally as well as substantively rational in both its establishment (lawmaking) and implementation (lawfinding). A legally rational order can be either created by the agreement of those subject to it or imposed upon them. The validity of its laws extends to those who exercise authority in the organization and whose power of command is conferred upon them by the laws. Members of the organization obey those in authority only insofar as they represent the organization's impersonal order.[47] *Rational-legal authority*, Weber observed, has become increasingly manifest in the modern world, in the state, capitalist firm, university, hospital, and political party.

The second basis of legitimacy is the fact that a rule is a tradition. The

172   Rules and Social Order

rule is long-standing, whose sacredness is attributed to its immemorial status. *Traditional authority* is the oldest and most universal type according to Weber. Those who believe in the validity of tradition obey those who hold the power of command in conformity with traditional rules. In contrast to rational authority, obedience is owed to the person in authority and takes the form of personal loyalty. In the pure sense, traditional rules are irrational. They are not deliberately enacted to achieve some specific end, and innovations are construed to be the discovery of what has always existed. In its ideal-typical sense tradition has no chance of becoming logically formalized. Insofar as rules enter into traditional lawfinding, they take the form of precedents. In the formal sense, traditional lawfinding resorts to irrational means like oracles, charismatic prophecy, and ordeals.[48]

The third basis of legitimacy originates in the extraordinary, exceptional, or exemplary characteristic of an individual who on that basis is defined as a charismatic leader. The rules he comes forth with are accepted as valid because of the belief in his charisma. Such a leader can be a prophet, military hero, or one having powers of healing or legal wisdom or thought to be of divine origin. The followers who believe in his charisma obey his person—a fact that distinguishes charisma from rational-legal authority. Charisma also is differentiated from the latter in that charismatic lawmaking is irrational, originating in divine revelation or inspiration. The norms are not abstract, formal principles; and consequently lawfinding proceeds on a case-by-case basis. Moreover, said Weber, *charismatic authority* stands in opposition to tradition, which the leader rejects in favor of new obligations.[49]

In sum, an order's legitimacy comes down to a belief either that its norms are rationally adapted to shared goals, or that they ought to be honored because they are old, or that they are valid because they are originated by an extraordinary individual. Like so many of Weber's concepts they are ideal-types, the validity of any given order being determined by a combination of all three beliefs.

Weber and Durkheim tried to explain the source of duty as a motive for upholding norms. They squarely faced the fact of authority and its role in human life. The sacredness of moral rules according to Durkheim converges with the charismatic origin of norms according to Weber. Despite this similarity, their discussions of these topics diverged in other respects. According to Durkheim, the authority of rules derives from the impact of society as a reality in and of itself. But for Weber legitimacy is

The Normative Order   173

to be traced strictly to historically conditioned subjective beliefs of individuals. Whereas Durkheim explored the universal functions of rules for individuals and society, Weber's historical perspective led him to identify the processes and causal factors involved in the rationalization of legitimate orders. He explored how the organizations of staff are related to the legitimating belief in authority,[50] an area of domination largely left untouched by Durkheim. Finally, Durkheim was convinced that science could be used to foster moral progress, whereas for Weber a moral science was a contradiction in terms.

Talcott Parsons attempted to integrate Weber's notions about rational action with Durkheim's concept of moral authority to build a systematic theory of the normative order—the principal controlling factor in the social system. In doing so he considerably broadened the scope of Weber's concept of legitimate order.

Norms and Values in the Social System

At one point in his writing Parsons gave the following definition of the norm:

> A norm is a verbal description of the concrete course of action thus regarded as desirable, combined with an injunction to make certain future actions conform to this course.[51]

After this definition he gave the example that soldiers should obey the orders of their officers. The definition and example express the familiar element of duty. Parsons then went on to elaborate a more extended conception of the normative.

A norm calls for a course of action that is directed toward an end. We can infer from the example, said Parsons, that an immediate goal of the rule is military efficiency. However, two logical possibilities present themselves. One is that obedience to orders is an end in itself, desirable for its own sake, in which case the norm requires an action having intrinsic value. The second is that military efficiency, although an end, is at the same time a means to some other end such as national security. Parsons held that norms usually involve both of these possibilities. When we raise the question of what further end a norm-oriented action

174   Rules and Social Order

accomplishes, we raise the possibility of a means-ends chain "upward" to some ultimate end, which is not a means to another.[52] Therefore, a norm for Parsons is a rule that requires an action that may be intrinsically worthwhile, but which also has an end that is also a means in a chain.

It is obvious that this concept of the normative includes elements other than those ordinarily associated with rules. The chain of means and ends logically suggests some *ultimate value*; for lacking the status of means, the final end in the chain is an ultimate that reflects a value. Parsons defined an ultimate value as that which members believe to be desirable for their society as a whole. An ultimate value thereby provides a definition of the good society.[53] In the above example the desirability of a society secure from enemies illustrates an ultimate value.

Norms, therefore, contribute to the realization of ultimate values. In turn, these values legitimate the norms and provide them with binding qualities.[54] In order to realize society's ultimate values is why, according to Parsons, individuals are obligated to comply with norms—a formulation that reflects the influence of Weber's inquiries into the legitimacy of law. According to Weber, as noted above, a law is oriented to some end; and especially legal authority is legitimate because it is substantively and formally rational. Its legitimacy derives from its legality and the fact that it is rationally adjusted to ends. Parsons thus incorporated the means-ends nexus in Weber's theory into his concept of the normative as a chain of means and ends grounded in ultimate values.[55]

This relationship between values and norms does not exhaust Parsons's concept of the normative. In the example at the outset, an immediate end achieved by the norm Parsons inferred to be military efficiency. Obedience to orders makes for efficiency. The army is a collectivity that is a part of society, and one of its collective goals is military efficiency. Hence, the norm achieves a goal of this collectivity, which at the same time is a means for achieving society's security. And this is one value in the latter's value-system. A rule contributes to the goal of a collectivity that is a subsystem of society and in so doing contributes to the realization of an ultimate value. The normative thus includes in its scope collectivities as well as society,[56] the means-ends chain encompassing both levels of social structure.

Moreover, neither should we lose sight of the individual soldier, who in complying with the norm carries out his military role.[57] Obedience to a command is the beginning of the means-ends chain. As a result, Parsons's concept of the normative finally embraces four units of social

The Normative Order   175

structure from the highest to the lowest: value, norm, collectivity, and role. We will always find in society these four levels. Strictly speaking, we should note, however, that normative culture consists of values and norms, which are models for collectivities and roles.

Let us take a closer look at the interrelationships among these structures. Values confer legitimacy on norms. A person obeys a norm which ultimately contributes to the realization of a value that he shares. Norms in turn specify values to concrete situations by defining obligatory courses of action in roles. Here one can see an analogy between the specification of a value by a norm and the application of a rule to a situation. It follows that values are always more general than norms. Moreover, a role defined by a norm is also a structure in a collectivity. Therefore, the enactment of a role not only starts a chain of means and ends, but at the same time expresses a value.[58] The role accomplishes the actor's goal, which contributes to the collectivity's goal and indirectly to an end of society.[59] It is also apparent that the means-ends chain is also a chain of influence in the opposite direction. For if norms are derived from values and individuals are obliged to comply with norms in the course of their roles, the predominant influence comes from values and "flows" through collectivities to roles. Parsons called this chain of influence a *cybernetic hierarchy of control.*[60]

Moreover, at the lower end of the hierarchy the goals of a collectivity also reflect its own value-system, which is consistent with that of the society to which it belongs.[61] For instance, military values are compatible with those of society conceived of as a totally integrated ideal-type.

For norms to connect roles and collectivities with values, they must first, said Parsons, designate those to whom they apply. Second, they must be enforced through rewards and punishments. Third, they must be continually interpreted in relation to concrete situations.[62] Insofar as these situations are contexts of roles in all sorts of collectivities, it follows that the everyday operation of society consist of a continuing interpretation of rules, somewhat analogous to the interpretation of laws of the state with regard to individual cases.[63] The need for interpretation grows as values undergo processes of generalization in order to legitimate norms that arise as a result of increasing social complexity, for example, industrialization.[64] Here Parsons adapted Durkheim's generalization that law and custom grow more abstract with complexity in the division of labor to his theory of evolution.

In this rather complicated analysis of the normative, it is evident that

176   Rules and Social Order

Parsons constructed a type of social organization based on the concept of rule. For their implementation, rules require vast cooperative efforts, oriented in one direction to values "above them" and in the other exerting a "downward" influence on collectivities and roles.

How does Parsons's conception of the normative relate to morality? One way to answer the question is to take the actor's perspective in the context of the social system. According to Parsons, a moral problem arises under two conditions. It arises first when an individual has to choose among competing courses of action with the aim of selecting that which best fits with all his needs. Here the choice is made with reference to the individual himself. A moral problem also arises when the individual is forced to choose an action with the aim of coordinating it with the actions of others, and in order to do this he is obliged to take account of their expectations and their needs. It is evident that in both cases moral choice involves the functional problem of integration.[65]

What sorts of moral decisions does one make when he integrates his actions with others? Parsons identified five types of choices, all of which are made either explicitly or implicitly. Should the individual treat others with respect to who they are or what they can do? This is the moral dilemma of *object modalities*. Should he place his own interests above theirs or subordinate his interests? This is the dilemma of *private versus collective interest*. Should he define those with whom he interacts with reference to general standards or treat them on the basis of his unique relationship to them? This, said Parsons, is the dilemma of *transcendence versus immanence*. Should he exploit them for his own gratification or restrain himself? This is the dilemma of *gratification versus discipline*. Should he orient himself to them as total persons or confine his interest to only a segment of their personalities? This is the dilemma of the *scope of significance of the object*. These decisions, Parsons claimed, are oriented to the pattern variables—moral norms that prescribe the proper set of choices in relevant situations.[66] When a combination of pattern variables is institutionalized, the members of a social system are under the moral duty to make the choices therein prescribed. The motive for compliance is duty.

As formal norms the pattern variables are obviously implicated in the concept of the normative. Providing obligatory definitions of roles, they contribute to the goals of collectivities and society and express ultimate values. They prescribe actions in means-ends chains. It follows that

The Normative Order   177

choices made in the course of roles, insofar as they follow such norms, integrate collectivities into society as a whole.

Parsons's notion of morality reflects the influence of Durkheim, who saw the end of a moral action as society's benefit. A moral arrangement, society cannot exist without morality. But the French sociologist was not very precise about the specific ways that moral acts maintain society. Equipped, however, with a rather detailed model of the social system's functions, Parsons was able to identify precisely how moral action benefits society. The key to morality's role is to be found in its accomplishment of the integrative function.[67]

It is this function that brings about order. Therefore, the principal contribution of norms to society is order. Parsons illustrated the integrative function of norms very simply. Consider a network of streets and roads heavily traveled by automobiles. Assume the space to be limited in relation to the volume of traffic. It would be impractical, Parsons theorized, to rely solely on the intentions and spontaneous decisions of drivers to coordinate their actions. If coordination depended solely on *ad hoc* choices, there would be a large number of collisions, at least more than now occurs. In order to integrate their actions, the drivers follow both conventions and laws, the latter being enforced by special personnel. There is an elaborate system of rules of the road, a legitimate order that controls the flow of traffic. In the absence of rules each would pursue his interests in such a way that would lead to chaos. Unintegrated by norms, private interests would lead drivers to achieve ends that are random in relation to one another. The resulting conflict, said Parsons, would approximate the miserable condition of man in the state of nature described by Hobbes.[68]

Traffic rules integrate society on one level, i.e., the level of action. They specify ultimate values in the sense that we have already seen. Moreover, each such value is part of a system, consistent with all the others; for culture, according to Parsons, tends toward pattern consistency.[69] The compatibility of the values in society's value system constitutes its highest level of integration. Consequently, under the postulate of pattern consistency it follows that actions at the bottom end of a chain, namely, actions in roles, are compatible.[70] If norms were to specify contradictory values, the actions oriented to them would conflict.

Like Durkheim, Parsons was also interested in the question of why individuals obey rules. Durkheim believed they are subtly aware of the constraining power of norms originating in an all-powerful society.

178   Rules and Social Order

Experienced as sacred entities, they command respect. Parsons stated that he agreed with Durkheim's conclusion that the principal reason why we do not steal is because the norm prohibiting it has become a part of us. We have internalized it; and when we violate it, we feel guilty.[71] Society self-consciously establishes methods to internalize its norms within its members.

Through a selective borrowing from Durkheim and Weber, Parsons fashioned a model of society as a system of normative determinism, its normative order prescribing choices that integrate the actions of its members. Durkheim's society as a moral reality became in Parsons's theory the self-maintaining social system that socializes its members into its moral codes. They accept the authority of society's rules as binding and comply out of a sense of duty. The norms defining how roles should be played are applications of society's value-system—the highest level of normative structure. The specification of values to roles and collectivities by norms is analogous to the enforcement of rules through lawfinding in Weber's sense. Collective goals achieved through normatively governed actions illustrate the principle of rationality, also derived from Weber. Norms are standards that rationally adapt means to well-defined collective ends. Hence, the social system operates not only according to a moral but also a rational determinism; and its normative order of values, rules, and collective ends is rationally differentiated such that society's functional requirements are continually met. Society's entire normative order is modeled on Weber's concept of the systemization of law. Morality and rationality thus combine to confer legitimacy on the rules.

Habermas on the Legitimation of Norms

Habermas sees logical problems in Weber's treatment of the rationalization of law, and his attempts to rectify them also have implications for Parsons's theory of the normative. Weber was wrong, says Habermas, in attributing the legitimacy of modern law to its legality.[72] As noted previously, Weber's concept refers to the procedures established in the enactment and application of law, in lawmaking and lawfinding. Such procedures are stated in constitutions and devised by lawyers. Thus, a particular law is legitimate if it was legally established; and a specific legal decision is legitimate if it was enunciated according to legal procedures.

The Normative Order   179

But, argues Habermas, the belief that an enacted law is legal cannot by itself confer legitimacy because it presupposes the legitimacy of legality itself. The assumption of the legitimacy of a legal order that lays down what is legal is a circular argument. Furthermore, Habermas refuses to accept as the basis of an order's legality the fact that it was brought into being either by agreement or by imposition as Weber said.[73] Thus, neither the fact that the United States Constitution was established by consensus nor the fact that the minority are compelled to go along with it is a satisfactory foundation of its legitimacy.

Habermas went on to contend that despite Weber's description of modern law as rational, he excluded from law a rational foundation. The criticism applies both to particular laws and the legal order as a whole. Weber explained the rationality of modern law strictly in terms of purposive rationality, emphasizing law as a rational means but omitting the rationality of the derivation of the end served.[74] For Weber a demonstration of law's substantive rationality is limited to testing for consistency among the values implied in the law and ascertaining the feasibility of achieving an end compatible with those values.[75] In contrast, Habermas argues that the legitimacy of a law is to be found in the methods of deriving the end it serves.[76] These methods are considered below.

Why, Habermas asks, did Weber err in identifying legality as an independent type of legitimate domination? The answer is to be found in Weber's observation of a kind of what Habermas calls a "secondary traditionalism" that develops in societies under the domination of rational law. With the ever-growing rationalization of making and enforcing law by experts, ordinary individuals become distanced from the law's rational foundations. They do not understand these foundations, and for them the empirical validity of law comes to rest on habit. Failing to understand, they rely on the legality of laws for the latter's legitimacy.[77] In other words, legality is a poor substitute for something better.

If legality is not the foundation, then what is the source of legitimate domination? In Habermas's opinion we can no longer rely on traditional world views such as religion, civil privatism, natural law, and familial-vocational privatism; for these grow weaker under the impact of science and other social changes.[78] Such systems of thought furnished legitimacy for traditional states and the early liberal capitalist societies. But they were really not genuine legitimations, but rather ideological justifications that merely assumed shared interests in the laws and militated against

180   Rules and Social Order

rational discussion of them.[79] Today, however, the legitimacy of the state is coming to rest on a rational consensus arrived at by its citizens. Legitimacy derives from the procedures that produce rational agreement among the public about laws established by the state.[80] What precisely are these procedures?

These procedures constitute what Habermas calls the *ideal-speech situation* characterized by a number of conditions. Those who are discussing a rule are free and equal in their rights. No one is restricted in expressing his opinion through power or the threat of sanction, the only force admitted into the dialogue being the force of the better argument. In Habermas's view, power distorts the dialogue. The exclusive topic of conversation is the validity of a norm, the only motive that of testing its claim to legitimacy. The test includes discerning abstract principles of justification that are compared in order to ascertain their consistency.[81] The only acceptable motive for participation in the dialogue is the search for truth. The ideal-speech situation excludes deception; no one tries to get the better of another through pushing his self-interest (a form of strategic action).

Everyone whose interests are affected by a norm has a chance to participate. Each is encouraged to discover and express his true interests insofar as they relate to the norm under discussion. Each has the right to defend and challenge the bases on which the validity of the rule is claimed. The test of the rationality of the consensus that forms is the discovery of a common (generalizable) interest advanced by the norm. This shared interest communicatively arrived at is found through the reasons advanced in the discussion of the validity claims raised. These are discursively redeemed,[82] which is to say met and answered.

The legitimacy of a law established through rational discourse does not include, says Habermas, compromise. Normative validity is not derivable from each group's relinquishing some interest to get an agreement but rather from a shared interest. Compromise is justified only when a balance of power obtains among the parties to the discussion and when their interests are not generalizable.[83]

Therefore, concludes Habermas, Weber was in error in denying the rationality of ends. The end served by a norm admits of truth, arrived at through a rational consensus that turns up a general interest. The universality of a general interest expresses a kind of objectivity.[84]

It follows that the legitimacy of an order is the product of the conditions of *communicative action*, which is defined as a speech situation whose goal is to arrive at a consensus through rational persuasion. What are these conditions? Consensus depends on mutual understanding; speaker and listener must understand a sentence the same way. In order that a hearer understand a speaker who is attempting to persuade him, he must know what to do to fulfill the speaker's wishes. He must also know why the speaker is justified in trying to persuade him. The second of these two conditions boils down to the speaker's fulfillment of a criticizable validity claim.[85] For the listener to understand, the speaker's reasons must be acceptable. Assume that a speaker is trying to persuade a hearer to follow a norm. In that case, the communicative action has as its purpose the establishment of legitimacy. Consequently, legitimacy arises from the structure of communicative action itself. And since, as Habermas tells us, an existing law is at all times subject to the necessity of withstanding criticism of its claim to validity, it follows that the entire normative order is in principle continually subject to challenge by the test of reason.

The dialogue that results in a rational consensus with regard to the validity of norms is, according to Habermas, a moral discourse. He thus sees the process of forming legitimacy as a moral enterprise. And according to his model of society, norms, values, goals, world views, and concepts of collective identity constitute the *lifeworld (Lebenswelt)* of society. They are symbolic structures that give the society its social integration.[86] From all this one can draw the implication that the formation of legitimacy through communicative action is a process in the formation of the lifeworld.

From the perspectives of communicative action and lifeworld Habermas also criticized Parsons's theory of the normative as the basis of order. Parsons constructed a theory of action on the concept of the isolated unit act of a single, hypothetical actor. Following Weber, he conceptualized the unit act as the selection of means to attain an end, which itself is the result of selection among ends. Here is the beginning of the aforementioned means-ends chain. But, said Habermas, these selections were explained by Parsons as functions of the normative, which he merely assumed to be shared. Values and norms, which are embodiments of moral authority that he borrowed from Durkheim, were assumed by Parsons and then postulated as the explanation of order. Thus, the normative accomplishes order through the integrative function. Through the normative Parsons attempted, in Habermas's view, to create a system of action out of the isolated unit act.[87]

182   Rules and Social Order

This, however, doesn't work. Parsons's theory of action is incapable of generating a concept of society. Instead of concentrating on the relation between means and ends in the unit act, which is a teleological conception, he should have focused on language as the mechanism through which individuals arrive at agreement about their goals and develop norms through raising and settling validity claims in rational discourse. Not having a way to explain the origin of normative integration, Parsons was compelled to introduce the cultural, social, and personality systems as independent sources of causal contributions to action. The actor thereby becomes an agency through which cultural norms, social role-expectations, and personality motives propel his action.[88]

However, if we give a theoretically central place to language and use the lifeworld as context, it becomes possible to explain mutual understanding (norms) as products of culture, society, and personality relied on as resources. Individuals make use of cultural traditions, social institutions, and personal competencies to arrive at understandings that coordinate their activities. Now we can explain, says Habermas, both the determinants of action and the existence of culture, society, and personality, which are produced through action. Communicative action thus provides the unity among the three systems. "*Without the conceptual bridge of a 'lifeworld' centered on communicative action culture, society, and personality simply fall apart.*"[89]

Habermas's criticisms come down to the point that Weber and Parsons did not extend the principle of reason to the selection of ends but confined rationality to the instrumental choice of means. Neither were they aware of the role of communication as the medium through which the ends of norms can be rationally formed. Despite these disagreements about the formation of legitimacy, Habermas's analysis reveals a fundamental continuity. He accepts the basis of legitimacy in the modern world as resting on rational thinking, which was the central theme of Weber's investigations and which Parsons incorporated into the theory of the social system.

Theory of the Normative Order

The preceding accounts converge on the idea that the most important cause of social order is to be found in the fact that individuals follow rules. Compliance with rules enables them to coordinate their actions to achieve goals that would otherwise be unattainable. Repeated again and again, these actions that conform to rules give the appearance of stability and make for predictability; for knowledge of rules and the situations to which they apply enables one to know what to expect.

What distinguishes rules from other plans of action is that they express the idea of the "ought." Consequently they are backed by sanctions, and one has no choice but to comply. Although it is an acknowledged fact that rewards and punishments are real factors motivating compliance, the preceding writers emphasized a sense of duty as a more significant motivation. The sense of duty is reinforced by the respect that derives from the consciousness that rules more or less express the collectivity's general will, a respect that is absent when the desire to avoid punishment is the sole reason for compliance.

Since obedience often requires the suppression of self-interest in favor of a more general interest, compliance has often been identified as an act of morality. Hence, theories of the normative order have interpreted such compliance within moral contexts. Obedience to authority is internalized within the character structure and has the consequence that failure of duty is experienced as guilt. The duty to comply is also expected when the bearer of authority is a person who derives his power of command from a rule.

The notion of authority raises the question of the legitimacy of a rule, and the theory of the normative order discovers such legitimacy in the end for which the rule was established and in the value expressed by the end. Hence, the "oughtness" of a rule is created and sustained strictly by the subjective orientations of individuals, who define it as "good" for society in terms of the social benefits that result from its purported end and underlying value. The rule's "goodness" is a source of its legitimacy.

Far from being self-contained entities, rules are interrelated to form normative orders. Their interrelationship in systems, which becomes especially visible in the rational codification of laws, points to the extent of consistency between the end of one rule and the ends of others. In the ideal-typical case, rules are totally consistent in means, ends, and values and totally determine the actions relevant to them. The logical integration of the normative order on the level of meaning produces an integration of society at the level of action. The order produced by a single rule extends, in the extreme case, to a total order produced by the interrelation of rules. Integration manifests not only as coordinated action but also as a feeling of solidarity arising from furthering the good of society through promoting socially useful ends; and theories that identify moral dimensions of conformity place the entire normative order in a moral context.

A normative order benefits not only society by integrating it, but also has advantages for its members. Durkheim especially emphasized the benefits for the individual of a constraint on the possibilities of his self-interest, which he interpreted as a force continually "pushing against" rules. The unchecked self-interest results in the collapse of normative orders through a loss of legitimacy; social order gives way to chaos, and predictability to the randomness of actions.

In the modern world normative orders are increasingly evaluated by members of society in terms of their objective rationality. How well do they achieve well-defined ends that benefit society? The criterion of rationality grows in importance as the belief that norms are established by gods declines. As generalized rules apply to broader ranges of situations, the interpretation of rules, which is also evaluated in terms of rationality, becomes more difficult. And at the same time, law enforcement becomes differentiated from lawmaking.

This overall conception, or various aspects of it, is widely held, either explicitly or implicitly, in sociological thinking. As we have seen, it is prominent in functionalism, but also evident in commonsense thinking. It has provided the basis for further theorizing and empirical research. It falls short, nevertheless, of explaining all aspects of social order; and therefore other theories have come into conflict with it.

6

The Construction of Order

The supremacy of rules for social order was broadly challenged in a twofold manner. First, the application of a rule to concrete situations, which is illustrated by what Weber called lawfinding, founders on facts inherent in those situations. Following a rule is not a process of logical deduction yielding unambiguous conclusions. The differences among situations falling under the jurisdiction of rules reduce the fit between rules and their contexts of application. Exceptions arise that limit their generality. When carried to an extreme, this process results in a complete denial of the existence of rules, which dissolve in the uniquenesses of each situation. To the extent that a rule is overwhelmed by particularities, situational constructions of meaning rush in to fill the gap between rules and contexts. In a sense, a rule is discovered in the attempt to apply it. These constructions limit the determinative impact of rules and have negative implications for a logically closed, self-contained normative order grounded in a small number of ultimate values. Order is rather the result of *ad hoc* constructions. This is the viewpoint of both the symbolic interaction theories and ethnomethodology.

The second challenge to the theory of the normative order came from those theories that focused on the rational pursuit of self-interest. According to these, social order is constructed by and arises from the interests of individuals as they see them. First, social order is a direct product of coincidences of interests, according to which what is to the interest of

186   Rules and Social Order

one individual is also to the interest of others. Such identity of interests is explained by identifiable factors both rooted in human nature and inherent in social circumstances. In pursuing their interests, individuals may follow maxims—rules learned from experience that they believe will accomplish their goals. But these maxims differ from rules in the normative sense in that they are not sanctioned as moral imperatives. Second, social order is also an indirect product of the national calculation of self-interest, which is thought to stand behind the origin and obedience to laws as their basic motivating factor. Laws, for example, are obeyed in order to avoid punishment. The necessity of the existence of sanctioned rules is a concession to the recognition that the identity of interests is incomplete, and here self-interest is forced to achieve social order in a roundabout way because of imperfections in facts that work toward an identity of interests.

The reduction of social order to the rational pursuit of self-interest collides with moral commitment as elaborated in the theory of the normative order. As we have observed, moral duty eschews self-interest and indeed suppresses it. In contrast, the theories advocating the principle of the rational pursuit of self-interest tend to define morality in precisely those terms. From all this it follows that the two approaches emphasize contradictory factors in the production of social order. The theory that most applauded self-interest was utilitarianism, which appeared before the rise of sociology; but many of its tenets are also expressed in contemporary social exchange theory.

Mead's Reconstruction of the Act

In coming to terms with Darwin, George Herbert Mead (1863–1931) formulated a theory of the act that identified elements of novelty and unpredictability. These elements have the consequence of limiting the effectiveness of rules as determinants of action and are to be found as characteristics of the *reflexive self*. It is this self that Mead believed most importantly distinguishes the human being from other animals.[1]

By the reflexive self is meant the self that is both a subject and an object. We are able, said Mead, to sweep ourselves into the orbit of our own experience. When we think about ourselves, the self is both subject and object. The self that thinks is also the self that is thought about. In its capacity to turn back upon itself, the self is reflexive. Not that we always possess a self. For when we become so absorbed in our experience of an external object that we do not think about ourselves, we lack a self at that time. When a person who is running away has his experience swallowed up in the objects about him, he lacks a consciousness of self.[2] When it does occur, however, the experience of self-consciousness is, according to Mead, the highest expression of consciousness.

Mead posed the question: How can a person get outside of himself experientially so that he can see himself as an object? The answer lies in his ability to take the attitude of others toward himself. The individual understands how others define him and thereby sees himself as an object from their perspective. Mead called this process taking the role of the other. The ability to take the other's role in turn arises with the individual's ability to communicate with symbols; for as the person speaks, his words arouse within him the same response as they arouse in the other.[3] In communicating with others he thus becomes aware of himself by covertly assuming their roles.

Mead broadened the notion of taking the other's role to include the perspective of society as a whole. When the individual takes the attitudes of all the other members of society toward one another and toward himself with reference to the organized activities of society, he takes, said Mead, the role of the generalized other. The attitudes of specific others are generalized to encompass those of others in general. As the person plays his roles in society, he experiences himself from the viewpoint of the generalized other. He objectifies himself through an abstract, general perspective. The unity of society as a whole gives him a unity of self.[4]

Mead analyzed the reflexive self into two phases—the "I" and "me." Whenever the person becomes conscious of himself, he has both an "I" and a "me." One is inconceivable without the other. The "I" is the subject of the action, the "me" its object. When the person acts, it is as an "I"; but the "I" acts with reference to a "me," which, as noted above, consists of the attitudes of others. When the "I" acts in relation to the attitudes of society in general, it acts, of course, in relation to the *generalized other*. Consequently, a self-conscious act is always social inasmuch as it is oriented to conventional expectations and attitudes. The "I," however, can never be directly experienced; for the individual cannot be directly aware of himself as he acts. He can only directly experience those objects to which his action is directed. Therefore, when he thinks about his "I" that just now acted, he must experience it as an object, namely a "me." Since he cannot turn around quickly enough to catch himself, the "I" of the past is always experienced as a "me," which has become a memory in the present. Never experienced as such but necessary to account for action, the "I" is a postulated construct according to Mead.[5]

Shared with others, his "me" fits the individual into society. It includes what the person is expected to do. The "I" on the other hand is what the person actually does, and there is a dialectic relationship between these two phases of the self. Although the "me" is the attitudes an individual shares with others, his "I" always acts in a way that is novel. Despite the standardization imposed by the generalized other, every individual is different by virtue of his "I." Neither does one know precisely, Mead went on to contend, how he will act until his act is completed and appears in his experience as a memory. Even with regard to so simple an act as walking, the taking of the expected steps puts the person into a situation that he never entirely anticipated. Take as another example a scientist. He is immersed in data to be explained, but he does not know how he will put the facts together, what hypothesis he will actually arrive at, until he does it. No one can predict how an event will turn out in all its details. Consequently, the "I" acts like a principle of uncertainty and constantly injects novelty into the social process. Whereas the "me" makes everyone similar, the "I" makes everyone different.[6] The self is pointed, so to speak, in contradictory directions.

The constructive uniqueness of geniuses like Jesus, Socrates, and Buddha, Mead went on to point out, was a product of the "I." Such leaders stand out against the generalized other and significantly modify it, yet the novelty is only an extreme of the small amount that occurs in every act. Moreover, novelty can be destructive, as illustrated by a violent mob.[7]

Mead's analysis of the self suggests implications for the role of rules. It is obvious that the "me" and the generalized other, although they include more, also include society's rules. The attitudes of others encompass their expectations of an individual, expectations enforced by sanctions. However, if the "I" always departs in unpredictable ways from the "me," it is an elusive, ubiquitous factor in the social order. Because of it, action can never be completely regulated by norms. Functionalism's normative order, therefore, is subject to continual subversion, modification, and change due to the spontaneous, unpredictable, creative power of the self. Its determinative power is limited.

The Construction of Order   189

The "I" is further defined in the context of Mead's theory of *reflective intelligence*. He formulated this theory against the background of an ideal-typical state according to which habits perfectly adjust individuals to their situations. Identical with the "me," habit reigns supreme. Under its force the person need neither make choices nor reflect about what he does; nor is he conscious of himself. With no problems to solve, he need not think; for thinking arises only when habit fails.

Habit does in fact fail, however, to bring about an adjustment whenever novel elements arise in a situation. The walk through the woods is interrupted by a ditch. The actor is now faced with a problem that demands a solution in order for normal routines to be carried out. The conflict with the preexisting habit initiated by a change in the situation inhibits the habit from realizing itself in overt conduct. As a consequence the individual engages in rational thinking, which involves indicating to himself through implicit vocal symbols new stimuli in the situation matched by their appropriate responses incorporated in the central nervous system. By attending to those stimuli responsible for the various parts of the previous habit, the person breaks up the action and eliminates the maladaptive elements. He constructs new, adjustive responses through attaching existing responses to stimuli combined in novel ways. The person imagines himself responding in these ways and conceptualizes their consequences as given in memory. The purposeful selection of stimuli creates new conceptual objects exercising control over the act. The imagination of alternative courses introduces a future orientation, which brings about control of the present by the future. The individual selects that imagined sequence of responses supposed to bring about a new adjustment to the changed situation. The selected course functions like a hypothesis to be tested in overt conduct.

These reflective processes involve a self as the person imagines himself putting into effect alternatives. Each ideational alternative involves the perspective of others, the taking of others' roles. Thus, selection involves an organization of perspectives. Insofar as imagination of alternatives proceeds through the implicit articulation of verbal symbols in an internal conversation, reflective thinking is a social activity through and through. This is one of Mead's central points.

The novel element in the situation, such as a barrier, emerged from the past but could not be predicted. Here is a counterpart to the unpredictability of the "I." It can, however, be retrospectively explained on the basis of the past in terms of its necessary, but not its sufficient,

190   Rules and Social Order

conditions. The fact that its sufficient conditions cannot be known explains why the novel element could not be predicted. The reconstruction of action required to solve problems created by unpredicted conflict is carried out by the "I." And the reason why the "I" fails to coincide with the "me" is that, according to Mead, every situation is impregnated with varying degrees of disruptive novelty. Were every previous action capable of effecting an adjustment by itself, then it would be possible for the self to be reduced to the "me."[8] But this is not so.

We draw two related conclusions pertaining to the role of rules in social order from Mead's analysis of the "I" and "me." First, under the assumption that the "me" includes those of society's expectations that are rules, namely, that the expectations in question are sanctionable "oughts," rules can never be totally determinative of social order. For the "me" is always accompanied by an "I." Second, action is always to some extent constructed, even in those situations to which rules apply. This implication follows from the contributions of the "I" to deviance, novelty, and change. Building on Mead's legacy of these two phases of the self, other symbolic interactionists emphasized the role of ongoing interpretations and reinterpretations of norms.[9]

The Ethnomethodological Conception of Rules

Although there are important differences, similarities also obtain between symbolic interactionism and ethnomethodology. Mead's "I" has its counterpart in Garfinkel's theory of the *account*, both of which limit the impact of a preexisting normative order. On the other hand, with regard to rules ethnomethodology takes a more radical position.

As Garfinkel sees it, the task of ethnomethodology is the discovery of the procedures individuals use to define their situations. How do individuals go about constructing interpretations of their activities and the activities of others? He contends that interpretations are achieved within the situations rather than carried over from the past. Definitions are thus ongoing constructions or "situated accomplishments."[10] Even the recognition by members of a family in the evening that they are the same family to whom they said goodbye in the morning is a situated accomplishment.[11] It is evident that Mead's "I" is continually at work. Garfinkel

The Construction of Order   191

calls such definitions "accounts," and the objective of ethnomethodology, therefore, is to give scientific accounts of these everyday accounts.

Ethnomethodologists, however, recognize a divergence between their perspective and that of the individuals they study. They conceive of accounts as constructions that "assemble" an occasioned corpus; the individuals being studied, however, attribute their own definitions of objects to such cultural givens as norms. In their minds these givens make possible a continuity among situations. Moreover, ethnomethodologists also point out that conventional sociologists also explain interaction in terms of such givens. To laymen and conventional sociologists the normative order appears as an objective reality. But to the ethnomethodologist, in contrast, persons' accounts of the objectivity of rules is itself a construction that results from their interpretive procedures.[12] It is up to the ethnomethodologists to describe and explain these procedures.

Garfinkel identified several characteristics of commonsense accounts, all of which have a bearing on rules. The everyday accounts individuals use to make sense of their situations are *indexical, reflexive,* and *loose.* The indexical expression has been discussed in chapter 2. Accordingly, the reader will recall that the meaning of an object is influenced by its context. Therein lies its indexicality. Consequently, the same terms in an account of one situation vary in meaning when used to give an account of another.

Garfinkel locates the reflexivity of an account in the fact that it is an aspect of the situation that it gives an account of.[13] The individual who defines an object as having a given quality acts toward it on that basis and thereby establishes it as having that quality. I give an account of my friend as being knowledgeable about a subject, and on the basis of that account I ask him a question. The act of consulting him establishes his knowledgeability. The account of his knowledgeability establishes what is real and organizes our relationship. Here is an analogy with Mead's example that the conduct of the cow eating grass creates the object of food.[14] Organizing the situation they give an account of, accounts are reflexives.

A third characteristic of accounts is their looseness. An account formulated to interpret one situation will not offer an equally valid interpretation of another even though it employs the same terms. The looseness of accounts is closely related to their indexicality. Neither can all the conditions under which an account holds up ever be specified. Therefore, in giving an account or formulating a plan of action, individ-

192   Rules and Social Order

uals are compelled to omit relevant information and take certain things for granted. Not all of the facts in a given situation that contribute to the meaning of an account can ever be stated. Consequently, the inability to state all relevant conditions of an account limits its transsituationality. Garfinkel sums up the inconclusiveness of accounts by noting that everyone giving an account is obliged to implicitly resort to assumptions like "*et cetera*," "unless," and "let it pass."[15] At best, an account of one situation can hold in a comparable one only in a general way.

It is apparent that these characteristics of all commonsense accounts are related, yet at the same time distinguishable. If an account acquires reflexivity by establishing itself in the situations that it accounts for and organizes, it nevertheless does so in a way unique to that situation. Thus, its reflexivity is independent of its indexicality. At the same time, each dimension affects how the other appears in any given context. The indexicality of an account endows its reflexivity with content.

Insofar as they appear as features of situations, rules, it is logical to assume, must also be accounted for by ethnomethodology. Let us, therefore, take a look at the ethnomethodological theory of rules in the light of the foregoing analysis of the features of accounts. Entering into accounts, rules ought to reveal indexicality, reflexivity, and looseness.

In view of the constructed nature of objects, the meaning of a rule is to be found within the situation in which it is applied. Consequently, the meanings of the terms of a rule vary from situation to situation; and the scope and applicability of rules are discovered within the occasions on which they are put into effect.[16] These variations make rules into indexical expressions.

How are such variations accomplished? In their research ethnomethodologists have identified a number of devices that interpret the meaning of a rule. In the first place, the meaning of a rule is elaborated in *ad hoc* ways to cover the particulars of a situation within which it is applied. The rule is "stretched" to fit the situation.[17] An example is Garfinkel's coding instructions, which the reader will recall were discussed in chapter 2. In the second place, the relevant events of a situation are reconstructed in such a way that they are made to fit the criteria of the rule. Wieder illustrates this with the example of symptoms of a disease. Rather than diagnosing the disease in terms of how its symptoms apply to a particular case, the person arrives at a diagnosis based on an imaginative reconstruction of the events that must have occurred to produce the symptom.[18] In this case the situation is reinterpreted to fit a rule rather than a rule being given an *ad hoc* interpretation to fit the facts. In the third place, those features and events of a situation that contradict a rule are ignored in order that the applicability of the rule is sustained. In the fourth place, the actions of others are explained (made accountable) by their conformity to rules that are given *ad hoc* elaborations. For example, Wieder's study of a halfway house found that staff members explained the conduct of parolees in terms consistent with the staff members' elaboration of the convict code. By giving *ad hoc* interpretations of the code, the staff arrived at inferences that linked diverse actions of inmates as following the code.[19] This method of finding the meaning of a rule also reconstructs situations to correspond to it.

These methods of interpretation illustrate not only the indexicality but also the reflexivity of accounts of rules. Take, for example, the behavior of parolees. Insofar as the staff was able to make sense of their actions as rational in terms of the convict code, such accounts furnished the bases for their orientations toward the parolees.[20] In good reflexive fashion the accounts of the staff became features of the organization they described and explained.

These commonsense methods of interpretation are illustrated in greater detail by Zimmerman's study of a public assistance agency.[11] One job of the receptionists in the agency was to assign welfare applicants to intake workers whose task was to determine their eligibility for various types of assistance. The receptionists were expected to coordinate the assignments in such a way that an orderly flow of work was maintained. In accomplishing this they were to apply a rule that assigned clients in the order of their appearance to intake workers listed on a vertical axis from top to bottom. When the worker at the bottom of column one was assigned a client, the next unassigned client was assigned to the worker at the top of the list but in column two. The implication was that this rule of top to bottom and left to right was a rational means to the end of an orderly flow of work. Despite the simplicity of this rule, it brings to light certain concepts relevant to the role of rules in general.

Zimmerman reported three instances when a receptionist suspended the rule. In the first, she assigned an applicant to an intake worker out of order because the worker designated by the rule was behind in her handling of a previous case. This caused a backlog. In the second, she permitted two clients, one of whom requested a specific worker, to switch places on the assignment list. In this instance the receptionist expressed disapproval, stating that this anomaly was not to set a precedent. In the

194   Rules and Social Order

third, receptionists routinely assigned "difficult" applicants to a specific worker known to be adept at handling such clients.

Zimmerman drew general conclusions from this study. Because of their abstract character, rules are incapable of covering every contingency. Therefore, they must be defined in terms of the occasions of their application. This "defect" cannot be rectified, said Zimmerman, by the development of informal rules to close the gap between the general and the particular. It is incorrect to invoke one rule to explain the interpretation of another.[22] In all three of the above instances the receptionists believed their decisions to deviate from the rule were justified. By temporarily suspending the rule, they were fulfilling its intent of maintaining an orderly flow of work.[23] They did not interpret these suspensions as violations but rather as actually satisfying the rule's provisions. They were prepared to defend their decisions. Thus, the value of order legitimated both the rule and its temporary abrogations. These anomalous situations cannot be theoretically interpreted, said Zimmerman, in terms of the rhetoric of compliance and deviation from norms. Any competent rule-user must construct what a rule means with reference to a larger organizational context.

Let us translate Zimmerman's account into Mead's theory of the act. The stacking up of applicants introduced a novel element, an element of conflict, in the organization's routine, which consisted of the orderly assignments of clients according to a rule. The backlog forced an innovative response to the failure of habit, a response that consisted of the suspension of the rule. Adherence to the rule would not have brought about an inadjustment of action; and therefore a self-conscious redefinition of rule in relation to situation was required. Reflective thinking carved out new objects, constructed novel meanings of the situation in order that the previous routine could be reestablished. The decisions to redefine the situation and suspend the rule were functions of the receptionists' "I's." The "me," on the other hand, was the rule itself. A logical continuity is thus apparent between Mead's theory and the ethnomethodological conception of rules.

Ethnomethodologists are fond of saying that for them rules are topics of study rather than resources (means) for explaining regularities.[24] Suspending the idea that norms account for recurrences in different situations, they therefore arrive at the conclusion that what remains is the *belief* by actors and conventional sociologists that norms are the cause of regularities. The consequence of this conclusion is that it becomes the goal of ethnomethodologists to explain this belief. Zimmerman's study illustrates this strategy. The receptionists believed that the rule of top to bottom and left to right produced an orderly flow of work. But they also believed that the suspension of that same rule in certain circumstances also maintained this order. At the same time, they held to the idea that the temporary suspensions were really not violations, but rather fulfillments of the rule. They interpreted the rule as the source of order. This, however, was really a belief in the *appearance* of order, which it had to be under the ethnomethodological assumption that rules are not the source of order. The appearance of order is an objective concept from the perspective of ethnomethodology. Zimmerman therefore set for himself the task of giving an account of the methods the receptionists used to create for themselves and others the appearance of order and the belief that it resulted from compliance with rules.

This approach to the problem of order stands in obvious contradiction to Parsons's functionalist account. For example, we cannot, according to Parsons, rely on the spontaneous decisions of automobile drivers to integrate their driving. A traffic order can be brought about only with the aid of rules, driving situations requiring a "me" rather than an "I." For Parsons, institutionalized rules of the road are objective determinants of order.

The focus of ethnomethodologists and some symbolic interactionists on the gap between rules and their context of application indicates limitations of the normative order's determinative power. Insofar as they bridge the gap, interpretations create order and are necessary because of limitations stemming from the nature of rules. The fact that the meaning of a rule is discovered in the attempts to apply it opens up the possibility of constructions other than those dictated by the rule's *a priori* meaning.

Since the creation of order occurs in situations that are normatively ordered, we can also expect individuals to create it in situations not under the jurisdiction of rules. A pervasive motive behind the creation of order in such situations evident to common sense is the rational pursuit of self-interest. But this motive also underlies conformity to rules. Thus, self-interest is directly related to social order as a constitutive factor and indirectly through its relationship to rules.

Let us, therefore, examine relevant aspects of the historic utilitarian theory, which explored this dual relationship of the rational pursuit of self-interest to social order. The reader will recall that utilitarianism constituted a second challenge to the theory of the normative order.

Bentham's Theory of Order

Jeremy Bentham (1748–1832), the leader of the utilitarian thinkers, explored the role of self-interest under the notion of *utility*. Although his thinking ramified in many directions, his primary concern was the relation between the principle of utility and law.

Bentham believed that in the uniform effects of pleasure and pain he had discovered consequences comparable to the laws of nature. He began his first great work with these words:

> Nature has placed mankind under the governance of two sovereign masters, *pain* and *pleasure*. It is for them alone to point out what we ought to do, as well as to determine what we shall do. On the one hand the standard of right and wrong, on the other the chain of causes and effects, are fastened to their throne. They govern us in all we do, in all we say, in all we think . . .[25]

Immediately after identifying the pursuit of pleasure and avoidance of pain as the wellsprings of action, Bentham translated these terms into happiness and unhappiness. Thus, the dominant tendencies in human action are the augmentation of happiness and the reduction of its opposite.[26] Although some do it with less exactitude than others, everyone calculates in order to augment his happiness.[27]

These propositions yield the famous principle of utility, which, according to Bentham, meant basically two ideas: (1) the recognition of the role of happiness in action, (2) the adoption of happiness as a criterion for the evaluation of action. With regard to the second, any action that increases to the fullest extent possible the happiness of all those whose interests are affected by it, including that of the actor himself, is positively regarded in the light of the principle of utility.[28] Later on, Bentham restated the principle in the light of the above to mean the greatest happiness for the greatest number.

Bentham therefore believed that the principle of utility not only reveals the causes of human action but also functions as the universal criterion of morality. For him the matter was obvious. Happiness is the only good, pain the only evil. And since every action is motivated to make the actor happy, no motive is intrinsically bad. It follows that insofar as an action actually brings about unhappiness, either to the individual himself or

The Construction of Order   197

others, the action is evil, despite the fact that, at the same time, the motive behind the action is good. Consequently, the moral worth of an act has to be judged strictly in terms of its effects.[29] The principle of utility is therefore a moral rule, which everyone, whether or not he recognizes it, employs as a standard of evaluation.[30] Bentham thus elevated the "is"of a law of human nature into the "ought" of a moral rule.

If utility is indeed a law of human nature, it ought to be possible to measure the quantities of various pleasures and pains and calculate their net balance. Bentham's positivism sought to carry over the precision of natural science to the science of human affairs. In order to obtain such measures, one must analyze each pleasure or pain into its various dimensions. Bentham identified four for each pleasure or pain experienced by the individual actor. First, each possesses a degree of intensity. Second, each has a duration. Third, each has a certainty or uncertainty of materializing. Fourth, each has propinquity or remoteness, i.e., how closely it follows the action producing it. Consequently, the value of a pleasure or pain produced by an act varies directly with its *intensity, duration, certainty,* and *propinquity.*[31]

An act, however, may have other consequences than the production of immediate experiences to the actor. In order to measure the values of these consequences, one must, said Bentham, take into account three other factors. The first is the *fecundity* of the action, which is the chance it has of being followed by sensations of the same kind. If the action has produced pleasure, its fecundity consists of the number of other pleasures that follow it. The second is its *purity,* which is the chance that the action is not followed by an opposite sensation. In other words, a pure act that produces pleasure is not followed by any painful consequence; neither if it is pure is a painful one succeeded by pleasurable consequences. The third factor is the *extent* of the action's impact, which is the number of others affected by it. The measurement of extent consists of the values of the six preceding dimensions of the pleasures and pains of all persons affected by the initial act.[32] Once all these pleasures and pains have been measured, it is possible to sum up their values and arrive at a net moral balance. Although Bentham conceded that putting this scheme of moral arithmetic into precise effect is not practical, nevertheless, it ought to be kept in mind as a general guide.[33] It can be thought of as a methodological type for measuring the fundamental law of human nature.

If a moral act promotes the individual's happiness, what factors prevent

198   Rules and Social Order

a person from obtaining happiness at the expense of someone else's unhappiness? Bentham identified three factors, all of which are prominent in the history of social theory. First, human nature is susceptible to benevolence, which is the pleasure one derives from being aware of another's happiness. This pleasure is sometimes called sympathy.[34] If I experience pleasure by making someone else happy, I shall promote his advantage. And if this action involves a sacrifice on my part, the other's pleasure must exceed my pain for the action to be good. The adjustment of pleasures thus brought about represents what came to be called a *sympathetic fusion of interests.*[35]

. Second, contributing to another's happiness and refraining from doing harm to someone (probity) promote the actor's happiness in a different way than sympathy. They make for good relationships with others, which everyone derives pleasure from, and a good reputation.[36] Achieving them is like placing deposits in a bank, which one can draw on in the future.[37] Consequently, again self-interest effects an adjustment of interests. These examples illustrate the principle of the *natural identity of interests.*[38]

Third, an *artificial identification of interests* comes into play when sympathetic fusion and the natural identity of interests are insufficient to achieve a total identity.[39] By adjusting interests artificially, Bentham meant bringing the activities of legislators and judges under the jurisdiction of the principle of utility to promote the greatest happiness of the greatest number.[40] Under the guidance of utilitarian theory legislators would enact laws that adjust interests in such a way that happiness would be maximized. In modern terminology, the fusion and natural and artificial identity of interests, insofar as they function the way Bentham indicated, serve to integrate action.

Let us illustrate the artificial identification of interests with Bentham's recommendations concerning penal law. The reform of law was the leading interest driving his social theory. In this context the greatest happiness for the greatest number is translated as the reduction of evil (pain) through the prevention of crimes. In order to prevent the offenses defined in law it is necessary to punish offenders. Here we are confronted, however, with the dilemma that because it inflicts pain, all punishment is evil.[41] Yet the goal of penal law according to utilitarianism is the reduction of pain. The only way to resolve the paradox is to institute punishment in such a way that it excludes an even greater evil, for a lesser evil is justifiable to prevent a greater. The immediate goal of punishment, therefore, is to prevent both the future offense of an offender

and the offenses of those who desire to imitate him.[42] The immediate
objective of criminal law is to deter crime, according to Bentham.

To achieve this objective, Bentham hoped to make punishments
proportionate to offenses. This was the fundamental principle of his
theory of crime and punishment. Accordingly, he devised specific rules
to effect this proportionality, all of which he based on the principle of
utility. The most important states, "The value of the punishment must
not be less in any case than what is sufficient to outweigh that of the
profit of the offense."[43] Profit refers to all the advantages a person reaps
or expects to reap from the offenses. Should the pain of punishment fall
below the pleasure derived from the offense, the punishment must fail in
its intention to deter. In that event, punishment would be, said Bentham,
inefficacious[44]—a result predictable from the utilitarian theory of motivation.

Bentham came forth with other rules to achieve the proportionality
between crime and punishment. A punishment should be no greater
than what is necessary to deter the offense in the future; for by causing
unnecessary pain, excessive punishment fails to produce as much happiness as possible. Another rule allows a judge to increase or decrease the
quantity of punishment to take account of varying sensibilities of offenders to pain,[45] for the same objective punishment may actually inflict
varying amounts of pain on different offenders. Other rules require that
punishments be increased to compensate for the fact that the profit of an
offense is both more certain and has greater proximity than the corresponding punishment.[46]

Bentham also applied the utilitarian principle to civil law. Take, for
example, the notion of obligation. Legal obligation, according to him, is
a service required by law. Whenever law creates a right on someone's
behalf, it creates a service obligation for someone else. For example, a
law requiring someone to come to the aid of a drowning person imposes
a service from him. Again, a legal obligation to bear arms imposes a
service for society's benefit. The principle of utility, Bentham argued,
compels any law imposing an obligation to result in a service that
produces pleasure in excess of the pain of the obligation. For obligation
is not something positive, but rather a restriction on liberty and therefore
a pain that therefore must be justified by its consequence of increasing
the sum total of happiness.[47] Of course, he who fails to fulfill his legal
obligations is subject to the punishment prescribed by penal law.

Thus, the artificial identification of interests is to be accomplished by

200   Rules and Social Order

rational methods in both civil and penal law according to the principle of utility. Providing a scientific theory of action, utilitarianism thought itself capable of guiding legislation that would have predictable results. On the assumption that every action is oriented to happiness, it is necessary only to make the consequences of certain acts painful enough to deter them. Bentham and other utilitarians thus determined to rebuild the legal order on the universal desire for happiness.

Bentham attempted to explain the existence of social order in terms of self-interest (he called it *egoism*). Even the sympathetic fusion and natural identity of interests come down in the final analysis to the actor's self-interests. Because these adjustive mechanisms are insufficient to bring about a total harmony, society is compelled to rely on law to bring it about artificially. The reason for this insufficiency is the failure of individuals to recognize the identity of their own well-being with that of others—a situation that practical utilitarianism will alleviate.

In achieving an artificial identity of interests, the legislative function is oriented to the principle of utility. According to this rational standard, laws are enacted whereby the pain of punishment exceeds the pleasure derived from the offense. Insofar as crime does not pay, interests are thereby adjusted. In theory at least, this requires that all the pleasurable and painful consequences of action be foreseen and compared through quantitative reduction given in Bentham's moral arithmetic. The law-making process is thereby subjected to a thoroughgoing rationalism; and the same motivation underlying any action, namely, self-interest, informs the act of compliance with law. People comply because deviation is not worth their while.

Bentham's attempt to model law strictly on the foundation of self-interest contrasts obviously with the concept of duty analyzed by such theorists of the normative order as Durkheim. It contrasts sharply with Durkheim's conviction that one who complies with a moral rule solely to escape punishment does not act morally; for whoever performs a moral act does not hesitate in order to calculate the utilitarian consequences. Accordingly, utilitarian advantage and moral discipline represent contradictory foundations of rules. In one case, self-interest supports the legal order; in the other, the legal order suppresses self-interest. In one case duty and self-interest coincide; in the other they diverge.

In the evolution of utilitarian thought the notion of the natural identity of interests achieved a preponderant position and reduced the emphasis Bentham placed on law.[48] Derived from the economic branch of utilitar-

The Construction of Order   201

ianism, this adjustive mechanism displaced the theory of the artificial identification of interests. The dominance of the natural harmony of interests was central to Spencer's version of utilitarian theory.

Spencer's Law of Equal Freedom

Herbert Spencer's (1820–1903) utilitarianism was more indebted to the economic branch under the leadership of Adam Smith than to the legal theories of Bentham. This will become evident below. According to Spencer, the ultimate purpose of the creation of the universe and the state of affairs toward which it is evolving is the greatest possible amount of happiness.[49] This formulation weds Bentham's principle of utility to universal progress.

The question now suggests itself: What constitutes happiness? It is, said Spencer, the satisfaction of all desires. But desires can be satisfied only through the proper exercise of the individual's relevant faculties, such as his eyes. Hence, all gratification stems from the exercise of faculties, both physical and intellectual. On the other hand, when a faculty like the stomach is not properly exercised, pain results.[50] An obvious consequence of this notion is that to be happy an individual must have the freedom to fulfill his desires by exercising his faculties. Spencer attributed this freedom to God's will.[51]

Since the purpose of creation is the greatest amount of happiness, it follows that all persons must have this freedom. However, with no limitation on anyone's freedom, individuals will inevitably clash in pursuing their respective ends. The freedom of one will interfere with the freedom of another. Therefore, we arrive at the principle that everyone may legitimately claim the fullest freedom for himself compatible with the freedom of everyone else. Spencer called this principle the *law of equal freedom*.[52] The word "equal" acknowledges that everyone has the same claim to happiness, which must be the case if progress consists of a movement toward the greatest possible happiness.

It is evident that the law of equal freedom, which Spencer thought to be a moral law, involves pain, for any restriction on anyone's effort to satisfy any desire is painful. Since the limits of our knowledge do not permit an exact calculation of the net balance of pleasure or pain in every case as Bentham claimed, all we can do in applying the law, said

202   Rules and Social Order

Spencer, is to limit the same freedoms of everyone that unduly restrict the free exercise of faculties.[53] It is better to restrict individuals too little than too much.

If everyone has the right to gratify his desires, where does the conviction that each ought to respect that right in others originate? Spencer found the answer in Adam Smith's theory of moral sentiments. According to Smith, each person possesses the faculty of sympathy, which excites in him the same feelings experienced by others. If someone feels pleasure as a result of an activity, an observer will also experience pleasure. He reacts sympathetically to the other's pleasure. In the form of sorrow or pity sympathy also extends to another's experience of pain. Consequently, when we recognize, reasoned Spencer, the pleasure of another's claim to the right to seek happiness as one we experience, we sympathize with the claim and are willing to respect it.[54] This is how sympathy upholds the law of equal freedom.

The effect of this law is increasingly evident as societies evolve from a military to an industrial organization. As militant societies assume the characteristics required by peace, the law of equal freedom finds more fertile soil in which to fulfill itself. Concomitant with the transition from the militant to the industrial type, the faculty of sympathy grows stronger in the human constitution at the expense of the predatory instincts[55]—a belief similar to Comte's belief in the growing dominance of altruistic over egoistic feelings. Thus, industrial progress is accompanied by the increasing strength of sympathy, which gives increasing support to the law of equal freedom. By another law, the *law of adaptation*, the human constitution undergoes change consistent with changes in social organization; and only after considerable adaptation is there conformity to the law of equal freedom.[56] Therefore, in accordance with the law of adaptation an increase in sympathy adapts individuals to the requirements of industrial society. The course of evolution for Spencer truly leads down the path of moral progress.

What characteristics of industrial society facilitate the law of equal freedom? Both individuation and mutual dependence increase. When everyone exercises his faculties to the fullest extent, he becomes different from everyone else. At the same time, a complex division of labor presents diverse opportunities for individual expression as industry makes available a wide range of jobs. A reciprocity obtains between the development of personal differences and the industrial division of labor, each facilitating the other.[57] At the same time, a growing interdependence among individuals accompanies individuation so that specialized activities intermesh. Industrial society thus creates a paradox: As the individual becomes different, he also becomes dependent. Separateness makes for union.[58] The happiness of each, obtained through the exercise of his faculties in a division of labor, depends on the happiness of all the others obtained in the same day. In fulfilling his function, each fulfills the functions of the larger social unit. A natural identity of interests results.[59] Thus, Spencer grounded this famous principle of utilitarian theory in the industrial division of labor.

In the light of what he thought to be the course of evolution, Spencer proceeded to determine what industrial societies *should* do. It is their first and foremost duty, Spencer emphasized, to protect the individuality of their citizens.[60] After all, if individuation is the means of happiness and happiness is the end of life, then this duty of the state follows from the utilitarian theory. How does the state do this? It protects individuality by guaranteeing justice, which Spencer defined as the preservation of the connection between acts and their results. In other words, justice requires that each receive those rewards that accrue from his own efforts; and it is the function of government to preserve justice in this sense.[61] Justice requires that no one, not even the state, deprive any person of the benefits of his own work. Here was a clear defense of *laissez-faire*. The state cannot justly adopt any policy that redistributes wealth. The only laws the state can legitimately enforce are those guaranteeing justice, and in doing so it upholds the law of equal freedom.[62]

Spencer found another justification for the limited role of the state in the interdependence of the industrial system. This interdependence produces a natural tendency for those who violate the law of equal freedom to suffer the consequences. Take, for example, the case of the tradesman who adulterates goods to increase his profit. His competitors are eventually forced to do the same, with the result that the rate of profit is eventually brought down by the entry of others into the business. Here is a deduction from a law of classical economics. In the meantime, adulteration catches on; and other businessmen do it. The consequence is that the original tradesman now suffers as a consumer.[63] With such examples Spencer made the case that up to a point the law of equal freedom is self-enforcing.

Spencer's model of industrial society incorporates the notion that social order is an ongoing construction based on self-interest. Motivated by the end of happiness, industrial man finds himself the job that best

204   Rules and Social Order

stimulates his faculties; and the mechanism that links him to an occupation is the freely formed labor contract. Voluntary decisions increasingly assume a contractual form. In this type of society the individual also gratifies himself by joining associations that reflect his interests, by purchasing commodities that suit his taste, and by exercising freedoms such as the freedom of expression. Through rational decisions he links his interests with those of everyone else. In accordance with sympathy and the natural identity of interests, it is to his well-being to promote his happiness in such a way as not to interfere with that of others. If through an irrational decision he does trample on the rights of others, the state will intervene to ensure that justice is done. With growing industrialization the function of the state shrinks to the point of purely negative regulation. It tells its citizens what they may not do rather than commanding what they must do. The consequence is that the law of equal freedom substitutes for a normative order, social order being largely the result of construction based on self-interest largely self-regulating.

Functionalist Critiques of the Utilitarian Theory of Order

The criticisms of utilitarianism were many-sided and came from a variety of sources, but here the concern is with the limitations that functional social theory detected in utilitarianism's explanation of social order. The functionalist criticisms involve the role of rules. Let us briefly examine the criticisms by Durkheim and Parsons, who adopted utilitarian notions as points of origin for their own theories.

It was to Spencer's claims that Durkheim's criticisms were mostly addressed. Durkheim noted that Spencer held that solidarity and cooperation in industrial society came about automatically as a result of the pursuit of self-interest. Everyone carries out some specialized function and thereby makes himself solidary with everyone else. Therefore, society need not intervene very much. The major connection among persons is the free exchange of services and goods for money, and the contract becomes the model for all social relationships.[64] Because of the key role Spencer attributed to the contract in adjusting interests, Durkheim examined this relationship in some detail and criticized Spencer on both empirical and theoretical grounds.

Spencer contended that as contractual relations in industrial societies increase in number the regulations of the state decline because interests become automatically adjusted through voluntary agreement. Durkheim's reply was that if one searches the historical record he will find that restitutive law (civil, constitutional, and administrative) actually grows. Take marriage as an example. In lower societies it is largely a private matter, but with the development of civilization it not only becomes hedged about with restrictions but also acquires positive injunctions from the state. In the West marriage was first regulated by the Church and then passed under the control of the state in a civil ceremony.[65] Hence, on purely empirical grounds Spencer's evolutionary theory can be criticized.

More pertinent, however, are Durkheim's theoretical grounds of criticism. Although marriage and adoption, for example, are contracts, noncontractual obligations are also involved in these relationships. This is true of any contract. When individuals form a contract, they bind themselves to obligations set by law—obligations they themselves did not originate as part of the agreement. For example, a seller may not exempt himself from making good on a hidden defect in the commodity. The law intervenes on the basis of its past experience with similar situations, defining rights and duties applying to circumstances that the contracting parties did not foresee. The rules of contract bring the past to bear on the present, which relieves the contracting parties of the necessity of having to construct everything from scratch. "Noncontractual" rights and duties, said Durkheim, are indispensable to cooperation; otherwise changing circumstances would change the interests underlying the agreement to begin with.[66] If someone borrowed money with the agreement to repay with interest at a certain date came upon an unexpected sum of money in the meantime, he would still be required to fulfill his end of the bargain. The inescapable fact here is that even a freely formed contract is not sufficient to establish cooperation without the intervention of legal rules.

Durkheim generalized about the inability of self-interest to bring about cooperation. If self-interest brings individuals together, it does so for only a few moments. Even in relationships of exchange, total harmony is only apparent, concealing latent or deferred conflicts that show up later. Consciences are not really brought together in a state of interpenetration. Where self-interest is the only factor linking individuals, they soon find themselves in a state of war.[67] Even in contractual relationships rules are

206   Rules and Social Order

needed, said Durkheim, to guarantee stability of cooperation.[68] Social order cannot be created by self-interest that replaces the normative order.

Parsons's critique of utilitarianism sustains Durkheim's conclusion that self-interest cannot generate order. With the economic side of utilitarianism in mind, Parsons charged that the theory adopted the model of a rational actor, who by using his reason figured out those means best adapted to the achievement of a given end, but failed to explain where the ends come from. As a consequence utilitarianism also failed to give an explanation of how the ends of one individual get to be integrated with the ends of others. Hence, concluded Parsons, utilitarian theory implied that ends are random. In other words, they remain unexplained.[69]

Parsons saw Hobbes as a forerunner of utilitarianism. Hobbes's model of man was the individual who rationally seeks his own interests. Since individuals in the state of nature lack any moral standards, they are not limited in their choice of means and are therefore free to use force and fraud to achieve their ends. As instruments of power, force and fraud are technically adequate to achieve private ends; and in the absence of moral restraint it is rational for everyone to acquire a plenitude of power. In this doctrine, commented Parsons, we find the logical outcome of self-interest as the sole motivating factor—a state of intermittent war. But, observed Parsons, war is not man's normal condition. It follows that Hobbes's theory lacks something typical of all theories that explain action in terms of self-interest.[70] And that something is moral rules reflecting shared values.

Parsons proceeded to analyze the limitations of Locke's theory insofar as it relates to the subject of order. Also a forerunner of utilitarianism, Locke disagreed with Hobbes's description of nature as a condition of war of all against all. Rather, there exists a natural law, discovered by reason, that forbids anyone from harming another and that requires each to respect the life, health, and property of others. Hence, in acting to obtain their ends, individuals are restricted by natural law from using force and fraud. Natural law, according to Locke, thereby provides the mechanism of integrating ends.

Also, by natural law everyone has the right to his own labor. When an individual "mixes" his labor with property, he has a right to it. He then exchanges this property for that produced by someone else's labor whereby each profits from the transaction because he receives more value than he could produce with his own labor. Exchange, therefore, and natural rights are the foundation of social order.[71] This was also the conclusion Spencer and other utilitarians arrived at. Classical economists such as Smith and Ricardo also adopted it. With natural law restraining everyone from violating others' rights to life, liberty, and property, individuals are free to form contracts to advance their interests peacefully.[72]

In criticizing Locke, Parsons identified the law of nature as an example of the natural identity of interests—a theory utilitarianism relied on for two hundred years. This theory, however, is metaphysical. Beyond scientific proof, it acts like a *deus ex machina*. The postulate of the natural identity of interests made it possible, said Parsons, for utilitarianism to avoid the problem raised by Hobbes of how order is possible. As already noted, however, the correct solution to the problem of order, according to Parsons, is the normative order. Man-made norms, not a metaphysical law of nature, are the conditions of social order. Parsons's critiques of utilitarianism in general turn out to be similar to Durkheim's criticisms of Spencer.

Utilitarianism in Homans's Exchange Theory

In building a version of what has come to be known as exchange theory,[73] George C. Homans avowed his purpose to introduce some intellectual order into the chaos of *ad hoc* generalizations drawn from commonsense experience about face-to-face behavior. The way to accomplish this is to logically deduce these generalizations from a small number of more general, higher-order propositions.[74] Although the term does not appear in Homans's formulations, these general propositions incorporate the notion of utility. And although he derived them from behavioral psychology and recognized their affinity with economics,[75] it can be shown that in some respects they converge with utilitarianism.

Homans put forth six general propositions. The first, which he calls the *success* proposition, reads as follows:

> For all actions taken by persons, the more often a particular action of a person is rewarded, the more likely the person is to perform that action.[76]

In other words, actions that achieve the interests of people are likely to be repeated. By reward, which includes food, shelter, money, and approval, Homans means a favorable result to the actor. If the action is either followed or accompanied by a consequence that is rewarding, the actor is likely to do it again. The more often, says Homans, an action has been rewarded, irrespective of the reason why it was first performed, the higher is the probability of its recurrence. In contrast, if a favorable consequence does not follow, the action is unlikely to be repeated. It is "extinguished." Homans observes that the interval of time between an action and its reward makes a difference. The shorter the interval the more likely it is to be repeated.

The second proposition, the *stimulus* proposition, relates to the effect of the circumstances upon the action. They can be thought of as causal contexts of action. It states:

> If in the past the occurrence of a particular stimulus, or set of stimuli, has been the occasion on which a person's action has been rewarded, then the more similar the present stimuli are to the past ones, the more likely the person is to perform the action, or some similar action, now.[77]

Like the success proposition, the stimulus proposition is expressed in quasi-statistical form. Had a fisherman, Homans illustrated, caught fish in a dark pool in the past, there is a high probability that he will fish in a dark pool in the future. This proposition assumes that an individual has the cognitive capacity to discriminate among stimuli and generalize from one stimulus-context to another.

Whereas the success proposition concerns the frequency of a reward obtained by an action, the third concerns the degree of its value. Thus, the *value* proposition states:

> The more valuable to a person is the result of his action, the more likely he is to perform the action.[78]

The more satisfaction an action yields, the more likely it is to recur. The greater the pleasure a past action brought to the individual, the more likely he is to act that way again. Another possible outcome implied by the proposition is that an action can result in a painful consequence to the actor. The action punishes rather than rewards. The value

The Construction of Order   209

proposition accordingly implies that the more punishing to a person is the result of his action, the less likely he is to perform it. A reward can be the avoidance of a punishment, and a punishment the withholding of a reward. Although it is impossible, says Homans, to generalize about which values individuals hold, knowledge of a person's values in particular circumstances is a good predictor of how he will act.

The possibility of punishment as the result of an action led Homans to reformulate the value proposition. Since the withdrawal of a reward is a punishment, one kind of punishment following from many actions is the reward relinquished by the impossibility of performing an alternative action. If a man goes fishing, he cannot play bridge at the same time. From economics Homans defines the reward of the best alternative that is foregone as cost. This definition leads to another, namely, profit as the excess of reward over the cost incurred. Now the value proposition is reformulated: The greater the profit a person receives from an action, the more likely is he to perform the action.[79] Here the calculus of satisfaction takes into account the comparison of alternatives.

The fourth proposition states the possibility of variation in the value of one reward on different occasions. Homans calls it the *deprivation-satiation* proposition:

> The more often in the recent past a person has received a particular reward, the less valuable any further unit of that reward becomes for him.[80]

The statement refers to the obvious fact of satiation. There is also a reverse implication that the less frequently a person has received a reward recently, the more value it will have. Hence, he will be very likely to act in order to acquire it. Food has more value for a hungry man than for one well fed. The proposition states a more general formulation of the principle of diminishing marginal utility.

The fifth, the *aggression-approval* proposition is stated in two parts:

> a. When a person's action does not receive the reward he expected, or receives punishment he did not expect, he will be angry; he becomes more likely to perform aggressive behavior, and the results of such behavior become more valuable to him.[81]
>
> b. When a person's action receives the reward he expected, especially a greater reward than he expected, or does not receive

210   Rules and Social Order

> punishment he expected, he will be pleased; he becomes more
> likely to perform approving behavior, and the results of such
> behavior become more valuable to him.[82]

An individual's expectation is determined by the rewards and punishments he did in fact receive or saw others receive in similar circumstances. If the aggression and approval as reactions to frustration and pleasure get rewarded, then these reactions, which are subject to the success and stimulus propositions, are likely to be repeated.

Finally, the sixth, the *rationality* proposition explains an individual's choice among alternative actions.

> In choosing between alternative actions, a person will choose that
> one for which, as perceived by him at the time, the value, v, of
> the result, multiplied by the probability, p, of getting the result,
> is greater.[83]

The person chooses what he believes will yield him the greatest value. Assume that he faces a choice between two actions, one of which will yield three units and the other two units of value. He estimates the probability of attaining the result in the first case as one out of four and that in the second case one out of two. Since $3 \times \frac{1}{4}$ is less than $2 \times \frac{1}{2}$, he will, if he acts rationally, choose the second. Homans points out that the rationality proposition incorporates the success, stimulus, and value propositions.

It is easy to discover in these propositions convergences with Bentham's theory of action based on utility. It is obvious from Homans's examples that reward is identical with Bentham's pleasure and punishment with pain. Therefore, the motivating factors in human action, according to Homans, are happiness and the avoidance of pain. He also agrees with Bentham that the interval of time between an action and its consequences, in Bentham's terminology the propinquity of a pleasure, has a bearing on the consequent happiness and thereby affects the probability of its recurrence. What Bentham called the "circumstances of production,"[84] which are causally related to an action, have their parallel in Homans's stimulus proposition. The value of a reward in his value proposition is readily analyzable into the intensity and duration that Bentham identified as dimensions of every pleasure and pain. Both writers expressed their theories of action in terms of the logic of probabil-

The Construction of Order   211

ity. Finally, Homans's concept of profit as the standard of choice among alternatives finds its counterpart in Bentham's famous calculation of the net balance of pleasure resulting from action. Thus, at many points Homans's propositions are translatable into the language of classical utilitarianism. In both cases human action is constructed on the basis of what the individual considers to be in his best interests.[85]

Homans tried to explain numerous generalizations about social behavior in terms of these propositions. By social behavior he meant those actions of individuals that are rewarded by other individuals with whom they are in immediate contact. As a heuristic device, he conceptualized social behavior as a relationship of exchange—one in which individuals trade rewards. He concluded that a good deal of social behavior can be so conceptualized, but certainly not all of it.[86] The concept of social behavior as consisting of exchanges of rewards gives Homans's theory another affinity with utilitarianism, especially in its economic version.

To illustrate the concept, consider Homans's example of workers in an office who are preparing reports. From time to time an inexperienced worker asks for help from one who is experienced, and the latter accedes to his request for advice. To reward him for his advice, the novice thanks him, thereby expressing approval. Approval, like money, says Homans, is a generalized reinforcer of a wide range of actions. In the above transaction we thus see an exchange of advice for approval—an exchange explicable in terms of the success, stimulus, and value propositions. For in past, similar situations, the inexperienced worker had requested information and received it. As he was rewarded, his request was successful. Here Homans also infers the stimulus proposition to be at work. Similarly, the experienced worker in his past had been rewarded for giving advice. In this office good advice rewards the request for it, and approval, in turn, rewards the rendering of it. Advice and approval had become values for the workers, which Homans concluded could be explained by the value proposition.[87] This simple exchange illustrates the formation of a relationship based on self-interest.

Homans attempted to explain other social behaviors—leadership, power, conformity, status, etc.—in terms of these propositions and exchange. Like the above example, they all illustrate the formation of relationships out of motives of self-interest. Homans, however, cautioned that the theory is not limited to a crude hedonism of materialistic values, for values that fetch rewards can be altruistic. Although the interests of someone else, they function at the same time as rewards to the actor[88]—

212   Rules and Social Order

a possibility reminiscent of utilitarianism's sympathetic fusion of interests. Experiencing pleasure in someone else's pleasure brings about an adjustment of interests.

Homans also analyzed norms in the light of his theory—an analysis that further clarifies his relationship to utilitarianism. One type of norm is established by a group that comes to the conclusion that an anticipated rule would yield a reward. Such a rule does not grow out of preexisting practice, and it is not the case of the "is" becoming an "ought." Homans illustrated it with a study of the restriction of output by workers in industry. Some workers decide what is a fair number of pieces of work to be produced in a given period. They create a work rule that limits production to what is fair with the intention of forestalling management from increasing the piecework rate. The motivation for this decision is the anticipated reward of the rule and the reason behind it. It is thought that the collective goal of the rule will outweigh in the long run the cost of foregoing higher pay by increasing production.

Homans categorized the conformers and nonconformers to the rule. One group of conformers obeyed the rule because they believed that the goal of the rule was in their interest. Another group did not believe in the norm's effectiveness but conformed in order to avoid the pressure and ostracism for noncomformity. A group of nonconformers withdrew from the group for the same reason. Another group "held out" because the rewards of nonconformity in their view outweighed the pain of the punishment inflicted by the conformers.[89] In every case the compliance or deviation was motivated by a rational calculation of the balance of rewards.

Homans distinguished a second type of norm that arises "naturally" out of the interaction among individuals. As time passes, members of a group recognize what they are doing and state it as a generalization of what ought to be done. They express this habitual behavior as a norm, which then becomes obligatory and sanctioned. What is, said Homans, is always in the process of becoming what ought to be.[90]

An example of this type is what Aristotle called *distributive justice*, which is a rule, according to Homans, followed by many persons in many societies. Even if it were not taught to the young, it would be reinvented again and again.[91] Distributive justice is a formula that determines the rewards individuals ought to receive. Consider two persons, P_1 and P_2 and two rewards, R_1 and R_2. Justice requires that their contributions (their *merit* in Aristotle's sense) express a ratio equal to that of their respective reward:

$$P_1 \qquad R_1$$
$$P_2 \qquad R_2$$

Thus, if P_1 makes twice the contribution to an exchange than P_2, he ought, if justice prevails, to receive twice the rewards (R_1) of P_2.[92]

Homans illustrated the rule with research conducted on a utility company. The ledger clerks thought they were being unjustly treated because they were being paid the same wages as the cash posters. Their duties, however, required more responsibility, which is a cost, and more seniority, which is an investment, than the duties of the cash posters. In this case reciprocity between reward and contribution called for by distributive justice was being violated.[93]

Homans further analyzed this rule in work settings. Rewards consist of what workers receive from a job, such as pay, status, and intrinsic satisfaction. The other side of the equation consists of what workers give to the job, i.e., their contributions or their "merit" measured in terms of level of responsibility, skill, and effort. This side of the equation also includes, according to Homans, the investments the person makes in the job, such as seniority and the costs incurred in making the contribution.[94] In arriving at notions of the equivalence of contributions, investments, and rewards, individuals compare themselves to others who are similar to them, to those who work in the same organization, and to those with whom they are in contact.[95]

Again we find parallels with utilitarianism; for it is evident that the rule of distributive justice is a more precise version of Spencer's law of equal freedom, and its underlying logic is typical of theories that emphasize the role of self-interest in social order. The rule of justice aims at establishing the condition that the interest of each is furthered by promoting the interests of others. According to it, the more I contribute to the end of a collectivity the more I contribute to my own interest. Consequently, interests are adjusted by the rule. Rules in general, therefore, are rational instruments for maximizing everyone's interests, one being to avoid the punishment that is a consequence of their violation.

In utilitarian thought self-interest also explains the achievement of order without rules, it being to everyone's interest to take into considera-

214   Rules and Social Order

tion the interests of others. This finds its parallel in Homans's example in which each worker had a conception of his own interest and acted on that basis and at the same time furthered the interest of the other. The exchange of advice for approval also contributed to the organization's goals. Not only were the actions of the two individuals integrated, but also the organization, all of which came about without anyone complying with a rule. The freely formed agreement, whose culmination is the legal contract, is the procedure by which interests are adjusted.

The Issue Reconsidered: Duty and Interest

In light of the preceding delineation of the issue, I conclude that normative orders must be upheld by both self-interest and moral duty. Such orders cannot be reduced to self-interest. That norms must satisfy interests if individuals are to comply is an obvious fact. Not so obvious, however, is the necessity of duty.

In order to maintain its legitimacy a rule must fulfill two criteria. First, its implementation must achieve its intended end; and how well it does so has an obvious bearing on the satisfaction of interests. That is, a rule must satisfy the criterion of substantive rationality. Second, it must originate in legal procedures. That is, it must satisfy the criterion of legality.

Although there are variations, it is obvious that rules are rarely totally rational, but rather fall short of their intended goals and culminate in unforeseen consequences whose costs often prove to be unacceptable.[96] Thus, to some degree they always fail the test of rationality and become vulnerable to a denial of their legitimacy. One limitation on their rationality is the difficulty of comparing the interests relevant to a rule in order to determine a net balance of advantages. In the language of Bentham this presupposes a comparison of pleasures and pains. But in the absence of a single universal standard, who can really be certain, as Bentham thought he was, that even in the case of a criminal act that the damage to the interests of the victim exceeds the gain to the offender as measured in terms of his interests? Imperfect understanding of how a rule will affect relevant interests makes it difficult to establish on purely rational grounds. Thus, the logical difficulty of the commensurability of values restricts the objective rationality of rules.

The Construction of Order   215

Even if we grant the assumption in any given case of unanimous agreement about a given norm and that the value of the interests served has been accurately calculated, as Durkheim pointed out, interests have a way of changing. And changing values of the interests involved hinder the prediction of results throughout the course of a project.

Chapter 9 further explores factors that limit rationality, but at this point we emphasize the irrationalities involved in the calculation of interests that lay the groundwork for moral commitment as a foundation of normative orders. For if rules are vulnerable to deficiencies on rational grounds, their survival requires another factor of justification. This factor is moral commitment. Obedience to the authority of rules is moral. Consequently, alongside of rationally sought ends that satisfy interests, moral duty rises to the occasion as a stabilizing factor in normative orders.

Consider the case of distributive justice, which, if we are to believe Homans, prevails widely as a sanctioned ideal and a formula for devising policies and norms. Homans correctly pointed out that disagreements invariably arise concerning the interpretation of merit, the weights of qualitatively different contributions, and what constitutes a reward, all of which are ultimately defined by a comparison of qualitative interests. In his analysis of the study of cash posters and ledger clerks, Homans pointed out that the managers, who failed to regard job autonomy as a reward, periodically would transfer the clerks to cash posting when the posters fell behind. They did not believe they were acting unjustly. But the clerks, who defined job autonomy as a reward, thought the transfers violated justice.[97] Differences in interpretation of values restricted the rationality of the formula calling for equivalence between reward and contribution.

The problem is compounded in the interpretation of entire normative orders. According to Parsons, a normative order tends toward pattern-consistency, its values forming a logically consistent, integrated system. At a lower level of generality, norms specify these values into roles. If the specification of a value is analogous to the interpretation of the terms of a norm, then it follows that value specifications will yield contradictory norms. The incommensurability of interests destroys the unifying effect of the underlying values in normative orders, just as they impair the homogenizing effect of norms on actions in roles.

In the light of these considerations it is realistic to conceive of rules as ideal-types, their terms, ends, underlying interests and values being

216 Rules and Social Order

constructs from which the orientations of those who think about them diverge. Therefore, the subjective orientations of those who follow rules and those who evaluate the compliance of others *must* diverge from a given rule. It follows that, insofar as interpretations enter into the contexts of their application, rules are bound to exist in a state of tension with the latter. This renders their outcomes problematical.

If moral commitment to rules is necessary to compensate for unavoidable irrationalities in the calculation and fulfillment of interests, the question arises as to its source. Why do individuals believe it is right to comply with a rule even when they cannot legitimate it solely in rational terms? The answer is to be found in the rule's legality. The sense of duty, which Durkheim defined as the willingness to obey without calculation of self-interest, is aroused by the belief that the enactment of a law conformed to procedural norms. Thus, the principle of legality furnishes a moral foundation of the normative orders of the state and other organizations.

The antinomies we have been analyzing are captured in terms of Weber's types of social action. Whereas the orientation to a rule in terms of its rationality is expressible in terms of Weber's ideal-type of purposive rationality *(Zweckrationalität)*, the orientation to a rule as an object of moral duty is captured by his ideal-type of value-rationality *(Wertrationalität)*. According to the former, the rationality of a rule is determined in terms of the clarity of its end, its effectiveness as a means to its end, and an evaluation of its secondary consequences. According to the latter, a rule is evaluated as an end in itself, compliance regarded as inherently right because of its legality. Legality elevates compliance into an absolute.

It is quite evident that these types of orientation to rules are contradictions. For if one holds it as an absolute duty to obey a law because it is legal, he does not base his action on an evaluation of its consequences with reference to his interests. On the other hand, the sole justification in terms of its consequences for various interests locates a rule strictly in the realm of the pragmatic. However, reality, as Weber pointed out, cannot readily be filtered into the terms of a type. Subjective orientations of particular individuals toward norms are constituted by varying mixtures of these dimensions, the distribution of which influences the empirical validity of a normative order. Consequently, morality and rational expediency combine to uphold the validity of rules.

The decline of religion as a support for tradition raises the question: How does legality compare with religion in producing commitment to moral duty? Let us rephrase the question more specifically with reference to distributive justice: Can a law incorporating this kind of justice generate the same level of commitment based on its legality as does the belief that there is a god who enforces justice through compensation in the afterlife? Under the assumption that secularization will continue to grow, the answer to these questions has a bearing on the future stability of normative orders. The questions imply the larger problem addressed by Comte and Durkheim in their attempts to build a science of morality.

In discussing social order, we have limited the considerations primarily to rules and how they are related to several other factors, the most important of which is self-interest. Order, however, can result from other factors, one being power. Also, it is obvious that rules depend on some degree of consensus—a fact that the preceding discussion merely took for granted. These two factors—power and consensus—are addressed in the following chapters as central to the controversy over consensus and conflict—an issue that is also closely related to the problem of order. In addition, as will be shown, legality and the substantive rationality of law also link the two issues.

PART FOUR

The Duality of
Consensus and Conflict

Consensus

It is fashionable to trace the origin of the consensus-conflict debate to a reaction in the 1950s against what some sociologists thought was an overemphasis by Talcott Parsons on the role of value-consensus in the social system. Some critics believed that Parsons had created a utopia rather than a model useful for scientific purposes largely because his theory depicted society as organized around a system of values maintained as an unrealistic consensus. Although it is true that the issue was raised to the level of debate recently, its various dimensions have appeared again and again in diverse contexts throughout the history of social thought. One can easily, for instance, recognize in the *Republic* Plato's concern with guarding the city-state against the ravages of conflict within the ruling class through a unity of outlook among its members.

The issue has struck the sociological imagination, for it involves factors that social theorists have long found to be of central interest in the study of societies. Stratification, power, authority, legitimacy, ideology, and change are important notions within the conceptual arsenal of sociology, but at the same time are relevant to matters of more practical interest such as the foundations of democratic and totalitarian regimes. In its wider ramifications, consensus and conflict are also relevant to the possibilities and constraints inherent within symbolic communication, where misunderstandings leading to conflict are possible.

This chapter and the one that follows do not reconstruct the history of

222   The Duality of Consensus and Conflict

this debate,[1] but rather examine the issue within the context of those social theories most affected. Many divergencies between functionalism and conflict theory can be shown to stem from the different emphases, both implicit and explicit, given to consensus and conflict with regard to the roles they play in the social order. Each of these factors functions as a criterion of relevance that selects other factors that go into a theory, with the result that lines of selectivity result in contradictory representations of society. Viewed in the light of functionalism and conflict theory, the issue in the final analysis comes down to which of the two models constructed on the foundations of these antithetical factors provides the closest fit to real societies.

The following discussion of the consensual foundations of functional theory is limited to the relevant formulations of Durkheim and Parsons. Although functionalism is the product of many contributors, they will be regarded as exemplars. As noted in previous chapters, the work of Parsons stands at the confluence of streams of functional concepts. At the same time, the concept of consensus is not exhausted by the body of functionalist theory; for functionalism takes communication for granted without providing an explanation of it. Therefore, I shall pay some attention to the relation of consensus to communication as worked out by Mead and Schutz, who stood within different theoretical traditions.

Collective Conscience and Representation in Durkheim

As we have seen in chapter 5, Durkheim held the end of a moral act to be the preservation of society. A moral action follows a rule that furthers the interest of society rather than that of the actor. Since moral rules are widely shared by members of a society, he drew the logical conclusion that the existence of society depends upon a moral consensus. That consensus is a necessary condition of social order is essentially the conclusion that Auguste Comte had already reached.[2] The idea that moral consensus is a necessary condition of social order is a postulate of functional social theory.

This postulate, however, is only the beginning of a more detailed analysis by Durkheim. Consensus is implied in his celebrated concept of the *conscience collective;* without the former the latter makes no sense. Composed of the totality of beliefs and sentiments common to average citizens of the same society,[3] the collective conscience is a source of the solidarity that makes them want to associate. The mechanical solidarity of the *conscience collective* is given by the formula that like attracts like; and, said Durkheim, everyone "knows that we like those who resemble us."[4] The resemblances he had in mind are not physical, but rather the similarities of thoughts and feelings. In other words, individuals like those who think and feel the way they do; and liking them they want to associate with them. Birds of a feather flock together. These similarities constitute a nearly total consensus in any given society and bring its members into relationships with one another.

The beliefs of the *conscience collective* are reflected in rules, whose violations are regarded as crimes and severely punished. Thus, the belief in the sanctity of the person finds its expression in the law against homicide. Such laws, said Durkheim, are so firmly implanted in the consciences of citizens, who expect everyone to know them, that any adult not sharing the underlying beliefs is considered to be pathological.[5] The different is identified with the abnormal.

These collective beliefs are so important to the integrity of individuals that they must be vigorously defended against challenges. Any belief that contradicts a collective belief acts like a disease that corrupts the individual. Causing psychic disorders, the offending belief upsets his equilibrium by colliding with the collective conscience. Contrary beliefs enfeeble collective beliefs. To protect the latter, the invader must be countered; and that is why society turns upon a person with offending beliefs with such hostility. Not only do the hostile reactions of the group defend the collective conscience against challenge, but the denial of its contraries through the act of punishment strengthens it.[6]

On the positive side, mutual affirmation of a collective belief by like-minded persons also strengthens the *conscience collective*—an effect that becomes more intense in large assemblies. In crowds the expressions of a sentiment can even reach the level of violence through mutual repercussions in the consciences of all. When someone asserts an idea that we accept, it superimposes itself upon our own belief, becomes fused with it, and reinforces its vitality. In large numbers these effects of mutual expression are compounded.[7]

One can elicit in Durkheim's analysis of the collective conscience the following formula: A collective belief is doubly maintained by a collective

224   The Duality of Consensus and Conflict

reaction against the expression of that which denies it and by a collective affirmation of it. The former underlies his theory of crime and punishment, and the latter his theory of religious ritual. This formula contains the seeds of equilibration and the pattern-maintenance and integrative functions identified by Parsons, for the collective conscience maintains itself and at the same time is a basis of solidarity and stability. Stable equilibrium, said Durkheim, depends upon consent.[8]

Durkheim went on to generalize that with the growth of the division of labor, the number of shared beliefs declines as individuals assume differentiated roles. However, this lessening of mechanical solidarity is accompanied by a growing organic solidarity that derives from functional interdependence. The *conscience collective* grows progressively indeterminate and less intense in its effects as the number of collective beliefs declines.[9] The solidarity accruing from consensus is partially replaced by another type.

In his classic study of suicide, Durkheim differentiated the concept of the *conscience collective* into various types of beliefs that he called *collective representations*; and much of his later work was devoted to an explication of them. In a previous chapter we noted that his research turned up statistics purporting to show that suicide was more prevalent among Protestants than Catholics and Jews; less prevalent among the married than the single, widowed, and divorced; and more prevalent during periods of political stability than during political crises like wars.

It can be demonstrated that a consensus of beliefs is a decisive factor in explaining the religious differences in inclinations to self-destruction. Why do Protestants under a variety of different circumstances commit suicide more frequently than Catholics and Jews? As we have seen, Protestants experience higher rates of egoistic suicide because their religious organizations are less integrated than Catholicism and Judaism. They are less integrated insofar as they impose fewer doctrinal beliefs upon their members. Traditional Christian beliefs (collective representations) have come under greater criticism within Protestantism than within Catholicism, for the Protestant is given greater encouragement to interpret his religious creed for himself. The cult of individualism has made greater inroads among Protestants. Like Catholicism, Judaism has also been better able to maintain the authority of its religious codes. Facing a threatening environment, it has maintained its doctrinal unity as a defensive posture. Hence, the latter two religions are more integrated than the former.[10]

Consensus   225

This explanation is one case at the basis of the larger generalization Durkheim drew that egoistic suicide varies inversely with integration. The proposition states a causal relationship: Declining integration is the cause of rising egoistic suicide. Furthermore, the integration of a group stems, according to Durkheim, from both the number and strength of its collective beliefs and practices.[11] On the other hand, integration is not to be found in the content of beliefs; the criteria of integration are formal rather than substantive. It is apparent that the integration Durkheim saw operating turns out to be the mechanical solidarity stemming from the collective conscience. The greater the vitality of a society's collective conscience, the greater is its integration and its resistance to egoistic suicide. Moreover, the greater the integration that decreases vulnerability to egoistic suicide, the greater the consensus of a group. Consequently, consensus acts as a guard against the pathology of high rates of egoistic suicide.[12] The large number of resemblances among Catholics and Jews increases their power of attraction.

Thus, it is not simply beliefs that integrate a group, but shared beliefs, i.e., collective representations. Durkheim's explanations of variations in suicide illustrate a general significance of consensus, which is characteristic of functional social theory. More than merely an organism, man has needs that transcend the purely physical ones so necessary for physical survival. He pursues religious, moral, political, and artistic ends. These supraphysical needs attach him to life beyond the purely physical and give him purposes for which to live. For example, the belief that God exists results in the need for the individual to participate in religious ritual. Collective representations originate in society, incarnate themselves within the individual, and serve the purposes of society. In the service of society, they endow the individual with purposes beyond himself. And when these collective representations lose their hold over him, the individual loses his reason for existence. When life is not worth living, any occasion becomes a pretext to leave it. Purely private beliefs, individual representations, that is, devised by the individual are not sufficient. That is why the cult of individualism leads to self-destruction. Thus, inasmuch as life-sustaining beliefs are collective, it is consensus that maintains the will to live. The greater the consensus, the stronger and more numerous the collective representations, the greater their preservative value.[13]

Durkheim went on to explain the role of other types of collective representations. These include the very categories of thought, such as space, time, number, class, and cause. Unlike religious creeds, the categories of understanding are fundamental to cognition itself. They underlie all other representations, for it is impossible to represent any thing or event without locating it in space and time and without representing it as a number.[14] The categories of thought include the universal properties of things. They too are produced in the mind of society, its morphology and institutions; and like religious beliefs and moral rules, they inhere in society itself. Society's very existence depends upon a logical consensus; for unless individuals possess similar conceptions of time, space, number, and class, they cannot understand one another. And if unable to understand one another, they will not associate.[15]

Durkheim surmised that, being collective representations, the categories should vary among societies, and that is precisely what he found in his studies of primitive societies. Take, for example, the category of class. All societies place objects within systems of classifications. The simplest case is illustrated by Australian tribes, each of which is divided into moieties. This bipartite classification of tribesmen is reflected in a bipartite division of nature: Objects such as sun, moon, stars, animals, and plants are put into one of two classes called by the same names as the moieties.[16] More complex classifications consist of inclusions of classes within others to form relationships of hierarchy. Whatever the system, however, the classifications applied to nature were derived from those applied to society.

Such categories are also concepts. To be sure, they are superordinate concepts that "dominate" and "envelop" all others. To have a concept of America, for instance, implies the concept of class, which distinguishes Americans from other classes of people. But the categories of thought are not the sole concepts. Concepts are what individuals in everyday life think in terms of. They are more stable thought formations than sensations and perceptions. They need not be very general, for we develop concepts of the characteristics of particular persons we know. Not only are concepts the content of thought, but they are also expressed in language. The ordinary words we use are concepts. As collective representations linguistic concepts have their origin in society. Thus, the same content is the basis of both thought and communication, the latter, according to Durkheim, consisting of an exchange of concepts whose unique role is to achieve a harmony of minds.[17]

The harmony of minds leads us back to mechanical solidarity. If the totality of beliefs and sentiments common to average citizens of the same society drives them to interact because like attracts like, then the categories of understanding and linguistic concepts contribute to solidarity. They help to form similitudes of belief and sentiment. At the same time, category and concept belong to the *conscience collective* and are derivatives of society. Consequently, the social consensus possesses the capability of self-expansion, for linguistic concepts increase the totality of belief and sentiment held in common.

The ideal is another type of collective representation. The value of anything is estimated, said Durkheim, in terms of its relation to an ideal. The negative evaluation of criminal assault, for example, is determined by both the intensity and strength of the idea of human dignity. Indeed, statistics of crime are an empirical indicator of the strength of that ideal. In the same way, the number of divorces, separations, and adulteries is an index of the conjugal ideal. Consequently, value-systems are generated by ideals, the former determined by the latter insofar as values embody ideals. Yet, argued Durkheim, since ideals vary among societies, it is once again obvious that they are collective representations originating in society. Reflecting ideals, values express a reality which is society itself.[18]

In times of great collective ferment and enthusiasm society forms its ideals. Products of collective excitement are illustrated by the Scholasticism of the twelfth and thirteenth centuries, the Reformation, the Renaissance, and nineteenth-century Socialism. During periods of collective effervescence, great ideals capture the mind, but only for brief periods; for no one can stand to be so completely dominated for long. Ideals then become memories; however, their power to dominate is periodically reviewed and renewed during religious or secular ceremonies. During these occasions reality moves closer to society's ideal.[19]

On such occasions of collective excitement, we observe Durkheim's principle of *collective affirmation*. The public expression of values reinforces them and intensifies them as commitments; and each, aware that a great number of others cherish the same ideals, gets caught up in the enthusiasm. An intense bond of mechanical solidarity is formed as individuals become conscious of their resemblances with a great many others. The principle of like attracts like manifests in an intense form.

Although the term *consensus* appears rarely in Durkheim's work, it lurks like an ever-present force not far below the surface. It is implicit in his explanations and concepts, especially in the word *collective*. A great

228   The Duality of Consensus and Conflict

force that binds individuals together, attaching them to one another and to society, is the solidarity that comes from the similarity of beliefs. The greater the number of similitudes of belief and the larger the proportion of social life regulated by them, the greater the cohesion. People seek out those with whom they have things in common and whose thoughts and actions run in similar channels. These similarities result from the imposition by society of its collective representations upon its members. The consensual nature of collective representations goes directly to the reality of society, which is the source of unity among individuals; and Durkheim never tired of reminding us that society is their source. Collective representations make it possible for people to live. They provide purposes that attach the individual to life, concepts with which he cognizes his world, and words with which he communicates. Routine processes familiar to everyone depend upon the concordance of minds fostered by collective representations.

Consensus in the Social System

Parsons incorporated Durkheim's collective representations into his theoretical formulations although he did not use the term. He had the members of the ideal-typically conceived social system sharing values, norms, beliefs, and language, but worked out the interrelationships among these factors more systematically than Durkheim. By tracing the roles they play within the social system, we can arrive at a more detailed understanding of the functions of consensus than Durkheim left us with.

THE DYAD

Considered as an ideal-type, the *dyad* consists of the interaction between two hypothetical actors, whom Parsons designated as *ego* and *alter*.[20] Parsons's basic premise is that for them to interact in an orderly way, i.e., for each to obtain gratification of his needs, they must come to agree about what the objects in their mutual situation mean. In other words, they must arrive at a consensus of definitions. The reason why obtaining a consensus is a problem is that because of his unsurpassed mental capabilities the human being is able to define a given object in many

Consensus   229

different ways. For ego and alter to agree, therefore, they are compelled to choose a congruent set of definitions from an infinity of possibilities. In order for them to cooperate in relation to a chair, for example, they must agree as to what a chair means.

They can either arrive at a consensus of definitions during the course of their interaction or bring to the situation a preestablished consensus. Especially in the case of the former does language, which is itself a set of shared meanings, play a crucial role. In either case, the consensual meanings of objects function, according to Parsons, as a cultural system that guides their actions toward each other. The notion of consensus thus contributes to the definition of culture as a scientific concept in Parsons's theory. Having a culture, ego and alter now know what to expect from each other. Their interaction becomes predictable and stable.

The cultural system is differentiated with regard to problems inherent in their situation. Some cultural standards apply to their external situation, others to the personalities of ego and alter. With regard to the external situation, shared standards define the cognitive nature of objects. Is this object large or small, heavy or light? Cognitive cultural standards yield the answers. With regard to the personalities of ego and alter, other standards define how objects in the external situation relate to their interests. Will this object gratify or frustrate ego's need? Appreciative cultural standards help them arrive at an answer. When they are in doubt about which cognitive and appreciative standards to use to establish meanings, the cultural system provides moral standards to evaluate them. These ensure that the cognitive and appreciative standards chosen will be compatible with the requirements of the interaction. In other words, these moral standards, such as the pattern variables, as we have seen, integrate the social system.

Having analyzed cultural standards into these types, Parsons went on to differentiate them "vertically." A standard (value-orientation) is differentiated into values and norms. Thus, there are cognitive values and norms, etc. The role played by these elements has been discussed in detail in chapter 5. The point to be emphasized here is that these units of culture and society are consensual according to Parsons's model of the social system. In the ideal-type the consensus is total. Furthermore, consensus underlies the entire normative order. Consequently, what we have called the normative determinism in Parsons's theory depends upon and presupposes the factor of consensus.

It is evident that cultural values in his theory correspond to Durkheim's

230 The Duality of Consensus and Conflict

conscience collective as the source of society's mechanical solidarity and norms generate the organic solidarity identified by Durkheim. In addition, feelings of solidarity obtain between ego and alter according to Durkheim's formula that like attracts like.

For the sake of order, the social system motivates its members to internalize its cultural codes, thereby perpetuating consensus. Here is Parsons's equivalent of Durkheim's theory that society incarnates itself in its members. Internalization has as a consequence the desire of the individual to orient himself to cultural standards willingly, even at the cost of sacrificing other of his interests. When ego and alter so orient themselves to gratify their needs to comply with as well as to fulfill the requirements of society, a cultural standard, in Parsons's terminology, has become institutionalized. Consensus is thus maintained both by personality need and social requirement and at the same time brings about solidarity.

INSTRUMENTAL ACTIVISM IN AMERICA

Armed with the concept of *consensual values*, Parsons attempted to delineate the core values of American society. If both dyad and society are social systems, then it should be possible to generalize from one to the other. Consequently, a society, which is a relatively self-contained, autonomous system, must incorporate within its structure a central system of values. Further, to the extent that a particular society is integrated, all the values institutionalized in its parts must be congruent with this core system. In modern society, especially America, Parsons thought he found such a value-system, which he referred to as *instrumental activism*.[21]

Instrumental activism prescribes the absolute desirability of America to impose an active mastery over its environments—its physical environment, other societies, and the personalities of Americans. Mastery over personality is a form of asceticism, which calls upon each individual to subordinate his need to objective tasks and submit to universalistic standards of judgments. The occupational sector, the world of work, is the arena in which this ethic of mastery is followed. Asceticism calls for the achievement of difficult goals as an intrinsic value and not merely as a means to some other end. A pluralism of worthy goals, to be achieved in science, industry, art, and the professions, translates the ideal of progress. Goal attainment must result from disciplined effort.

Achievement is that of individuals, not collectivities, which serve merely as contexts for the former. The importance of individuals, according to Parsons, corresponds to the individualistic trend in American culture, which militates against the promotion of the welfare of collectivities as an end in itself.[22] "Institutionalized individualism" accounts for commitment to freedom and equality.[23] Instrumental activism views organizations and authority through a pragmatic lens; these are expected to justify themselves strictly as means to the achievements of individuals. Parsons's compact characterization assimilates traditional American ideals to the abstract notion of instrumental activism.

Instrumental activism itself explains other institutions. It legitimates, for instance, the family, whose function is to transmit this value-system to forthcoming generations. It also legitimates the university, whose function is to create the knowledge upon which high achievement depends. Overall, this value-system is institutionalized in diverse contexts and its consequences evidenced in unlikely ways ranging from the free market to the tenure system in universities.

Instrumental activism was spawned by and continues to be grounded in a complex of religious ideas that may be summed up by the phrase the "liberalization of Calvinism."[24] Following Weber, Parsons held that Calvin's doctrine of predestination was transmuted into the assumption that an individual's moral worth could be interpreted as a sign that that individual had been selected by the Lord for salvation. On the other hand, an evil life could be construed as a sign of his damnation.

What is the moral life? Such a life is devoted to the ascetic practice of a secular occupation as a calling. The moral elect compose an invisible church, a holy community destined by the Lord to bring into existence by human agency His Kingdom on earth. Here we find the activism in instrumental activism. Originally in Calvinism there were collectivist and individualist themes, but it was the latter, said Parsons, that eventually predominated in America.

Tracing the development of Calvinism in North America, Parsons found a number of modifications in a liberal direction. The individualism in the doctrine, namely, that each person in his own right stands before God's judgment, became institutionalized as an orientation within the world of work. The holy community, appearing in New England and Virginia, gradually became consolidated as the nation-state under God, whose building was to be the product of individual achievement. As the original emphasis on predestination grew weaker, the radical elitism of

232   The Duality of Consensus and Conflict

Calvinism declined; for a strict dichotomy of citizens into elect and damned was incompatible with a democratic value-system. The abandonment of predestination, however, did not destroy religious commitment, which was sustained by faith. The invisible church became a communion of souls in faith.

These doctrinal liberalizations on American soil were accompanied by separation of church from state and by denominational pluralism. Religious toleration was even written into the United States Constitution. These ideas and structures proved to have an astonishing capacity to include generations of Catholic immigrants within the nation-state, for all who lived under the God of Israel and Jesus Christ were eligible to become members of the holy community.

The inclusion of non-Protestants in the American community through pluralism and toleration reveals a consensus of form that permits a diversity of substance. Although variations in belief, ritual, and ecclesiastical organization are to be found in the many churches, there is broad agreement among Americans on the idea of live and let live. Pluralism and religious tolerance are purely formal principles which generate in a kind of dialectical fashion the very differences in substance that they are willing to accept, containing diversity within an overall context of unity. Toleration incorporates a consensus of form that limits conflict. Yet, if we are to believe Durkheim, live and let live does not result in the mechanical solidarity that stems from a genuine similitude of beliefs and sentiments.

RELIGION IN THE SOCIAL SYSTEM

Parsons's analysis of the relation between Calvinism and instrumental activism reflects a general theory about the relationship between religion and social system. The culture of every society is grounded in a world view, some general conception of the human condition, which legitimates its standards. What better reason is there for accepting a rule than the fact that it was instituted by God? As an ultimate frame of reference, a world view is the "limit of the intelligible"[25] for interpretation of norms. The meanings of the cultural tradition are consequently grounded in general, ultimate meanings of a philosophical-religious system of beliefs.[26]

Of special importance is the relationship of these beliefs to the moral standards, for morality finds its origin in religion. Religious beliefs synthesize existential assertions beyond scientific proof about the nature of the world with value-commitments to certain kinds of action within it.[27] One example is Calvin's God, who created the world as His vineyard that man is to cultivate in accordance with an ascetic ideal. At the level of religious thought, cognition, cathexis (interest), and evaluation (moral choice) merge to form a matrix for cultural meanings at more specific levels.[28] In light of their formative function for the cultural tradition, Parsons labeled religious beliefs *constitutive symbolism*.[29]

Religious beliefs in the social system are consensual. With Durkheim's study of Australian totemism before him, Parsons corroborated the role of religious ritual in creating and maintaining solidarity.[30] Those who share religious beliefs and rituals comprise a moral community, and the interaction between common ritual and shared belief augments the cohesion stemming from each.

EQUILIBRIUM

The social system, therefore, is organized around a normative order legitimated by a philosophical-religious world view. Insofar as the system depends on a concordance of beliefs, values, and norms, it must, argued Parsons, incorporate mechanisms that maintain consensus. The search for these mechanisms leads directly to equilibrium.

A system in stable equilibrium is one in which deviations from a given state of it are counteracted such that the original state is restored. Equilibrium gives the system the capacity to maintain itself. The state of the system Parsons identified as the focus of equilibrium is its normative culture—its institutionalized values and norms. Insofar, therefore, as a social system remains in static equilibrium, its normative commitments are maintained.[31] Taking the dyad as the simplest social system, Parsons drew the generalization that the first law of social process is the maintenance of the complementary of ego's and alter's expectations.[32] Ego and alter tend to continue to follow the norms that regulate them once those norms have been established. In other words, so long as the first law of social process holds, equilibrating factors need not come into play.

There are, however, two kinds of factors that threaten equilibrium whose nullification reestablishes equilibrium. First, there is the necessity that before an actor can play his role the way others expect him to, he

234   The Duality of Consensus and Conflict

must learn how; for before learning a role, he is bound to act in ways that deviate from expectations. Therefore, the first great mechanism of equilibrium is *socialization*—a process that includes both learning how to fulfill a role as well as acquiring the desire to fulfill it. Socialization of actors into their roles, moreover, is not a process done once and for all, but continues in response to changes in the situations in which roles are played.[33]

The second kind of factor that tends to disrupt equilibrium is changes that continually occur in the actor's personality that diminish his motivation to conform. These changes lead him to deviate. Factors that forestall an individual with inclinations to deviate from actually deviating and those that return him to the path of conformity once he has deviated from a norm are mechanisms of *social control*. They are *equilibrating mechanisms*.[34] According to Parsons, the most fundamental mechanism of control is the sanctions inherent in interaction itself. When ego fulfills his obligations, alter rewards him with approval; and when he fails in these, alter punishes him with disapproval. In that case alter also fails to conform to what is expected of him; and this failure of alter to play his role frustrates ego's attainment of his own goal. Mutual frustration is a consequence of the fact that interaction is a form of cooperation in a division of labor in which each actor depends on the other.[35]

Should ego fail to comply with standards, alter expresses disapproval. Although alter may point out to ego the advantages of conformity or provide some support so as not to drive him "beyond the pale," alter lets him know that he is "out of line." Diffuse forms of punishment in everyday interaction include the expression of overt disapproval, the embarrassed silence, and the failure to fulfill reciprocal obligations. Formal punishment of criminal acts through legal isolation of the criminal reinforces in the minds of others the beliefs and sentiments that support the law. At this point Parsons identified Durkheim's theory of crime and punishment as indicating an equilibrating mechanism.[36] Other such mechanisms Parsons discussed include psychotherapy, rituals of bereavement, and safety-valve mechanisms.

Socialization and control, therefore, are the mechanisms that tend to maintain the static equilibrium of the social system. It follows that for American society as a whole these equilibrating processes insofar as they are effective defend the theme of instrumental activism from erosion. In upholding values and norms, they perpetuate normative consensus; for it is agreement about these that gives the system its structure and distin-

Consensus   235

guishes it from other social systems and from the personalities of its members. In this sense socialization and social control maintain the boundaries of the social system. What gives the latter a structure distinct from personalities is its normative culture, which is a unity by virtue of the fact that it is consensual.

Parsons cautioned, however, that in any particular system of interaction, i.e., the "real world," processes that reestablish equilibrium are only a tendency. Integration of motivation with shared standards is incomplete, and equilibrium merely limits the consequences of deviant motivation.[37] Some anomie is always present.

Static equilibrium is only one possibility, for equilibrium can be a moving (dynamic) one. A social system in moving equilibrium institutionalizes the value of change in a given area.[38] Here the norms prescribe a certain kind of change, with the result that actors who play their roles properly bring about change. One example is the community of scientists, which institutionalizes the accumulation of knowledge. The growth of cognitive knowledge may invalidate existing knowledge and cause conflict; however, its growth is expected, predictable, and orderly. Another example of moving equilibrium is the relationship between parent and child, for a changing relationship involving such things as authority and responsibility is expected. Change in a moving equilibrium is an orderly process as the system reaches one equilibrium after another. Like static equilibrium, moving equilibrium expresses a value-consensus.[39]

POWER AND POLITY

Parsons's theory of the modern state grows logically out of the matrix of the interaction within the dyad. If society is a social system writ large, then its basic processes ought to be detectable in a dyad. Both society and small groups engage in political processes. Although ego and alter make choices with the aid of cultural models brought forward from other contexts and developed over the course of their interaction, their relationship is not spun out from a total cultural determinism. In order to cooperate, they must continually choose their collective goals, although, to be sure, these are compatible with the relevant appreciative and moral norms. Likewise, the larger society must continually define its collective goals in accordance with its values and norms.

Parsons's political theory attempts to explain how the polity (the state)

236   The Duality of Consensus and Conflict

carries out the goal-attainment (G) function for society. Typical collective goals defined by modern polities are the maintenance of internal order, protection of territorial integrity, and the administration of welfare.[40] The structures of the polity that carry out these activities are the executive-administrative, legislative, and judicial bodies. In explaining how the polity defines collective goals and mobilizes the means to achieve them, Parsons analyzed the role of such classical political factors as authority, power, the franchise, leadership, and electorate. The democratic political system assumes the existence of consensus, and Parsons attempted to explain how consensus about goals is formed. His functional political theory contrasts sharply with that conceived by the conflict tradition.

To carry out the G function, the polity must have *authority* and exercise *power* on a routine basis. Political authority is the right of those in certain positions to exercise leadership and to exert over members of society those controls necessary for the achievement of collective goals.[41] Vested in political offices, it is the legitimate right of incumbents to fulfill their duties. Power, on the other hand, is identified as the actual decisions made in the fulfillment of political duties. It is the actual exercise of authority. Authority is the static element of position, whereas power is the dynamic element of role. Parsons set forth a more detailed definition of power as follows:

> Power, then, is generalized capacity to secure the performance of binding obligations by units in a system of collective organization when the obligations are legitimized with reference to their bearing on collective goals and where in case of a recalcitrance there is a presumption of enforcement by negative situational sanctions—whatever the actual agency of that enforcement.[42]

This rather lengthy definition incorporates a number of somewhat diverse elements. First, it states exactly what power accomplishes, namely, the obtainment of the cooperation of citizens for the achievement of the goals established by the polity. Second, having the capacity to assemble resources to achieve a variety of goals, power is generalized. Third, the obligations that power secures, such as registering for a draft, are legitimate with reference to the values of society. The goals defined by the polity put these values into effect. Hence, the assumption follows that most individuals will comply with them. Fourth, those, however, who do refuse their obligations will be forced to comply or will be punished by the polity if they refuse.

Parsons's definitions of power and authority unite factors hitherto separated in social thought. They blend the consensus underlying voluntary fulfillment of duty and the conflict underlying coercion by the state. Furthermore, his definition implies that power is a capacity confined in its uses on behalf of the whole society, most of whose members agree with its goals; and dissenters, who are a distinct minority, must legitimately give way to the majority.[43]

Force is one kind of power. As a physical exercise, it is illustrated by placing someone in a city jail against his will. Although the democratic state possesses a monopoly on the use of force—only the polity or those it authorizes to do so may use force—it need not routinely rely on force; for the demands it lays upon citizens are legitimate.[44]

Parsons further clarified the nature of power by drawing analogies between it and money. Money and power, surprisingly enough, are both media of exchange, the former procuring goods and services, the latter the obligations of citizens. Both measure the values of things they procure, money being a measure of the value of goods and services that exchange for it and power a measure of the effectiveness of the policies of the polity. As individuals repose confidence in money and are willing to accept it as a medium of exchange, so citizens have confidence in the polity and are willing to accept its decisions. Money is ultimately grounded in the intrinsic value of gold, while power is grounded in the intrinsic value of physical force. Gold and force are the backups of last resort of money and power. Neither has intrinsic value, for neither money nor power can be consumed. Finally, money and power are generalized media, each being capable of acquiring a variety of valued things.[45]

As a medium, power "flows" out of the polity and into the other three functional subsystems of society.[46] Parsons's political theory is formed within the content of the model of society as consisting of interchanges among its four functional subsystems. According to this model, each subsystem obtains the resources (Parsons called them *inputs*) it needs to fulfill its function for society as a whole from the other three. In return, each subsystem reciprocates by giving inputs to the others, which they require to fulfill their functions. Thus, there is a system of exchanges of inputs among the four subsystems. This system of exchanges is complemented by an exchange of *outputs* (products) among the same four

238   The Duality of Consensus and Conflict

subsystems. Accordingly, the polity receives from the pattern-maintenance subsystem (he later called it the *fiduciary system*) the input of
legitimation of its authority. And from the economy it obtains the
facilities (he called this input *control of productivity*) to implement its
policies.[47]

It is in his analysis of how the polity relates to the *societal community*,
however, that Parsons touched directly upon the formation of political
consensus. Incorporated in this analysis are traditional democratic ideas
that are also compatible with functional logic.

The societal community is that subsystem of modern society that
specializes in the integrative (*I*) function, whose most relevant structure
for Parsons's political theory is the *democratic association*.[48] The processes
that occur between polity and democratic association constitute what
Parsons called the *political support system* and involve an exchange of
factors.[49] Citizens in the democratic association vote for candidates for
political office, which Parsons interpreted as grants of power. The right
to vote is a form of authority, and the vote itself is a form of power. Votes
are power because they are binding; the loser must relinquish office
under the threat of coercion. Votes are power also in that they confer it
upon the winners, who as political incumbents have the right to exercise
it. In elections, therefore, power as a medium flows in the form of ballots
from the democratic association to the polity.

Once elections determine the winners, they have the authority to
select goals binding on everyone. No matter how many votes a candidate
receives, there is only one winner. This is how political support in the
form of voting power ultimately forms a consensus on collective goals. A
minority with respect to any given political decision is expected to comply
because democratic norms, such as a "one man one vote," have been
adhered to. The hierarchy of power and authority in the polity (some in
government have more than others) is matched by the aggregation of
votes in an election according to the norm of majority rules. Hence, a
hierarchy of power arises out of the formal equality of votes. The right of
a fully qualified citizen to vote and have his vote equal any other in
power is grounded in America's instrumental activism, which legitimates
these norms.

Political officeholders use these grants of power to define collective
goals and formulate political decisions that incorporate them. These
decisions, backed of course by the possibility of coercion, are forms of
power that in a sense flow back to the citizens, who are obliged to

comply. Thus, here is a "circular flow" of power. Voters confer it upon leaders, who return it in the form of decisions such as laws.

Inasmuch as they are binding, political decisions acquire legitimacy. One source of their legitimacy is, as noted above, the fact that formal political norms, such as those governing elections, have been adhered to. This source is legality, discussed in the preceding chapters. Decisions, nevertheless, affect individuals and groups in different ways. Some pay a higher price as the result of a law while others gain, for the democratic association is a highly differentiated structure of interests. As a result, political leaders attempt to acquire legitimacy for decisions by persuading the electorate that a given policy is in the overall interest of society. Thus, Parsons identified another symbolic medium, i.e., *influence*, which operates along with power in the political support system. The political process cannot rest upon power alone, but also upon influence as a source of consensus.

Like power, influence flows from polity to democratic association and back again. Candidates for office try to persuade voters of the benefits of certain broad, general policies and offer to assume leadership for such policies. Citizens, on the other hand, influence political incumbents to adopt various policies. The influence in the form of citizens' demands returns to them in the form of leaders' defending and justifying policies in the light of society's value-system. In sum, the political support system overall consists of two interchanges between polity and democratic association: Policy decisions exchange for interest-demands, and political support exchanges for leadership responsibility.

Parsons's political theory assimilates democratic notions with sociological functionalism. Society's goal-attainment function is fulfilled by a polity that operates according to democratic norms like the secret ballot, formal equality of votes, freedom of discussion, and the accountability of politicians. Political policies incorporated into laws and administrative decisions are formulated and implemented with a maximum of harmony and minimum of conflict because they acquire the legitimacy of consensual political norms and the central values they reflect. Correspondence of collective goals with society's values is achieved through the necessity of leaders to argue their cases and persuade a democratic association. Democratic norms also are legitimated by society's values. Thus, the cybernetic hierarchy of values, norms, and goals that characterizes an integrated social system is preserved through political mechanisms.

Political consensus is formed with the framework of a consensus on political norms and within the context of a consensus on social values.

Rather than disrupting the system, power achieves the general welfare; for the conflict inherent in coercion is subordinated to the legitimacy of power exercised on behalf of society. The hierarchical dimensions of power are muted by the necessity of a democratic state to exercise it through a system of interchanges over political boundaries. The exercise of power is judged by a democratic electorate in terms of its conformity to standards of effectiveness. The polity fulfills its functions through an interdependence with the other functional subsystems, which takes the form of balances in an exchange of inputs and outputs. These balances are logical extensions of the checks-and-balances system of American democratic theory, and in them the concept of system equilibrium finds another expression. Enmeshed in this system of interchange, the potential of the polity to exploit is severely limited. Overall, the way in which the polity defines and implements goals and the conditions that it must meet make it truly a form of popular sovereignty that expresses the will of the people. The capacity of the American political system to generate a consensus on collective goals contributes to the nation's mechanical solidarity.

THE SOCIETAL COMMUNITY

The electorate in Parsons's exposition of the political system belongs to the societal community. As mentioned above, it is the societal community, a more inclusive structure, that has primacy of integrative function. Along with the fiduciary system, economy, and polity, it takes its place as the fourth of the functional subsystems of modern society.

A differentiated structure, the societal community includes all individuals in society who are considered to be its full members.[50] Complete membership includes those who have full opportunity to participate in all areas regulated by society's norms and to realize in their lives its core values. Two examples of persons in the United States excluded from membership are aliens and blacks. The latter are still in the process of being included, but for them full membership has not yet been attained.[51] With regard to membership, a distinction needs to be made between those to whom society's normative order applies and those allowed to participate in all areas governed by it. The latter are first-class citizens, who form a *gemeinschaft*.

Consensus   241

Membership is more precisely defined with reference to the entire normative order of society, i.e., all of its norms, including those applying to everyone and those that differentiate members in a division of labor. A part of the normative order of great importance is the legal system. Parsons's concept of the societal community in large part overlaps with Durkheim's concepts of mechanical and organic solidarity. The delineation of this functional subsystem cuts across the others; for workers in a business firm are subject to economic norms, which are also parts of the total normative order. Consequently, a worker belongs both to the economy and societal community. Here, the problem of loyalty arises; for in a totally integrated society, the loyalty of the individual to his firm must be reconciled with his loyalty to the societal community. Also, the employee must adjust his loyalty to the firm with his loyalty to other collectivities such as the family.[52] Mechanisms that resolve problems of competing loyalties and interests are obviously integrative mechanisms. The societal community specializes in the integrative function.

Membership carries full citizenship rights; and following T. H. Marshall, Parsons identified a historical sequence of rights that were gradually extended. Although the extension originally occurred in Europe, the same sequence with modifications is evident in America's history.[53] Three kinds of rights yield a clearer notion of what Parsons meant by the societal community. First came the civil (legal) rights of security of person and property, freedom of speech, religion, assembly, and the equal protection of the laws. Although able to participate in areas such as one's chosen religion, some were still excluded from the polity. Political rights then came with the near-universal extension of the franchise and the right to hold office. Finally, social rights of financial welfare, medical care, and education enabled more people to hold prestigeful occupations and to participate in "cultural" activities. These rights are still being extended to American blacks, recent examples being elimination of the poll tax and the Civil Rights Act. Parsons called the process of extending membership in the societal community *inclusion*.[54]

Societal membership is connected to instrumental activism. If an individual is to achieve active mastery, if he is to achieve difficult goals in the professions, business, and politics, he must have access to higher education, to health, to the franchise—in short, to the full panoply of rights. In the totally integrated society, norms governing the distribution of rights are integrated with the core system of values. They put the values into effect. As noted above, members of this community subordi-

242   The Duality of Consensus and Conflict

nate their loyalties to other collectivities to the societal community; and priorities of loyalty contribute to the solidarity of the nation.[55]

The societal community, according to Parsons, lends a further connotation to the notion of consensus. In modern societies consensus is not limited to agreement on values, norms, goals, and religious legitimations, but allows whoever wants to take advantage of it the opportunity to implement instrumental activism—with minor exceptions such as children and aliens. Inclusion extends opportunities for individuals to realize values in their lives.

On the other hand, Parsons recognized that even with total universality of rights, some would be better able than others to realize values. He presented several reasons for this,[56] one of which being an especially important issue in the consensus-conflict debate. Although the societal community is a solidary structure with normative consensus, it is also differentiated by religion, race, ethnicity, voluntary associations, and occupation—differences that must be welded into a unity. Especially relevant to its unity are those differentiations that stratify it, for *stratification* can readily cause conflict. Consistent with his overall approach, Parsons set forth the functional theory of stratification.

It is easy to demonstrate in modern European history a decline in ascribed inequalities, e.g., hereditary aristocracy, and a growth in equality of rights.[57] These historical trends force on the defensive those who today defend inequality, and it is up to them to justify it. How can any kind of inequality be defended? Parsons's answer links the institutionalization of stratification to the existence of social order.[58]

To begin with, it ought to be noted that the very civil, political, and social equalities that have become institutionalized lead to various inequalities. A number of examples make the point. The right to form contracts inevitably results in some investments yielding higher returns than others, the result being that some individuals make more money than others. Freedom to form labor contracts results in some getting better jobs than others. Freedom of religion leads to a diversity of religious affiliations varying in prestige. The right to vote leads to winners and losers in the race for political office. Finally, mass education results in different levels of academic achievement, leading to differences in upward mobility and cultural participation.[59] Paradoxically, inequality in outcomes results from equality of opportunities.

From this mixture of equality and inequality Parsons extracted a formula that explains the stratification of the societal community. It is a

Consensus   243

community of equals who have the right to win unequal rewards from a base of equality of opportunity so long as the differences result from achievements legitimated by their functional contributions.[60] Stratification arises out of a matrix of equality of opportunity, which is a derivative of instrumental activism,[61] and at the same time contributes to the functions of modern society. Equality precedes inequality, and the latter must be functional. Inequalities resulting from lack of equal opportunity, on the other hand, undermine instrumental activism and are illegitimate. It is all right for someone to get rich so long as his wealth results from his achievements that are functional to society.

To obtain a clearer picture of the functional theory of stratification, consider the individual in a bureaucracy. Each member, ideally considered, must be accorded control over the facilities (means) necessary to play his role, which can be blast furnaces or church pews depending on the bureaucracy. One especially important facility is authority, which is always hierarchical; he who has authority has the right to wield power. Also to be allocated are rewards of money and approval. These are functionally necessary to motivate the individual. Differentially distributed, facilities and rewards stratify a bureaucracy.

The phrase "necessary to play his role," however, is too vague. How many facilities and rewards are sufficient for a role? In addressing the question, Parsons found two principles governing their distribution, namely, the importance of the role and the competence of the individual who plays it. A role's functional importance is determined by which of the four functional subsystems it belongs to. One whose function is the most direct expression of the bureaucracy's value-system is more important than one whose duties are further removed.[62] For instance, since the business firm is organized about the value of efficiency, roles that are most crucial for the production of utility are the functionally most important. In a political bureaucracy, by contrast, the paramount organizing value is effectiveness, embedded most directly in policy-making roles. Consequently, functional importance is determined in accordance with the standard of value-relevance. There are also standards that measure the competence with which an individual fulfills his duties, and somehow the standards applicable to different duties must be correlated to determine the relative competence of performance.[63] In sum, overall stratification of an organization in terms of facilities and rewards is based on value-determined functional contributions and achievements.[64]

These principles can be generalized to society as a whole. Whereas

244   The Duality of Consensus and Conflict

the role is a stratification unit within a bureaucracy, the latter is a unit within society. The question now arises: What governs the flow of facilities and rewards to a bureaucracy, which it in turn distributes to its members in roles? The answer is essentially that given in the functional formula: functional contribution measured by value-relevance to society.

Accordingly, business firms that are most efficient will earn the greatest share of property and money, concluded Parsons. They benefit society by producing generalized facilities that can be put in the service of private and collective goals. They meet very well the value-standard of utility. A polity that meets the test of effectiveness in delineating and achieving collective goals will increase its authority and power. In the pattern-maintenance sector, universities that excel in the production of knowledge will accumulate resources and high rank. Pattern-maintenance organizations are evaluated in terms of integrity as a value-standard, which corresponds to the criteria of utility and effectiveness. Finally, associations belonging to the societal community that persuade individuals to become members and realize selected values acquire prestige and influence. The value-standard that stratifies these associations is solidarity. Those contributing most to the solidarity of the societal community get the highest rank.[65] In sum, collectivities belonging to the various functional subsystems are ranked in accord with how closely they conform to the standard that is relevant to the function they specialize in. It is evident that Parsons's functional theory of the stratification of rewards converges with the norm of distributive justice.

At this point the functional explanation of stratification manifests a continuity with Weber's interpretation of Calvinism. Active mastery of the world, the cultivation of the Lord's vineyard, is worthy in the eyes of Calvin's God. The negative of God's approval is the moral unworthiness of the lazy. Parsons's theory substitutes the flow of facilities and rewards for the approval of the Lord, for in the modern world the impersonal allocations of the stratification system replace salvation as the motive for achievement.[66] By rewarding achievement, stratification upholds instrumental activism, which is functional for America. Finally, insofar as stratification rewards conformity to this value-system through distributing rewards in proportion to contribution measured by it, America ultimately rests on the principle of justice. This is a hidden implication of Parsons's functional theory of stratification.[67]

SOCIAL EVOLUTION

Responding to the charge that a functional social theory emphasizing consensus and equilibrium cannot account for social change, Parsons resuscitated the essentials of Herbert Spencer's theory of social evolution. Parsons's theory of change preserves the social system's normative consensus within the four-function paradigm.

The structure of any society, said Parsons, is a historical result of recurrent but progressive cycles of change. The recurrent cycle is to be thought of as an ideal-typical sequence, with complexities in real situations not contained in the type. It does not follow, of course, that a given society must experience the same evolutionary path as others, but only that whatever its present evolutionary status, it must have experienced the cycle a number of times. Moreover, a particular society may not evolve, it may regress, or it may borrow innovations from other societies. The endpoints of the evolutionary continuum are the most primitive society and the modern, highly differentiated society.[68]

The cycle of change consists of four processes.[69] First in the cycle is *differentiation*. A collectivity or group of them divides into two structures—a process of binary fission. A familiar example is the separation of factory from household during the industrial revolution. Whereas under the domestic system textile production occurred within households and was accomplished by family members, the industrial system transfers this work into the factory. Now a person, usually the male, belongs to two collectivities, a kin group and an organization of production. If differentiation is really evolutionary it must result in *adaptive upgrading*, which is the second phase of the cycle. The society has won greater control over its environments because each collectivity can better fulfill the function it now specializes in than before differentiation occurred. The factory is a more efficient unit of production than household, upgrading the entire society, which now has more facilities at its disposal.

With differentiation arises the need for the collectivities to undergo *integration*, the third phase of the cycle. For example, the employment contract specifies the hours the employee is to spend in the factory and thereby regulates the relationship between it and his household with respect to time. Whereas previously the worker sold the products made by his family on the market, now he purchases with wages what his family needs from the market. Wages function as integrator of kinship

246   The Duality of Consensus and Conflict

with workplace. These examples are merely illustrative of a series of adjustments that integrate the two structures. Integration often involves the inclusion of individuals into the societal community.

Parsons called the fourth phase of the cycle *value-generalization*, which incorporates what Durkheim observed in the growth of organic solidarity. The new structure that has separated from its more diffusely organized matrix is brought within the meaning of the society's value-system and made legitimate. The values are applied to the new collectivity, which is interpreted as a specification of them. For this to happen, however, the values must be made more abstract and general. The industrial workplace, for instance, is explained as a legitimate specification of instrumental activism: Hard industrial effort contributes to God's kingdom on earth. As a result, the concept of active mastery is informed by connotations it previously lacked.

In the extension of values to new structures and contexts, value-generalization preserves normative consensus. Although Parsons conceded that in reality the cycle of change causes conflicts and strains, structural changes occur without upsetting core values.[70] As the cycle repeats itself in history, new evolutionary breakthroughs, such as religion, stratification, money, bureaucracy, and universal law, yield enormous increments in adapting upgrading.[71] As evolutionary cycles and breakthroughs recur, a society grows progressively more differentiated in structure and function. Nevertheless, value-generalization acts as an equilibrating mechanism to maintain the stability of normative consensus despite potentially disruptive social change.

Of the four phases, value-generalization is of the greatest relevance to consensus. The process preserves stability through extending values to new structures, bringing them into the orbit of consensus. Parsons pointed to the inclusion of non-Protestants, even secular humanists, into the societal community of America as an example.[72] Civil rights were extended to anyone willing to accept American law and the principle of religious toleration; but in the process of inclusion, religious conceptions became stated more abstractly. Parsons cited America's civil religion as an example of value-generalization.[73] Civil religion defines God, not in specifically Christian terms, but in the abstract as the Supreme Being who endows individuals with inalienable rights. More abstract formulations include religiously diverse groups within the religious consensus. Value-generalization makes it possible for groups to form solidary unities without relinquishing their beliefs.

CONCLUDING REMARKS ON PARSONS

The preceding is a selective analysis whose aim is to reveal the role of consensus in Parsons's theory of the social system. Once again I have chosen Parsons as the principal exponent of sociological functionalism, and so the analysis elucidates the centrality of this factor in an important theoretical tradition of sociology. The exposition makes clear the full extent to which cooperation (the social system is really the cooperation of individuals) depends upon a consensus of several factors—cognitions, goals, values, rules, and general views of things. Although every agreement came into existence at some historical time and therefore had to be constructed, Parsons's main emphasis is on a preformed cultural system, whose historical origin for the most part remains unexplained but assumed. Consequently, the role played by consensus is incorporated in a modified cultural determinism originating in a taken-for-granted consensus.

Although Parsons never wrote a treatise on conflict, he introduced this factor here and there in his formulations as one that disturbs the social system, one that produces strain within it, tearing down its order. The destructive consequences of conflict correspond to the commonsense recognition that conflict gets in the way of cooperation. To him, conflict is the antithesis of consensus. Whereas Parsons and other functionalists have explored how consensus generates a cooperative order, the conflict theorists have outlined the consequences of conflict in social life. We shall see in the following chapter how a concentrated theoretical focus on this factor draws a picture of society that contradicts that painted by functionalism.

Consensus and Symbol According to Mead

George Herbert Mead demonstrated that sharing perspectives depends upon a psychological capacity given to the human being as a result of the evolution of the central nervous system. Shared perspectives, that is, consensus, are possible only among humans. For Mead the basis of this capacity and the distinctiveness of human life are explained by the *significant symbol*.

The animal relates himself to other animals only through nonsignifi-

248   The Duality of Consensus and Conflict

cant gestures. One dog barks, the other dog growls, the first dog runs. The gesture of one becomes the stimulus for the adjustive response of the other. The barking dog does not anticipate the other's response of anger; interaction proceeds only on an instinctive basis. At the human level interaction becomes self-conscious, for the human being is able to respond cognitively to his own gesture the way another person might. His ability to anticipate the other's attitude toward his own gesture converts the gesture into a significant symbol.[74]

As symbol, a word evokes the same meaning in the minds of speaker and listener. In fact, Mead identified mind as consciousness of subjective meanings elicited by symbols, which can be words, actions, or objects.[75] Insofar as a symbol evokes shared meanings, it is social; and the human mind is a social product.[76] And insofar as the individual's self has a similar meaning to him as to others, his self is also social. Placing himself in the position of the other, the individual conceptualizes himself the way the other does. He becomes an object to himself by taking the role of the other. Hence, the self is also a social product.[77] The conclusion that mind and self are social products, arising through symbolic interactions, is the main point of Mead's social psychology.

For a social act to occur, the individual must take the role of the other. He must look at an object as the other does. Before he acts, he must formulate an idea of what the other will do in relation to the object and what he will do, role-taking being accomplished through symbols. Thus, the social act is conceived in imagination before it occurs. The overt act of one individual occurs within the context of the roles of all the others. Mead's imaginative role-taking, the taking of the attitude of the other, is similar to the norm in Parsons's theory; while the overt taking of a role finds its equivalent in the role according to Parsons. When roles are conceived in relation to one another, we get in Mead the social system of Parsons. And insofar as the overt act corresponds to the imagined role in the minds of both individuals, the latter, in Parsons's terms, is institutionalized. Mead's analysis of the social act reveals equivalences with Parsons's theory of the social system.

In the transmutation of non-significant gesture into significant symbol, we discover the psychological foundation of consensus. A symbol evokes one meaning in several minds, and therein consists a mutual understanding about an object. Were it not for minds operating with symbols, consensus would not be possible. Mead generalized the possibility of similar attitudes toward an object by individuals to society as a whole and thus developed the concept of the *generalized other*. Not only does one take the role of a particular other, he also takes the attitude of the generalized other toward objects and toward himself.[78] It is clear that the generalized other overlaps Parsons's cultural system.

Intersubjectivity in Schutz's Phenomenology

Alfred Schutz left us with a more detailed and thorough analysis than Mead of how shared perspectives are possible. In attempting to clear up ambiguities in Weber's notions of *Verstehen* and social action, Schutz borrowed extensively from Husserl's phenomenology. Schutz located the process of understanding in the possibilities inherent within the face-to-face relationship. Genuine subjective understanding (*Verstehen*) is most likely to occur, and then only in degrees, in that context. Although mutual understanding does not always result in accord, without the former the latter, at least in the long run, is unlikely.

How one goes about understanding another, said Schutz, is to be found in the characteristics of the direct, face-to-face relationship.[79] This structure locates the origin of everyone's knowledge of the social world, for everyone's knowledge of those whom he has never met ultimately derives from the stock of knowledge acquired in face-to-face relationships.

What happens in this relationship is summed up in Schutz's phrase, the "general thesis of the alter ego." Two individuals who find themselves in a direct relationship mutually experience three contextual factors: They share a common time, space, and situation. The fact that each can point to the same object makes their situation into a "communicative common environment," which unites their streams of consciousness.[80] Although each views an object from a slightly different spatial perspective, they also share a common space and an objective time measured by the clock. They participate in a community of the "here," and "now." Moreover, within this objective space-time, each experiences his own inner, objective time as a duration, which he gets a sense of as he turns his attention away from the objective situation toward the inward flow of his experience. The latter includes perceptions, memories, anticipations, fantasies, and plans of future actions. An ego, therefore, alternates his attention between exterior objects and his subjective experiences.

Within a shared spatio-temporal context the face-to-face relationship

250   The Duality of Consensus and Conflict

is constituted by several levels of awareness that Schutz distinguished analytically. When ego becomes conscious of the physical presence of alter and conscious that he has a stream of subjective experience, alter becomes a "thou" to him. Alter's body, including his words (signs), is recognized as a field of expression for his inner experiences. A thou-orientation, however, does not involve an understanding of what goes on in alter's mind, but only that alter has a mind. For his part, if alter experiences ego as a "thou," then this reciprocal thou-orientation becomes a "we-relationship." For instance, both persons watching a bird in flight are aware that the other is perceiving the same object as he; and each is aware that the other has this awareness. Each notices the movements of the other's head as the flight progresses. Nevertheless, this coordination of their experiences does not involve an understanding of what actually goes on in the other's mind. It is within this "we-relationship," however, that mutual understanding can occur.

Let us now assume that the two participants are also talking about the bird in flight. Now there is communicative intent, whose success is measured by how well each grasps the subjective, intentional meanings of the other. At this point Schutz drew a distinction between *objective* and *subjective* meaning. An interpretation placed by ego on the words uttered by alter that reflect ego's own experiences of those words constitutes the words' objective meaning. Objective meaning reflects ego's understanding of his own experiences of those words. Furthermore, contained within the definition of objective meaning is that content which any speaker of the language would interpret the words as carrying. This kernel of content is part of the language as an "ideal objectivity,"[81] namely, the dictionary definitions of words abstracted from their use by particular individuals in specific settings. In his objective interpretations of alter's utterances, ego relies on the meanings of the language as an ideal objectivity. Subjective meaning, by contrast, is the actual subjective meaning of the words to alter as he uses them. The extent to which ego gets behind the objective meaning of signs to arrive at their subjective meaning measures the degree to which genuine intersubjective understanding emerges within the we-relationship.

An optimum outcome of the we-relationship requires not only an interpretive effort by ego but also expressive effort by alter. Just as ego's objective interpretations reflect his own past experiences, so alter's words reflect *his* past experiences. Each has during the course of his life reflected upon his experiences and synthesized them into contexts of

Consensus   251

meaning of which the relevant ones are brought to bear on the here and now of a we-relationship. Alter must convey his unique contexts of meaning, constituted during the course of his biographical history, to ego—a process facilitated by any personal knowledge he possesses of ego. Like ego he can begin with the objective meaning of words as ideal objectivities. In other words, for intersubjective understanding to occur, alter's *expressive schema* must merge with ego's *interpretive schema* mediated through the meanings of words as *ideal objectivities*.

The question now becomes: How does the coordination of an interpretive schema with an expressive schema come about? Schutz looked for a solution in the immediacy of the face-to-face relationship. As alter speaks, ego experiences his meanings as they are constituted. A grasp of the process of meaning-constitution yields a greater understanding (*Verstehen*) than a grasp of the completed act as product. As ego hears alter's words and catches the expressions on his face, ego's observations keep pace with alter's stream of consciousness as it transpires. Ego lives within alter's lived experiences so that their streams of consciousness are simultaneous and flow in parallel directions. They "grow old together."[82] As alter's meanings are established through a series of intentional acts of discourse, ego's knowledge of him continually grows and is revised. He is able, sometimes in a flash, to grasp alter's in-order-to motive, i.e., the end that alter is attempting to achieve through his utterances. If ego is unclear about what alter means, he can point to an object in their mutual environment and ask questions about it.

While ego attends to alter's expressions, he lives within their common stream of consciousness. While totally attuned to alter's words, living within alter's contexts of meanings, he knows alter better than alter knows himself (at that time). If, however, he reflects upon what alter says, if he interprets it retrospectively in the light of his own contexts of meaning, then he temporarily withdraws from the relationship. He steps outside the we-relationship and "freezes" it. At that point ego interprets alter's intentional expressions in terms of objective meaning. The more ego becomes aware of the we-relationship, the less he is involved in it; for the more he thinks about it the more alter is transformed into a mere object of thought. This insight parallels Mead's observation that the individual when totally absorbed in an external situation does not think about himself; at that point he lacks a reflexive self.

On the other hand, intersubjective understanding as Schutz analyzed it remains a limiting conception. It is essentially an ideal-type, never

252   The Duality of Consensus and Conflict

totally realized in practice. The reason for the approximate nature of understanding is that no two individuals have identical streams of thought. The person to be understood interprets his own experiences according to contexts of meaning built up over his past life. For a person to understand another's experience precisely, not only would his past experiences have had to duplicate the latter's experiences but also his meaning-contexts. In other words, the person attempting to understand the other would have to be the other if complete understanding were to occur.

Even the direct relationship varies in degree of directness. The thou-experience can be intimate or distant, intense or faint, or of varying degrees of immediacy. The other can be at the center or periphery of attention. Nevertheless, the further removed one's experience is of another concretely present in a we-relationship, the less is the probability of intersubjective understanding. At the other extreme from the direct relationship is the purely indirect relationship, within which the individual thinks about a purely anonymous contemporary—a fellow American. In constructing the meaning of such a person, the individual substitutes a purely objective interpretation for a subjective understanding. The latter is abandoned and the meaning given is objective; the individual interprets his own experience of others built up from his own past.[83] These objective contexts of meaning, however, are heavily shaped and constructed from his previous direct relationships. One's view of the world of anonymous contemporaries is in general determined by and its validity attributable to his past we-relationships.[84]

Insofar as consensus finds its foundation in mutual understanding, agreement is traceable, either directly or indirectly, to the context of the direct relationship. It is within the face-to-face relationship that the general thesis of the alter ego holds, according to which one can live through the other's experience in its immediate present. Nevertheless, limits to understanding are established by the inevitable differences in the biographically determined situation of the participants. No two individuals have identical biographies; nor as a result do they have identical senses of what is relevant in their mutual situation. It follows that the more similar their experiences are, the greater the mutual understanding. On the other hand, the greater the differences between their systems of relevances, the smaller the probability they will understand one another. Complete disparity in conceptions of relevance and

Consensus   253

contexts of meaning makes a universe of discourse impossible. In that case consensus becomes impossible.

What Parsons took for granted was a fundamental social scientific problem for Schutz: How is mutual understanding possible?[85] Taking for granted the possibility that ego and alter are able to understand each other's orientation, Parsons then logically concluded that each can grasp what the other expects of him. On that basis norms impregnated with values arise that take on the status of imperatives for the way ego and alter define their situation and interact within it. A consensus on normative definitions made possible by mutual understanding integrates their actions. For Schutz, understanding poses a problem; and that is why he devoted a good deal of analysis as to how it comes about. His comprehensive discussion leaves us with a more thorough grasp of the prerequisites for consensus, for mutual understanding is its necessary condition.

Nevertheless, his analysis of face-to-face interaction and the indirect relationship adds a problematic dimension to understanding. For Durkheim, Parsons, and Mead, consensual elements are objective givens, there to be internalized through socialization. A norm is a norm, the same for everyone in society, whose meaning is invariant even for those to whom it does not apply. The collective representation, the core value, and the generalized other give society a unity of consensus, integrating its members around shared elements that make it possible for them to work together. If, however, we are to believe Schutz that mutual understanding, even among those intimately related, is a limiting conception and that a person indirectly known is constituted as an entity solely in terms of objective meaning and anonymous typification, then how do we know that a contemporary American whom we have never met will play his role in accordance with a norm? Insofar as an individual's conception of an anonymous other, e.g., a postal clerk, is constructed on the basis of his previous direct relationships sedimented into a unique biographical history, the generalized other becomes a variable and loses some of its generality.

Nevertheless, Schutz enhanced our understanding of how understanding occurs. The model of the coordination of streams of experience is the interaction among those sharing time and space in which the immediately given organism is the objective arena for expression of subjectively intended meaning. In the grasp of the other's intentional meanings, individuals can arrive at common ways of defining their situations.

The Role of Consensus

This selective discussion reveals in some detail the role of consensus in social relationships. A necessary condition of consensus is mutual understanding that brings about a kind of psychological unity among individuals. Essential to this complex process is language, which itself is a consensual system of semantic content and grammatical rules. The functional theory of the social system assumes this linguistically created mutual understanding. Accordingly, the primary consensual element in social life is language.

Other consensual elements are embodied in language, which codes cognitive beliefs, values, norms, and goals. These are the categories of ideas that individuals must agree upon if they are to cooperate successfully. In order to cooperate, they must come to an agreement about what goal they want to achieve. They must develop a cognitive consensus about the means to achieve it, which include the allocation of tasks and the facilities needed to accomplish them. A division of labor in turn incorporates instrumental and solidary relationships among those carrying out roles within it. Finally, there must be agreement about how the benefits of the goal are to be distributed. If the act is to be repeated again and again or if the goal requires a long time to achieve, then the problem of maintaining commitment and effort becomes critical. Norms backed by sanctions must be established. In these shared conceptions we find the essentials of the functional requirements of Parsons's social system.

Although specialization and the accumulation of knowledge occur and new evaluations, goals, and norms emerge, the consensual foundations according to the functional model do not change from the small group to the large society. With functional theory's selective focus, the model of modern society is constructed as one in which shared knowledge, evaluations, and goals are voluntarily created with a minimum resort to coercion. There is even agreement about the stratification of society in terms of power, resources, and rewards. Money, a relatively free market, persuasion, and appeal to shared values contribute to social function. When normative consensus is threatened, it is defended by equilibrating mechanisms. Social change occurs within an overarching consensus and is relatively painless. All in all, the functional model corresponds in its essentials to classical democratic theory.

This theory, especially in the work of Parsons, has been constructed and elaborated in complexity in the attempt to explain the formation and maintenance of consensus in modern democratic society. Parsons's analysis of political influence, the connection between Calvinism and instrumental activism, the inclusion of religious diversity in the societal community, the market as allocator of unequally distributed resources all illustrate how society comes to grips with its functional necessities. Also, Durkheim's penetrating investigations of anomie were reactions to the collapse of consensus in Europe, and his analyses of solidarity clarified the consequences of consensus. Symbolic interactionism and social phenomenology do not yield a detailed delineation of a total society; however, their minute investigations of communication provide a foundation for the functional model.

To be sure, stability is always subject to the threat of failure to develop the necessary consensus. These failures lead directly to the factor of conflict, which in varying degrees is destructive of the cooperative order. What functionalists regarded as a residual factor, however, became the central preoccupation of conflict theory.

Conflict

Conflict theory has shown more interest in the clash of interests than in the consensus of values, the former having the status of a postulate in an ideal-typical formulation. The conflict of interests is of overriding importance even if it is conceded that the concept of interest includes benefits to other groups than one's own.[1] On the other hand, an all-encompassing value-consensus turns out to be an illusion perpetuated by ideologies that paper over real differences among individuals and groups. For conflict theory, what is of theoretical concern is not a symbolic system shared by ego and alter that enables them to cooperate, but rather that they seek mutually exclusive goals. Conflict over ends and contradictions among values dominate their relationship. Parsons's pattern-maintenance and integrative functions do not figure prominently in explanations.

The abstraction of conflicts and contradictions as objects of scientific focus results in the construction of theories that yield a very different picture of society than that sketched by consensual assumptions. Durkheim's collective representations, moral rules, and mechanical solidarity are replaced by contradictory beliefs, values, and interests that generate hostility. The overwhelming importance of power as a rational instrument to achieve goals displaces authority and persuasion as techniques of adjustment. Institutions and formal organizations, especially state and stratification, are cast in a different light, their structures and dynamics

258   The Duality of Consensus and Conflict

being explained as consequences of struggles among groups to obtain power, material resources, and the dominance of particular values. Consensus and cooperation within groups and organizations are interpreted as subordinate factors, explained strictly as means for participation in conflict with other groups.

Although the discussion of conflict is historic, many of the formulations during the past thirty years that can be considered as versions of conflict theory take as their point of origin a critical posture toward the consensus assumption underlying functionalism. In view of the self-understanding of much of recent conflict theory as critical of functionalism, the following discussion is organized so as to emphasize the points of opposition between the two theories. This criterion for organizing ideas is consistent with the notion of a controversial issue.

As Dahrendorf pointed out, the antiquity of the contrast between consensus and conflict is indicated by the contrasting definitions of justice put forth in Plato's *Republic*, which foreshadow notions explained in greater detail by subsequent thinkers.[2] Nevertheless, a logical beginning for the discussion of conflict is the relevant ideas of the English philosopher Thomas Hobbes (1588–1679); for it was he whom Parsons criticized for advancing a faulty solution to what the latter thought of as the problem of order. My discussion of conflict then proceeds to identify contrasts, some explicit and intentional, others implicit, between the concepts and generalizations of the conflict model and those of functional theory. Parsons's disagreement with Hobbes is followed by the inconsistent generalizations of Marx and Parsons. Also considered is Weber's separation of factors he believed Marx erroneously conjoined. Dahrendorf's criticisms of Parsons's theory identify other dimensions of the controversy; and Collins's attempt to build a total sociology on the foundation of conflict, heavily dependent on Marx and Weber, implies a thoroughgoing repudiation of consensus and function as adequate foundations. In the last section I identify an underlying dimension of the issue, which may put a new light on the entire controversy.

The Hobbesian State of Nature

The causes of conflict are to be found in the nature of man. Impressed by the science of Galileo, Hobbes fashioned a mechanical model of man as matter in motion. What is the heart but a spring, the nerves but strings, and the joints but wheels giving motion to the body?[3] In analogizing the human being to an engine, he imported mechanistic materialism into social science.

Hobbes translated scientific materialism into the human level as a rather crude stimulus-response psychology. An object stimulates a motion internal to the organism, which is subjectively experienced as a passion. If the passion is an appetite or a desire, the human machine moves toward the object; if an aversion, the machine moves away from it. Thus, the type of passion stimulated by an external object determines the individual's direction. From desire and aversion, Hobbes derived a range of more specific passions. For example, the objects men desire they love; those they dislike they hate. When men expect to be hurt by an object, they fear it; when they expect to avoid harm by resisting it, they have courage. An object that an individual expects to obtain in the future is viewed with hope. An object that the person does not expect to obtain is viewed with despair. Continual hope is self-confidence.[4] Thus, desire and aversion differentiate into a spectrum of passions whose objects occur either in the past, present, or future and are located either within or outside the individual. Hobbes's passions are really states of feeling elicited by the evaluation of things.

From this mechanistic model Hobbes derived notions of good and evil. Any object desired by an individual is good; any object of his aversion is evil. It follows that good and evil are strictly relative to the individual and also vary over time.[5] Hobbes's relativism did away with moral absolutes as expressed in previous conceptions of the law of nature. Furthermore, he downgraded reason from a faculty leading to moral truths to one strictly instrumental to the fulfillment of desire. Rather than repress desire for the sake of a moral purpose, reason becomes its instrument. The general aim of the human being is continual success in the satisfaction of desire, a state of affairs that Hobbes identified as happiness.[6]

Happiness, however, was difficult to attain in man's natural condition before government was formed. This state of nature is the condition that would prevail in the absence of state and civil society. It has a twofold logical status in Hobbes's writings. Insofar as its characteristics can be deduced from the absence of government, it is hypothetical. Yet insofar as approximations to it can be glimpsed, it is real.[7] Within nature either as reality or hypothetical condition, the consequences of Hobbes's model become clear. Because men are approximately equal in mental and physical faculties, they all have equal hope of attaining their ends. Therefore, if any two men desire the same thing which both cannot have, they become enemies. Their passions move them against each other. Competition for scarce objects is justified by the right of self-preservation—a right everyone is endowed with by nature. Accordingly, everyone has a right to those things he considers necessary to preserve his life. And since there is nothing he cannot make use of to preserve himself, everyone has by the right of self-preservation a natural right to everything.[8]

Morally justified competition therefore leads to intermittent war in nature. The famous Hobbesian state of nature is the war of all against all. If everyone has a right to everything, each has a right to take it from others. Having dissolved absolute good and evil into shifting desires and aversions, Hobbes saw no moral restraints against the use of any means to obtain an end. In nature man is amoral. The resulting war is aggravated by fear; for if everyone has the right to take another's property by force, everyone is in a state of fear. In order to protect himself, therefore, everyone seeks power. Power is built up through alliances, but such cooperation is at the call of shifting constellations of interests. Men cooperate to despoil others of their wives and possessions; but after victory their common interest dissolves, and they fall out.[9] Thus in nature there is a ceaseless struggle in which reason devises the most effective methods, such as force and fraud, of accumulating power.

Besides competition and fear, a third factor that Hobbes called *glorying* makes its contribution to war. Everyone desires others to think as well of him as he thinks of himself. Consequently, each is ready to destroy another who treats him with contempt, for status is essential to self-preservation.[10] As a result, war, caused by competition, fear, and glory, militates against security, industry, navigation, building, science, and art. In short, in nature man is unhappy, for his desires are not well gratified in an impoverished culture. It was in this context that Hobbes wrote the immortal words: ". . . and which is worst of all, continual fear, and danger of violent death: and the life of man, solitary, poor, nasty, brutish, and short."[11] Such is the state of nature.

Fear and unhappiness are incentives for escape from nature. Reason responds to the challenge by discovering certain laws of nature, which are moral maxims that when followed yield peace by removing man from his natural condition. The first three natural laws are the most important.[12] The first enjoins men to seek peace. The second instructs them how to achieve it. It commands each to renounce his right to everything and to relinquish as much of his liberty to move against others as they are willing to renounce of theirs to move against him. The third, which Hobbes called justice, requires men to abide by their covenants (agreements). The third obviously refers directly to the second; once having agreed to a mutual renunciation of certain rights or liberties, men are obliged to honor their agreements.

The trouble, however, is that in nature not all men keep their promises; and if one refuses to honor his contract with another, the latter by keeping his end of the bargain endangers his self-preservation. Since he cannot renounce this right, he is not obliged to honor his part of the bargain. Thus, the only way to enforce contracts is to appoint a sovereign power that compels everyone to abide by his agreements. This power is the state, which comes into being through contract. Accordingly, everyone enters a contract with everyone else to transfer the rights referred to in the second law of nature to either a monarch or a sovereign assembly. Hobbes preferred the former over the latter. The king, then, who is not a party to the contract, is the recipient of the enormous powers vested in everyone by the natural right of self-preservation. Now, only the king can move against anyone; whereas before the contracts that establish the state were formed, everyone could move against everyone else. Having absorbed all those powers into itself, the state is a great monster, a leviathan.[13]

The state puts into legal enactments the natural laws that reason discovers.[14] Including gratitude, accommodation, arbitration, equity, pardon, and mutual respect, these laws of nature maintain peace and enable everyone to augment his happiness. The laws of the state substitute for the decisions of individuals in the state of nature, and thus everyone is better off.

Because the monarch is not a party to the contract, he cannot be removed from office for violating it. Nothing the king does can be criticized by citizens, who through contract have authorized all his acts. No one can object to a policy because in that case some person or group would be required to judge whether a citizen or the king were right, which would elevate that group to a position higher than the latter.[15] But the concept of sovereignty itself implies there can be no higher power than the sovereign. Through such arguments, Hobbes denied anyone the right to protest against the state. Even an oppressive king who preserves

262   The Duality of Consensus and Conflict

peace is preferable to the anarchy of nature. The contracts that institute the state confer upon it all the usual legislative, judicial, taxing, and foreign powers.

Hobbes's theory diverges significantly from Parsons's political theory in the role of coercion. The monarch achieves the goal of peace through coercive power, and his subjects obey his laws because of fear of punishment. For Parsons the coercive element of power, muted by the willingness of citizens to obey political decisions because they are the expressions of shared values, is of minor importance. The power of the polity rests upon legitimacy. The monarch, in contrast, forms policies instrumental to peace through terror; and his subjects put up with this as the lesser of two evils, the other being the anarchy of nature. Hobbes's own words speak to the point:

> The only way to erect such a common power . . . is to confer all their power and strength upon one man or upon one assembly of men . . . and therein to submit their wills, every one to his will, and their judgment to his judgment. This is more than consent or concord; it is a real unity of them all. . . . For by this authority given him by every particular man in the commonwealth, he hath the use of so much power and strength conferred on him that by terror thereof, he is enabled to form the wills of them all.[16]

At this point Parsons called into question the adequacy of the entire utilitarian theory of the state.[17] Society must select a number of goals, not solely that of security; and these must acquire the commitments reflected in a consensus of values they express. Society cannot be reduced to rational choice alone.

The role that Hobbes laid out for the sovereign marks the introduction of a pervasive theme in conflict theory. Those who have political power stand in opposition to those subject to their power. The state employs coercion to carry out its will while consensus recedes into the background.

In addition, the Hobbesian state of nature, which political power is intended to rectify, is a classic outline of the clash of unregulated interests resulting from an egoistic model of man. Here an anomaly appears, for the right of everyone to preserve himself by any means represents a concord of minds. Everyone agrees on the universality of the right of self-

Conflict   263

preservation, yet this leads to conflict. It thus becomes apparent that the correspondences between consensus and cooperation and disagreement and conflict are not total.

Marx and Conflict

It is more to Karl Marx, however, that contemporary formulations of conflict owe their provenance. Although the differences between the Hobbesian and Marxian versions should not be minimized, there appear in Marx's theory analogues with the former. For Marx as for Hobbes, self-interest, greed, and infinite expansion of material desire motivate individuals. Stimulated by greed, conflict is a ubiquitous factor as men go about producing commodities. Whereas Hobbes was interested in conflicts over the consumption of goods, Marx was more impressed by conflicts during their production. Both held the state to be a coercive apparatus.

CONFLICT IN THE DIVISION OF LABOR

Like Hobbes, Marx called attention to the material side of man's life. In order to live, human beings must feed and clothe themselves, find shelter, and propagate their species; and any history of mankind must duly take these factors into consideration.[18] Thus, men engage daily and hourly in two acts of self-reproduction: They produce material necessities from nature, and they reproduce themselves sexually. These reproductive acts contain the basis of Marx's materialistic interpretation of history.

Both of these types of reproduction are cooperative activities.[19] Sexual reproduction requires cooperation of man and woman within the family. The conquest of nature for the means of subsistence requires cooperation in an economic division of labor. Marx referred to these relationships as the "social relations of production." With growth in population and economic development, however, the family becomes subordinate to the economy; and the latter turns out to be the most important determinant of total societies.[20]

The trouble is that both sexual and economic divisions of labor lead to certain inequalities, although those in the economy are the most

264   The Duality of Consensus and Conflict

decisive ones for the society as a whole. In the first place, labor itself is unequally distributed.[21] In earlier historical forms, for example, some individuals begin to perform intellectual work while others do manual tasks. Here is a qualitative inequality in labor that Marx thought to be significant. Intellectual functions were performed by priests and those who supervised labor. Also, there have always been quantitative differences in the amount of work individuals do. In the second place, the products of labor come to be unequally distributed. The result is that differences materialize among individuals in their ability to control both consumables and the material instruments of production (tools). Even in the family, Marx observed, the husband controlled the labor of the wife, a relationship that constituted the earliest form of slavery. Inequalities in labor and property that arise in the social relations of production turn out to have far-reaching consequences.

One such consequence is *domination.*[22] Those who perform intellectual functions and who control the material instruments are able to exercise power over others in the division of labor. They are able to dictate to others and realize their economic interests. These forms of domination intensify in relation to the increase of other factors in the division of labor. As production employs more man-made capital, the division of labor grows more differentiated and complex as work becomes more specialized and the tasks divided. As material capital accumulates, its control grows ever more concentrated, a process that Marx called the separation of capital from labor.[23] Hence, the growth of complexity increases inequalities in work and property and the accumulation of power.

In commodity production increasing domination is matched by increasing *alienation*—a factor of great importance in Marx's materialist interpretation of history. Alienation is an attitude, a mode of perception, which is manifest in several ways. In the first place, the producer becomes alienated from the very commodities produced by his own labor power. "Congealed" in commodities, labor assumes an objectified form. Although a commodity is the product of labor, the worker looks upon it as an objective, alien power hostile to his own interests. He defines the world of commodities as an external force that controls his existence, determines his fate, and makes him into a slave. Although having produced commodities, he is denied their possession. If he does not possess them, someone else must; and that someone else is he who can dispose of the material instruments of production. It follows that the ownership of property and the alienation of labor are indissolubly linked.[24] Property turns out to be a determinant of domination that contributes to alienation.

Alienation is a dynamic process. The greater the production of commodities through the application of larger amounts of material capital, the more powerful becomes this alien world. In his theory of capitalism, Marx worked out the precise ways in which capital accumulation alienates labor. For example, increases in the volume of commodities devalues the worth of labor and leads to unemployment.

In the second place, the worker is alienated from the activities of his own labor. Those who own the instruments of production are in a position to dictate the tasks of labor, which strips the worker of his autonomy. Forfeiting the control of his own work to another, the worker loses his freedom and views his own work as an alien power. Especially under capitalism, labor is coerced and dictated rather than voluntary and spontaneous. Like the commodity, labor has effects that work against its own interests. Marx identified the degradation of labor in controlled, routinized production as a form of self-alienation.[25] The greater the domination involved in commodity production, the greater is the alienation of labor.

Marx's analysis thus far reduces to these essentials: Except under communism, production imposes an unequal distribution of burdens and benefits. These inequalities result from inequalities in the distribution of work and the control of property, which in turn result in domination and alienation. Especially important is the control of property, which in capitalism takes the form of private individual ownership. Domination and alienation grow more pronounced as the division of labor grows in complexity and as the instruments and materials of production accumulate. Marx placed strong negative evaluations on these effects and arrived at the startling conclusion that human beings are victims rather than beneficiaries of the division of labor. The latter abounds in exploitation.

SOCIAL CLASS

Inequalities in labor, power, and property become manifest as class differences among those within the system of production. The basic determinant of class, according to Marx, comes down to the legal

266   The Duality of Consensus and Conflict

ownership of property in the form of the material instruments of production. Insofar as the distribution and consumption of goods depend upon their mode of production, it follows that property owners also dominate the entire economy. Ownership of capital thus separates the higher from the lower classes; and ownership of different forms of capital, such as land and industry, divide the owners of property themselves into classes. It is clear that the phenomenon of social classes is based on the aforementioned factors in the division of labor.

Thus, the division of labor places individuals in situations where their opportunities and burdens are largely determined by property. It is therefore appropriate to speak about class situations conditioned by the distribution of property ownership, with corresponding interests embedded in the structure of the division of labor. These *objective class interests*, however, precede their recognition by those who find themselves in similar class situations.[26] When they do come to a recognition of their common interests, that is, when the latter become aspects of their conscious experience, then those individuals constitute a *class for itself*.[27] Before acquiring that consciousness, however, they form only a *class in itself*. *Class consciousness* is the decisive factor, a necessary condition, for overt class conflicts. Conditioned by inequalities in the division of labor, class interests are always opposed. The wealth of one social class is the poverty of another. With the notion of contradictory class interests, Marx universalized economic conflict; for every division of labor calls forth a social class which suffers burdens but is denied advantages, and in capitalism this class is the *proletariat*.[28]

Marx illustrated how types of property ownership relate to forms of class conflict with examples.[29] Tribal ownership, the first form, corresponds to a hunting and fishing division of labor. At higher stages of this economic mode, there also occur some cattle breeding and agriculture. An extension of the family, it includes patriarchal chieftains, ordinary tribal members, and slaves as three distinct classes. Tribal slavery, according to Marx, turns out to be an extension of the slavery latent within the family. When tribes unite to form cities either by agreement or conquest, the division of labor grows more complex. Then the antagonism between citizens and slaves grows more intense. The citizens, holding slaves as communal property, unite to keep them in subordination.

At the same time there develops within the city-state movable and immovable private property (land). At first, private property appears as an abnormal type in a society dominated by communal property. But as the former grows, the latter decays. Private property brings with it other conflicts, such as conflict between country and city and among city-states representing contrasting interests of town and country. As private property spreads, the division of labor within city-states grows more differentiated.

Such examples illustrate how changing modes of production result in changing class configurations. Changes from hunting to agriculture involve changes in ownership, which in turn alter class situations and conflicts. New modes of production replace the old, and new classes and constellations of interests displace previous ones. Class antagonisms intensify with growing complexity in the division of labor, and economic "progress" never occurs without the intensification of conflict.

Class consciousness, as we have seen, does not immediately develop from interests inherent in class situations. Those in common situations become aware of shared interests in the process of defending themselves and become solidified through struggle. Marx pointed to the struggle of the burghers of the Middle Ages against the nobility.[30] Living in cities and engaging in commerce, the burghers fought to free themselves from feudal restrictions imposed by the nobility. The conflict, observed Marx, between merchants and nobles reflected a conflict between commercial and landed capital. Living off dues and rents from landed estates, the nobility dominated the feudal system, which was a different mode of production from the emerging system spearheaded by the *bourgeoisie*. Although in competition with one another, burghers joined together and formed associations of cities to defend their interests. These activities made them class conscious.

In the capitalisms of his time Marx identified the three major classes of wage-laborers (proletariat), capitalists (bourgeoisie), and landowners.[31] The latter two classes own industrial capital and land respectively, whereas laborers own no property and are therefore forced to sell their labor power for a wage. As small manufacturers, artisans, and peasants sink into the proletariat, the main cleavage in capitalist societies divides bourgeoisie from proletariat.[32] Marx predicted that the workers would gradually organize against the bourgeoisie, organizing first factories, then trades, and finally entire regions. Resorting to strikes, arson, and riots, they will eventually become conscious of themselves as a class.[33] Their battle will take on a political dimension, for it will also be directed against the state.

268   The Duality of Consensus and Conflict

THE STATE

Marx's theory of the state provides another legacy to the conflict tradition. In the contest between consensus and conflict for theoretical supremacy, the state looms as an important factor because it possesses a monopoly of power. Who controls it is a matter of controversy within the consensus-conflict debate.

Marx's theory of the state must be understood in the context of his materialist conception of history. Accordingly, society is divided into *base* and *superstructure*, the former exerting a determinative influence on the latter. The economic base is comprehended by the modes of production, consisting of the aforementioned social relations and the material forces of production (tools, raw material, and technology). The superstructure is composed of classes, legal order, family, state, and higher ideas expressed in religion, philosophy, and ethics.[34] Although base and superstructure influence each other, the modes of production exert the predominant impact. Engels left no doubt that the decisive factor in organizing the entire society is its economic base.[35] Therefore, the state must be explained in terms of the economic base.

A clear idea of the function of the state can be found in Engels's account of its origin.[36] The state entered history at the tribal stage of historical development. It follows that the state is not a universal institution. The modes of production of tribal society yielded a surplus above what was required for mere physical survival. Surplus eventuated in the exchange of commodities, which in turn provided a model for the exchange of humans. Accordingly, slavery was introduced into history. These changing modes of production intensified class antagonisms, which tribal society was unable to contain because its political organization was based on *gentes* (clans) rather than territory. Engels called societies with these economic and political structures *gentile societies*.

Gentile society, according to Engels, was unable to contain intensified class conflicts generated by surpluses, exchange, and the division of labor. To prevent these conflicts from shattering society, the state emerged in order to confine them within manageable bounds. Gentile society was unable to exert sufficient political control over a demarcated territory as it had in the past when gentes inhabited given areas. Mobility had, moreover, upset the correspondence between gens and territory; and the territorial state filled the breach. But unlike the control exercised by clans, which expressed the interests of the whole tribe, the state represented only the interests of the privileged classes. For example, the public power of ancient Athens represented the interests of the free citizens against the slaves. Previously the whole society had organized itself as a cohesive armed force, but this was no longer possible with the appearance of class cleavages.

Athens illustrates a fundamental principle of Marxist political theory. Despite its origin in the intent to contain class conflicts, the state is typically controlled by the dominant class for the realization of its own interests. That class captures control and uses the state as an instrument to hold the lower classes in subjection. Consequently, the exploitation and alienation arising in the economic division of labor are perpetuated in a political form. To be sure, sometimes a state takes on the semblance of impartiality when conflicting classes reach a stalemate in their struggle for power. Generally, however, it stands above society as an external, alien power. Political alienation in the state parallels alienation in the economy; both state and commodity are experienced as hostile powers not subject to human control. The Greek and Roman city-states allied themselves with slave owners, the feudal state with nobles, and the capitalist state with the bourgeoisie, said Engels.

Marx's discussion of the state complements Engels's account of its origin. Although all states are conditioned by property, the modern state more than any other is based on private ownership of property. Therefore, it is dominated by the bourgeoisie, who loan it money and manage the national debt. Indeed, its very function is to guarantee the integrity of private property. The laws enacted that pertain to property were not the outcome of an independent communal will, said Marx. They did not grow out of the will of the people, but rather reflected the conquest of feudal by commercial and industrial property. Strictly in the interests of the bourgeoisie, the legal order of property is entirely independent of the community.[37]

Contemporary Russia furnishes another example of alliance between state and class. There the nobles owned more land than the peasants, yet paid only one-fifteenth of the annual land tax as the latter, Marx pointed out. The average size of the estates held by the nobility was much larger than the average land holding of the peasants.[38] As noted above, one does not, however, need to limit himself to antidemocratic states to find such alliances. Although democracy is the most advanced form of the state, even there the class struggle will erupt in revolution. That a state has formally democratic constitutions does not render it representative of the

270   The Duality of Consensus and Conflict

general will nor insulate it from the power of the upper class, for democracy is the last form of the bourgeois state.[39] In the context of the role of the bourgeoisie in history, Marx and Engels wrote the famous words: "The executive of the modern State is but a committee for managing the common affairs of the whole bourgeoisie."[40] Born out of class conflict and nourished by its intensification, the democratic state, far from being an impartial arbiter, is a weapon in the class struggle.

The general outlines of Marx's conflict theory of the state are thus clear: Man is not by nature a political animal, for the state originates in societies at a particular stage of their historical development. The state's intended function is to contain the destructive potential of conflicts among social classes, but it realizes this function only under rare circumstances. In the course of time, states typically default by taking sides as political leaders support the propertied classes by sustaining a social order congenial to their interests. Hence, the state ends up representing a part of the whole against the rest. This generalization also applies to those states with formal norms of democracy; consequently no state is actually founded on the principle of popular sovereignty. As a result, the state relies on coercion as one of its principal supports. Because the state in history enters as part of the class struggle, it will disappear in communist society, where there are no classes.

Marx derived this "economic elite" model of the state from the materialist interpretation of history. Its premise of a relationship between base and superstructure yields the conclusion that the social relations of power and conflict in the former become manifest in the latter. Economic conflict generates political conflict, and economic dominance is translated into political power. Alienation from commodity and work in the base is paralleled by alienation from the state in the superstructure.

IDEOLOGY

According to the materialist interpretation, abstract thought in the form of religion, philosophy, and ethics is conditioned by the modes of production. In analyzing the role of such systems of thought, Marx stood Hegel "right side up" by inverting the relationship the latter saw between thought and history. The role that thinking plays in society according to Marx was applied in later conflict theory, especially to the state.

The class that comes to dominance in the class struggle bends the state to its will. Political power, however, is not its only prop. By acquiring control over the means of mental production, the ruling class represents its interests as the general interest.[41] The system of thought that represents the part as the whole takes the form of an *ideology*. The question then becomes, What is an ideology?

Marx's historical account yields the beginning of an answer. When the division of labor became complex enough for some to do only manual work and others to think, ideological dimensions penetrated society's religious and ethical ideas.[42] Until then these ideas more or less accurately reflected the relationships of production. But with the separation of intellectual and physical labor, the ideas of specialists in thinking such as priests no longer corresponded to what was going on in the division of labor. Their ideas failed to capture the conflicting interests among various categories of labor and the contradictions between base and superstructure. Religion and mythology glossed over these conflicts and in a sense "concealed" them. Ideological dimensions turn out to be distortions that enter into religion, philosophy, and moral theories. Marx identified priests as the first ideologists in history.[43]

Thus, the idealistic superstructure becomes permeated by ideological dimensions in the course of the division of labor. What, more specifically, constitutes ideological thinking? This type of thinking, said Marx, abstracts certain aspects of reality, omits the remaining, and then conveniently forgets the abstract character of ideas, claiming to give a faithful representation. This is precisely, said Marx, what Hegel did, who abstracted thinking from its material base and then, forgetting the latter, treated thought as though it were the determinant of all history.[44] Ideological thinking distorts reality through omission; it refracts rather than mirrors. When religion, philosophy, and ethics become "pure theory," they cast a veil of illusion over the society they describe and present an inverted representation of individuals and their circumstances.[45] In concealing the real interests of the lower classes, they create, for example, a false consciousness. In order, therefore, to grasp reality rather than its semblance in ideology, one must go back to the modes of production out of which ideological thinking arose. Ideologists themselves are not always aware of their presuppositions and of the way they actually create ideas.[46] Ideology cannot, therefore, be totally reduced to conscious deception.

Marx gave examples of the entanglement of ideas in class struggles, even though the latter are formulated as pure theory. In the past, when

272   The Duality of Consensus and Conflict

kings, aristocrats, and bourgeoisie were contending for supremacy, the doctrine of the separation of powers became the dominant notion of political philosophy. When aristocrats dominated society, the concepts of honor and loyalty predominated. When the bourgeoisie assumed the dominant position, the notions of freedom and equality came to the fore. When one class becomes the ruling class in the state, its ideas then become the ruling ideas in society. The class that controls the material means of production, according to Marx, also acquires control of the means of mental production.[47]

Ideologists either belong to the ruling class or are loyal to it. In producing ideas, they create illusions about that entire class and represent its interests as coincident with those of society. They elevate prevailing notions to the status of universals. The classical economists, for example, set forth the doctrine that the laws of supply and demand that govern a free market are natural laws.[48] That doctrine gives legitimacy to the bourgeois mode of production. Ideologists stabilize society by legitimating the existing division of labor and structure of power.

Thus, the power of the ruling class, although arising from property, does not rest on property alone. Society's economic and political arrangements, which favor the upper class, are also reinforced by ideologies. These, however, are not critically formed but are unconsciously motivated deceptions. Ideas relevant to the formation of public policy are not expressions of public opinion, but are formed rather by class interests that shape it. Their latent function is to perpetuate the dominance of the ruling class, but their expressed purpose is to create valid representations of reality. The relationship of ideologies to conflict is twofold. First, they repress overt conflicts by concealing clashes of interests. Second, when the veil of illusion is penetrated by a counterideology, ideological conflicts are reflections of real conflicts in society. Consistent with these generalizations, later versions of conflict theory link ideology closely to the state and explain it as supplying a pseudolegitimacy to the latter.

REVOLUTION

The analyses of class conflict, state, and ideology foreshadow Marx's theory of revolution, which is also a derivative of the materialist interpretation. Revolutions arise out of conflicting class interests that originate in the base and rapidly transform the superstructure, propelling societies through stages of development. Revolutions against society and state by oppressed classes are the real engines of historical change.

Before a revolution can occur, said Marx, certain objective conditions must prevail. In their absence, the mere desire of individuals to revolt will not produce a revolution.[49] Revolutionary conditions consist of conflicts between the material forces and the social relations of production. What Marx meant here is that the way the material instruments of production are distributed in accordance with the legal order of property restrains further development of production even though the technology, raw materials, and machines are available. The social relations, said Marx, act like fetters on the material forces of production.[50] The contradiction between material forces and social relations appears as part of a configuration of conditions. The society is polarized into an oppressor and oppressed class. Polarization is so extreme that the oppressor concentrates within itself all the evils of society, while the oppressed class is able to represent its interests as identical with society as a whole. This kind of polarization, said Marx, prevailed at the time of the French Revolution between nobility and clergy on the one hand and the bourgeoisie on the other.[51]

It is clear that such conditions materialize from lawlike changes in the economic base. Marx held that no social order perishes until all the productive forces that typify that stage of development have been realized. Further, no new order replaces its predecessor until the seeds of its material characteristics have appeared within the latter.[52] These two laws of historical change collectively describe a society with maturing modes of production reaching their apex while in the process generating the contradictory characteristics of the order that will replace it. Originating in class struggles, revolutions push societies through developmental stages—the Asiatic, ancient, feudal, and bourgeois modes of production.[53] Reorganizations, of course, occur in the superstructure that accompany the changes in the modes of production.

Marx complained that all past revolutions merely altered the distribution of labor and power without abolishing the class system itself. The victors appropriated the material means of production, but remained subservient to the division of labor.[54] They replaced one minority rule with their own. Even when, however, the majority of people took part, their efforts turned out to be at the service of the victorious minority; for the latter was always able to foster the ideology of representing everyone's interest.[55]

274   The Duality of Consensus and Conflict

In contrast, the communist revolution against capitalism will abolish the class system itself[56] by socializing the material instruments of production.[57] Having located the structure of domination and oppression in the ownership of property, Marx drew the conclusion that by vesting it in the total community domination would disappear. He went on to speculate vaguely about the communist utopia, in which the state disappears and man finally overcomes alienation. At last the human being escapes victimization by the division of labor and attains freedom.[58]

In sum, the materialist interpretation explains social change as the result of opposing interests generated in the division of labor. These form the bases of social classes, whose struggles culminate in a series of revolutions that replace one social order by another that is governed by different principles. Conflicting economic interests are generalized to the other institutions in accordance with the theory of base and superstructure. These clashes of interests take the form of destabilizing contradictions in the social order. The changes are not random but follow a rough, sequential order of stages toward perfection. A fundamental principle of this theory of revolution for conflict theory is that conflict is the major cause of change.

Marxism and Functionalism

These two theoretical traditions come into collision in regard to the following question: How can the differences inherent in a division of labor be adjusted so they do not result in conflicts that destroy it? Functionalists like Durkheim and Parsons conclude, as we have seen, that a reconciliation of diversity can be accomplished through the formation of norms. Society carries out its functions according to such norms as universalistic competence and distributive justice that take on the connotations of moral imperatives. Generalized mechanisms such as money, markets for material and labor, power, influence, and the appeal to value-commitments allocate materials and persons to roles and facilitate in other ways their performance in a division of labor. Like the norms that define roles, these mechanisms command consensus.

On the other hand, Marxists have always been skeptical about the effectiveness of these factors so long as the control over material means is concentrated. Norm-formation under the existence of power always results in norms that further the interests of those in power. In the long run, these norms cannot be sustained by consensus. Antagonistic interests, although suppressed in the short run, will destroy the division of labor in the long run. Therefore, in answer to the above question, Marx concluded that the differences inherent in a division of labor can be adjusted only in communist society, where differences in the ownership of property are eliminated.

These contrasting answers lead to other differences. According to Parsons, control over property (facilities) must be unequal because those with the competence to perform roles that make possible the survival of the society must be given the means necessary to do the job. These include authority and power. Consequently, the imperatives for the existence of society require that it be stratified. Stratification, therefore, brings about the adjustment of differences. Inequalities in facilities and rewards are legitimated by a consensual understanding of their necessity for the realization of common values. Those at the bottom of the ladder are socialized into believing that the norms and values that put them there are legitimate. However, according to Marx, it is these very inequalities that will destroy society; for all stratification originates from power rather than from functional necessity. Power seeks the gratification of self-interest rather than the achievement of collective goals. Inequalities can be sustained in the short run by power and ideology but are inevitably destructive in the long run.

The Marxist theory of the state explains its role as an extension of the power of those dominant in the stratification system. The state is the political means for realizing the interests of the dominant class, which does not have with other classes a shared, legitimate value-system. The unadjusted differences in the division of labor in the course of time evoke the exercise of political power, but not in an evenhanded way. Even formally democratic states do not really rest on popular sovereignty.

Functional social theory, on the other hand, is logically constrained by its commitment to consensus to explain the state as another functional necessity. Its role is to achieve collective goals that correspond to the values of the majority, at least most of the time. It balances conflicting interests through persuasion and the appeal to values. In mediating among conflicting interests, it acts like the referee of an athletic contest, who calls decisions in accordance with the rules of the game that give each side an equal chance of winning. Popular sovereignty is an achievable ideal.

276   The Duality of Consensus and Conflict

In contrast to Marx, who inverted Hegel, Parsons through the cybernetic hierarchy sustained Hegel's theory of the primacy of ideas. Grounded in consensual world views, values are determinants rather than reflexes of material processes of production. As guiding principles of the organization of society, they legitimate that organization. As a result, its stability rests mainly in the fact that society satisfies its members by bringing reality into correspondence with consensual values. On the other hand, according to Marx, ideologies do not form blueprints for society as a whole. Instead, they justify the inequalities of property, power, and reward in the presentation of a distorted picture. Ideologies cloak society with a pseudolegitimacy and are open to challenge by counterideologies. Originated by thinkers whose loyalties are to the ruling class, ideologies do not originate in public opinion but "trickle down" to shape it.

Functional social theory attributes an efficacy to processes of equilibrium that maintain values. Historical change tends to be slow, cumulative, and consistent with values. Thus, the cultural heritage of society is preserved while at the same time change contributes to its adaptation. This kind of change contrasts with revolutionary transformations that result in novel social orders that follow different principles.

Under the influence of the notions of consensus and conflict, the same concepts in functionalism and Marxism take on different connotations. From the perspective of Marx, for instance, it makes no sense to identify actions of a revolutionary class as forms of deviance; for there is no universal, consensual standard in society that can be taken as a measure. In contrast, the exploitative connotations of the term social class are absent in Parsons's use of the term. Another example of divergent connotations of the same term is given by the notion of ideology. Incorporated in Parsons's definition of this concept is a system of beliefs held in common by members that achieves society's evaluative integration[59]—a definition clearly devoid of the function that Marx identified. Similar divergences in connotation are apparent in other concepts, such as democracy, power, and legitimacy. In addition, concepts central to one theory are totally lacking in the other, such as class consciousness, false consciousness, and functional prerequisite. Therefore, what is a problem for one theory is not a problem for another; and concepts within these different scientific traditions are linked in different ways.[60]

Contradictory generalizations about state, stratification, change, etc.

Conflict   277

drawn from the theories of Parsons and Marx contain the outlines of the controversy over consensus and conflict. As we shall see, other formulations having relevance to the controversy turn out to be expansions and corrections of these delineations.

Status Groups as Conflict Units

In defining *status group* as ideal-type and distinguishing it from class, Weber enlarged our understanding of conflict. The principal cleavages in society are not always the results of conflicting class interests as Marx had so brilliantly argued, but are often the consequences of conflicts among status groups. These groups are the key to a model of society implicit in Weber's historical investigations that at once reveals oversimplifications in Marxism and at the same time poses a challenge to functionalism.

What Marx conjoined, Weber separated. For Marx the higher classes through their relations to the modes of production acquire not only power and wealth but also status. For Weber, however, a perfect correspondence between wealth, status, and power is an oversimplification that must be disposed of by a proper analysis of their interrelationships. Some power, for instance, confers dishonor rather than status. Weber pointed to the American political boss as an example.[61] Neither does every group with high status possess wealth; for some clergy, as an example, live a prestigeful life in poverty. In addition, not all power can be traced to economic factors; for high status can acquire economic power, thus reversing Marx's causal sequence. An example is the inherited estate of the knight.[62] These examples prove that it is essential to make analytical distinctions among class, status, and power; only then can their interrelationships be studied.

What is a status group? A status group consists of those who share a distinctive style of life that is a negative or positive source of honor, prestige, or esteem.[63] The word negative in this definition implies that some status groups are objects of contempt rather than esteem. The key to the prestige of a status group is its members' style of life, whose conventions they recognize as the code of the group.

Well-known factors define a style of life. Family background is an obvious, inherited aspect of a style of life. The prestige of an occupation

278   The Duality of Consensus and Conflict

is another factor that shapes the distribution of status. Residence, membership in clubs, and formal education, especially one aimed at the cultivation of a gentleman, go into a mode of living. In contrast to members of a class who are similarly situated with respect to the modes of production, members of a status group are similarly situated with respect to modes of consumption. There is a tendency for members to restrict their associations through endogamy and commensalism to those of their own circle in order to uphold their status. Status groups tend to become closed. In order to uphold its prestige, the group also enforces the conventions of its style of life through all sorts of sanctions. Members of status groups with high prestige derive a sense of dignity through complying with its conventions.

Thus, in the way Weber defined them status groups are organized around values, such as the conduct of an occupation, literary education, military service to the state, and religiosity. With regard to these groups, Weber drew the generalization that in defending and extending their values they come into conflict with one another. Sometimes the victors are able to get their values accepted as the cultural ideals of an entire society or civilization. Examples are the Confucianism of literati, the Hinduism of Brahmans, and the asceticism of Protestant sects.[64] One method to realize their material and ideal interests was to acquire monopolies over the activities and materials they needed to practice their style of life. History furnishes examples of legal monopolies such as the entailment of estates, the right to bear arms, the right to wear certain costumes, and the right to practice particular occupations.

Weber emphasized the fact that these conflicts are not class conflicts. Whereas Marx had defined class in relation to the modes of commodity production, Weber defined class in relation to the market for commodities and labor. Those who are similarly situated with reference to the market constitute a class. A class, then, consists of individuals who have similar opportunities to realize various life chances through commodities or income from the market. For example, those who own property can sell it for money, which then can be exchanged for consumables or capital or invested in stocks or bonds. Those who possess services or skill sell it on the labor market for a wage.

It is evident that Weber's definition of class is narrower than Marx's. Classes, accordingly, cannot come into existence until labor and commodity markets develop. Marx's modes of production, in contrast, is a more general concept, which refers to an entire economic order including production, distribution, and consumption of goods with or without a market. For Marx slaves of the past were a class; but according to Weber slaves who are not free to sell property and their labor are not a class, but a status group. Yet Weber agreed with Marx that the possession of property forms a fundamental division between "propertied classes" and "acquisition classes," the latter having only services to sell. Within these two classes numerous subdivisions based on types of property and level of skill exist.

Weber observed that those who find themselves in a similar class situation may or may not unite to advance their economic interests. They may or may not develop class consciousness. Whether or not such a "communal action" is forthcoming and how many individuals get involved depend on various factors. Consequently, the Marxist class struggle is only a probability for Weber. Nevertheless, those class struggles that did occur throughout history fall roughly into a historical sequence. The earliest was between property owners and debtors in antiquity—peasants in debt to urban creditors. Then came price wars over the price of bread and other commodities basic to life. Beginning in antiquity and lasting throughout the Middle Ages, these price conflicts occurred between the propertied, who put these necessities on the market, and the propertyless, whose interest was in cheap commodities. Finally, the basic conflict today is over the wages paid to labor.

Although fundamentally different, the economic and status orders are, according to Weber's analysis, related in complex ways. The prestigeful status group refuses to admit those with no other qualifications except economic power and wealth; the parvenu has everywhere been rejected. The group will, however, admit his descendants if they conform to its conventions. The antithesis of class and status is manifest in the fact that if economic power alone could confer status, the status order, resting on style of life, would be threatened at its very foundations. In that case, the wealthiest individual would be accorded the highest status. On the other hand, property, although not sufficient, may be one necessary criterion for belonging to the status group. Also, the members of different classes can belong to the same status group.

Status groups are related to the market in diverse ways, according to Weber. History gives numerous examples of status groups that hindered the development of the market. The inherited estate of the feudal nobility could not be sold. Essential to the market is bargaining over the price of goods, which the honor of the high status group eschews. In addition, occupational groups are status groups, whose claims to prestige are based on the style of life they make possible and not on the wealth they acquire. Some occupations of status groups of high prestige decree a life of poverty for their incumbents. It is also possible for two occupations to yield the same average income, yet vary in prestige. In sum, Marx's economic determinism turns out to oversimplify the relationship between class and status. Although related, the economic order and the status order do not coincide.

In these amendments to Marx, Weber demonstrated that class struggles are not the principal conflicts in history; for they are often overridden by conflicts among status groups. These conflicts, oriented to ideal values, sometimes even hinder the development of classes and the economic power of property. Neither do all individuals place the same value on economic acquisition, and the man who is willing to die for his god cannot be explained as economically motivated. The solidarity of the status group arises often from noneconomic values. Held as absolutes, ideal values of different status groups come into conflict; and Weber saw no way that these conflicts could be resolved in terms of utilitarian or scientific criteria. Science cannot decide which are true.

It was at this point in his construction of the social system that Parsons contradicted Weber; for he believed as we have seen, that an individualized ascetic Protestantism appearing in the guise of instrumental activism captured the mind of Western societies to become their cultural ideal. Having emerged victorious in the contest of values, instrumental activism furnishes the common value-system around which these societies are integrated. What Parsons did was to reinterpret within the framework of a consensual model a principle of conflict enunciated by Weber.

Dahrendorf's Critique of Parsons

Ralf Dahrendorf (1929–) has criticized from a conflict perspective Parsons's theory of the social system as a form of utopianism that has been detrimental to social research. His analysis of the shortcomings of the social system has become a classic statement in the consensus-conflict controversy. Among other criticisms, Dahrendorf charged that Parsons did not construct the social system with the end of providing explanations

Conflict   281

of specific facts or of solving riddles suggested by human experience. Not being anchored in the concrete world, the social system turns out to be a utopia.[65] Dahrendorf's challenge contains methodological as well as substantive dimensions.

Like the utopias of Plato, Owen, and Marx, the social system has not been constructed out of any familiar reality. It does not consist of a limited number of variables abstracted from the real world because of their presumed relevance for explaining a particular problem, but consists rather of a purely logical interrelation of parts. As a result, the social system is a model of an imaginary world, useless for providing generalizations. A prime illustration of lack of contact between social system and concrete societies is the former's universal consensus of values. The evidence is overwhelming, said Dahrendorf, that no real society has ever enjoyed such a consensus. And if such a society could be found, it would lack conflict because conflict always involves clashes of values. A society without conflict is also unrealistic.[66]

Having value-consensus, the theory of the social system cannot explain conflicts caused by structural contradictions. Instead, what Parsons came up with is the deviant, who is either incapable of conforming or who is pathologically motivated to violate the social system's values. In either case, said Dahrendorf, because of the sociological inadequacy of his theory Parsons was forced to implicitly resort to individual psychology to explain the disruption caused by the deviant.[67]

Furthermore, any changes in the system's structure are neutralized by its mechanisms of social control that reestablish equilibrium.[68] Another unreal element, equilibrium implies that the social system does not change. It contains, to be sure, recurrent processes such as reproduction, socialization, and role allocation; but these leave its structure basically intact. Moreover, since it is self-sufficient and isolated, it is hard to see how it can be changed from the outside. Hence, the social system lacks a history.

Yet, Dahrendorf conceded, highly general, abstract models can be useful in explaining specific problems, one being why educational achievement is thought by so many to be so important.[69] For such a problem Parsons's theory might be useful. Nevertheless, there is another general model that represents a new departure that stands in logical opposition to Parsons's integration model. Dahrendorf referred to it as the *coercion model*, which can conceivably solve problems that the social system is unable to penetrate.

To draw the contrasts, Dahrendorf formulated each model in a highly

282   The Duality of Consensus and Conflict

oversimplified form and as a logical opposite of the other.[70] In juxtaposing them he conceded that both are essential for sociological analysis but that each is relevant to different scientific problems. Each expresses a different "face" of society. The integration model, which is a simplified codification of the social system, is as follows:

> (1) Every society is a relatively persistent, stable structure of elements.
> (2) Every society is a well-integrated structure of elements.
> (3) Every element in a society has a function, i.e., renders a contribution to its maintenance as a system.
> (4) Every functioning social structure is based on a consensus of values among its members.[71]

The coercion model states:

> (1) Every society is at every point subject to processes of change; social change is ubiquitous.
> (2) Every society displays at every point dissensus and conflict; social conflict is ubiquitous.
> (3) Every element in a society renders a contribution to its disintegration and change.
> (4) Every society is based on the coercion of some of its members by others.[72]

Although the integration model oversimplifies Parsons, the coercion model oversimplifies Marx. In effect, the coercion model generalizes the class conflicts and contradictions that Marx saw in past and present societies to all the elements that compose any society. With ubiquitous conflicts making for recurrent instabilities, the only factor holding a society together is coercion (power). These models reveal the logical tension between Marxism and functionalism.

Dahrendorf's Theory of Class Conflict

In order to prove the superiority of the coercion over the integration model for explaining certain problems, Dahrendorf went on to build a theory of class conflict upon that model. He also claimed that with the coercion model he could provide a better explanation than Marx's theory.

His explanation modified Marx's ideas in the light of changes that have occurred in industrial societies since Marx wrote and which he did not foresee.[73] Armed with this model and with Marx as a foundation, Dahrendorf formulated a theory of class conflict. It is quite apparent, he stated, that the integration model is inadequate for this problem.

The structure within which class conflict occurs is the *imperatively coordinated association* as defined by Max Weber, exemplified in the modern state, economic enterprise, church, and trade union.[74] Consequently, any society composed of these organizations is subject to class conflict. If a society has fifty such associations, it has the potential for that many class conflicts.[75] Although conflict assumes many forms, it is class conflict that is the focus of Dahrendorf's explanatory attempt.[76]

In accord with the strategy of revising Marx, he adopted a different basis of class. Possession or exclusion from property is not the foundation of social class. Rather, the basis of class is the possession or exclusion from authority. As a result, those in positions of authority in these associations form an upper class, at least potentially. And those who are subject to authority form a lower class. Whereas Marx believed that power arises from the ownership of property, Dahrendorf concluded that the control over property stems from the possession of authority. That authority is more general than property is illustrated by the clergy, who have ecclesiastical authority, but lack control over the instruments of production. The trouble with Marx's theory, said Dahrendorf, is that it is inconsistent with the trend toward separation of ownership from control in the economy.[77] The managers, not the stockholders, control corporate property; and, therefore, Marx must be revised.

Let us, then, reconstruct more specifically his theory of class conflict from the coercion model. According to this model, authority in imperatively coordinated associations, even though legitimate, must ultimately generate conflicts between those who wield it and those subjected to it. Authority must have this consequence because it is an element of society, and according to the model all elements of society are in conflict. Conflict and disintegration, not authority's integrative function, reveal society's ugly side, said Dahrendorf.[78]

On the basis of several assumptions, Dahrendorf argued that conflicts arise out of this distribution of authority when certain empirical conditions materialize. He assumed that embedded in the roles of those who hold authority are interests that contradict interests embedded in the roles of those who obey.[79] The interest latent within roles of authority is

284   The Duality of Consensus and Conflict

that of maintaining the existing structure, whereas the interest latent within roles of subjection is that of changing it.[80] It is obvious that these *latent interests* correspond fairly closely to what Marx called objective interests. Rather than resulting from a differential distribution of property, however, they originate in a differential distribution of authority.

If role incumbents become aware of their latent interests and consciously adopt them as goals, they become transmuted into *manifest interests*.[81] Those in subjection adopt their latent interest in changing the system of authority as their conscious goal, while those with authority consciously defend it. As psychological realities, manifest interests can now be studied on the ideological level as a conflict between doctrines that maintain the legitimacy of authority and doctrines that undermine it.[82] Again the continuity of Dahrendorf with Marx is evident, for the transmutation of a latent to a manifest interest corresponds to the acquisition of class consciousness.[83]

Individuals who share roles with similar latent interests constitute what Dahrendorf called a *quasi group* within the association.[84] Those members of a quasi group who then become conscious of their latent interests form an *interest group*, the former being a recruiting field for the latter.[85] Interest groups are real groups with shared goals and organization; and within the context of Dahrendorf's theory, they turn out to be social classes that engage in class conflict.[86] This two-class model of associations corresponds to Marx's polarization of society.

Dahrendorf concluded that the emergence of classes from quasi groups is not inevitable. Here he rejected Marx.[87] Some quasi groups remain quasi groups. For an interest group to form, certain empirical factors must materialize. In identifying three types of such factors, Dahrendorf qualified the theoretical model of coercion with empirical facts. One factor consists of the social conditions of organization, such as the concentration of a quasi-group in one space, which enables its members to communicate. A second factor is technical. To become a class, a quasi-group must acquire a charter with rules, officers, and material premises. Especially important are leaders. A third factor consists of the political conditions of organization. The state, for example, must permit a group to organize.[88]

Dahrendorf's assumption that contradictory perspectives toward authority have an existence in roles apart from the orientations of their incumbents implies a critique of functional theory. He compared these objective perspectives to Parsons's role-expectations,[89] and the assumption leads directly to the conclusion that the legitimacy of authority is always precarious. Somehow, to those who are excluded from it, authority is suspect and its functional contribution not sufficient to sustain it. Given the aforementioned social, technical, and political conditions, which really are not the causes of the loss of its legitimacy, those subject to authority are predisposed by its very nature to oust those who have it. Dahrendorf thus transposed Marx's notion of objective economic interests conditioned by property to the sphere of authority. Yet, at the same time he denied that social organization is possible without domination and subjection. The result is that organization is continually unstable.

Having thus explained the origin of class conflicts, he went on to explain variations in their intensity and violence.[90] The intensity of conflict is the extent to which individuals are involved in it, the amount of energy they expend, or the costs they are willing to pay to win. In other words, intensity is really the amount of value they place on the conflict. Violence is the extent of physical or other kind of damage the classes inflict on each other. These two dimensions are not necessarily correlated. Thus, a conflict can be very intense but nonviolent, or violent but with little intensity. For example, with a legal apparatus to regulate conflicts between management and labor, the violence is likely to be reduced. Yet, such conflicts can at the same time reach a high intensity. Here Dahrendorf once again rejected Marx, who believed violence to be inherent in class conflict.[91]

Dahrendorf identified well-known factors that explain these variations. When two or more conflicts are *superimposed*, their intensity increases. Superimposition occurs when the same individuals are in positions of authority and positions of subjection in the associations where conflicts occur. For example, if the managers of industry also control the state and the industrial workers are merely citizens who are not in political office, the superimposition of political upon economic conflict intensifies both. The personnel in authority in industry and state need not coincide exactly for one conflict to superimpose itself on another. All that is necessary is that there be a connection between them. Conflicts intensify when the same individuals confront one another in different situations of conflict. Superimposition, according to Dahrendorf, leads down the road to a polarized society.

In the configuration of conflicts, *pluralism* is the opposite of superimposition. Rather than one conflict being superimposed on another, conflicts cut across one another. For example, those in authority in the

286   The Duality of Consensus and Conflict

church are mere citizens of the state and those with political authority are mere laymen in the church. It is evident that pluralism diminishes intensity because those subject to authority in one association have a chance for gratification in another, and those who confront one another in one sphere of conflict are allies in another.

Mobility also affects intensity. It is *intragenerational mobility*, the movement of individuals into and out of positions of authority during the course of their lives, that Dahrendorf found most relevant. When carried to an extreme, intragenerational mobility prevents the formation of social classes in an association, for there is a continuous rotation of members into and out of authority. A good example is a rotating chairmanship. At the other extreme, there is no intragenerational mobility when those in authority and subjection maintain their positions indefinitely. These hypothetical endpoints define a scale of mobility that correlates inversely with intensity. For instance, industrial workers are unlikely to attach a high amount of importance to class conflicts if they themselves expect to move into positions of authority.

The violence of class conflict is determined primarily by the extent to which conflicts are regulated. For a conflict to be properly regulated, each class must recognize that a legitimate conflict exists while at the same time refusing to concede victory to the other side. Classes can then form. Once organized, they are in a position to agree on procedural rules, such as when and where to meet and how to reach decisions. Such rules, which suppress violence, are the most important regulators of conflict.

Marx believed that violent class conflicts were the engine of historical change. Once again Dahrendorf saw other possibilities than Marx. Not only is it possible for structural changes to be caused by other conflicts than those among the social classes, but changes in imperatively coordinated associations resulting from class conflict often assume different forms. First, change can come in the form of a total exchange of personnel, whereby all those in authority lose their positions to those formerly in subjection. Dahrendorf called this possibility a *very sudden structural change*. Second, a *less sudden change* consists of a partial exchange of personnel with regard to authority, and it is possible for changes in personnel to take place without any changes in the policies of the association. Third, structural change can vary in *radicalism*. Radical change consists of changes in policy of the imperatively coordinated

Conflict   287

association. In distinguishing between sudden and radical change, Dahrendorf separated elements that Marx had combined.

Overall, this theory of class conflict assumes the inevitability of contradictory interests with respect to a scarce value. In this it is typical of conflict theory in general. The scarce value in this case is authority. Those who lack it want it, and those who have it refuse to relinquish it. Yet at the same time the imperatives of organization require that someone have it. It follows that the social order is continually plagued by the "outs" trying to get "in," which leads to a kind of circulation of elites. Social organization thus carries within it the seeds of recurring instability. Conflicts between "ins" and "outs" vary in intensity and violence in relation to certain factors. Another possible outcome of class conflict than shifts in leadership is a shift in policies. Those in authority remain in their positions, but they adopt different policies. The implication, however, is that this radical change is forced upon the leaders as a result of class struggle. These policies, accordingly, are not the products of consensus.

When he began to construct the theory of class conflict, Dahrendorf proclaimed the integration and coercion models to be of equal theoretical utility. Later on, however, he revised his opinion. The coercion model is more general than the former by virtue of the fact that it has the capability of explaining any phenomenon that the latter can explain. Hence, it is superior and ought to replace the integration model.[92]

To demonstrate this superiority with regard to a specific problem, Dahrendorf examined stratification and its relation to the state in light of the coercion model. At the outset he agreed with Durkheim and Parsons that every society is a moral order of norms, but then he took a different path. Wherever there are norms, there will be both conformity and deviance. Moreover, positive and negative sanctions will also be found; for it is rewards and punishments that maintain a normative order rather than moral commitments internalized into personalities.[93] Rationally seeking their self-interests, people comply with norms to obtain rewards and avoid punishments—a motivation compatible with the coercion model.

The rewards for conformity to the normative order of society come principally in the form of prestige and money, which are the currencies of stratification. For example, under a piecework system the younger workers are likely to win more rewards than the older, the outcome of which is a stratification of money and prestige in the factory. In cases of

288   The Duality of Consensus and Conflict

violations of the laws of the state, punishments, of course, include deprivations like imprisonment as well as loss of revenue and prestige. The conclusion Dahrendorf drew from these facts is that the normative order itself is the universal creator of stratification.[94] There are always some who will be able to excel in meeting the demands of society and others who will fail by virtue of their deviations.

Because, however, conformity depends upon sanctions, there must be individuals with the power to impose them. The nucleus of all power, concluded Dahrendorf, is the ability to inflict punishment; and power is necessary because no normative order rests upon consensus. When a sociologist tries to discover who has the power to impose punishments and distribute rewards, he will find the answer in the political officehold-ers and the upper classes. They are the ones not only with the power to uphold norms but also with the power to formulate them in accordance with their own values. Stratification, therefore, arises from norms, sanctions, and power.[95] Inequality always involves the gain of one group at the expense of another and as a consequence generates protest and historical change.[96]

Consequently, stratification results from power rather than function. Since norms are necessary but can be upheld only by rewards and punishments, an elite of power is required to enforce the normative order. In accomplishing this, it raises some to high position and degrades others. Thus, power logically precedes stratification; and the norms it creates and upholds are those congenial to its own values. Here Dahren-dorf comes to the conclusion already arrived at by Marx and Weber that minorities establish the values that set the tone of society.

Legitimation as Domination

In the tradition of critical theory, Jürgen Habermas also emphasized that the very existence of the normative order is a source of stratification. Although, like Dahrendorf, Habermas is aware of norms as sources of stratification and domination, like Durkheim and Parsons he recognizes the role of legitimation in sustaining them. Rather than clothing norms with moral authority, however, legitimations, according to Habermas, are forms of power.

It is the *advanced capitalist societies* that Habermas is especially

Conflict   289

concerned with. What distinguishes them from the *liberal capitalisms* that were their predecessors is the intervention of the state into the economy to prevent crises. The political-administrative systems of the advanced capitalisms intervene, for example, to control the supply of money; subsidize capital-scarce enterprises like agriculture and science; build and maintain infrastructures of roads, housing, and education; and maintain the welfare of citizens through social security and unemployment insurance. Political intervention into the market compensates for the latter's failures and thereby keeps class conflicts latent.[97] Were it not for a polity that compensates for capitalism's inadequacies, the social classes would intensify their conflicts. The implication is that the modern state enacts the role marked out for it by Marx and Engels.

Political intervention into the capitalist economy must, however, be legitimated. And the sources of legitimation reveal quite a bit about the dynamics of advanced capitalism. Habermas identified formal norms and informal conventions that have long functioned as legitimations of the state's efforts to "steer" the economy. The purely formal norms of democracy, the most important being the right to vote, are of certain relevance to the legitimating process. As long as political leaders comply with democratic rules, their policies receive a stamp of legitimacy.

It is certain informal expectations that make up democratic culture, nevertheless, that Habermas believes to be peculiarly effective. At informal levels, democratic culture enjoins citizens not to become too involved in political decision making. Through the franchise they confer power on elites whom they then ought to leave pretty much free to make authoritative decisions. Habermas calls this abstinence from more active involvement *civil privatism*.[98] Another legitimating convention is *familial-vocational privatism*, which also limits the political role of citizens. It consists of a cluster of values, namely, successful pursuit of a career through hard work, the cultivation of leisure, and the acquisition of money for consumption.[99] So long as the state fulfills its steering function in such a manner that citizens are successful in their jobs, satisfied in their consumption, and happy in their leisure, they remain content with the political system. The trouble is, however, argues Habermas, that these traditions are weakening. This could eventuate in crises for advanced capitalist societies.[100]

In addition to these privatisms, other beliefs legitimate advanced capitalist states. Bourgeois ideologies of the past, such as parliamentari-

290   The Duality of Consensus and Conflict

anism, popular sovereignty, and natural law provided legitimations for the liberal capitalisms.

Unlike civil and familial-vocational privatism, these ideologies justified direct citizen participation in politics but distorted reality in their assertions that the interests of individuals are shared ("generalizable" in Habermas's language). Such claims are counterfactual and have the effect of actually suppressing these interests by distorting reality. Bourgeois ideologies are, however, functional for the maintenance of the political authority in advanced capitalism, proving the validity of political norms while preventing citizens from thematizing and discussing them rationally. Insofar as they foreclose the consideration of alternatives, they are a form of power.[101] Furthermore, the political norms in advanced capitalist societies rest also upon force; and citizens both fear the sanctions that the state can impose and realize their powerlessness.[102]

Another legitimating ideology recently come to prominence is science. Habermas's analysis of this role of science gives a further understanding of how ideologies are forms of power. In emphasizing science's ideological function, he elaborated upon a central theme of the Frankfurt school. Especially since World War II political decisions have become "scientized." By this term Habermas includes both the broad impact of science and technology and the specific willingness of politicians to take the advice of scientists.[103] Natural science and the technology it has spawned have been so successful in raising the material level of life that politicians and citizens are willing to listen to scientists. The problem is, however, that embedded in scientific recommendations are not only the means to achieve goals but the goals themselves. Yet the goals suggested by scientists are not, according to Habermas, thoroughly and explicitly discussed in political forums. As a result, they conceal interests that conflict with other interests. Military secrecy, for example, rules out systems for inspecting nuclear tests.[104] Also, technologies of space set their own demands. Overall, scientific technology is harnessed to the growth of material progress and an unreflected-upon perpetuation of capitalism.[105]

Science and other technologies are forms of power. They are power insofar as they prevent the raising of questions, such as ones concerning, for example, the unequal distribution of rewards and opportunities. By conveying a distorted picture of social reality that submerges conflicts among interests under an inauthentic consensus, they encourage acquiescence in a class system and smother an awareness of alternatives. They deaden the will to change toward a better life. Insofar as they foreclose possibilities, ideologies freeze a status quo that is not grounded in legitimate consensus emerging from rational discussion.[106]

This analysis stands within the Marxist tradition of ideological distortion and false consciousness. Habermas measures the political systems of the capitalist societies against the standard of a rationally based will of the people and finds them wanting. The test of democracy is whether it legislates policies based on a rational consensus formed within the ideal-speech situation.

Factors that inhibit expression or prevent speakers from becoming aware of their interests prejudice rational discourse and produce forced consensus. To arrive at generalized interests, people must come to a realization of what they really want. Capitalist ideologies prevent the attainment of rational consensus by repressing awareness of individuals' true interests. They facilitate false consciousness. Capitalist societies conform, in the words of Habermas, to "the model of the suppression of generalizable interests."[107] As older ideological traditions such as natural law and civil privatism decline in their influence, advanced capitalisms may suffer from a legitimation crisis.[108] In such a crisis the state will not receive the mass loyalty necessary to steer the economy.

In shifting the ground of legitimacy from substantive values to linguistic procedure, Habermas comes into conflict with functionalism's principal source of legitimacy. For Parsons, the legitimacy of the democratic polity is grounded in instrumental activism, which itself is a reflection of ascetic Protestantism. But these religio-philosophical systems of past regimes, says Habermas, are becoming less effective. The ideology of achievement, for instance, which states that rewards are distributed according to individual achievement (distributive justice), is losing its force through social change.[109] Also, the procedural norms of democracy as grounds of justification are insufficient. The legitimation of political domination cannot be equated with the norms for the democratic organization of domination.[110] Rather, the grounds of legitimation must be sought in the kind of communicative interaction capable of producing a rational consensus. Habermas's solution in the final analysis comes down, as we have indicated above, to citizens talking to one another in the appropriate manner.

Collins's Conflict Sociology

Many of the concepts and propositions of the conflict tradition have been woven into a theoretical synthesis by Randall Collins (1941–), whose ambitious goal was to reorganize sociology around conflict as its master concept. Collins predicates his synthesizing attempt upon the stated assumption that the ample volume of research conducted by sociologists has already yielded a substantial number of empirically supported generalizations. What needs to be accomplished is to integrate them into an explanatory theory. The concepts that Collins most relies on to achieve this goal are *conflict* and *power*.

Collins applies these concepts to the domains of stratification and organizations, which he believes are the areas upon which a conflict sociology can be founded. He chose them because they have been so much researched by sociologists and because so many other factors of social life, such as political opinions, deviance, religious beliefs, consumption, and methods of child raising, have been shown to be linked to them. Moreover, stratification and organizations are themselves interrelated. Occupations, which are the most important determinants of social class, are the basic units of organizations, at least in the modern world. It follows that every organization contains an order of social classes. Consequently, the theories of organization and stratification overlap and reinforce each other[111] and can function as sources to integrate a large range of factors into a general conflict theory.

Nevertheless, there is more to Collins's overall strategy. He attempts to interpret the generalizations about stratification and organizations within the framework of an *a priori* general conflict theory in which conflict and power are decisive concepts. Collins called this theory "the basics of conflict theory." He pieced it together from the ideas of prominent social theorists. Accordingly, conflict sociology ultimately derives from the integration of previously established generalizations into a conflict theory constructed from previous theories. Conflict sociology is a synthetic product.

In order, therefore, to get an understanding of conflict sociology, one has to look at its foundations in the basics of conflict theory. This theory can be reconstructed, Collins tells us, in terms of a number of propositions.[112] (1) Human action is explained by the pursuit of individual self-interest. (2) The interests of individuals conflict. (3) Each individual is inclined, given the right circumstances, to use violence or its threat to achieve his interests. These means are forms of coercion (power). Thus, the realization of self-interest occurs within social contexts of coercion. Collins refers to these propositions as *cynical realism*, whose origin he traces to Machiavelli and Hobbes.

(4) Property can also be utilized as power in the conflict among interests, and the control over material instruments forms participants in these conflicts into social classes. Here Collins acknowledges Marx's contributions. Classes are social relationships, which implies that individuals cooperate; but cooperation comes into being as a way for individuals to increase their power.

(5) In order for individuals to cooperate, they must develop shared beliefs. These arise from solidarity, which in turn stems from rituals of all sorts. The insight that shared beliefs originate from solidarity-producing rituals Collins attributes to Durkheim and Goffman. The social order, however, is not the result of one encompassing *conscience collective* as Durkheim said, but many miniature ones. (6) It follows that shared ideas are created in order to exercise power. For individuals to go against others, they increase their power by joining with others. In order to cooperate, in turn, they develop some consensus dictated by a coincidence of interests. Therefore, shared ideas are determined in the final analysis by power.

With regard to the role of ideas, Collins sees the relevance of Weber's investigations of conflicts among status groups. (7) The victorious group in these conflicts imposes its own beliefs and values as the dominant ones. Inasmuch as the latter are the beliefs and values of the victors, they occupy the top positions in the system of stratification. Possessing the means of mental production, they use these beliefs and values to create and maintain their power. Both Marx and Weber, Collins reminds us, analyzed the role of ideas in domination.

(8) Self-interest is constituted not only of material values and power, but also status. Everyone toils to maximize his status, which is comparable to the glory motive according to Hobbes. Each tries to get the better of the other. In order to accomplish this, individuals attempt to shape the realities experienced by others. Each tries to get power over how others define situations. Here, ritual plays a role by contributing to the reality-forming process. In this context Collins indicates the contributions of Mead, ethnomethodology, and phenomenology to the analysis of the construction of reality.[113]

294   The Duality of Consensus and Conflict

(9) Power, however, (Collins in this context refers to coercion), always generates a reaction of antagonism from those against whom it is exercised. This is true because the experience of being coerced to do something is intrinsically unpleasant. Thus, the resort to power in the pursuit of self-interest increases conflict and also results in struggles for power. The antagonism elicited by being the object of power is matched by the feeling of exultation on the part of those who exercise it. Individuals like to dominate others; and power, therefore, is sought as an intrinsic as well as instrumental value.

Reciprocally related, conflict and power play central roles in this theory, and both are connected to an egoistic model of man. Various factors of long-standing interest to sociologists, such as property, shared ideas, solidarity, and ritual, turn out to be forms of power contributing to conflict rather than to consensual order. Whereas according to functionalism individuals voluntarily cooperate to achieve their goals, Collins's theory accounts for cooperation as a means to engage in conflict. Factors that the former assumes as contributing to consensus and stability the latter assumes as contributing to conflict. Once cooperation is established, it is power that sustains it—a conclusion that accords with Dahrendorf's coercion model. Whereas Mead and Schutz analyzed how language makes possible shared perspectives, Collins emphasizes reality construction as a manipulative effort in the continuing attempt to establish superiority. Once again, the same concepts are imbued with different and often contradictory interpretations because they are interconnected in different ways within different theories.

Collins's *a priori* theory of conflict is reflected in his explanation of the numerous dimensions of stratification and formal organization, and the dimensions he finds to be important in the latter are suggested by the former. As noted above, occupations determine classes and thus stratify organizations into distinct social classes. What is the most important fact about an occupation in an organization?

Collins's answer is unambiguous. The most important fact is how much power it confers upon its practitioner. Although Marx's proposition that the dividing line between classes is property has some truth to it, the most general case, especially today, is the division of classes determined by the right of some occupations to give orders. The most important factor of organization, therefore, is domination. The greatest effect of an organization on an individual's behavior and his most important experiences are whether he gives orders or receives them. Collins wholeheartedly agreed with the benchmark that Dahrendorf drew of organizational authority as the dividing line between classes. Accordingly, three classes (although Dahrendorf delineated only two) can roughly be delineated: those who give orders to many, but take orders from none or few; those who both give and take orders; and those who merely take orders. The first group, an upper class, includes executives. The second, a middle class, includes middle-level bureaucrats, technicians, and white-collar workers. The third, a working class, includes manual workers.[114]

Thus, the decisive role of power in the *a priori* theory of conflict is reflected in organizations. Who exercises power is not only the most telling aspect of occupations but also of organizations. Since power establishes stratification, the importance of power establishes the primary importance of organizational stratification. It enables individuals to enact rituals of superiority. They can extract responses of "yes sir" and "no sir" from those to whom they give orders. In the spirit of Goffman, Collins describes him who gives orders as assuming a bearing of "upper-class assuredness, cool composure, and unconscious arrogance."[115] He controls definitions of reality to his own advantage. On the other side, he who receives orders adopts a demeanor of listening politely and deferring, at least for the moment. His behavior resembles the animal cowed by another and brought to its heels.[116] Unequal to his superior in the power to gratify his interests, he is forced to capitulate in the contest for domination and status. These rituals of deference are always, implicitly at least, fraught with conflict.[117]

Why is occupational power so important? It is important, according to Collins, because it is causally related to other factors. First, power determines the networks of communication in organizations, i.e., who interacts with whom and how often. Second, the power that goes with an occupation confers a certain amount of income and wealth on those who practice it. Third, power determines the nature of work; and those who give orders can push the dirty, undesirable jobs on those who have no power.[118] Fourth, occupational power determines the culture of the classes. This is the most important of the four effects. Collins traces the sources of the value-systems of the upper, middle, and working class to the giving and receiving of orders.[119] These are examples of power shaping ideas.

This analysis of the effects of power illustrates the synthesis of empirical generalizations in the light of the *a priori* conflict theory. The decisive role of power derives from the latter, and the causal connections between

296   The Duality of Consensus and Conflict

it and other factors are supported by citations from previous research. Organizational power, however, in the light of the theory has to be connected to conflict. Collins addresses this in his analysis of the modes of control the organization exerts over its members.

According to the basics of conflict theory, organizations are to be conceptualized as composed of individuals seeking their own interests. These reduce to material interests, as illustrated by money; power; and status, which is determined by compliance with certain ideals (values). These interests coincide with Weber's concepts of class, party, and status. So much that goes on in organizations, Collins argues, is explicable by these conflicting types of interest.[120] And it turns out that each also corresponds to one of the three modes of organizational control investigated by Etzioni. Accordingly, one form of control is coercion. A second occurs through material rewards, such as money. A third is exercised through appeal to the norms and values of the organization. Each of these, however, produces conflict.

Coercion (power) produces conflict because, as stated in the theory, it is unpleasant to experience and always produces antagonistic reactions. There is also, however, a great deal of empirical evidence to support this generalization. One who coerces another always alienates him. If they have the resources, those who are coerced fight back. If they lack the means to overtly resist, they either put forth a ritual, minimal compliance or engage in passive resistance if they cannot escape. If escape is possible, they will leave the organization. Collins notes that throughout history prisoners and slaves were noted for their dull, perfunctory compliance with commands when they lacked the opportunity either to escape or rebel.[121]

When a person with power relies strictly on money or some other tangible value to get someone to comply with his orders, the latter will try to do as little as possible for the greatest amount of money he can get. He will try to manipulate the situation to his own advantage because his only interest is in acquiring as much as he can get. His performance inevitably brings him into conflict with the other. Management tries to combat this acquisitive behavior through piecework systems, but Collins notes that the research shows that workers devise informal means to subvert the intent of systems that tie reward to productivity.[122]

Normative control secures compliance insofar as the one who complies does so because he believes in the organization's values and goals. He is willing to perform an assigned task as a means to the achievement of a collective goal. It would seem that normative control stems from consensus. But Collins draws other conclusions. Those who are normatively oriented are likely to be found in leadership positions. The reason for this is to be found in the complexity of the relation between power and ideals. Leaders have power, which they ostensibly wield to implement the ideals of the organization. But, says Collins, it is the power itself that is the reward for the pursuit of organizational goals; and leaders work for the latter in order to enjoy the former. The leaders' power depends upon the existence of organizational values and goals, which are upheld by that power. That is why the powerful are always enacting rituals such as one finds in a court of law. These rituals define the reality of the normative order, which induces individuals to conform to it.[123] The upholding of the organization's values and norms results in sustaining the power of its leaders.

The reason why those at the top of an organization are committed to its normative order explains why those at the bottom are not. Deprived of power, they have nothing to gain by such commitment. Therefore, the controls that secure their performances are coercion and material reward. Here, however, we encounter a dilemma. To secure normative commitments from those at the bottom in order to escape the negative consequences of coercion and utilitarian control, those with power must share it. But giving those at the bottom "a piece of the action" flattens the hierarchy and results in a loss of efficiency.[124] Here Collins tacitly acknowledges the functionality of power.

How does normative commitment result in conflict? The powerful argue about what the ideals, policies, and goals of the organization ought to be and what they mean. Each member of the power-elite tends to specify and interpret them to suit his own interests. That explains the controversies over religious dogmas, political ideologies, and even scientific theories.[125] Consequently, the normative order itself is a source of controversy; for it is something to argue about.

Collins's overall conflict sociology, which stands in stark opposition to functional theory, emphasizes that shared elements—values, norms, and goals—result from the pursuit of conflicting interests through the use of power rather than from consensus. They are definitely not formed as a consequence of agreement about system imperatives. Once an order of values and norms is formed as the result of the interests backed by the greatest power, it is also sustained by the latter. Often, however, the victory of one set of interests over others is incomplete; therefore, the

298   The Duality of Consensus and Conflict

order is riddled with continuing conflicts and power struggles that make it more or less unstable. Although cooperation occurs and things get done, the order depends more on power than consent. Some accept what they get and do what they do because they have no alternatives, but those at the top get more out of the order than those at the bottom.

Rituals do not generate a mechanical solidarity in Durkheim's sense, but rather function as a form of power that sustains those ideals, rules, and goals most congenial to those who enact the rituals. Rituals thus are manipulative, being resources to get control of the way everyone constructs reality. They do not express society's reality as Durkheim said, but rather the view of things shared by those in charge. Punctuating everyday interaction, rituals are not confined to state occasions.

The role of power extends beyond the coercion of the occasional deviant from a consensual order, for it is the most important prop of a pseudolegitimate order. Reward and punishment, distributed by those at the top, not moral commitment, are what maintain a normative order. Conflicts caused by power are complicated by the fact that power is acquired as an end in itself as well as for its value as a means in the pursuit of other interests. In general, Collins's conflict sociology expresses many of the classic themes of conflict theory.

Functions of Conflict

Building on the insights of Georg Simmel, Lewis Coser (1913–) has disputed Parsons's conclusion that conflict is antithetical to social order.[126] Quoting Simmel, Coser states that in close relationships, those in which ego and alter are totally involved, dissociating tendencies coexist with associating ones. Normative consensus and solidarity are accompanied by feelings of hatred and hostility which render these relationships ambivalent.[127] When negative feelings result in overt conflicts, these are likely to be very intense because they engage the total personality. Also, previous repressions of hostility contribute to the intensification of conflicts once they erupt.[128] Hence, there is a kind of dialectic of opposites in those relationships which Parsons analyzed as affective and diffuse.

Despite their ubiquity, hostility and conflict, however, do not always destroy the group. They need not be dysfunctional. At this point, Coser, following Simmel, goes on to identify specific ways in which conflicts

Conflict   299

maintain and even strengthen groups. These can readily be conceptualized as instances of integration and pattern maintenance in Parsons's
social system. If, for example, a member of a group could not express his
hostility or his dissent, he might simply withdraw because of unbearable
frustration. Conflict traceable to these motives integrates the group.
Closely related to this "clearing of the air" are the various safety-valve
institutions provided by societies to release hostility so that the individual
can continue to play his roles.[129] Also, a distinction ought to be made
between those conflicts that threaten the very basis of a relationship and
those that involve peripheral issues. Thus, conflicts between husband
and wife over whether to have children must be distinguished from those
over how to spend a vacation. By resolving tension, conflicts over
marginal issues may be functional; but those that strike at the consensual
foundation of the relationship are dysfunctional.[130]

   Coser is led to another distinction among conflicts with regard to their
functional possibilities. Loosely organized societies, those that are plural-
istic, permit their members to belong to all sorts of voluntary associations
such as labor unions, religions, and ethnic associations. Conflicts consequently are likely to be "crisscrossing" rather than superimposed. Thus,
two individuals may oppose each other on an issue within a group but
may also belong to another which stands united against a third with
reference to another issue. In this case, the first conflict that divides them
tends to be neutralized by the second which unites them. Conflicts that
crosscut one another are like waves, the troughs of some coinciding with
the crests of others. Less disruptive than superimposed conflicts, these
tend to stabilize a society.[131] Here again conflict contributes to integration.

   The above conflicts occur within groups and societies. Coser turns his
attention to external conflicts. When one group threatens another, the
latter's members grow more cohesive and united in their efforts to defend
themselves. They pull together. Indeed, the strengthening of integration
in the face of external conflict is a consequence so apparent that societies
actually search for real enemies or invent them in order to maintain their
cohesion. Erstwhile antagonists forget their differences to face a common
enemy.[132] Another integrating effect of external conflict is the creation of
coalitions of hitherto unconnected allies who join together to confront a
common threat.[133] Even war, the most extreme conflict, is subject to
norms that limit the violence; and these rules tend to become elaborated
and eventually give rise to new ones. Each side develops an interest in

300   The Duality of Consensus and Conflict

limiting the destruction.[134] The formation of rules to minimize conflict is an obvious convergence with Parsons's solution to the problem of order.

Such generalizations illustrate the integrative function of conflict. Coser identifies other effects of conflict that contribute to what would be considered pattern-maintenance in the context of Parsons's theory. In struggling against opposition, a group is compelled to arrive at a clear definition of its goals and values. In the course of conflict it becomes more fully conscious of how its values differ from those of its opponent and at the same time achieves a heightened sense of self-identity. This boundary maintenance is illustrated, says Coser, by Marx's theory of how classes constitute themselves through conflict.[135] While engaged in external conflict, a group is compelled to be less tolerant of internal dissent and therefore defines its norms more clearly so as to achieve victory. Norms define the limits of tolerance and restrict dissent so as to further the cause.[136] While the clarification of its values furthers pattern-maintenance, the clarification of its norms and the suppression of dissent contribute to integration.

Coser's propositions derived from Simmel weaken the dichotomy thought by some to obtain between functionally sustained order and conflict destructive of order. Not all conflict is dysfunctional, and some conflicts have precisely the consequences of building up the internal order of collectivities, strengthening them, and integrating hitherto unrelated collectivities. In the light of Simmel and Coser, consensus and conflict progress from strict antithesis to partially overlapping factors in regard to their effects.

The Issue Reconsidered: Power and Authority

Let us address the consensus-conflict controversy by revising the boundaries between functionalism and conflict theory, for any theory can be legitimately criticized if it illegitimately extends the explanatory power of the dimensions it abstracts from reality and legislates false explanations as a result.

The concepts of authority and power delineate such boundaries. In the context of preceding discussions, by authority is meant compliance motivated by duty, the source of authority being experienced as legitimate. This we have already seen. In contrast, by power is meant the mobilization of resources to impose one's will against resistance, compliance by the weaker with the will of the stronger, which is not experienced as legitimate by the weaker. We put forth a dual contention: (1) Conflict theory exaggerates the role of power and minimizes the role of authority; (2) functionalism exaggerates the role of authority and minimizes the role of power. The former mistakenly extends the scope of power, whereas the latter mistakenly extends the scope of authority.

Conflict theory's emphasis on power is traceable to the postulate of conflicting interests, the assumption of irreconcilable conflict setting the tone. This is especially evident with regard to the state and other political organizations. Consequently, the most significant fact about the modern state is the inevitability of conflicting interests between political leaders and citizens. The former are therefore compelled to rely on power in order to establish their values and maintain control. Conflict theory has it that political elites make use of coercion through the instruments of violence on the one hand and an ideological control of thinking on the other. With regard to the latter, religious and secular world views are accordingly reduced to the status of distortions whose major purpose is to secure mass allegiance.[137] In either case conflicting interests are not removed but merely controlled through threat of coercion and cultivation of a pseudolegitimacy. Even the democratic state achieves only a modicum of representativeness resulting from a balance of power among groups with approximately equal resources.[138] Conflict theory then relies on these generalizations to explain the dynamics of other organizations.

This interest-mobilization theory fails to take into account the distinction Weber drew between the formal and substantive rationalities of a legal order. In the light of this distinction policies can be evaluated, as we have seen, both with respect to their goals and their legality, the latter including the procedural rules that place individuals in positions of authority. An achievement of the modern state is the institutionalization of procedural rules. Consequently, as noted in chapter 6, conflicts over substantive issues can well coexist with consensus (here we speak in terms of degree) on the formal validity of procedural norms. Belief in a political order's legality reduces the need for a purely ideological control that deliberately distorts reality. There is room for disagreement so long as policies are legal. Here an analogy with language becomes apparent: Individuals can disagree about what they say but at the same time concur on the linguistic rules that enable them to say it. The failure of conflict theory to give legal authority its due exaggerates the state's reliance on its coercive apparatus and ideological resources while minimizing its legitimacy.[139]

That laws are made and applied according to "rules of the game" contributes to the type of moral unity Durkheim saw as originating from the *conscience collective* and that Parsons incorporated into his model of the social system. Nevertheless, the belief that an order is legal need not depend upon a precise understanding of relevant procedures as written in constitutions, even those of democratic states and organizations. What is decisive, on the other hand, is the *assumption* that lawmakers are playing by rules.

Let us assume that democratic procedures of lawmaking in the ideal case give every relevant view an equal chance of being considered and at the same time reject the assumption that with regard to any given issue there is a "true" general interest. Instead we assume that all relevant views merely express particular substantive interests. Accordingly we equate the general interest with a legal outcome, and the general interest is defined in terms of legality itself.

In the United States an underlying consensus on procedural authority is reinforced by the legitimacy of tradition, the Constitution having survived for 200 years.[140] What evokes outrage among Americans is an awareness that some law or policy or some appointment or election, has violated legal norms. The intensity of the anger often exceeds that aroused by a law whose goal or consequences are abhorrent. A consensus on legality (again we speak in a relative sense) is a substitute for violence, which contradicts conflict theory's generalization that a state achieves the general interest only when contending groups with equal power neutralize one another. Although legality may have originated out of a balance of power, once institutionalized as a criterion of legitimacy it militates against the use of violence to achieve collective goals.[141]

There is another significant dimension of the relationship between power and authority related to the larger issue. If we are to believe Weber, some legitimate orders are imposed rather than established by voluntary agreement; and what originates as an order imposed by ruthless force, Weber went on to say, in the course of time acquires legitimacy among those who resisted it.[142] This generalization can be illustrated by American slavery, whose authority came to be accepted by some slaves.[143] Imposition by power shifts through a series of transitions to submission on the grounds of expediency to acceptance of an order's legitimacy.

Changing motives for compliance blur the distinction drawn by theory between authentic legitimacy and false consciousness. Thus, there is a tendency for power to transform itself into authority, which implies that the factors maintaining an order do not coincide with those that established it. The criteria for the existence of consensus may not be relevant to the conditions of its formation, and failure to recognize these possibilities exaggerates the role of conflict. The scope of these generalizations is not limited to the state; they also apply to other formal organizations and therefore require a corresponding revision of interpretations of the latter.

Squarely based on the postulate of consensus, Parsons's theory identifies legality as a source of the polity's legitimacy. Located in the pattern-maintenance subsystem (Parsons later came to call this the fiduciary subsystem), the United States Constitution, supported by judicial interpretation, furnishes the inputs of legitimation to the polity's authority and legality to the power of its offices.[144] Legality thus appears among the interchanges between polity and pattern-maintenance system. In addition, the substantive rationality of law finds its place in Parsons's theory among the interchanges between polity and societal community. Policy decisions originating in the polity exchange for interest demands originating in the societal community, and leadership responsibility in the polity exchanges for political support in the societal community. It is obvious that these inputs and outputs are evaluated with reference to substantive criteria.

Identification of the political with the goal-attainment function has the consequence of generalizing the former to all of society's subsystems. For Parsons every one of society's subsystems is compelled by its functional requirements to arrive at political decisions, even when its functional primacy is not goal attainment. Every large economic firm, for example, has political roles requiring legitimation and develops a "constitutional system"[145] of legal procedures. Consequently, we should find in such organizations the same conditions obtaining in the political electorate, namely, a coexistence of legality with substantive disagreement, of consensus on procedures with conflict over policies.

Despite the legitimating function of legality, Parsons located the principal source of legitimation of society's normative order in a religious world view, which, as the reader will recall, he called constitutive symbolism. Agreeing with Robert Bellah, he concluded that a civil religion prevails as a viable system of beliefs in America today.[146] In integrating Bellah's thinking into his own theory, Parsons also saw a

304   The Duality of Consensus and Conflict

convergence between civil religion and individualized, liberalized Protestantism.[147] Civil religion or liberalized Protestantism thus turns out to be America's constitutive symbolism. According to Bellah, a widely held belief in the existence of a nonpartisan God is shared by Protestants, Catholics, and Jews—a God Who from the very beginning adopted Americans as His chosen people and America as the promised land. Washington, Franklin, and Jefferson all saw the hand of God guiding the new continent's experiment in republican government. Throughout American history, Bellah goes on to say, civil religion furnished powerful symbols of national solidarity that generated deep commitments to achieve collective goals such as the abolition of slavery.[148] Parsons's argument comes down to the fact that civil religion, originating in a liberalized Calvinism, legitimates the state today.

Parsons theorized that every cultural pattern has cognitive, expressive, and evaluative dimensions, which "merge" because they are all somehow modes of *differentiation* from a *common matrix*.[149] The common matrix, which is the equivalent of constitutive symbolism, is a religio-philosophical conception of ultimate reality. For Parsons it follows that the entire normative order makes sense in terms of the latter and takes on legitimacy in those terms.

It is necessary, however, to draw a distinction between the act of deriving a policy from a religious system and invoking God as a legitimation for one determined on other grounds. America's civil religion has too little substance and too few tenets upon which to base political decisions. And the concept of God has been invoked for contradictory policies; both defenders and opponents of slavery appealed to the same deity.[150] Furthermore, the lack of seriousness with which religion is taken today leads to the conclusion that constitutive symbolism lacks the viability sufficient to generate a consensus on substantive issues.[151] Instrumental activism stemming from Calvin's God is an inadequate premise upon which to base the specifics of political policy. Here it is well to recall Durkheim's search for a secular substitute for religion as a foundation of morality. One should also recall that the writers of the Constitution deliberately ruled out religion as the foundation of the state, basing it instead on legal procedures. If everyone is at liberty to worship God as he sees fit, how can religion provide the kind of consensus capable of generating political decisions?

We contend, on the contrary, that no single view of the world, whether religious in the strict sense or secular, such as the dialectic of history,[152] functions the way Parsons analyzed the relationship of society to its cultural system. As individuals play their roles and as politicians go about their deliberations, an infinite variety of justifications enter into the context of thought that make action intelligible. It is unlikely that any single shared conception of the world so dominates individuals' orientations to their society as to furnish a legitimating matrix of choice. Meaning-contexts also change, even in the face of similar situations. The cultural system's constitutive symbolism is thus an insufficient base for the derivation of society's substantive political goals and the collective goals of its subsystems.

These propositions compel the conclusion that functional theory exaggerates the amount of substantive authority in modern societies. This conclusion is reinforced by Parsons's conflation of power and authority; for, placed in the service of collective goals, power by definition cannot serve individual ends, including those that undermine society's value-system. Conceptual suppression of the egoistic possibilities of power clears the way for the notion that inequalities, being necessary to accomplish tasks, are based purely on functional principles. Hence, whereas conflict theory exaggerates the role of power, the consensus side of the issue exaggerates the role of authority.

The claim that a resolution, or at least a partial one, of the issue of consensus and conflict hinges on the distinction between authority and power is an oversimplification. The relationship, however, between these two pervasive facts of social existence is certainly of great relevance, and I am convinced that a more detailed historical analysis of their relationship would reveal a more accurate understanding of the relationship between consensus and conflict. Legal authority, for example, is a cement that limits the potentially destructive effects of substantive conflicts in all sorts of organizations. Because, however, any explanation of social facts necessarily involves abstraction, it is just as easy through focusing on some elements and omitting others to build a model of society as continually threatened with destruction through conflict as it is to build one of society secure in lasting cooperation.

The Limits of Rationality

Looking back upon these issues, we become aware of a unifying theme. The theme is the relationship between rationality and the factors that restrict it in both social science and social life. I by no means contend that all the dimensions of the issues considered in this work can be reduced to the conflict between rationality and its limiting factors, but only that it recurs, sometimes explicitly, sometimes below the surface, in various arguments involved in the issues. The claim of a total reduction would be an oversimplification. The phrase "the limits of rationality"[1] expresses the idea that reason, a powerful force in the modern world, is nevertheless circumscribed in its influence. In this context it is appropriate to distinguish between subjective rationality, which is rationality from the perspective of an actor, and objective rationality, which is the degree to which an action is rational as assessed by an observer. The limitations referred to are those revealed by an objective perspective. Some of them are analyzed in the writings of Max Weber—the social scientist centrally concerned with the rationalization of life.

The limits of rationality appeared most explicitly in the analysis of the relationship between moral duty and self-interest. According to that analysis, it was demonstrated that commitment to norms based on their legality is a source of duty required to make up for deficiencies in their substantive rationality and that these two factors stand in a relationship of tension within normative orders. Beyond that, formal rationality, i.e.,

308   The Duality of Consensus and Conflict

legality, and the substantive rationality of ends reappear in the discussion of the issue of consensus and conflict. The theme we have been discussing remained implicit in the discussion of positivism and antipositivism, where the role of interests in social theory was touched upon. It was also brought out that certain erroneous conclusions can be traced to the reification of society; and, as we shall demonstrate below, conceptualizing society as a transcendent reality has resulted in an exaggeration of its rationality in certain theories.

Rational action and its qualifications, therefore, are manifestly apparent and latently present and intertwined with various aspects of the issues addressed in this volume. Let us therefore examine these relationships in greater detail by exploring further some ground already covered.

The Limits of Positivism Again

It is instructive to return to the hypothetico-deductive model in the positivist conception, with Parsons's delineation of theory as the exemplar. The reader will recall that for him a proper theory consists of logically interrelated propositions with the characteristics of analytical laws. A proposition, said Parsons, either states a fact or expresses a relationship between facts; and the logical relations among propositions makes a social theory into a logically closed, integrated system. An important consequence of logical integration is that any change in our knowledge of important facts relevant to a theory requires a revision of the entire theory.[2]

This last statement implies how Parsons defined the importance of facts. A factual discovery, Parsons claimed, is important if it requires an extreme revision of the theory to which it is relevant—a revision made possible by the theory's integrated character. The reverse implication, which Parsons did not draw in this context, is that those facts that add more weight to the evidence supporting a given theory are also important. In any case, logical necessity demands that facts requiring the revision of a single proposition also require a revision of other propositions in the theory. An integrated theory is analogous to a system of mathematical equations, in which change in one numerical value changes the values of others.

Parsons thought that no matter how interesting a novel fact appears to

The Limits of Rationality 309

common sense, if it does not revise theory it is scientifically trivial. What is trivial or important from a practical point of view, said Parsons, may be just the opposite from a scientific point of view. He gave the example of the discovery of a small deviation of a star from its calculated position, which although trivial practically nevertheless effected a revision of astronomical theory. From this method of determining importance, Parsons drew the obvious conclusion that the direction of scientific interest is theoretically determined.[3] In other words, theory is the sole guide to the scientist. "Theory not only formulates what we know, but also tells us what we want to know, that is, the questions to which an answer is needed."[4] Reciprocity obtains between fact and theory; being in a relationship of interdependence, neither is cause of the other.[5]

In chapter 2 we questioned the practicality of integrated social theory on logical grounds. Here we question the notion of scientific interest driven solely by logical criteria. In the final analysis sociologists judge the importance of facts and generalizations in terms of their ideas of what is important as determined by their values. Although embracing as a guiding principle a theory that reflects their sense of the significant based on their values, they, like Parsons, attempt to make the case that their judgments of theory are solely dictated by scientific considerations. For instance, they challenge the validity of a theory when, in fact, it relates to a subject that fails to engage their interest. Nevertheless, in scientific investigation the domain of facts and the relevant dimensions of the social world are initially determined by nonrational considerations. This argument, of course, is grounded in Weber's concept of value-relevance.

Let us briefly illustrate the argument with contrasts between Dahrendorf's and Parsons's analyses of democracy. Under the selective influence of the concept of class conflict, Dahrendorf called attention to sources of conflict in the democratic state. The conflicts he indicated stem from the attempts of those outside of the categories of functionaries he included in the structure of domination in the state to change the distribution of political authority. First, the minority in the legislature, who are in a state of conflict with the majority, attempt to get their interests enacted into law. By Dahrendorf's definition they do not belong to the ruling class so long as they remain on the losing side of issues that get adopted. Second, interest groups in the electorate, such as labor, agriculture, and business, contend with one another to obtain the legal adoption of their programs. Third, political parties compete for votes to elect candidates to office and to secure their policies. Although Dahren-

310   The Duality of Consensus and Conflict

dorf's analysis is more extended than this brief summary, the principal explanation of how democracy works remains that the political process is a continual struggle between those who have and those who lack authority. Class conflict is the dynamic that Dahrendorf singled out for his analysis of democracy.[6]

In contrast, Parsons, as chapter 7 indicates, identified democracy's dynamic as the acquisition of the power necessary for the polity to mobilize resources to achieve collective goals. Power comes in the form of generalized support from citizens who express a broad confidence in the society's general direction as marked out by its political leaders. A broad consensus exists between leaders and citizens. Conflict in elections is minimized by two important factors turned up by extensive political research. One is widespread consensus on the rules of politics, such as the acceptance of defeat by those on the losing side in elections and their recognition of the legitimacy of the winners. A second factor curtailing conflict is a crisscrossing structure of solidarities, which lessens hostilities between those who disagree about candidates and policies. Overall, consensus is what Parsons singled out in analyzing democracy.

Students of politics will readily recognize that these different accounts relate to the same system; and most would probably agree with the above generalizations, which are not really contradictory. Nevertheless, Dahrendorf's and Parsons's divergent interests in conflict and consensus, which are reflected generally in their sociological writings, selected different dimensions as typical of the system. Although touching on conflict, Parsons focused primarily on consensus; although touching on consensus, Dahrendorf focused primarily on conflict.

I draw several conclusions from the foregoing. In the first place, the generalizations enunciated by Dahrendorf and Parsons were shaped by presuppositions, not deduced from hypothetico-deductive theory in accordance with logical rules, but rather from their value-informed interests in consensus and conflict.[7] These are presuppositions rather than deductions from theory. In the second place, these interests led to differing conclusions through the selectivity they exerted. In the third place, it is impossible to determine which of the generalizations have logical priority. It is impossible to establish which are scientifically superior by locating them within the framework of an integrated theory as Parsons defined it.[8] In the fourth place, each set of generalizations adds to our knowledge of democracy by giving a more comprehensive understanding gained from diverse perspectives rather than a cumulation of knowledge according to which one idea is logically built on others.

The uncontrollability of conceptions of the significant by purely logical criteria limits the rationality of the social scientific enterprise. This fact also challenges the identification of consensus within the scientific community as a criterion of progress. For if the subjects of investigation and the identification of relevant facts are determined by differing notions of what is significant, reaching agreement on what constitutes scientific progress is hard to achieve. Informed by logically unrelated interests, scientific findings do not cumulate. As we shall see below, a similar source of difficulty in reaching consensus also complicates rational action in practical life.

Rationality and the Reification of Social Structure

The assumption that society is a transcendent structure, a collective actor, paves the way for the conclusion that it is a rational structure. The reification of society permits an observer to impute characteristics to it that cannot be found within individuals or to attribute to it individual characteristics in an exaggerated form. Let us illustrate this with Durkheim's classic study of totemism.

The central thesis of the study is that the animal that serves the clan as its totem is a transfigured symbol.[9] The kangaroo, for example, symbolizes the clan, which is experienced under a religious guise. Thus, as the men of the clan ritually kill and eat the totem, the communal feast, although interpreted by them as an act of renewing the sacred powers of the totem within their souls, is actually, according to Durkheim, a transfiguration of the renewal of society's moral power within them.[10] The totem in reality stands for the society of the worshipers. The fact that it symbolizes both the sacred force of the totemic principle and the clan is explained by the fact, said Durkheim, that totem (god) and clan are in reality one and the same.[11] The power of the totem is the power of society.

It is the ritual, therefore, that is for Durkheim religion's most important element. The intensity of religious experiences formed under the

312   The Duality of Consensus and Conflict

impact of ritual renders individuals acutely aware of society's presence. The beliefs and sentiments of each are synthesized into truly collective beliefs and sentiments of transcendent power and energy. These *sui generis* collective representations are the collective thoughts of the clan itself, which enable society to become conscious of itself.[12] Thus, during the ritual propagation and consumption of the totemic species, the clan is created as a transcendent reality, even continuing to exist as its members carry out routines apart from religious ceremonies, but in an enfeebled state.[13] Although during rituals individuals become acutely conscious of its existence, they are always aware of society's presence.[14]

The question now suggests itself: Why do individuals represent society with religious symbols? More specifically, why do members of the clan think of it as a totem? Durkheim pointed to the complexity and roundabout paths followed by social influences. Lacking science, ordinary persons are unable to grasp society's real nature and how it exerts its authority. They therefore attribute its moral authority to supernatural entities. Were they capable of grasping society and its effects directly, they would not invent beliefs that attribute its effects to gods.[15] In that case the members of the clan would not have devised myths about the totem.

Man's consciousness of society through religious symbolism provides the clue to religion's universal function. In representing society symbolically, individuals strengthen the bonds that attach them to it.[16] Their attachment to society strengthens their capacity to obey its moral precepts and renews their confidence to submit to its discipline. For it is not the god who originated rules but society itself, and without morality neither clan nor members could survive.

In living the religious life, therefore, man is not the dupe of an illusion;[17] for there is a real object that answers to religious beliefs, namely, society. The fundamental truth of society's real existence, said Durkheim, overrides the "secondary errors" in religious beliefs,[18] such as unscientific explanations of natural events.

In this context the reader will recall that Durkheim's society is a reality *sui generis*—a structure with supraindividual properties. The theory of religion depends upon this conceptualization, for if society were merely an abstraction it would not be possible to give a rational interpretation of religious beliefs. Religious symbols would turn out to be transfigurations of individuals rather than a transcendent entity. Religion consequently would degenerate into an irrational institution—a tissue of erroneous beliefs lacking a real basis. And indeed the absence of a basis in reality is exactly what the students of religion whom Durkheim criticized held, namely, that religion projects human characteristics onto mythical beings.[19]

Consequently, Durkheim's reification paved the way for the notion that religion has a rational foundation. He claimed that no institution can rest upon an error that is necessary to make it possible; for if it were not based on the nature of things, it could not have triumphed in the face of facts. For Durkheim this was a general postulate of sociology[20] and facilitated the conclusion that although religious beliefs that contradict science will continue to retreat, the universal necessity of ritual will guarantee their continuation in some form. Sociology lends its authority to this inescapable conclusion because it demonstrates the *sui generis* reality of society.[21]

The quest to save the principle of reason also informs Parsons's functionalism. Parsons held that society is maintained through the accomplishment of its indispensable functions, each of which can readily be thought of as a highly general end. Take integration as an example. The integration of its members and subcollectivities is a social system's generalized goal. Conceived of as an end of the system, integration is achieved through increasingly rational means during the course of social evolution. Thus, the *I* function is solved by more adequate solutions in the form of such processes as rational adjustments of disputes, rational allocation of facilities, and a stratification system increasingly based on a just system of rewards. These methods can be regarded as forms of the working out of the law of increasing rationality as Parsons stated it.[22]

It is easier to exaggerate the amount of rationality in a reified society than in a concept of society recognized as an abstraction. Although it is apparent that individuals act irrationally, the social system as a distinct entity is rational. In contrast, when society is identified with selected characteristics of its members, rational action is best thought of as an ideal-type. This, of course, was Weber's approach. Parsons, on the other hand, adopted the alternative conception of the social system as a distinct entity with unique functions, distinguishable from those fulfilled by personalities.

It is also evident that the social system's rationality is enhanced if it is constructed as being organized in terms of a small number of consensual values, or even better, in terms of a single, generalized value. For in that case the rationality of choices can be measured with reference to their

314   The Duality of Consensus and Conflict

contributions to the implementation of a single value. Here rational processes complement the means-end chain incorporated into Parsons's model. As noted above, Parsons thought he discovered such a value in the pattern of instrumental activism—the historical outcome of Calvinism in America.

Consequently, the concept of society as a unique, self-maintaining entity organized around a single, generalized value upon which there is consensus lays the foundation for the attribution of rationality to society so conceived. Reification, value-consensus, and rational action are mutually supporting. On the other hand, a functional theory that takes an individualistic point of view regarding social structures, according to which consequences of subjective rationality are strictly functional and dysfunctional for individuals, rules out the notion, which Parsons adapted from Durkheim, of society inexorably progressing toward supraindividual goals and in the process binding individuals to its will.[23]

Rationality and Consensus

Let us pursue the relation of consensus to rational action further. It is evident that the latter depends upon the former as its necessary condition. The formation and implementation of a policy, for instance, depends upon the agreement of those concerned on its goals, the necessary means, what secondary effects will occur, and how they are evaluated. Conflicts and compromises over these factors impair the success of the concerted effort necessary to put the policy into effect.

Let us explore some barriers to the achievement of consensus first with reference to Jürgen Habermas's conception of universal pragmatics and second with reference to Alfred Schutz's analysis of the face-to-face relationship. We look at these ideas in a somewhat different perspective than previously.

As noted in chapter 5, a communicative action, according to Habermas, is one in which the participants attempt to reach agreement concerning the validity of a norm. The attempt can be successful under the right conditions and assumes either that a previous consensus has broken down or was nonexistent at the outset. The listener has explicitly raised a validity claim about the correctness or appropriateness of a norm upon which the speaker's view is predicated. Habermas gave as examples of topics of such discourse a jury verdict, a reprimand, and a command issued by a superior. To come to an understanding about such decisions the participants are obliged to discuss the validity of the norms upon which they are based.[24] Was the jury's decision based on justifiable laws that were correctly applied? Consensus, according to Habermas, is intrinsically possible given the conditions of an ideal-speech situation as he constructed it.[25] In order that disputed validity claims be satisfied, the speakers raise the discourse to the more general level of underlying norms, in which recognized needs are legitimated in terms of abstract, ultimate principles. Needs are endowed with legitimacy insofar as they are generalizable, i.e., all participants in the dialogue want them satisfied. Consequently, a rational consensus about a norm whose effect is to satisfy such needs is possible.

Habermas's optimism, however, about the possibility of consensus must be qualified in the light of the distinction Weber implied between rational and scientific thinking. Rational thinking involves the deliberate choice of a goal relative to other possibilities in the light of relevant values and predictable consequences. Action informed by this thinking has subjective rationality. Nevertheless, no matter how deliberately the end is chosen, the choice cannot be objectively validated in terms of the canons of science. It is not subject to empirical criteria. To be sure, its instrumentality, Weber noted, can be scientifically justified if it is a means to a further end; but ultimately it reflects a value or view of the world that can only be presupposed. There is no way for science to decide, for example, whether scarce goods should be distributed according to the rule of distributive justice or according to need. Weber was convinced that world views conflict and can only be nonscientifically selected. In the final analysis the world is ethically irrational.[26]

Despite the fact, therefore, that the ideal-speech situation is a response to what Habermas believed were limitations of Weber's analysis of rationality, it cannot guarantee consensus. When practical discourse is raised to the level of ultimate principles in order to justify programs for practical action, it runs afoul of the logical truth that there are no empirical criteria for the selection of ends. Since there are no scientific criteria to determine which needs are generalizable, practical discourse, as Habermas conceived it, is just as likely to eventuate in arguments to justify conflicting policies as to produce a rational consensus regarding legitimate needs.

Let us explore further the relationship between consensus and under-

316   The Duality of Consensus and Conflict

standing. For in order for individuals to come to an agreement, they must grasp one another's viewpoints. It is equally obvious that obstacles to mutual understanding impair the consensus necessary for rational decisions. In this context we return to Alfred Schutz's analysis of intersubjective understanding—an analysis that reveals intrinsic limits to this indispensable process.

Chapter 7 set forth Schutz's general thesis of the alter ego. In the direct, face-to-face relationship, I can observe your lived experiences as they actually take place. Our streams of consciousness "intersect," and we "coexist" in a simultaneity as we grow old together. The time of this growing-old-together is not objective, scientific time, which is divided into quantitative units, but rather subjective, inner time, or duration, as Schutz put it. Each of us experiences his own duration and that of the other. In this relation I can become aware of the other's lived experiences as he talks to me and even those of his experiences, such as facial expressions, that he does not notice. I can comprehend the other's intentional acts as they occur in a step-by-step manner. This comprehension, Schutz observed, coincides with what Weber meant by observational understanding.

Nevertheless, the fact of my experiences of your experiences does not imply that our streams of consciousness are the same despite the fact of their temporal simultaneity. For when I interpret my experiences of your experiences, I place them in contexts of meaning that have been constructed out of my past lived experiences. You, on the other hand, place your lived experiences in meaning-contexts constructed out of your past lived experiences. Those meaning-contexts (interpretive schemes) differ from mine because, our biographies being different, we are different persons. For us to be the same individual, I would have had to live through all your experiences exactly as you did and interpret them within the same contexts of meaning as you did and in the same order. But this is absurd. Even more, when you talk to me, I may reflect upon and interpret experiences of yours that you do not reflect upon. From all this Schutz concluded that understanding another completely is an unfulfillable ideal, a limiting case. No one is able to observe another's subjective experience precisely the way he does.[27]

Inherent barriers to understanding rooted in the nature of ongoing experience provide the context for Schutz's analysis of the difficulties of those rational acts that depend on cooperation. In specifying the conditions of such a rational project, Schutz stated that if the end of my action depends upon another's action, then he must completely understand the way I envisage my action. That would require that he comprehend my goal, how it relates to my other goals and life-plans, the means that I find to be causally adequate and how they interfere with my other goals, and the secondary consequences of the act as I anticipate and evaluate them. In other words, rational action must be projected identically in the subjective experiences of those involved. This degree of concordance, argued Schutz, is impossible because of the uniqueness of everyone's biographically determined experience. How my goal, for instance, related to my life-plans cannot be understood by my partner.[28] Consequently, the rationality of concerted action runs up against inherent limits within direct communication.

Novelty and Rationality

We return to George H. Mead for an analysis of novelty, which has a bearing on the determinateness of the social order. Although Mead saw a connection between novel events and the relevance of the scientific method, his analysis also implies a limitation on the rational process. As we have pointed out in chapter 6, Mead contended that reflective thinking arises when habit encounters a situation with an unexpected departure from past experience. The unanticipated novelty interrupts the completion of the habit, whose adjustive capacity is hindered by the novelty. The individual is therefore compelled to reconstruct the situation in order to devise a modification of the habit to achieve the goal representing a continuity with the past.

Mead went on to say that the novel element—an emergent—could not have been foreseen. Only when the present has elapsed into a past, when the "now" has become a "just now," does the actor become conscious of the past in order to explain the present with a view of accomplishing a future act. He examines the past in order to explain the anomaly. But genuine novelty implies that, although the event could not have occurred without the necessary conditions obtaining in the past, the latter did not contain it. In other words, the past contained the necessary but not the sufficient conditions of its occurrence. Therefore, when the attempt is made to explain the novel event, the past has to be reconstructed as other than it really was. In the process the actor reconstructs that part of the

318   The Duality of Consensus and Conflict

world necessary to make the novelty into an essential, routine element, i.e., to fit it into the world so that it ceases to be a novelty.[29]

Thus, all history is a reconstruction whose purpose is to solve problems that interfere with present adjustments. Historical reconstruction is based on hypotheses formulated to identify the necessary conditions in the past that make possible the novel event and which are tested against the resultant acts that occur in the future. Hence, past, present, and future are bound together to establish continuity in experience.[30] Mead recognized, nevertheless, that knowledge given in historical construction is never totally adequate for the solution of present problems.[31]

Accordingly, the emergent that disrupts the adjustive power of habit, although it could not have been predicted, can be explained in retrospect. Not only does the present depend on the past, but the past as reconstructed depends on the perspective generated by the present. At the same time, the situation in which the anomaly presents itself is affected by the action that results from the modification of the habit. In changing himself to bring about an adjustment, the individual also changes the situation.[32] Overall, it is the emergence of novelty that makes time possible. Past and future arise in experience so that the individual can adjust to the unexpected.

This analysis of the relation between novelty and time is readily expressible in terms of Mead's social psychology. The "me" represents continuity with the past and the force of habit. The "I," which is always present as part of the self, represents the emergent novelty in action, a discontinuity with the past. As a response to novelty, the "I" expresses what is problematic against the background of what is taken for granted— the "me." The "I" is the principle of rational adaptation to the omnipresence of emergence. And in the process of bringing about adjustment, the "I" also influences the community. Hence, organism and environment affect each other. In most cases the deviation of the "I" from the "me" and the changes therein introduced into society are minimal. Nevertheless, Mead tells us that the social changes introduced by great historical figures are merely extreme cases of the latter.[33]

Let us identify an interrupted habit with an action oriented to a rule. On the basis of Mead's theory of emergence it follows that the rule, no matter how carefully crafted, cannot eventuate in total uniformity. For whoever is oriented to a rule is compelled to reinterpret the past in the face of present novelty. Correlated with the magnitude of novelty, the reinterpretation I have in mind may include a revision of the rule's intended meaning as originally formulated and involve a modification of its underlying values and view of the world. Consequently, the unpredictability of the emergent undermines the rational basis of the rule. Although the "I" is the rational self that reconstructs normative orders, its necessity is traceable to an unavoidable irrationality in social orders.

One can detect traces of Mead's analysis in the theorizing of ethnomethodologists and their interpretations of research. A convergence is apparent. As we have pointed out in chapter 6, ethnomethodologists found that when individuals in the course of their duties were trying to decide what happened they often invented alternative sequences of past events that would have led up to the facts as they appeared in the present. They then selected one of these sequences as the explanation. Thus, in a Suicide Prevention Center those charged with the task of determining causes of death would assume courses of past events and past circumstances and choose from among them in order to select the "correct" cause from among the "labels" natural death, accidental death, suicide, and homicide. Of uppermost importance was the construction of past courses that maintained continuity with the present and that conveyed a semblance of rational decision that could be justified in the future. The past was reconstructed to fit present anomalies. In interpreting the research, Garfinkel implied that the concern with what actually happened in any given case was subordinated to the appearance of continuity between hypothetical reconstruction of what might have happened and facts that happened to become available in the present.[34]

Garfinkel's interpretations correspond to Mead's belief that what is important about a past is not what it was when it was a present, but what it was in relation to a present. His interpretation also converges with Mead's observation that once an emergence has been fit into a historical reconstruction, it becomes less of an emergent;[35] for the goal is to create a view of the world that fits novel events into it as essential elements. Since they could not be predicted from the pasts that were presents at the time, the reconstructed order therefore must take the form of a rewriting of the past.

Mead's theory has obvious implications for rational thinking. Although the reconstruction of the past to account for novelty is a rational activity, the inability to predict the novelty implies a world that lacks total determinacy. It follows that policies and norms designed to bring into being future states can never achieve their intended goals. Yet the difference between the intended and actual tends to be obscured by retrospective interpretation, which sustains the illusion that social order is more rational than it really is. It has, in other words, more subjective than objective rationality. To be sure, only some divergences that occur in the world between intention and outcome are singled out as significant; but the difference between those considered to be significant and the less-noticed deviations and their reinterpretations by the "I" in ordinary life is only one of degree.

If, according to Mead, the past is always a reconstruction of events that were necessary conditions of a present in order to cope with unforeseen novelty, then the past can never be reconstituted in memory exactly as it was when it was a present.[36] Mead's theory of time paved the way for Alfred Schutz's phenomenological analysis of past, present, and future experiences—an analysis that further clarifies novelty. One can find similarities between Schutz's and Mead's treatment of the temporal aspects of action. The former borrowed from the latter.

An action in progress, according to Schutz, presents itself to conscious experience differently than the act anticipated before it began and differently than the completed act resurrected as a memory. Things always look different the morning after. Why is this so?

Whereas an action in progress is directly experienced, an act anticipated is imagined as already completed. When an individual, therefore, plans an action in his phantasy, i.e., develops a project, he conceives of it in the future perfect tense. Although the anticipation looks to the future, it is also permeated by a sense of pastness, in contrast with the experience of an action taking place in the present. Hence, these experiences are differentiated in terms of a temporal conception.

What are the characteristics of an act projected in imagination? Although projects vary in the amount of detail and degree of clarity, they can never attain the detail and clarity of the experience of an act already completed. This is explained by the fact that no matter how rational the project, the actor conceives the means and end only in their typical form. They cannot be projected in their occurring uniqueness. The anticipated act is thus "empty in content," omitting the uniqueness of its actual occurrence and context. This uniqueness corresponds, at least to some extent, with the novelty identified by Mead. As a result, the act completed is bound to diverge from the act projected.

There is another explanation, according to Schutz, for the divergence. While the action is in progress, the actor's stock of knowledge changes to correspond with changes in his interests and structures of relevance. At the conclusion of the act he has "grown older" and is a different person. Now he can look back on the completed act in memory and compare it with his project. He can fill in the gaps in the project and judge whether the act is a success in the light of the project. Whatever his judgment, however, the completed act experienced as a memory looks different than the act experienced as an anticipation. As Schutz put it: ". . . in the common-sense thinking of everyday life whatever occurs could not have been expected precisely as it occurs, and that whatever has been expected to occur will never occur as it has been expected."[37] Schutz's thinking here is translatable into Mead's discussion of novelty.

These generalizations state factors, some existing in the situation and others within subjective experience, that limit the rationality of an action, no matter how rationally conceived. In this context, irrationality is measured by the discrepancy between the plan and the outcome of the action oriented to it.

Such discrepancy varies, affected by the loose concepts of common-sense thinking.[38] Commonsense terms are contextually qualified, and therefore the meanings of success and failure vary among individuals. That is one explanation why individuals come to contradictory evaluations of a policy, some judging it a success because it has achieved its intended goal, others calling it an unmitigated failure because it has not.

Legitimacy and the Limits of Rationality

These limitations suggest the question of how well decisions and policies will continue to furnish legitimacy to normative orders as ever-greater demands are placed upon them. A recurring topic in social theory, legitimacy looms as a central concept in the discussion of the issues considered in Parts Three and Four of this work. Although the legitimacy of the state, for example, rests upon a consensus regarding the legality of its procedures and the strictly legal enactment of laws, substantive rationality with regard to its goals, as we have seen, also contributes to its legitimacy.

Today the state attempts to achieve a broad spectrum of ends. One of its most important, highly generalized ends in the light of historical trends is the increase of individual freedom. This phenomenon, of course, has been inextricably bound up with the guarantee of human rights. Although spearheaded by the state, individual freedom has spread into nearly all areas of life. Given the value that members of society place on it, the state and other normative orders must meet the continuing challenge of freedom in order to preserve their legitimacy.

Freedom, however, involves the state in ramified activities in order to create its conditions. For example, mass transportation systems increase freedom by making possible jobs that widen the range of possibilities for individuals to fulfill their work obligations. Again, the restriction of arbitrary authority to exclude persons on the basis of ascriptive qualities by the institution of rational rules increases the freedom of those subject to authority. Fostering the conditions of freedom, however, requires policies and their bureaucratic implementation that face the aforementioned limitations on their rationality. Legal rationality, for example, involves the rule of law; but, as we have seen, the implementation of a rule is not so simple a matter as it may seem. Although many of the factors coming to light as limitations on rational processes were uncovered by microsociological theories,[39] they are nonetheless generalizable to large numbers of individuals formally organized. This follows from our previously defended individualist conclusions.[40]

Herein resides a dilemma for modern structures of authority. They are obliged to cope with the contradiction of claiming the rationality necessary to achieve unlimited individual freedom, yet at the same time these claims founder on inherent limits of rational action, with the possible loss of legitimacy. A related danger is that people's boundless faith in the capacity of reason to achieve any end will lead down the path of disillusionment—a disillusionment not so easily dispelled by a social science subject to some of the same limitations as commonsense thinking.

Notes

Introduction

1. Thomas S. Kuhn, *The Structure of Scientific Revolutions*, 2d ed., enlarged (Chicago: The University of Chicago Press, 1970), 20–21.

Chapter 1

1. Thomas Hobbes, *Leviathan*, ed. Michael Oakeshott (New York: Collier Books, 1962), 45.

2. Ibid., 70–71.

3. See Talcott Parsons, *The Structure of Social Action: A Study in Social Theory with Special Reference to a Group of Recent European Writers*, (Glencoe, Ill.: The Free Press, 1949), 2d. ed. 473–87, for a brief overview of this development.

4. In this regard Parsons in 1961 wrote: "Probably the greatest consensus exists regarding the applicability to our discipline of the general canons of scientific method. The battle about whether science is possible in the field of human social behavior may be said to be over in its main phase, however much may remain to be settled in many of the subtler points, particularly the borderline problems" (Talcott Parsons, "An Outline of the Social System," in *Theories of Society: Foundations of Modern Sociological Theory*, vol. 1, ed. Talcott Parsons et al. [Glencoe, Ill.: The Free Press, 1961], 32).

5. Philosophers have written voluminously about the positivist model of science and have addressed the problem of the relationship of the social to the natural sciences. My discussion cannot go into what philosophers have written. Nevertheless, their analyses provide a context for it, and various philosophical ideas are represented through their having been absorbed by the writers.

324   Notes

6. Auguste Comte, *The Positive Philosophy*, trans. Harriet Martineau (New York: Calvin Blanchard, 1855), 25–26.

7. Ibid., 45–47.

8. Ibid., 45–46.

9. Ibid., 46.

10. Ibid., 48–49.

11. Ibid., 48.

12. Ibid., 464.

13. Ibid., 474–75.

14. Ibid., 485–86.

15. Ibid., 826–27.

16. Ibid., 486–87.

17. Ibid., 819–20.

18. Auguste Comte, *System of Positive Polity*, vol. 1, trans. John Henry Bridges (New York: Burt Franklin, 1875), 30–31.

19. Ibid., 32–35.

20. Ibid., 6.

21. Ibid., 21–23, 42–43.

22. Ibid., 351, 354.

23. Ibid., 345–46.

24. Ibid., 351–53.

25. Ibid., 13, 27–28.

26. Comte, *Positive Philosophy*, 37–38.

27. Steven Lukes, *Emile Durkheim: His Life and Work* (New York: Penguin Books, 1973), 68.

28. Emile Durkheim, *The Rules of Sociological Method*, trans W. D. Halls, repr. *The Rules of Sociological Method and Selected Texts on Sociology and Its Method*, ed. Steven Lukes (New York: The Free Press, 1982), 63, 71.

29. Ibid., 175.

30. The mode of existence of the social fact is discussed in chapter 3.

31. Durkheim, *Rules*, 31–32.

32. Ibid., 36–37. Also see his debate with the historian Seignobos. Ibid., 212–17, 228.

33. Ibid., 35–36, 70–72.

34. Ibid., 80–83.

35. Ibid., 110–11.

36. Ibid., 74–75. Although he did not complete the task, Durkheim believed it is possible to define types of societies, "social species" as he called them. All societies belonging to a type possess common characteristics. See ibid., chap. 4.

37. Ibid., 108–9, 110–11.

38. Ibid., 134.

39. Ibid., 147–49, 215.

40. Emile Durkheim, *Suicide: A Study in Sociology*, trans. John A. Spaulding and George Simpson (Glencoe, Ill.: The Free Press, 1951), 208–10.

41. Durkheim, *Rules*, 150–51, 183.

42. Ibid., 151–52.

43. Durkheim, *Suicide*, 208–10.

44. Emile Durkheim, *The Division of Labor in Society*, trans. W. D. Halls (New York: The Free Press, 1984), 63–65.

45. Ibid., 127, 139–41.

46. Ibid., 165–66.

47. Durkheim, *Rules*, 33.

48. He incorporated causality in the definition of sociology: "Sociology (in the sense in which this highly ambiguous word is used here) is a science concerning itself with the interpretive understanding of social action and thereby with a causal explanation of its course and consequences" (Max Weber, *Economy and Society: An Outline of Interpretive Sociology*, vol. 1, ed. Guenther Roth and Claus Wittich [New York: Bedminster Press, 1968], 4). It is interesting to note that he classified sociology as a science. Nevertheless, as the following discussion will show, Weber's overall conception of social science was permeated by antipositivist notions.

49. Max Weber, *Roscher and Knies: The Logical Problems of Historical Economics*, trans. Guy Oakes (New York: The Free Press, 1975), 194–96.

50. Max Weber, " 'Objectivity' in Social Science and Social Policy," repr. *The Methodology of the Social Sciences*, trans. and ed. Edward A. Shils and Henry A. Finch (Glencoe, Ill.: The Free Press, 1949), 79.

51. Weber, *Roscher and Knies*, 147–48.

52. Ibid., 196, 278.

53. Ibid., 170–71. Weber gave an example of the triviality of formalizing common-sense rules: "Whoever displays pleasure at someone's distress is likely to become unpopular." Ibid., 171.

54. Weber, " 'Objectivity' in Social Science and Social Policy," 79–80.

55. Max Weber, "Critical Studies in the Logic of the Cultural Sciences: A Critique of Eduard Meyer's Methodological Views," repr. *Methodology*, 164–66, 171–74.

56. Max Weber, "The Meaning of 'Ethical Neutrality' in Sociology and Economics," repr. *Methodology*, 1.

57. Ibid., 11.

58. Ibid., 13.

59. Ibid., 11–15, passim.

60. Ibid., 18–21; " 'Objectivity' in Social Science and Social Policy," 52–54.

61. Parsons separated his voluntaristic theory from what he called positivist theories of action. See Talcott Parsons, *Structure of Social Action*, 60–82. Nevertheless, the following discussion will demonstrate there are positivist dimensions to Parsons's strategy for building theory.

62. Ibid., 730, 753–54.

63. Ibid., 753–56.

64. Ibid., 34–35.

65. Ibid., 36.

66. In practice, said Parsons, it is difficult to distinguish between means and conditions. Factors in an actor's situation are usually both. For instance, an automobile is a means to reach a destination, but also an object to which the driver must adjust. He has only a partial control over it, and he did not create it. Ibid., 44.

67. Ibid., 43–45, 74–77.

326   Notes

68. Ibid., 751–52. The later development of Parsons's theory is an attempt to discover the laws of social action.

69. Ibid., 36–38.

70. Talcott Parsons and Edward A. Shils, Introduction to "Values, Motives, and Systems of Action," in *Toward a General Theory of Action*, ed. Talcott Parsons and Edward A. Shils (Cambridge: Harvard University Press, 1962), 50–51.

71. Parsons, *Structure of Social Action*, 734–35.

72. Ibid., 754–55.

73. Talcott Parsons, "Social Systems," repr. *Social Systems and the Evolution of Action Theory* (New York: The Free Press, 1977), 177.

74. He borrowed from Pareto, who derived the model of the system from mechanics, and from biologists such as Bernard, Cannon, and Emerson. Pareto's influence came through the physiologist L. J. Henderson. Talcott Parsons, "On Building Social System Theory: A Personal History," repr. *Social Systems and the Evolution of Action Theory*, 27–28.

75. Talcott Parsons, "The Present Status of 'Structural-Functional' Theory in Sociology," repr. *Social Systems and the Evolution of Action Theory*, 101–2; "The Relations Between Biological and Socio-Cultural Theory," repr. *Social Systems and the Evolution of Action Theory*, 118–19.

76. However, the unity of biology and sociology has its limits, for human action systems constitute a *sui generis* reality. This notion corresponds to Comte's belief that, although nature reveals continuity, there is also gradation. The sciences cannot be reduced to one common denominator.

77. Parsons, "The Present Status of 'Structural-Functional' Theory," 111–13; "The Relations Between Biological and Socio-Cultural Theory," 119–20.

78. In conceptualizing the system Parsons also drew on physical systems, such as the solar system. In these cases one finds again interdependence, uniformity, and self-maintaining processes (equilibrium). See Parsons and Shils, "Values, Motives, and Systems of Action," 107–8.

79. Talcott Parsons, "A Paradigm of the Human Condition," in *Action Theory and the Human Condition* (New York: The Free Press, 1978), chap. 15.

80. In this regard Parsons wrote: "Logical integration or systematization is in this sense a matter of degree. The ideal, however is a system of propositions so related that their logical interdependence is complete, so that all the propositions in the system can be rigorously derived from a set of primary postulates and definitions. Few schemes of scientific theory have approached this goal, but it remains the ideal and provides essential critical canons" (Parsons, "An Outline of the Social System," 32).

81. George C. Homans, *The Nature of Social Science* (New York: Harcourt, Brace & World, 1967), 4–5.

82. Ibid., 8.

83. Ibid., 8–11.

84. Ibid., 15.

85. Ibid., 22–23, 25.

86. See Peter Halfpenny, *Positivism and Sociology: Explaining Social Life* (London: George Allen & Unwin, 1982), 62–66.

87. Homans, *The Nature of Social Science*, 23–25.

Notes 327

88. Ibid., 26–27.

89. George C. Homans, "Contemporary Theory in Sociology," in *Handbook of Modern Sociology*, ed. Robert E. L. Faris (Chicago: Rand McNally, 1964), 951.

90. Ibid., 953–55.

91. Ibid., 955–56.

92. Homans, *The Nature of Social Science*, 28–31, 79–80.

93. Ibid., 19–20.

94. Ibid., 85.

95. Homans formulated propositions based on the research provided by behavioristic psychology. See George C. Homans, *Social Behavior: Its Elementary Forms*, rev. (New York: Harcourt, Brace & World, 1974), chap. 2.

96. Homans, *The Nature of Social Science*, 90–96.

97. Ibid., 98–99.

98. Ibid., 95.

99. Homans wrote as follows: "If the central problem of the social sciences is to show how the behavior of individuals creates the characteristics of groups, we should pay particular attention to the situation in which social phenomena can be most convincingly explained by psychological propositions" (ibid., 108).

100. Comte, *Positive Philosophy*, 38.

101. Robert K. Merton, *Social Theory and Social Structure*, rev. and enl. ed. (Glencoe, Ill.: The Free Press, 1957), 95–96.

102. Ibid., 97.

103. Ibid., 97–99. With regard to the last point, one cannot be certain that a correct prediction from a theory is explicable by it. For example, if A (theory), then B (prediction) occurs; but even though its occurrence was predicted by A, it could have been brought into being by C. Not to recognize this, said Merton, is to commit the fallacy of *affirming the consequent*. Ibid., 98.

104. Ibid., 64–67, 99–101.

105. One of the most famous of Merton's paradigms is the paradigm for functional analysis in sociology. Ibid., 50–54.

106. Ibid., 93–94.

107. Ibid., 89–92, 114–15.

108. Ibid., 92–93, 115–16.

Chapter 2

1. The terms historical sciences, social sciences, cultural sciences, and humanities were often used synonymously by German scholars of Weber's era. The specific disciplines included under them were also grouped under the inclusive term *Geisteswissenschaften* (sciences of mind) in contradistinction to the natural sciences. In much of Weber's methodological writings he makes little discrimination among these disciplines. Insofar as there is a division of scientific labor, however, the social sciences, which include economics and sociology, specialize in establishing empirical regularities and history in the causal analysis and explanation of individual actions, personalities, and

328　Notes

structures. Nevertheless, the social sciences are logically subordinate to history. This distinction will be clarified in the course of the discussion. See Max Weber, *Economy and Society: An Outline of Interpretive Sociology*, vol. 1, ed. Guenther Roth and Claus Wittich (New York: Bedminster Press, 1968), 19.

2. Max Weber, *Roscher and Knies: The Logical Problems of Historical Economics*, trans. Guy Oakes (New York: The Free Press, 1975), 55–57; " 'Objectivity' in Social Science and Social Policy," repr. *The Methodology of the Social Sciences*, trans. and ed. Edward A. Shils and Henry A.Finch (Glencoe, Ill.: The Free Press, 1949), 72–73.

3. Weber, *Roscher and Knies*, 57; " 'Objectivity' in Social Science and Social Policy," 72–73.

4. In line with developments in logic, Weber referred to the objects and configurations that are conceptualized by social science as "historical individuals." Weber, " 'Objectivity' in Social Science and Social Policy," 79. These include collective phenomena like a particular bureaucracy and the American Civil War as well as particular individuals.

5. Weber, *Roscher and Knies*, 57–58.

6. Ibid., 58.

7. Weber, " 'Objectivity' in Social Science and Social Policy," 72.

8. Value-relevance does not negate ethical neutrality. Once the social scientist has selected the object of investigation in accordance with his values, the inquiry proceeds in a purely scientific manner. Personal evaluations remain, or ought to remain, apart from an objective analysis. Max Weber, "The Meaning of 'Ethical Neutrality' in Sociology and Economics," repr. *The Methodology of the Social Sciences*, 21–22.

9. Weber, " 'Objectivity' in Social Science and Social Policy," 72, 76.

10. Ibid., 80–81.

11. Weber, *Roscher and Knies*, 102–4.

12. Weber, " 'Objectivity' in Social Science and Social Policy," 72–77.

13. Ibid., 84.

14. Weber, *Roscher and Knies*, 64.

15. Weber, " 'Objectivity' in Social Science and Social Policy," 88.

16. Ibid., 92.

17. Ibid., 89–90.

18. Ibid., 90.

19. Ibid., 94.

20. Ibid., 97–99.

21. Ibid., 90.

22. Ibid., 91.

23. Ibid., 100–101.

24. Ibid., 95–96.

25. Ibid., 94.

26. Ibid., 105.

27. Ibid., 90, 92.

28. Ibid., 101–2.

29. Weber, *Roscher and Knies*, 57.

30. Ibid., 101–5.

31. Weber's definition of sociology emphasizes the causal possibility of interpretive understanding. See note 48 in the preceding chapter.

Notes   329

32. It should be reiterated that these generalizations do not express the kind of nomological knowledge given in natural laws. Rather, they are relatively lacking in precision, yield ambiguous interpretations, are not axiomatized, are implicitly used, and often derive from everyday experience. Ibid., 170–73. Some examples given by Georg Simmel, who also faced the problem, illustrate some of these points made by Weber. Take the presupposition that democracies prevent abuse of power because those in office fear recall in the next election. Yet one can find cases where just the opposite happens. Those who hold political power for a limited time exploit their offices ruthlessly for precisely that reason. Or take the case of agricultural workers in Russia after serfdom was abolished. A historian concluded that they did not like their freedom because the lord, who now paid wages, was not compelled to employ them permanently. On the other hand, Prussian data show that before serfdom was abolished, the peasants did not work hard. Two contradictory "laws" must be invoked to explain each of these historical facts. See Georg Simmel, *The Problems of the Philosophy of History: An Epistemological Essay*, trans. and ed. Guy Oakes (New York: The Free Press, 1977), 49–50.

33. Weber, *Roscher and Knies*, 125–28.

34. Ibid., 125–29.

35. Ibid., 142; *Economy and Society*, 94, 100.

36. Weber, *Roscher and Knies*, 186–88; *Economy and Society*, 24–26. There is an imaginary experiment in this example. The scientific observer imagines that had the actor employed "objectively correct" means, the result would have been different. This implies, of course, that the means actually used were an adequate cause of the result. See the preceding chapter for a discussion of the imaginary experiment.

37. Talcott Parsons, *The Structure of Social Action: A Study in Social Theory with Special Reference to a Group of Recent European Writers*, 2d ed. (Glencoe, Ill.: The Free Press, 1949), 730. Also see 603, 607, 610, and 614–16 of this work for Parsons's criticisms of Weber on the ideal-type.

38. He expressed the deductive possibilities of action theory in the following: "The socially relevant values are certain particular features of the situation of the actor, his ends and the like. . . . All deduction from theory can do is to help us mutually verify different sets of data by drawing their respective implications for each other. And if, for example, we have the values in a given case for three variables out of four in the system we can, given the requisite logical or mathematical technique, deduce that of the fourth" (ibid., 736).

39. Parsons, *Structure of Social Action*, 507.

40. Ibid., 600–601.

41. In this context Parsons wrote: "This implication is necessary to avoid a completely relativistic consequence that would overthrow the whole position." Ibid., 601.

42. Alfred Schutz, *Collected Papers*, vol. 1, *The Problem of Social Reality*, ed. Maurice Natanson (The Hague: Martinus Nijhoff, 1962), 58–59.

43. Ibid., 53, 58–59.

44. Ibid., 62–63.

45. Ibid., 38–40; Alfred Schutz, *Collected Papers*, vol. 2, *Studies in Social Theory*, ed. Arvid Brodersen (The Hague: Martinus Nijhoff, 1964), 65–69.

46. Schutz, *Collected Papers*, vol. 1, 43.

47. Ibid., 43, 62.

330   Notes

48. The difference is also apparent in other productions, such as a literary work or painting. The subjective meaning of a literary product consists of the thought processes of the writer when he wrote it, whereas an objective meaning or interpretation of it is illustrated by an observer's classification of it into a general literary style. The latter reflects the observer's experience rather than the experience of the writer. See Alfred Schutz, *The Phenomenology of the Social World*, trans. George Walsh and Frederick Lehnert (Evanston, Ill.: Northwestern University Press, 1967), 133–34.

49. Ibid., 180–81, 221.

50. See chapter 7 for Schutz's analysis of understanding in the direct relationship.

51. Schutz, *Phenomenology of the Social World*, 181–82, 220–22.

52. Ibid., 184–86, 223–24.

53. Schutz, *Collected Papers*, vol. 1, 44.

54. Schutz, *Phenomenology of the Social World*, 236.

55. Ibid., 225, 234–35. Weber presented two criteria for the scientific validity of an explanation of the course of an action. The first he called adequacy on the level of meaning. An observer's interpretation of an actor's subjective meaning is adequate on the level of meaning if it corresponds to habitual modes of thinking and feeling. The second he called casual adequacy. An interpretation is causally adequate if according to generalizations based on experience the action will probably recur. The overt action and state of mind must correspond in order to have a valid explanation. See Weber, *Economy and Society*, 11–12. Through a rather complicated argument, Schutz attempted to demonstrate that adequacy on the level of meaning and causal adequacy are convertible. If a type fulfills one of these two criteria, it also fulfills the other. It should be noted that Weber applied these criteria to explanations whereas Schutz applied them to ideal-types.

56. Schutz, *Phenomenology of the Social World*, 188–94. The reader will recall in this context Weber's observation that the more general the scope of a concept the less its meaning. The ideal-type loses in meaning what it gains in clarity and precision.

57. He described the relationship between the type and the scientist as follows: "The relationship between the social scientist and the puppet he has created reflects to a certain extent an age-old problem of theology and metaphysics, that of the relationship between God and his creatures. The puppet exists and acts merely by the grace of the scientist; it cannot act otherwise than according to the purposes which the scientist's wisdom has determined it to carry out. Nevertheless, it is supposed to act as if it were not determined but could determine itself" (Schutz, *Collected Papers*, vol. 1, 47).

58. Schutz, *Phenomenology of the Social World*, 232–33.

59. Ibid., 228, 236, 238.

60. He defined sociology as follows: "The primary task of this science is to describe the processes of meaning-establishment and meaning-interpretation as these are carried out by individuals living in the social world. This description can be empirical or eidetic; it can take as its subject matter the individual or the typical; it can be performed in concrete situations of everyday life or with a high degree of generality" (Schutz, *Phenomenology of the Social World*, 248).

61. Harold Garfinkel, *Studies in Ethnomethodology* (Englewood Cliffs, N.J.: Prentice-Hall, 1967), 4, 11.

62. Ibid., 5–7. Also see Thomas P. Wilson, "Normative and Interpretive Paradigms in Sociology," repr. *Understanding Everyday Life: Toward the Reconstruction of Sociolog-*

Notes   331

ical Knowledge, ed. Jack D. Douglas (Chicago: Aldine, 1970) for a more detailed analysis of the methodological problems occasioned by the contrast between objective and indexical expressions.

63. Garfinkel in collaboration with Egon Bittner, " 'Good' Organizational Reasons for 'Bad' Clinic Records," in *Studies in Ethnomethodology*, 186–87.

64. Ibid., 198–200.

65. Ibid., 200–201.

66. Ibid., 201–2, 203–5.

67. Ibid., 202–3. Also see Harold Garfinkel, "Studies of the Routine Grounds of Everyday Activities," repr. *Studies in Ethnomethodology*, 39–40.

68. See Wilson, "Normative and Interpretive Paradigms," 68–69, 74–77; Don H. Zimmerman and Melvin Pollner, "The Everyday World as a Phenomenon," repr. *Understanding Everyday Life*, 94–96.

Aaron Cicourel has criticized quantification by sociologists on this ground. Valid counting depends upon equivalence classes. Aaron Cicourel, *Method and Measurement in Sociology* (New York: The Free Press, 1964), 26–27. Logical equivalence is determined by three laws: (1) *Reflexivity* means that A is equivalent to A. (2) *Symmetry* means that if A is equivalent to B, B is equivalent to A. (3) *Transitivity* means that if A is equivalent to B, and B is equivalent to C, then C is equivalent to A. Ibid., 288. Although these laws can be met when measuring births, deaths, age, and marital status, measuring factors with meaning runs afoul of the properties of equivalent classes. A given attitude is not always an A and equivalent to itself, for what it means varies with context. In such cases, imperfect correspondences obtain between quantities of the properties of attitudes and the characteristics of the system of numbers applied to them. Ibid., 10–11, 194–95.

69. Harold Garfinkel and Harvey Sacks, "On Formal Structures of Practical Actions," repr. *Contemporary Sociological Theories*, ed. Alan Wells (Santa Monica: Goodyear, 1978), 295–96, 307–9.

70. Garfinkel, *Studies in Ethnomethodology*, 18–21.

71. Ibid., 21–24.

72. Regarding the sciences as falling into three distinct classes oversimplifies Habermas's scheme. It is more accurate to consider three types of scientific inquiry, a given science predominantly oriented to one mode but relying on the others. Natural sciences like physics are oriented mainly to empirical-analytical methods, whereas social sciences make use of both empirical-analytical and hermeneutic methods. See Jürgen Habermas, *Knowledge and Human Interests*, trans. Jeremy J. Shapiro (Boston: Beacon Press, 1971), 185–86, and "A Review of Gadamer's *Truth and Method*," repr. *Understanding and Social Inquiry*, ed. Fred. R. Dallmayr and Thomas A. McCarthy (Notre Dame, Ind.: University of Notre Dame Press, 1977), 356, for the dual nature of social science. As examples of critical science, Habermas points to psychoanalysis, some aspects of philosophy, and social theory insofar as it follows certain methods and addresses certain topics. Focusing mainly on antipositivist modes of social inquiry, the following discussion of Habermas's theory of science is selective.

73. Jürgen Habermas, *Theory and Practice*, trans. John Viertel (Boston: Beacon Press, 1974), 7–8.

74. Ibid.

75. Habermas, *Knowledge and Human Interests*, 129–31. He drew the example from Charles Saunders Pierce.

332   Notes

76. Ibid., 123–26, 162, 191; *Theory and Practice*, 19–22.

77. Ibid., 161–62, 191.

78. The knowledge-constitutive interest of the critical sciences is emancipation from unrecognized, repressive cultural traditions. Habermas would like to see the social sciences become more critical. See Habermas, *Theory and Practice*, 19–20. See chapter 8 below for discussion of repressive traditions.

79. Habermas, *Knowledge and Human Interests*, 212–13, 305–6; *Theory and Practice*, 19–20.

80. Habermas, *Theory and Practice*, 7–8; *Knowledge and Human Interests*, 34–35, 176.

81. Habermas, *Theory and Practice*, 76–81.

82. The criticisms appear in Jürgen Habermas, *Zur Logik der Sozialwissenschaften* (Frankfurt: Suhrkamp, 1970), 195–220, passim.

83. Habermas, "A Review of Gadamer's Truth and Method," 351–52.

84. Habermas, *Knowledge and Human Interests*, 309–10; "The Analytical Theory of Science and Dialectics," in *The Positivist Dispute in German Sociology*, trans. Glyn Adez and David Frisby (New York: Harper & Row, 1976), 134–36.

85. Jürgen Habermas, "The Hermeneutic Claim to Universality," repr. Josef Bleicher, *Contemporary Hermeneutics: Hermeneutics as Method, Philosophy and Culture* (London: Routledge & Kegan Paul, 1980), 183.

86. Jürgen Habermas, *The Theory of Communicative Action*, vol. 1, *Reason and the Rationalization of Society*, trans. Thomas McCarthy (Boston: Beacon Press, 1984), 123.

87. Habermas, *Knowledge and Human Interests*, 309–10.

88. Ibid., 260–66.

89. Habermas takes it as obvious that understanding also depends upon the correct application of the grammatical and semantical rules of the language. See chapters 5 and 9 for more detail about the validity claims raised in his conception of the ideal-speech situation.

90. Habermas, *Theory of Communicative Action*, 106.

91. Ibid., 108, 110.

92. Ibid., 111–20, 130–38. The ideal-speech situation is central to Habermas's conception of a critical social theory. Also see Jürgen Habermas, *Legitimation Crisis*, trans. Thomas McCarthy (Boston: Beacon Press, 1975), 110–11. Achieving consensus regarding the validity of meaning is an attempt to overcome the relativity of context-bound meanings.

93. Garfinkel and Bittner, " 'Good' Organizational Reasons," 189.

Chapter 3

1. Alfred North Whitehead, *Science and the Modern World* (New York: The New American Library, 1925), 18–19.

2. Ibid., 52–54, 57.

3. The term *methodological structuralism* should not be confused with the structuralism of the French anthropologist Lévi-Strauss. It should also be recognized that this long-standing dispute has been discussed under different terms, including individualism

versus collectivism, nominalism versus realism, and atomism versus holism. See Piotr Sztempka, *Sociological Dilemmas: Toward a Dialetic Paradigm* (New York: Academic Press, 1979), 288. The word *methodological* in the phrases indicates that contrasting conclusions about the reality of social structures have implications for the methods employed by the sociologist.

4. Emile Durkheim, *The Rules of Sociological Method*, trans. W. D. Halls, repr. *The Rules of Sociological Method and Selected Texts on Sociology and Its Method*, ed. Steven Lukes (New York: The Free Press, 1982), 39.

5. Emile Durkheim, "Individual and Collective Representations," trans. D. F. Pocock, repr. *Sociology and Philosophy*, intro. J. G. Peristiany (Glencoe, Ill.: The Free Press, 1953), 4–5.

6. Ibid., 6.

7. Ibid., 7.

8. Ibid., 10–11.

9. Ibid., 13.

10. Ibid. 23–32; Durkheim, *Rules*, 38–45, 130, 251–52.

11. Durkheim, *Rules*, 131–35, 147–50, 162.

12. Ibid., 119–20.

13. Ibid., 124–25, 134–35.

14. Ibid., 69–70, 171–72.

15. Ibid., 35–39, 69–72. In these remarks about the thing-like character of the social fact, it is evident that Durkheim's structuralism reinforces his positivism.

16. Ibid., 43–47, 51–52.

17. Ibid., 59.

18. Emile Durkheim, *Suicide: A Study in Sociology*, trans. John A. Spaulding and George Simpson (Glencoe, Ill.: The Free Press, 1951), 146.

19. Ibid., 148–51.

20. Ibid., 43–46.

21. He supported this conclusion also by statistics. The rates within societies show a startling stability over long periods. As objective indicators of the state of society, they reflect its stability. Ibid., 46–52.

22. Durkheim applied similar logic in rejecting other psychological facts, such as insanity, alcoholism, heredity, and imitation. See ibid., bk. 1, chaps. 1, 2, and 4.

23. Durkheim, *Suicide*, 208–16.

24. Ibid., 218–21, 228, 234, 239–40. The principal subtype of altruistic suicide is *obligatory* altruistic suicide. The other two subtypes, the *optional* and the *acute*, are really derivatives of the first. Optional death occurs to avenge one's honor, or out of vainglory, or from jealousy. Although not obligatory, these deaths confer prestige. In acute altruistic suicide, the victim takes his life out of a sense of religious obligation or to be with his god. Ibid., 222–27. With regard to military suicide, the army teaches the soldier to set little store on himself and place himself beneath the group.

25. See ibid., 246–58 for a discussion of anomic suicide apart from the institutional contexts in which it occurs.

26. Ibid., 243–44.

27. Ibid., 269–73.

28. Ibid., 322–23.

334   Notes

29. It can be shown that many of Durkheim's other investigations depend upon the strategy of what I have been referring to as methodological structuralism. Especially his explanation of religion assumes the existence of society.

30. I refer here, of course, to notions of individualism. For example, Marx wrote the following: "The premises from which we begin are not arbitrary ones, but real premises from which abstraction can only be made in the imagination. They are the real individuals, their activities and the material conditions under which they live, both those which they find already existing and those produced by their activity" (Karl Marx and Friedrich Engels, *The German Ideology*, repr. *The Marx-Engels Reader*, 2d ed., ed. Robert C. Tucker [New York: W. W. Norton, 1978], 149).

In the same vein Marx wrote: "History is nothing but the succession of the separate generations, each of which exploits the materials, the capital funds, the productive forces handed down to it by all preceding generations . . ." (ibid., 172).

Once again it should be recognized that contradictory tendencies appear in complex systems of thought. What follows is an ideal-typical analysis of structuralist tendencies in Marx's work. Some of the material regarding Marx in this chapter appears in greater elaboration in relation to other theoretical issues treated in this volume.

31. Marx and Engels, *German Ideology*, 198–99.

32. Karl Marx, "Preface," *A Contribution to the Critique of Political Economy*, repr. *The Marx-Engels Reader*, 4.

33. Marx and Engels, *German Ideology*, 154.

34. That economic relationships combine to form a collective actor whose actions are independent of the actions and wills of individuals is also evident in the following: "The social power, i.e., the multiplied productive force, which arises through the cooperation of different individuals as it is determined by the division of labour . . . not as their united power, but as an alien force existing outside them, of the origin and goal of which they are ignorant, which on the contrary passes through a peculiar series of phases and stages independent of the will and the action of man, nay even being the prime governor of these" (Marx and Engels, *German Ideology*, 161).

35. Ibid., 160.

36. Karl Marx, *Capital: A Critique of Political Economy*, vol. 1, trans. Ben Fowkes (Harmondsworth, England: Penguin Books, 1976), 92.

37. Marx and Engels, *German Ideology*, 160.

38. Marx succinctly presented it in "Preface," *A Contribution to the Critique of Political Economy*, 4–5.

39. Ibid., 4.

40. Marx and Engels, *German Ideology*, 159–61.

41. For a more complete discussion of Marx on classes, see chapter 8.

42. Karl Marx, *The Poverty of Philosophy*, repr. *The Marx-Engels Reader*, 218.

43. Karl Marx, *The Eighteenth Brumaire of Louis Bonaparte*, repr. *The Marx-Engels Reader*, 608.

44. Before a revolution occurs objective conditions must have materialized in the economic base. The mere desire to revolt is not a sufficient condition. See Marx and Engels, ibid., 165; Marx, *Poverty of Philosophy*, 218.

45. The determinative impact of social class on individuals is expressed by Marx: "On

the other hand, the class in its turn achieves an independent existence over against the individuals, so that the latter find their conditions of existence predestined, and hence have their position in life and their personal development assigned to them by their class. . . . This is the same phenomenon as the subjection of the separate individuals to the division of labor . . ." (Marx and Engels, *German Ideology*, 179).

46. Karl Marx, *The Class Struggles in France (1848–1850)* (New York: International Publishers, 1964), 39–40.

47. Ibid., 41–42.

48. Ibid., 51–52.

49. After the April elections produced a moderate, bourgeois-dominated constituent assembly, the republic adopted policies that contradicted the interests of the workers, one being retrenchment of the national workshops. Erstwhile allies in February, the lower sections of the bourgeoisie and the proletariat turned against each other.

50. Engels admitted that when the February revolution erupted he and Marx had expected it to end in a proletarian victory. Friedrich Engels, Introduction to *Class Struggles in France*, 12–13.

51. Marx, *Class Struggles in France*, 42–44. Engels agreed with this explanation.

52. An example is the Mobile Guards formed by the government. These were recruited from the unemployed of Paris and helped to crush the workers' revolt in June. Ibid., 50–51.

53. Ibid., 72.

54. Engels, Introduction, 16.

55. Ibid., 15.

56. Marx, *Class Struggles in France*, 90.

57. Ibid., 123–24, 125–26. The inexorable march of the proletariat toward a future recognition of its class interests was given in a previous writing: "It is not a matter of what this or that proletarian or even the proletariat as a whole *pictures* at present as its goal. It is a matter of *what the proletariat is in actuality* and what, in accordance with this *being*, it will historically be compelled to do. Its goal and its historical action are prefigured in the most clear and ineluctable way in its own life-situation as well as in the whole organization of contemporary bourgeois society" (Karl Marx and Friedrich Engels, *The Holy Family: A Critique of Critical Criticism*, repr. *The Marx-Engels Reader*, 134–35).

58. Talcott Parsons, "A Paradigm of the Human Condition," in *Action Theory and the Human Condition* (New York: The Free Press, 1978), 375–78.

59. Ibid., 417, 420–22. Binary fission is integral to his theory of personality development. For this theory see Talcott Parsons and Robert F. Bales, *Family, Socialization and Interaction Process* (New York: The Free Press, 1955), especially chaps. 2–4.

60. Parsons, "Paradigm of Human Condition," 380, 388–89.

61. Talcott Parsons et al., "Some Fundamental Categories of the Theory of Action," in *Toward a General Theory of Action*, ed. Talcott Parsons and Edward A. Shils (Cambridge: Harvard University Press, 1962), 9–10.

62. Ibid., 19–20.

63. Ibid., 20–22.

64. Ibid., 17, 20, 22; Talcott Parsons and Edward A. Shils, with the assistance of James Olds, "Values, Motives, and Systems of Action" in *Toward a General Theory of Action*, 192–94.

336 Notes

65. Talcott Parsons, *The Social System* (Glencoe, Ill.: The Free Press, 1951), 6.

66. In his latest work Parsons distinguished the behavioral system from both organism and personality. It is essentially the individual's intelligence conceived with reference to Piaget's personality theory. See Parsons, "Paradigm of Human Condition," 383; Charles W. Lidz and Victor Meyer Lidz, "Piaget's Psychology of Intelligence and the Theory of Action," in *Explorations in General Theory in Social Science*, vol. 1, ed. Jan J. Loubser et al. (New York: The Free Press, 1976), chap. 8.

67. Talcott Parsons, "An Outline of the Social System," *Foundations of Modern Sociological Theory*, in *Theories of Society*: vol. 1, ed. Talcott Parsons et al. (Glencoe, Ill.: The Free Press, 1961), 60–62.

68. Ibid., 38; Talcott Parsons and Gerald M. Platt, *The American University* (Cambridge: Harvard University Press, 1973), 438–39.

69. Parsons and Platt, *American University*, 33–40, 267–72.

70. Parsons, "Outline of the Social System," 61–62. See pages 435–42 in Parsons and Platt, *American University*, for the complete set of interchanges among behavioral organism, personality, society, and culture.

71. Talcott Parsons, *Societies: Evolutionary and Comparative Perspectives* (Englewood Cliffs, N.J.: Prentice-Hall, 1966), 28. Parsons analogized the cybernetic hierarchy with the control exerted by a thermostat, which with little energy controls a heating apparatus that expends much more energy. See Parsons, "Paradigm of Human Condition," 374–75.

72. See chapter 7 for a more detailed discussion of how the social system's functions are accomplished.

73. He originally called this function *latency*. See Talcott Parsons, Robert F. Bales, and Edward A. Shils, *Working Papers in the Theory of Action* (New York: The Free Press, 1953), chaps. 3 and 5.

74. Parsons, "Outline of the Social System," 39.

75. Talcott Parsons, "On the Concept of Political Power," repr. *Sociological Theory and Modern Society* (New York: The Free Press, 1967), 300.

76. Ibid., 300–301.

77. The discussion of adaptation is taken from Parsons, "Outline of the Social System," 39–40.

78. Ibid., 41.

79. Ibid., 40–41.

80. Ibid., 58–59.

81. Parsons, *Social System*, 77.

82. Parsons and Shils, "Values, Motives, and Systems of Action," 219.

83. The societal community is the structure of society that specializes in the *I* function. In having a "primacy" of function, it parallels the polity and economy.

84. Talcott Parsons, "Social Systems," repr. *Social Systems and the Evolution of Action Theory* (New York: The Free Press, 1977), 185; "Outline of the Social System," 38.

85. Talcott Parsons, "Social Structure and the Symbolic Media of Interchange," repr. *Social Systems and Evolution of Action Theory*, 233.

86. Parsons, "Outline of the Social System," 57–58.

87. Parsons, Bales, and Shils, *Working Papers in the Theory of Action*, 218–19.

88. Ibid., 187.

Notes 337

89. Pattern-maintenance is the focus of the social system's equilibrium. This notion is addressed in chapter 7.

90. Talcott Parsons, *The Evolution of Societies,* ed. Jackson Toby (Englewood Cliffs, N.J.: Prentice-Hall, 1977), 8–9.

91. Ibid., 9.

92. Parsons, *Social System,* 436–47, 440.

93. Ibid., 430–31. Also see "The Sick Role and the Role of the Physician Reconsidered," repr. *Action Theory and Human Condition,* 18–19.

94. Parsons, *Social System,* 477.

95. Ibid., 434–35.

96. Ibid., 460–62.

97. Ibid., 462, 476.

98. Ibid., 314–15.

99. Parsons, "Outline of Social System," 59.

100. Parsons, *Social System,* 476.

101. See Robert K. Merton, *Social Theory and Social Structure,* rev. and enl. ed. (Glencoe, Ill.: The Free Press, 1957), chap. 1 for his paradigm for functional analysis. Pages 50–54 present a codification of the paradigm. Merton recognizes the value of Parsons's *AGIL* scheme for functional sociology. See Epilogue in *Contemporary Social Problems,* eds. Robert K. Merton and Robert A. Nisbet, 2d ed. (New York: Harcourt Brace & World, 1966), 800–801. Parsons's functions of the social system illustrate the concept of functional prerequisite in Merton's paradigm, namely, some requirement of the system under observation that must be met if the latter is to persist.

102. Merton, *Social Theory and Social Structure,* 32.

103. For example, Merton wrote the following about psychological and sociological ambivalence: "Although the sociological and psychological kinds of ambivalence are empirically connected, they are theoretically distinct. They are on different planes of phenomenal reality, on different planes of conceptualization, on different planes of causation and consequence" (Robert King Merton and Elinor Barber, "Sociological Ambivalence," repr. *Sociological Ambivalence and Other Essays* [New York: Free Press, 1976], 7).

In identifying group properties, he again leaves little doubt that individuals and groups form distinct levels of reality: "It should be noted that this [definition of membership] is being stated as a property of the *group,* not in terms of idiosyncratic variations of definitions by particular individuals" (Merton, *Social Theory and Social Structure,* 311).

One of Merton's stipulations for structural analysis in sociology is that it must deal with both micro- and macrosocial phenomena. In this context he quotes a physicist who makes the claim that matter on a small scale obeys different laws than those that apply to it on a large scale. Drawing an analogy between social and physical sciences, he cites with approval a passage from Turner, who espouses the idea that emergent properties materialize on the level of the macrosocial. Merton, *Sociological Ambivalence,* 123–24.

104. Robert K. Merton, "The Social–Cultural Environment and Anomie" in *New Perspectives for Research on Juvenile Delinquency,* eds. Helen L. Witmer and Ruth Kotinsky, no. 356 (U.S. Department of Health, Education, and Welfare, Children's Bureau Publication, 1956), 25–26, 28, 39.

105. Merton, *Social Theory and Social Structure,* 132–33.

338   Notes

106. Ibid., 133–34.
107. Ibid., 134–35.
108. Ibid., 162, 164–66.
109. Ibid., 144–54, 162–63.
110. Ibid., 144–47.
111. Ibid., 141–44. Merton cautions that not all deviance is dysfunctional. Sometimes, for example, individuals who violate norms come forth with better means of arriving at goals. They become accepted and enable society to better adapt to its environment. Ibid., 182–83.
112. Ibid., 149–51.
113. Ibid., pp. 152–53.
114. Ibid., pp. 155–57. Merton summarized the types of adaptation to the cultural structure as follows (see ibid., 140)

A Typology of Modes of Individual Adaptation

Modes of Adaptation	Culture Goals	Institutionalized Means
I. Conformity	+	+
II. Innovation	+	−
III. Ritualism	−	+
IV. Retreatism	−	−
V. Rebellion	+	+

115. Ibid., 179–80.
116. Jürgen Habermas, *Legitimation Crisis*, trans. Thomas McCarthy (Boston: Beacon Press, 1975), 14.
117. Ibid., 9–10; Jürgen Habermas. *Toward a Rational Society*, trans. Jeremy J. Shapiro (Boston: Beacon Press, 1970), 92–93.
118. Habermas, *Legitimation Crisis*, 4; Thomas McCarthy, "Introduction," *The Theory of Communicative Action*, vol. 1, *Reason and the Rationalization of Society*, by Jürgen Habermas (Boston: Beacon Press, 1984), xxvi–xxvii.
119. Habermas, *Legitimation Crisis*, 4–5.
120. Ibid., 4–5.
121. Habermas believes the principal reason for the survival of capitalism is the intervention by the state, and it is state intervention that distinguishes advanced from liberal capitalism. See ibid., 33–34.
122. McCarthy, Introduction, xxvi–xxvii.
123. Habermas writes: "Whereas social integration presents itself as part of the symbolic reproduction of the lifeworld—which depends not only on the reproduction of memberships (or solidarities) but also on cultural traditions and socialization processes—functional integration amounts to a material reproduction of the lifeworld that can be conceived as system maintenance" (Habermas, *Theory of Communicative Action*, vol. 1, xxvii, as quoted by McCarthy).
124. McCarthy, Introduction, xxvi.
125. Habermas, *Legitimation Crisis*, 5.

126. Ibid., 34–35.
127. Ibid., 38–39.
128. Ibid., 36–37.
129. The following diagram expresses most of the factors of interchange: (Habermas, *Legitimation Crisis*, 5).

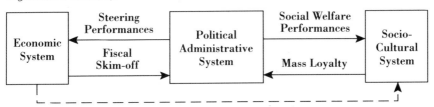

Rough parallels obtain between these interchanges and those identified by Parsons:

Habermas	Parsons
1. Fiscal skim-off	1. Control of productivity
2. Steering performances	2. Opportunity for effectiveness and allocation of fluid resources
3. Mass loyalty	3. Legitimation of authority
4. Welfare performances	4. Included under policy decisions
5. Motivation for role-performances	5. Labor capacity
6. Goods and services	6. Commitment to production of goods

See Parsons, "On the Concept of Political Power," 350, for the system interchanges. Habermas's sociocultural system combines Parsons's societal community (I) and his fiduciary (pattern-maintenance) system (L). See chapter 7 for a discussion of the inputs and outputs according to Parsons.

130. Habermas, *Legitimation Crisis*, 3, 147–48 (note 9).
131. Ibid., 3–4.
132. Ibid., 9–10, 13–14.
133. The methodological structuralism is muted and not so pronounced as in Durkheim's formulations.

Habermas warns that systems theory can readily be overextended and must be balanced by the model of society as lifeworld. Ibid., 14.

134. Ibid., 25–26, 28–29, 45–46.
135. Ibid., 46–48, 61–62.
136. Ibid., 61–63.
137. Ibid., 46, 62.
138. Ibid., 71–72.
139. Ibid., 70, 73.
140. Ibid., 75, 81.
141. Ibid., 75, 78–80.
142. McCarthy, "Introduction," xxxi–xxxiii.
143. Habermas, *Legitimation Crisis*, 75, 84.
144. He summarizes the scheme of crises as follows (ibid., 45):

Point of Origin	System Crisis	Identity Crisis
Economic System	Economic Crisis	——
Political System	Rationality Crisis	Legitimation Crisis
Socio-Cultural System	——	Motivation Crisis

145. Habermas does, however, incorporate other of Weber's conceptions of rationality, such as *Wertrationalität* (value-rationality) and the rationalization of world views, into his analysis of the sociocultural system. Habermas, *Theory of Communicative Action*, vol. 1, 168–78, 339–43.

Chapter 4

1. See Steven Lukes, *Emile Durkheim: His Life and Works* (New York: Penguin Books, 1973), 301–2.

2. Gabriel Tarde, "Sociology," repr. *On Communication and Social Influence*, ed. and trans. Terry W. Clark (Chicago: The University of Chicago Press, 1969), 79–80; "Sociology, Social Psychology, and Sociologism," repr. *On Communication and Social Influence*, 120–22.

3. Tarde, "Sociology, Social Psychology, and Sociologism," 115.

4. Ibid., 116–17.

5. Ibid., 117–18.

6. Ibid., 119–20.

7. Ibid., 122–24.

8. Ibid., 113–14, 135; "Sociology," 95–96; *The Laws of Imitation*, trans. Elsie Clews Parsons (New York: Henry Holt and Company, 1903), xvi, 24, 114–46.

9. Tarde, "Sociology, Social Psychology, and Sociologism," 125.

10. Tarde, "Sociology," 95–96.

11. Ibid., 103–4.

12. Tarde, *Laws*, 14–15.

13. Ibid., 68.

14. Tarde, "Sociology, Social Psychology, and Sociologism," 125.

15. Tarde, *Laws*, 15–16.

16. Gabriel Tarde, "Quantification and Social Indicators," repr. *On Communication and Social Influence*, 222–26.

17. Gabriel Tarde, *Penal Philosophy*, trans. Rapelje Howell (Montclair, N.J.: Patterson Smith, 1968), chap. 6.

18. Georg Simmel, "How Is Society Possible?" trans. Kurt H. Wolff, repr. *Georg Simmel, 1858–1918*, ed. Wolff (Columbus: The Ohio State University Press, 1959), 337–39.

19. Ibid., 340–42.

20. Ibid., 342–43.

21. Ibid., 343–45.

22. Ibid., 345–46, 347.

23. Ibid., 346–47.

24. Ibid., 351–53, 355. These apriorities do not exhaust the meaning of the term *form* in Simmel's writings. Perhaps the most familiar refers to the forms of sociation, which are those reciprocal interactions such as competition, superordination, conflict, division of labor, and the forming of parties, that the sociologist abstracts from the contents of interacting individuals. Simmel, "The Problem of Sociology," repr. *George Simmel, 1858–1918*, 314–15, 317. The sociologist studies the appearances of these forms in diverse contents at different times and places, their development, the displacement of one by another, and the conditions under which they appear. Ibid., 331–32.

25. Simmel, "The Problem of Sociology," 329–30.

26. The Enlightenment advocated freedom from the legal restrictions of the ancien régime. Once the privileges of the higher estates, the control over commerce by the guilds, the legal obligations to the Church, and the feudal obligations of peasants were removed, the essence of men, "natural man," would naturally unfold. Equality would be achieved inasmuch as all shared a common essence. Individualism was thus identified with freedom from the restrictions that forced individuals into unequal positions; and freed from artificial restraints, they would realize their individualities. Georg Simmel, *Fundamental Problems of Sociology (Individual and Society)*, repr. *The Sociology of Georg Simmel*, ed. and trans. Kurt H. Wolff (New York: The Free Press, 1950), 64–65, 72–73.

27. Ibid., 78–84.

28. Ibid., 74.

29. Ibid., 58–59.

30. Ibid., 58.

31. Durkheim wrote as follows: "In fact, only society can pass a collective opinion on the value of human life; for this the individual is incompetent. The latter knows nothing but himself and his own little horizon; thus his experience is too limited to serve as a basis for a general appraisal" (Emile Durkheim, *Suicide: A Study in Sociology*, trans. John A. Spaulding and George Simpson [Glencoe, Ill.: The Free Press, 1951], 213).

32. Simmel, *Fundamental Problems of Sociology*, 59–61.

33. Georg Simmel, *The Web of Group Affiliations*, trans. Reinhard Bendix (New York: The Free Press, 1955), 140–41.

34. Ibid., 150–54, 162–63.

35. Georg Simmel, *Sociology: Studies of the Forms of Societalization*, repr. *On Individuality and Social Forms*, ed. Donald W. Levine (Chicago: The University of Chicago Press, 1971), 252.

36. Ibid., 290–91.

37. Ibid., 254.

38. Georg Simmel, *The Philosophy of Money*, trans. Tom Bottomore and David Frisby (London: Routledge & Kegan Paul, 1978), 349–50.

39. Ibid., 284–86.

40. Ibid., 295–98.

41. Ibid., 312–14.

342   Notes

42. Ibid., 313.

43. Ibid., 314–15.

44. Emile Durkheim, "Individual and Collective Representations," trans. D. F. Pocock, repr. *Sociology and Philosophy*, intro. J. G. Peristiany (Glencoe, Ill.: The Free Press, 1953), 25–26.

45. Durkheim wrote, "In the fusion from which it results all the individual characteristics, by definition divergent, have neutralized each other." Ibid., 26.

46. The relationship of Weber to Marx in its totality is too extensive to be taken up in this section and in many of its aspects is irrelevant to the issue treated in this chapter. The following treats only those aspects of the relationship between these thinkers that are directly relevant.

47. Max Weber, *Economy and Society: An Outline of Interpretive Sociology*, vol. 1, ed. Guenther Roth and Claus Wittich (New York: Bedminster Press, 1968), 4.

48. Ibid., 8.

49. Ibid., 58 (note 6).

50. Ibid., 5–6.

51. Ibid., 8–9.

52. Ibid., 9–10.

53. Ibid., 13–14.

54. Ibid., 26–27.

55. Ibid., 40–42.

56. Ibid., 42–43.

57. See my discussion of Weber on class in chapter 8.

58. Weber, *Economy and Society*, vol. 2, 928–30. At this point Weber criticized Marx's conclusion of the inevitability of class struggles and revolution: "However, this fact must not lead to that kind of pseudo-scientific operation with the concept of class and class interests which is so frequent these days and which has found its most classic expression in the statement of a talented author, that the individual may be in error concerning his interests but that the class is infallible about its interests" (ibid., vol. 2, 930).

59. Ibid., 931.

60. Max Weber, " 'Objectivity' in Social Science and Social Policy," repr. *The Methodology of the Social Sciences*, trans. and ed. Edward A. Shils and Henry A. Finch (Glencoe, Ill.: The Free Press, 1949), 103. Weber wrote as follows: "We will only point out here that naturally all specifically Marxian 'laws' and developmental constructs . . . are ideal-types. The eminent, indeed unique, *heuristic* significance of these ideal-types when they are used for the *assessment* of reality is known to everyone who has ever employed Marxian concepts and hypotheses. Similarly, their perniciousness, as soon as they are thought of as empirically valid or as real . . . 'effective forces,' 'tendencies,' etc. is likewise known to those who have used them" (ibid., 603).

61. George C. Homans, "Bringing Men Back In," repr. *Institutions and Social Exchange: The Sociologies of Talcott Parsons and George C. Homans*, ed. Herman Tuok and Richard L. Simpson (Indianapolis: Bobbs-Merrill, 1971), 102–4, 106.

62. Ibid., 110–11, 115–16. Also see George C. Homans, "Contemporary Theory in Sociology," in *Handbook of Modern Sociology*, ed. Robert E. L. Faris (Chicago: Rand McNally, 1964), 967–70.

Notes   343

63. These are discussed in some detail in chapter 6.
64. George C. Homans, *Social Behavior: Its Elementary Forms*, rev. ed. (New York: Harcourt Brace Jovanovich, 1974), 194–96. Homans traced the explanation to the factor of power and ultimately to the general psychological propositions. Status is a resultant of power, which in turn is explicable by the stimulus and rationality propositions.
65. Ibid., 196–98.
66. Ibid., 341–42.
67. Ibid., 346.
68. Ibid., 343–45.
69. Ibid., 346–49.
70. Ibid., 342–43.
71. See chapter 7 in this volume for a more detailed discussion of Parsons's account of stratification.
72. George C. Homans, "Commentary," in *Institutions and Social Exchange*, 370.
73. Homans, *Social Behavior*, 307–8.
74. Society is not a collective actor. Although one can speak of a social stock of knowledge, it consists solely of the subjective experiences of individuals. Alfred Schutz and Thomas Luckmann, *The Structures of the Life-World*, trans. Richard M. Zaner and H. Tristram Englehardt, Jr. (Evanston, Ill.: Northwestern University Press, 1973), 262–63.
75. Alfred Schutz, *The Phenomenology of the Social World*, trans. George Walsh and Frederick Lehnert (Evanston, Ill.: Northwestern University Press, 1967), 3–9, 13–15.
76. This concept overlaps with Parsons's concept of role-expectations as discussed in the preceding chapter.
77. *The Theory of Social Action: The Correspondence of Alfred Schutz and Talcott Parsons*, ed. Richard Grathoff (Bloomington: Indiana University Press, 1978), 30.
78. Ibid., 30–32.
79. Ibid., 34–36.
80. Alfred Schutz, "Common-Sense and Scientific Interpretation of Human Action," repr. *Collected Papers*, vol. 1, *The Problem of Social Reality*, ed. Maurice Natanson (The Hague: Martinus Nijhoff, 1962), 21–22; "Choosing Among Projects of Action," repr. *Collected Papers*, vol. 1, 69–72.
81. Schutz, "Common-Sense and Scientific Interpretation of Human Action," 22–24.
82. Ibid., 22–23.
83. Ibid., 23–24.
84. Alfred Schutz, "The Dimensions of the Social World," repr. *Collected Papers*, vol. 2, *Studies in Social Theory*, ed. Arvid Brodersen (The Hague: Martinus Nijhoff, 1964), 30.
85. Schutz, "Common-Sense and Scientific Interpretations of Human Action," 31–33.
86. Ibid., 25; Schutz, "The Dimensions of the Social World," 32–33.
87. Schutz, "The Dimensions of the Social World," 54. Also see "Common-Sense and Scientific Interpretations of Human Action," 25–26.
88. Schutz, "Common-Sense and Scientific Interpretations of Human Action," 26.
89. Alfred Schutz, "Symbol, Reality and Society," repr. *Collected Papers*, vol. 1, 315–16.

344   Notes

90. Ibid., 315–16.

91. Schutz, "Common-Sense and Scientific Interpretations of Human Action," 23.

92. Reification has been an object of discussion by sociologists, a good deal of which focuses on the role it plays as identified by Marx. A distinction, however, must be made between the reification committed by individuals in everyday life as described by social theory and that which is built into various social theories themselves. It is the latter that is of concern here. Commonsense reification is explained by phenomenological theory as the result of the individuals' forgetting that a social order, experienced as an objective entity, was originated by and continues to be constructed by human beings. For them it takes on the character of a thing. They then falsely conclude that causality flows only from society to its members. This is similar to the reification that is closely related to the alienation occurring within capitalism according to Marx. See Peter Berger and Stanley Pullberg, "Reification and the Sociological Critique of Consciousness," History and Theory, 4, no. 1 (1964), 200–201; Peter L. Berger and Thomas Luckmann, The Social Construction of Reality (Garden City, N.Y.: Anchor Books, 1967), 60–61, 89–91, 197–98.

Although Berger and Luckmann are mainly concerned with commonsense reification, they also recognize a reifying tendency in sociological theory, especially functionalism. Ibid., 186–87. It is my view, however, that the two reifications have different origins. It should also be noted that the term has been defined in several different ways. See Burke C. Thomason, Making Sense of Reification: Alfred Schutz and Constructionist Theory (London: Macmillan, 1982), 88–94.

93. Talcott Parsons, The Structure of Social Action: A Study in Social Theory with Special Reference to a Group of Recent European Writers, 2d ed. (Glencoe, Ill.: The Free Press, 1949).

94. Ibid., 738–40, 742–43.

95. Ibid., 743.

96. Ibid., 746–47.

97. It should be noted that Parsons was cognizant of the pitfall of reification and cautioned about it. For instance, he wrote: "Second, it has been stated repeatedly that precisely in so far as the whole is organic its parts or units are not real entities but abstractions. Hence their use requires a particularly high degree of caution to avoid the kind of reification which creeps in when this is forgotten . . ." (Structure of Social Action, 747–48).

At various points Parsons disclaimed the reality of the social system. But on the other hand he made opposite claims. It is really a question of how he actually constructed the theory and the latter's assumptions and implications.

98. This analysis of the social relationship is indebted to Dr. Harley Upchurch.

99. Emile Durkheim, "Course in Sociology: Opening Lecture," repr. Emile Durkheim On Institutional Analysis, ed. and trans. Mark Trangott (Chicago: The University of Chicago Press, 1978), 50–51.

100. Emile Durkheim, The Rules of Sociological Method, trans. W. D. Halls, repr. The Rules of Sociological Method and Selected Texts on Sociology and Its Method, ed. Steven Lukes (New York: The Free Press, 1982), 31.

101. Durkheim, "Individual and Collective Representations," 25–26.

102. According to Parsons, the personality does accomplish the AGIL functions. My

Notes   345

formulation, in contrast, holds that the personality functions are sufficient to explain the interaction. See Talcott Parsons, "An Approach to a Psychological Theory in Terms of the Theory of Action," *Psychology: A Study of a Science*, ed. Sigmund Koch, vol. 3 (New York: McGraw-Hill, 1959), 659–797.

103. Peter Blau's work is a good example of the various social levels. At the beginning of his book, he stated his objective as the explanation of the emergence of complex structures out of face-to-face interactions. This overriding objective, Blau states, distinguishes his exchange theory from the exchange theory of Homans. Peter M. Blau, *Exchange and Power in Social Life* (New York: John Wiley & Sons, 1967), 1–4.

104. Durkheim, "Individual and Collective Representations," 30–31.

Chapter 5

1. Plato, *Laws*, repr. *The Dialogues of Plato*, vol. 5, trans. B. Jowett (New York: Oxford University Press, 1892), 8–9.

2. Plato, *The Republic of Plato*, trans. Francis Macdonald Cornford (London: Oxford University Press, 1945), 43–44.

3. Auguste Comte, *System of Positive Polity*, vol. 1, trans. John Henry Bridges (New York: Burt Franklin, 1875), 73; *The Positivist Philosophy*, trans. Harriet Martineau (New York: Calvin Blanchard, 1855), 500–501.

4. Comte, *Positive Polity*, vol. 1, 75–76, 77–78.

5. Ibid., 74.

6. Comte, *Positive Polity*, vol. 2, trans. Frederic Harrison, 8–9.

7. Ibid., 12, 14–15.

8. Ibid., 227–28.

9. Ibid., 18–20.

10. Ibid., 48.

11. Comte, *Positive Polity*, vol. 4, trans. Richard Congreve, 621–23.

12. Emile Durkheim, *Moral Education: A Study in the Theory and Application of the Sociology of Education*, trans. Everett K. Wilson and Herman Schnurer (New York: The Free Press, 1961), 23, 25–26.

13. Emile Durkheim, "The Determination of Moral Facts," repr. *Sociology and Philosophy*, trans. D. F. Pocock, intro. J. G. Peristiany (Glencoe, Ill.: The Free Press, 1953), 42–44.

14. Ibid., 44–45; *Moral Education*, 29–35.

15. Durkheim, "The Determination of Moral Facts," 49–51; *Moral Education*, 54–59.

16. Durkheim, "The Determination of Moral Facts," 51–53; *Moral Education*, 59–63.

17. Durkheim, *Moral Education*, 81–82.

18. Ibid., 70–72, 85–86, 88–92.

19. Durkheim, "The Determination of Moral Facts," 44–47; *Moral Education*, 96–99.

20. Durkheim, *Moral Education*, 120–22.

346   Notes

21. Ibid., 38–41.

22. Ibid., 41–46. See chapter 3 for the application of moral restraint to Durkheim's research on suicide. The idea of restraint of desire as a means toward happiness is not original with Durkheim. It is found, for example, in the thought of Plato and Aristotle, who identified the control and balance of desires (appetites) as moral elements.

23. Ibid., 37.

24. Emile Durkheim, *Professional Ethics and Civic Morals*, trans. Cornelia Brookfield (Glencoe, Ill.: The Free Press, 1958), 14–15, 24.

25. Emile Durkheim, *The Division of Labor in Society*, trans. W. D. Halls (New York: The Free Press, 1984), 231–33.

26. Durkheim, "The Determination of Moral Facts," 60–62. "Replies to Objections," repr. *Sociology and Philosophy*, 64–65, 66.

27. Among other types of repetitive courses of action, Weber defined usage, custom, and actions oriented to self-interest. The fact that furniture movers advertise when leases expire illustrates the latter. Max Weber, *Economy and Society: An Outline of Interpretive Sociology*, vol. 1, ed. Guenther Roth and Claus Wittich (New York: Bedminster Press, 1968), 31. The lack of standard terminology is evidenced by divergences between Durkheim's and Weber's usages. For instance, Durkheim's custom is similar to convention according to Weber. See Durkheim, *Division of Labor*, 24–26, 39.

28. Weber, *Economy and Society*, vol. 1, 31–33.

29. Ibid., 31–33.

30. Ibid., 34–35.

31. According to Weber, a state is a political organization that is largely successful in its claim to exercise a monopoly of physical force in a given territory. When physical coercion is carried out by another organization within the territory, that coercion is permitted by the state. See Weber, *Economy and Society*, vol. 1, 54.

32. Ibid., 313–15, 316–18.

33. Ethics for Weber are those rules considered as ethical by the members of a society or a group. As binding rules they have empirical validity. Some ethical precepts are conventions, while others have attained the status of laws. Not all conventions and laws, however, are considered as within the realm of ethics. In the final analysis, what norms are ethical is to be decided with reference to the definitions of a given society. Ibid., 36. These remarks imply that ethics is a variable part of the legitimate order and is more restricted in scope than Durkheim's concept of the moral.

34. Weber, *Economy and Society*, vol. 1, 319–21.

35. The types are diagrammed as follows:

Lawmaking		Lawfinding	
Formal	Substantive	Formal	Substantive
Irrational	Irrantional	Irrational	Irrational
Rational	Rational	Rational	Rational

36. Frazer reported an example of an irrational procedure to determine guilt. Among

a tribe of equatorial Africa the belief prevailed that if the wives of hunters did not abstain from sex while the latter were on the hunt, the hunt would be unsuccessful. When success was not forthcoming, the wives were given poison to determine who was unfaithful. The one who succumbed was judged to be guilty. Here is an example of irrational lawfinding. See Sir James George Frazer, *Aftermath: A Supplement to the Golden Bough* (New York: The Macmillan Company, 1937), 21–22. An example of formally irrational lawmaking is the revelation of law by an inspired prophet such as Moses or Jesus. A deity takes possession of the charismatic individual and reveals law through him. Weber, *Economy and Society*, vol. 1, 321–22; vol. 2, 439–41, 758.

37. Weber, *Economy and Society*, vol. 2, 653–57. Weber called this substantively irrational adjudication *kadi* justice. Ibid., 806, note 40.

38. Ibid., 815, 829.

39. Ibid., 671–72, 678–79.

40. Ibid., 811.

41. Ibid., 736.

42. Rheinstein illustrated Weber's conception of logical rationality. Jurists in both civil and common law wrestled with the problem of how to treat a corporation all of whose stock falls into the possession of one person. A formally rational approach might argue that since a corporation is a plurality of stockholders, when all stock falls into the hands of a single individual it ceases to exist as a corporation. An analysis of the definition of a corporation justifies this conclusion. On the other hand, a substantive approach might argue that a corporation with one owner does not cease to exist. It does not cease to exist because the corporation was legally established to foster the goal of mobilizing capital through limited liability; and this goal is also a legitimate one for a single individual. Max Rheinstein, Introduction to *Max Weber on Law in Economy and Society*, ed. Rheinstein and trans. Edward Shils (Cambridge: Harvard University Press, 1966), lii–liii.

43. Rheinstein's example illustrates this contradiction between rationalities.

44. Weber, *Economy and Society*, vol. 2, 883–84.

45. Ibid., 655–56, 657–58.

46. To fill in the gap a law was passed in 1900 making the taking of electric power a crime. Ibid., 885, 896–97.

47. Weber, *Economy and Society*, vol. 1, 36, 215, 217–18; vol. 3, 948, 954.

48. Weber, *Economy and Society*, vol. 1, 36, 37, 215, 216, 226–27.

49. Ibid., 37, 215, 243–44.

50. The preceding treatment did not go into this aspect of Weber's studies in any detail.

51. Talcott Parsons, *The Structure of Social Action: A Study in Social Theory with Special Reference to a Group of Recent European Writers*, 2d ed. (Glencoe, Ill.: The Free Press, 1949), 75.

52. Ibid., 75.

53. Talcott Parsons, "Durkheim's Contribution to the Theory of Integration of Social Systems," repr. *Emile Durkheim, 1858–1917: A Collection of Essays with Translations and a Bibliography*, ed. Kurt H. Wolff (Columbus: The Ohio State University Press, 1960), 122.

54. Ibid., 124; "An Outline of the Social System," in *Theories of Society: Foundations*

348   Notes

of Modern Sociological Theory, vol. 1, ed. Talcott Parsons et al. (Glencoe, Ill.: The Free Press, 1961), 43, 44.

55. Parsons argued that the ideal-types *Zweckrational* and *Wertrational* underwent a shift in meaning in Weber's work. As a result, Weber came to identify the former with the interest in putting the correct means to the service of an end without consideration of ultimate values. Also, *Wertrationalität* shifted from absolute value to ultimate value. Hence, Parsons concluded, *Zweckrationalität* in Weber's mind came to refer to the intermediate sector of the chain of means and ends and *Wertrationalität* to the ultimate end and value. Thus, Weber, Parsons argued, in effect arrived at his (Parsons's) idea of the normative. Parsons, *Structure of Social Action*, 653–54, 660.

56. Parsons, "Durkheim's Contribution," 124–25.

57. Ibid., 125. Parsons distinguished three types of norms. A *relational norm* defines the content of a role, i.e., how it should be played. It guides the selection of ends and means. It constitutes the role. A *regulative norm* merely imposes restraints on what individuals are permitted to do in realizing their interests. For example, traffic rules do not prescribe where a driver goes but merely some things he must do to get there. A *cultural norm* requires individuals to hold a certain belief without expecting them to put it into practice. Laymen, for instance, are expected to accept the validity of scientific knowledge without themselves playing scientific roles. See Talcott Parsons, *The Social System* (Glencoe, Ill.: The Free Press, 1951), 51–56.

58. Parsons, "Durkheim's Contribution," 127–28.

59. One must bear in mind, however, that in enacting a role the individual is compelled to adapt the norm relevant to the conditions of the situation. There is, said Parsons, a tension between the ideal of a norm and the conditions of the world that affect its fate.

60. Talcott Parsons, *Societies: Evolutionary and Comparative Perspectives* (Englewood Cliffs, N.J.: Prentice-Hall, 1966), 113–14. See chapter 3 for another cybernetic hierarchy identified by Parsons in the action system.

61. Parsons, "Durkheim's Contribution," 138–39.

62. Ibid., 123.

63. In Parsons's sense norms include the laws of the polity. His theory tends to describe the entire society in all its processes as oriented to norms. This is manifest in the relationship between two hypothetical actors. Since the outcome of ego's action depends on alter's reaction, it behooves the former to anticipate the latter's expectations of what is proper behavior on ego's part. "At the very beginning the expectations may be purely predictive, but very soon they acquire a normative content." Talcott Parsons and Edward A. Shils, "Values, Motives, and Systems of Action," in *Toward a General Theory of Action*, ed. Talcott Parsons and Edward A. Shils (Cambridge: Harvard University Press, 1962), 154. In other words, early on interaction becomes oriented to rules backed by sanctions.

64. Talcott Parsons, "Comparative Studies and Evolutionary Change," repr. *Social Systems and the Evolution of Action Theory* (New York: The Free Press, 1977), 307–13.

65. Parsons and Shils, "Values, Motives, and Systems of Action," 60, 70–72.

66. Ibid., 80–84, 170–72. The pattern variables in the order given in the text are as follows: ascription–achievement, self-orientation–collectivity-orientation, universalism–particularism, affectivity–affective neutrality, diffuseness–specificity. They have moral

significance in that the choices affect opportunities, causing such outcomes as a person's being deprived of a job because of race (ascription), an individual assuming extensive obligations toward another (diffuseness), and the duty of a professional to place the interest of a client before his own (collectivity-orientation).

67. See chapter 3 for the social system's functions. Parsons himself analyzed the relation as he saw it between Durkheim's theory and his own concept of the normative. Durkheim arrived at the identity of the social milieu and moral rules. The latter are obligatory and rest on common values, which turn out to be the ultimate values of society—those reflected at the top of the means-ends chain in Parsons' account. Parsons also argued that Durkheim arrived at conclusions that recognized the same relevant elements in Weber's *Wertrationalität*, which are those ultimate values of society.

68. Talcott Parsons, "Order as a Sociological Problem," in *The Concepts of Order*, ed. Paul G. Kuntz (Seattle: University of Washington Press, 1968), 373–75.

69. Parsons, *The Social System*, 15–16.

70. The consistency of ultimate values, which is the core organizing principle of any society, contradicts Weber's conviction that the various spheres of values are in a relation of irreconcilable conflict. What is true may be neither beautiful nor good, said Weber. Therefore, one is forced to choose among conflicting values, and science is incapable of providing help. See Max Weber, "Science as a Vocation," repr. *From Max Weber: Essays in Sociology*, trans. and ed. H. H. Gerth and C. Wright Mills (New York: Oxford University Press, 1958), 147–48.

71. Parsons, "Order as a Sociological Problem," 378–79.

72. Jürgen Habermas, *The Theory of Communicative Action*, vol. 1, *Reason and the Rationalization of Society*, trans. Thomas McCarthy (Boston: Beacon Press, 1984), 255–56. Also see *Legitimation Crisis*, trans. Thomas McCarthy (Boston: Beacon Press, 1975), 97–98.

73. Habermas, *Theory of Communicative Action*, 265–66.

74. Ibid., 262. Weber, as we have seen, held ultimate values to be irrational and not susceptible to the criteria of science. Parsons concurred with Weber.

75. Habermas, *Legitimation Crisis*, 105–6.

76. These procedures are not those given in the notion of legality.

77. Habermas, *Theory of Communicative Action*, 266.

78. These world views are considered in chapter 8.

79. Habermas, *Legitimation Crisis*, 112–13.

80. Jürgen Habermas, "Legitimation Problems in the Modern State," repr. *Communication and the Evolution of Society*, trans. Thomas McCarthy (Boston: Beacon Press, 1979), 184.

81. Ibid.

82. Habermas, *Legitimation Crisis*, 101, 105, 107–8, 110.

83. Ibid., 112. Habermas's concept of legitimacy is an implicit contradiction of Weber's statement that a legitimate order can be imposed. For if the minority is forced to submit to a law, it fails to express their interests. It fails the test of a general interest. Ibid., 111.

84. Weber and his followers are also wrong, says Habermas, in terminating their scientific interest with investigating the *beliefs* in legitimacy. What a critical theorist ought to do is make an independent assessment of an order's legitimacy with reference to

350   Notes

the criterion of rational consensus. For one suspects, Habermas goes on to say, that when citizens define a rule as valid, they have "good reasons," Hence, science can objectively distinguish legitimate from illegitimate domination resulting from a forced consensus. Habermas, "Legitimation Problems in the Modern State," 188, 199–200, 202. At this point Habermas departs from Weber's notion of a value-free science.

85. Habermas, *Theory of Communicative Action*, 297–305

86. Habermas, *Legitimation Crisis*, 3–5.

87. Jürgen Habermas, "Talcott Parsons: Problems of Theory Construction," *Sociological Inquiry*, vol. 51, no. 314 (1981), 177–79.

88. Ibid., 180–81.

89. Ibid., 183.

Chapter 6

1. George H. Mead, *Mind, Self, and Society: From the Standpoint of a Social Behaviorist*, ed. and with Introduction by Charles W. Morris (Chicago: The University of Chicago Press, 1934), 135.

2. Ibid., 136–37.

3. Ibid., 138–39.

4. Ibid., 154–55.

5. Ibid., 194–96, 199, 203.

6. Ibid., 176–77, 198–99, 210–11.

7. Ibid., 215–18.

8. George Herbert Mead, *The Philosophy of the Act*, ed. and with Introduction by Charles W. Morris (Chicago: The University of Chicago Press, 1938), 367–76. Also see *Mind, Self, and Society*, 90–100 for an account of reflective intelligence.

9. The "I" and "me" left a dual legacy to symbolic interactionism. On the one hand, interactionists have pointed to the role as determinant, whose theoretical source is, of course, the "me." On the other, they have emphasized interpretations of objects constructed within the situation, which reflects the "I." Herbert Blumer, for example, has said again and again that meanings of objects are the results of interpretations arising within the processes of interaction. Meanings are established in the light of particular situations. It follows that joint action is a product of continual constructions. Although Blumer concedes that one must recognize that every action has a continuity with previous actions and that meanings carry over from one situation to another, nevertheless, it is the ongoing constructions whose importance impresses him. Herbert Blumer, *Symbolic Interactionism: Perspective and Method* (Englewood Cliffs, N.J.: Prentice-Hall, 1969), 4–5, 16, 20, 55.

To critics who point to the rules whose preformed meanings carry over and thereby explain regularity, Blumer replies that even where rules apply, actions are outcomes of interpretations because the rules must be interpreted. Ibid., 17–19. Furthermore, joint action under the jurisdiction of rules is subject to uncertainties, for a rule may be suspended or transformed in meaning to fit the exigencies of concrete situations. The necessity of interpretation is one case of the more general proposition that all established meanings are reinterpreted. Blumer, *Symbolic Interactionism*, 5.

10. In line with Garfinkel, Zimmerman and Pollner use the phrase "occasioned corpus" to emphasize the constructed character of the way a situation is defined and organized. They write: "By use of the term *occasioned corpus*, we wish to emphasize that the features of socially organized activities are particular, contingent accomplishments of the production and recognition work of parties to the activity. We underscore the occasioned character of the corpus in contrast to a corpus of member's knowledge, skill, and belief standing prior to and independent of any actual occasion in which such knowledge, skill, and belief is displayed or recognized. The latter conception is usually referred to by the term culture" (Don H. Zimmerman and Melvin Pollner, "The Everyday World as a Phenomenon," repr. *Understanding Everyday Life: Toward the Reconstruction of Sociological Knowledge*, ed. Jack D. Douglas [Chicago: Aldine, 1970] 94).

11. Ibid., 96.

12. Ibid., 96–99.

13. Harold Garfinkel, *Studies in Ethnomethodology* (Englewood Cliffs, N.J.: Prentice-Hall, 1967), 7–10. Also see Warren Handel, *Ethnomethodology: How People Make Sense* (Englewood Cliffs, N.J.: Prentice-Hall, 1982), 35–39 for a discussion of the reflexivity of accounts. This book presents a clear picture of ethnomethodology.

14. Mead, *Mind, Self, and Society*, 215.

15. Garfinkel, *Studies in Ethnomethodology*, 2–4.

16. D. Lawrence Wieder, "On Meaning by Rule," in *Understanding Everyday Life*, 109.

17. Ibid., 134; Don H. Zimmerman and D. Lawrence Wieder, "Ethnomethodology and the Problem of Order: Comment on Denzin," in *Understanding Everyday Life*, 291.

18. Wieder, "On Meaning by Rule," 128–29.

19. Zimmerman and Wieder, "Ethnomethodology and the Problem of Order," 292–93.

20. Ibid.

21. The following summary is taken from Don H. Zimmerman, "The Practicalities of Rule Use," in *Understanding Everyday Life*, 226–38, *passim*.

22. Ibid., 223.

23. In the first and third cases the flow was maintained by avoiding or reducing backlogs. In the second the receptionist decided not to risk an argument, which would have disrupted the work process. The third instance of suspending the rule was kept secret. Receptionists and workers believed their supervisors would have disapproved of the practice, although they themselves believed in its legitimacy.

24. Zimmerman and Wieder, "Ethnomethodology and the Problem of Order," 287–89; Zimmerman and Pollner, "The Everyday World as a Phenomenon," 96–97, 100–101; Garfinkel, *Studies in Ethnomethodology*, 32–33.

25. Jeremy Bentham, *An Introduction to the Principles of Morals and Legislation*, ed. J. H. Burns and H. L. A. Hart (London: The Athlone Press, 1970), 11.

26. Ibid.

27. Ibid., 173–74.

28. Ibid., 11–12.

29. Ibid., 100–101.

352   Notes

30. Ibid., 13–14.
31. Ibid., 38–39.
32. Ibid., 39.
33. Ibid., 40.
34. Ibid., 44.
35. Elie Halevy, *The Growth of Philosophical Radicalism*, trans. Mary Morris (Boston: Beacon Press, 1955), 14. This source presents an insightful analysis of the utilitarian movement.
36. Bentham, *Introduction to Principles of Morals and Legislation*, 284–85.
37. Jeremy Bentham, *Deontology Together with a Table of the Springs of Action and the Article on Utilitariansim*, ed. Annon Goldworth (London: Oxford University Press, 1983), 184–86.
38. See Halevy, *Growth of Philosophical Radicalism*, 16–17.
39. Ibid., 17.
40. Bentham, *Introduction to Principles of Morals and Legislation*, 158.
41. Ibid., 163.
42. Ibid., 158.
43. Ibid., 166.
44. Ibid.
45. Ibid., 169.
46. Ibid., 169–70.
47. Jeremy Bentham, *A General View of a Complete Code of Laws*, repr. *The Works of Jeremy Bentham*, vol. 3, ed. John Bowring (New York: Russell & Russell, 1962), 179–81.
48. Halevy, *Growth of Philosophical Radicalism*, 477–78.
49. Herbert Spencer, *Social Statics: The Conditions Essential to Human Happiness Specified, and The First of Them Developed* (New York: Robert Schalkenbach Foundation, 1954). 367–68.
50. Ibid., 67–68, 368.
51. Ibid., 68–69.
52. Ibid., 69.
53. Ibid., 72–75.
54. Ibid., 89–91.
55. Ibid., 367–72.
56. Ibid., 96.
57. Ibid., 395–96; *Principles of Sociology*, ed. Stanislav Andreski (Hamden, Conn.: Archon Books, 1969), 538–39.
58. Spencer, *Social Statics*, 396–97.
59. Ibid., 402–3, 407–8.
60. Spencer, *Principles of Sociology*, 538.
61. Ibid., 540–41.
62. Spencer, *Social Statics*, 226, 228.
63. Ibid., 400.
64. Emile Durkheim, *The Division of Labor in Society*, trans. W. D. Halls (New York: The Free Press, 1984), 149–50.
65. Ibid., 155.

Notes   353

66. Ibid., 158–59.
67. Ibid., 151–52.
68. Ibid., 160–61.
69. Talcott Parsons, *The Structure of Social Action: A Study in Social Theory with Special Reference to a Group of Recent European Writers*, 2d ed. (Glencoe, Ill.: The Free Press, 1949), 56–60.
70. Ibid., 89–94. See chapter 8 of this volume for a more extended treatment of Hobbes.
71. Ibid., 95–96, 98–100.
72. Ibid., 96–101.
73. Homans objects to this label and prefers that his approach be recognized as an application of behavioral psychology to human interaction. See George C. Homans, *Social Behavior: Its Elementary Forms*, rev. ed. (New York: Harcourt Brace Jovanovich, 1974), 56.
74. As discussed in chapter 1, this strategy accords with the positivist conception of social science.
75. Homans, *Social Behavior*, 67–68.
76. Ibid., 16.
77. Ibid., 22–23.
78. Ibid., 25.
79. Ibid., 31.
80. Ibid., 29.
81. Ibid., 37.
82. Ibid., 39.
83. Ibid., 43.
84. Bentham, *Introduction to Principles of Morals and Legislation*, 80–81.
85. These examples are not intended to imply that Homans's theory is reducible to utilitarianism. There are differences, but here interest focuses on the similarities.
86. Homans, *Social Behavior*, 56.
87. Ibid., 53–57.
88. Ibid., 28.
89. Ibid., 99–108.
90. Ibid., 98.
91. Ibid., 248–50.
92. Ibid., 248–49.
93. Ibid., 242–48.
94. Ibid., 245–46.
95. Ibid., 252–53.
96. Herbert Spencer cited case after case of unintended consequences of legislation. For example, under the Poor Law pauperized workers had their incomes supplemented from the local taxes. But the businesses of the employers were taxed to help raise these funds. Consequently, in order to keep afloat, the employers reduced wages further to pay the taxes. Another example given by Spencer to illustrate the irrationality of law was basing the salaries of schoolteachers on the performances of their students. This led to a system of drill and cramming, which put undue pressure on the "dull and weak" children. The damage to children over twenty years was so great, said Spencer, that the

354   Notes

government was in the process of abandoning the policy. Furthermore, the health of some teachers was also ruined under the pressure. Herbert Spencer, *The Man Versus the State* (Caldwell, Idaho: The Caxton Printers, 1940), 27–28, 30.

97. Homans, *Social Behavior*, 243–46.

Chapter 7

1. See Thomas J. Bernard, *The Consensus-Conflict Debate* (New York: Columbia University Press, 1983) for an account. The controversy overlaps with several others previously analyzed in this volume. The investigation of rules and morality encountered consensus; for, as Durkheim told us, a moral rule presupposes agreement. The same can be said about values, goals, and religious beliefs. Here, however, the consensual nature of these phenomena, which was not at the center of attention before, becomes the central focus.

2. Comte identified agreement upon beliefs as the basis of the unity of societies. One task of social statics, said Comte, is the analysis of the elements that produce such consensus. The problem with modern societies, he lamented, is that the absence of a unifying system of beliefs results in crisis and chaos. Having contributed to the intellectual anarchy are Catholicism, Protestantism, and deism, each of which attacked certain aspects of tradition, depriving men of intellectual continuity. Catholicism attacked the beliefs of antiquity, Protestantism those of the Middle Ages, and deism all religious affiliations. The recent revolutionary principle sweeping Europe acknowledges no spiritual authority beyond individual reason. Comte drew from all this the conclusion that the only way to regenerate mankind is to propagate positivist theory and its derivative, the Religion of Humanity, which will provide a unity of beliefs. See Auguste Comte, *The Positive Philosophy*, trans. Harriet Martineau (New York: Calvin Blanchard, 1855), 36–37; *System of Positive Polity*, vol. 4. trans. Richard Congreve (New York: Burt Franklin, 1877), 320–21.

3. Emile Durkheim, *The Division of Labor in Society*, trans. W. D. Halls (New York: The Free Press, 1984), 38.

4. Ibid., 60–61, 64.

5. Ibid., 34.

6. Ibid., 54. Durkheim was careful to recognize a balance of forces. Our greater agreement with an opponent may override our antagonism toward him.

7. Ibid., 55.

8. Emile Durkheim, "Preface to the Second Edition," *Division of Labor*, xxxi–xxxiii.

9. Ibid., 122–23, 172–73, 226–27.

10. Emile Durkheim, *Suicide: A Study in Sociology*, trans. John A. Spaulding and George Simpson (Glencoe, Ill.: The Free Press, 1951), 152–55, 158–59, 170.

11. Ibid., 170.

12. Ibid., 366–70.

13. Ibid., 170, 211–16.

Notes   355

14. Emile Durkheim, *The Elementary Forms of the Religious Life*, trans. Joseph Ward Swain (New York: The Free Press, 1965), 21–22.

15. Ibid., 30–32.

16. Emile Durkheim and Marcel Mauss, *Primitive Classification*, trans. Rodney Needham (Chicago: The University of Chicago Press, 1963), 10–12.

17. Ibid., 479–87.

18. Emile Durkheim, "Value Judgments and Judgments of Reality," repr. *Sociology and Philosophy*, trans. D. F. Pocock, intro. J. G. Peristiany (Glencoe, Ill.: The Free Press, 1953), 87–95.

19. Ibid., 91–92.

20. This account of the dyad is based largely on Talcott Parsons, *The Social System* (Glencoe, Ill.: The Free Press, 1951), 1–15, 30–42.

21. See Parsons, *Social System*, 182–91 and Talcott Parsons and Gerald M. Platt, *The American University* (Cambridge: Harvard University Press, 1973), 40–45. Parsons originally called this value-system the universalist-achievement pattern.

22. Parsons, *Social System*, 183.

23. Parsons and Platt, 41–42.

24. Talcott Parsons, "Christianity," repr. *Action Theory and the Human Condition* (New York: The Free Press, 1978), 200–201. Calvinism itself was an event in the development of Christianity, which in turn finds its roots in Jewish and Greek thought. Parsons interpreted the religious aspect of modern societies in the context of this larger historical development. The following account is taken from the above source, especially pages 195–204.

25. Talcott Parsons, Introduction to "Part Four: Culture and the Social System," in *Theories of Society: Foundations of Modern Sociological Theory*, vol. 2, ed. Talcott Parsons et al. (Glencoe, Ill.: The Free Press, 1961), 970.

26. Following Durkheim, other functional theorists have also analyzed the legitimating role of religiously embedded conceptions of cosmic order. Values are never self-legitimating but conceived by members of society as integral aspects of a world order. Robert Bellah's civil religion is of relevance in this context. Also see Kingsley Davis, *Human Society* (New York: The Macmillan Company, 1949), chap. 19, and Edward Shils, *Center and Periphery: Essays in Macrosociology* (Chicago: The University of Chicago Press, 1976), 3–7.

27. Parsons, *Social System*, 367–68.

28. Parsons, "Introduction," in *Theories of Society*, vol. 2, 971.

29. Parsons and Platt, 17. Parsons borrowed this term from Bellah.

30. Talcott Parsons, "Durkheim on Religion Revisited: Another Look at *The Elementary Forms of the Religious Life*," repr. *Action Theory and The Human Condition*, 223.

31. Parsons drew an analogy between social equilibrium and the equilibrium in natural and organic systems. If two planetary orbits were to move closer to each other than is compatible with the state of the solar system, equilibrium would be restored if other changes occurred to eliminate the inconsistency. See Parsons and Shils, eds., *Toward a General Theory of Action*, p. 108. A more instructive example is the organism, whose temperature remains constant despite variations in the temperature of its environment. Mechanisms such as perspiration return bodily temperature to normal when a deviation occurs. Parsons sometimes substituted the term homeostasis for equilibrium.

356 Notes

Talcott Parsons, "Some Problems of General Theory in Sociology," repr. *Social Systems and the Evolution of Action Theory* (New York: The Free Press, 1977), 230, 233, 235.

32. Parsons, *Social System*, 205.

33. Ibid., 205–6.

34. Ibid., 206.

35. Talcott Parsons et al., "Some Fundamental Categories of the Theory of Action: A General Statement," in *Toward a General Theory of Action*, ed. Talcott Parsons and Edward A. Shils (Cambridge: Harvard University Press, 1962), 15–16.

36. Parsons, *Social System*, 274–75, 303, 310–12.

37. Ibid., 298.

38. Ibid., 36, 491–92.

39. Parsons set forth another concept of equilibrium, defined as a balance of input and output exchanges among society's functional subsystems. See Talcott Parsons, "On the Concept of Political Power," repr. *Sociological Theory and Modern Society* (New York: The Free Press, 1967), chap. 10.

40. Talcott Parsons, "The Political Aspect of Social Structure and Process," repr. *Politics and Social Structure* (New York: The Free Press, 1969), 327.

41. Ibid., 371–72.

42. Parsons, "On the Concept of Political Power," 361.

43. Parsons, "The Political Aspect of Social Structure and Process," 326; "On the Concept of Political Power," 353.

44. Talcott Parsons, "Some Reflections on the Place of Force in Social Process," repr. *Sociological Theory and Modern Society*, 265–66, 286–87.

45. Parsons, "On the Concept of Political Power," 360–66, 401–2.

46. See chapter 3 for a discussion of the functions and structures that fulfill them.

47. For the complete system of interchanges see Parsons, "On the Concept of Political Power," especially 347–54.

48. The following discussion is primarily based on Parsons, "The Political Aspect of Social Structure and Process," 329–38.

49. The following is a slightly abridged representation of the political support system:

		Policy Decisions P	
	In to I		
Factors			
		Interest-Demands I	
	In to G		I
G			Democratic
(Polity)			Association
		Leadership Responsibility I	
	Out to I		
Products			
		Political Support P	
	Out to G		

Factors are system inputs; products are system outputs. P stands for power, and I stands for influence. See "On the Concept of Political Power," 399.

Notes   357

50. Talcott Parsons, *Societies: Evolutionary and Comparative Perspectives* (Englewood Cliffs, N.J.: Prentice-Hall, 1966), 10; "Full Citizenship for the Negro American?" repr. in *Politics and Social Structure*, 253.

51. "Full Citizenship for the Negro American?" 252.

52. Talcott Parsons, *The System of Modern Societies* (Englewood Cliffs, N.J.: Prentice-Hall, 1971), 12–13.

53. Parsons, "Full Citizenship for the Negro American?" 259.

54. Ibid., 258–64.

55. Ibid., 253–54.

56. See *Social System*, 184–85 for some reasons.

57. An exception to the decline of ascription is the nuclear family, whose unity and functions require that children be assigned the rank of their parents. Rank ascribed to the nuclear family as a unit limits equality of opportunity; but nothing can be done about this, said Parsons, short of abolishing it. This is precisely what Plato advocated for the ruling class in the *Republic*. See Parsons, *Social System*, p. 188; Talcott Parsons, "Equality and Inequality in Modern Society, or Social Stratification Revisited," repr. *Social Systems and the Evolution of Action Theory*, 327–29.

58. Parsons, "Equality and Inequality in Modern Society," 322–33, 326–27.

59. Ibid., 334, 335, 338–39, 347.

60. Ibid., 346.

61. Equality and freedom, said Parsons, are values of "institutionalized individualism," which is a part of instrumental activism. Parsons and Platt, 41–42.

62. Talcott Parsons, "A Revised Analytical Approach to the Theory of Social Stratification," *Class, Status, and Power: A Reader in Social Stratification*, ed. Reinhard Bendix and Seymour Martin Lipset (Glencoe, Ill.: The Free Press, 1953), 100–103.

63. Ibid., 108–9, 116.

64. Ibid., 103–4. Parsons admitted that these principles are in specific cases difficult to apply for a number of reasons. See ibid., 101–2, 108–9.

65. Parsons, "Equality and Inequality in Modern Society," 346–61.

66. Davis and Moore emphasize the motivational function performed by material rewards in their earlier theory of stratification. Kingsley Davis and Wilbert E. Moore, "Some Principles of Stratification," repr. *Class, Status and Power: Social Stratification in Comparative Perspective*, 2d ed. ed. Reinhard Bendix and Seymour Martin Lipset (New York: The Free Press, 1966), 47–53.

67. It must be noted, however, that this conclusion assumes the institutionalization of full equality of opportunity.

68. Parsons, *Societies: Evolutionary and Comparative Perspectives*, 93.

69. Ibid., 21–25.

70. Ibid., 23.

71. Talcott Parsons, "Evolutionary Universals in Society," repr. *Sociological Theory and Modern Society*, chap. 15.

72. Talcott Parsons, *The System of Modern Societies*, 98–99.

73. Talcott Parsons, "Religion in Postindustrial America: The Problem of Secularization," repr. *Action Theory and the Human Condition*, 308–9; Parsons, "Christianity," 203–4.

74. George H. Mead, *Mind, Self, and Society: From the Standpoint of a Social*

358   Notes

Behaviorist, ed. Charles W. Morris (Chicago: The University of Chicago Press, 1934), 42–48.

75. Ibid., 48, 118, 120–21.

76. Ibid., 49–51.

77. Ibid., 137–40.

78. Ibid., 154–55.

79. The following discussion is based mostly on Alfred Schutz, *The Phenomenology of the Social World*, trans. George Walsh and Frederick Lehnert (Evanston, Ill.: Northwestern University Press, 1967), Sections 19–20, 24–27, 33–34. It supplements the analysis in chapter 4 of Schutz as a methodological individualist.

80. Alfred Schutz, *On Phenomenology and Social Relations: Selected Writings*, ed. Helmut R. Wagner (Chicago: The University of Chicago Press, 1970), 164–65.

81. Schutz, *The Phenomenology of the Social World*, 33.

82. Schutz, *On Phenomenology and Social Relations*, 166.

83. Schutz identified transitional relationships between the direct and the purely anonymous indirect relationship. Examples are a telephone conversation, a relationship between reader and writer, thinking about a person one has met in the past but is not present now, and the relationship of a person to one whom he has never met, but who is being described by someone who has. Schutz, *The Phenomenology of the Social World*, 104, 180–81.

84. Ibid., 177, 181–84.

85. Schutz, *On Phenomenology and Social Relations*, 55–56.

Chapter 8

1. See Thomas J. Bernard, *The Consensus-Conflict Debate: Form and Content in Social Theories* (New York: Columbia University Press, 1983), 207–8 for the concept of benefit as a bridge between interest and value.

2. Ralf Dahrendorf, "In Praise of Thrasymachus," repr. *Essays in the Theory of Society* (Stanford, Calif.: Stanford University Press, 1968), 129–32.

3. Thomas Hobbes, *Leviathan*, ed. Michael Oakeshott (New York: Collier Books, 1962), 19.

4. Ibid., 47–51

5. Ibid., 48–49.

6. Ibid., 42–43, 53.

7. Ibid., 100–101.

8. Ibid., 98–99, 103.

9. Ibid., 98–99, 130–31.

10. Ibid., 99.

11. Ibid., 100.

12. Ibid., 103–4, 113.

13. Ibid., 132–33.

14. Ibid., 199–200.

15. Ibid., 135.

Notes 359

16. Ibid., 132.

17. Talcott Parsons, *The Structure of Social Action: A Study in Social Theory with Special Reference to a Group of Recent European Writers*, 2d ed. (Glencoe, Ill.: The Free Press, 1949), 93.

18. Karl Marx and Friedrich Engels, *The German Ideology*, repr. *The Marx-Engels Reader*, 2d ed., ed. Robert C. Tucker (New York: W. W. Norton, 1978), 155–56.

19. Ibid., 157.

20. Ibid., 156.

21. Ibid., 159–60.

22. Ibid., 190.

23. Ibid.

24. Karl Marx, *Economic and Philosophical Manuscripts of 1844*, repr. *The Marx-Engels Reader*, 71–73, 77–80.

25. Ibid., 73–74.

26. Karl Marx and Friedrich Engels, *The Holy Family: A Critique of Critical Criticism*, repr. *The Marx-Engels Reader*, 134–35.

27. Karl Marx, *The Poverty of Philosophy*, repr. *The Marx-Engels Reader*, 218.

28. Marx and Engels, *German Ideology*, 192–93.

29. Ibid., 150–54.

30. Ibid., 178–79.

31. Karl Marx, *Capital*, vol. 3, repr. *The Marx-Engels Reader*, 2d ed., ed. Robert C. Tucker (New York: W. W. Norton, 1978), 441–42.

32. Karl Marx and Friedrich Engels, *Manifesto of the Communist Party*, repr. *The Marx-Engels Reader*, 479–80.

33. Ibid., 480–81.

34. Marx and Engels, *German Ideology*, 163–64; Karl Marx, Preface to A *Contribution to the Critique of Political Economy*, repr. *The Marx-Engels Reader*, 4.

35. Friedrich Engels, *Letter to Joseph Block*, repr. *The Marx-Engels Reader*, 760–62.

36. Friedrich Engels, *The Origin of the Family, Private Property, and the State*, repr. *The Marx-Engels Reader*, 751–59.

37. Marx and Engels, *German Ideology*, 186–88.

38. Friedrich Engels, "On Social Relations in Russia," repr. *The Marx-Engels Reader*, 666–67.

39. Marx and Engels, *Critique of the Gotha Program*, repr. *The Marx-Engels Reader*, 538–39.

40. Marx and Engels, *Manifesto*, repr. *The Marx-Engels Reader*, 475.

41. Marx and Engels, *German Ideology*, 161.

42. Ibid., 154.

43. Ibid., 159.

44. Ibid., 174–75.

45. Ibid., 154.

46. Ibid., 165.

47. Ibid., 173.

48. Karl Marx, *Foundations of the Critique of Political Economy*, repr. *The Marx-Engels Reader*, 225–26.

49. Marx and Engels, *German Ideology*, 165.

50. Marx, "Preface," 4–5.

360   Notes

51. Karl Marx, *Contribution to the Critique of Hegel's Philosophy of Right*, repr. *The Marx-Engels Reader*, 62–63.

52. Marx, "Preface," 4–5.

53. Ibid., 5.

54. Marx and Engels, *German Ideology*, 191–92.

55. Friedrich Engels, Introduction to Karl Marx, *The Class Struggles in France*, repr. *The Marx-Engels Reader*, 560–61.

56. Marx's massive analysis of capitalism in *Capital* attempted to demonstrate the trends in that system that are leading to the objective conditions for a proletarian revolution to succeed.

57. Marx and Engels, *Manifesto*, 490–91.

58. Marx, *Economic and Philosophical Manuscripts*, 81–93.

59. Talcott Parsons, *The Social System* (Glencoe, Ill.: The Free Press, 1951), 349.

60. Thomas S. Kuhn, *The Structure of Scientific Revolutions*, 2d. ed. (Chicago: The University of Chicago Press, 1970), 149.

61. Max Weber, *Wirtschaft und Gesellschaft*, repr. *From Max Weber: Essays in Sociology*, ed. and trans. H. H. Gerth and C. Wright Mills (New York: Oxford University Press, 1958), 180.

62. Ibid., 193.

63. The following discussion of status groups is based largely on Weber, *Wirtschaft und Gesellschaft*, 180–194 and Max Weber, *Economy and Society: An Outline of Interpretive Sociology*, vol. 1, ed. Guenther Roth and Claus Wittich (New York: Bedminster Press, 1968), 302–7. My treatment of Weber on status-group conflicts owes much to Reinhard Bendix's analysis of Weber's image of society. See Reinhard Bendix, *Max Weber: An Intellectual Portrait* (Garden City, N.Y.: Doubleday & Company, 1960), chap. 8.

64. Weber's study of the Prussian *Junkers* furnishes a good example of a status group that set the tone of an entire society. They sat in the House of Lords and Representatives, staffed the Prussian civil service, and composed the officer corps of the army. Diplomacy was entirely in their hands, and the fraternity system in the universities was oriented to the *Junker* style of life. Their impact on Prussia was projected onto Germany as a whole when it became politically united under Prussian leadership. In the nineteenth century the *Junkers* came into conflict with two other status groups. One was the peasants on their agricultural estates, whom they replaced with cheaper day laborers to whom they owed no obligations beyond the wage. Second, their attempts to increase the profits from their landed estates were motivated by their desire to maintain status superiority and match the consumption of the economically rising bourgeoisie of the cities. Max Weber, "The Relations of the Rural Community to Other Branches of Social Science," repr. *From Max Weber*, chap. 14, passim.

65. Ralf Dahrendorf, "Out of Utopia: Toward a Reorientation of Sociological Analysis," repr. *Essays in the Theory of Society* (Stanford, Calif.: Stanford University Press, 1968), 113, 121–22.

66. Ibid., 114–16.

67. Ibid., 116.

68. Ibid., 116–17.

69. Ibid., 123–24.

70. Ralf Dahrendorf, *Class and Class Conflict in Industrial Society* (Standord, Calif.: Stanford University Press, 1959), 159–65.

71. Ibid., 161.

72. Ibid., 162.

73. Ibid., 36.

74. Ibid., 167.

75. Ibid., 213.

76. Ibid., 204, 208.

77. Ibid., 136–38.

78. Ibid., 172–73.

79. Ibid., 177–78.

80. Ibid., 176.

81. Ibid., 178.

82. Ibid., 176.

83. Ibid., 179.

84. Ibid., 180.

85. Ibid., 180–82.

86. Ibid., 204.

87. Ibid., 123.

88. Ibid., 182–87.

89. Ibid., 177.

90. The following discussion of intensity and violence is taken from Dahrendorf, *Class and Class Conflict*, 210–31, passim.

91. Dahrendorf, *Class and Class Conflict*, 134.

92. Ralf Dahrendorf, "In Praise of Thrasymachus," repr. *Essays*, 149–50; "The Origin of Inequality," repr. *Essays*, 173.

93. Dahrendorf, "Origin of Inequality," 167–70.

94. Ibid., 169–70.

95. Ibid., 172–75; Dahrendorf, "In Praise of Thrasymachus," 134–35.

96. Dahrendorf, "Origin of Inequality," 177–78.

97. Jürgen Habermas, *Legitimation Crisis*, trans. Thomas McCarthy (Boston: Beacon Press, 1975), 33–38.

98. Ibid., 76–77.

99. Ibid., 37, 77.

100. Ibid., 75–84.

101. Ibid., 112–13.

102. Ibid., 96.

103. Jürgen Habermas, *Toward a Rational Society*, trans. Jeremy J. Shapiro (Boston: Beacon Press, 1970), 62.

104. Ibid., 78.

105. Ibid., 60.

106. At this point Habermas's analysis articulates with his theory of universal pragmatics—a delineation of the conditions that define the ideal speech situation whose goal is authentic agreement. Existing norms ought to be evaluated in the light of this ideal situation as a standard of truth and legitimated as a product of rational consensus. Here the activist side of Habermas's thought, aimed at change toward the good life, comes to the fore. See my previous discussion of universal pragmatics in chapter 5.

362   Notes

107. Habermas, *Legitimation Crisis*, 111–14.

108. Ibid., 47–50.

109. Ibid., 80–81.

110. Jürgen Habermas, "Legitimation Problems in the Modern State," repr. *Communication and the Evolution of Society*, trans. Thomas McCarthy (Boston: Beacon Press, 1979), 187–88.

111. Randall Collins, *Conflict Sociology: Toward an Explanatory Science* (New York: Academic Press, 1975), 41. This work contains a good deal of material not directly related to conflict. Collins was not able to integrate everything into conflict theory. My discussion is highly selective by focusing on some of its contributions to conflict.

112. Ibid., 56–61.

113. Ibid., 44.

114. Ibid., 62–64.

115. Ibid., 68.

116. Ibid., 67.

117. Ibid., 164–65.

118. Collins makes it clear that these three factors are causes in their own right and not merely effects of occupational power. For example, income is one determinant of life-style independent of power.

119. For example, Collins sees causal relationships between the routine giving of orders and the upper-class values of expecting obedience and deference, assuredness, arrogance, sociability, and dignity. Ibid., 67–69. The cultures of classes, says Collins, convert them into status groups in Weber's sense.

120. Collins, *Conflict Sociology*, 289.

121. Ibid., 298–99.

122. Ibid., 299–300.

123. Ibid., 301–3.

124. Ibid., 302.

125. Ibid., 315.

126. Lewis Coser, *The Functions of Social Conflict* (New York: The Free Press, 1956), 20–31. Coser sees Parsons as foremost among those theorists who regard conflict as a destructive factor, subversive of social structures. Coser sets for himself the task of extracting propositions about conflict from Simmel's *Conflict* and modifying them in the light of subsequent theoretical and empirical work in order to correct a one-sided emphasis on the maintenance of order.

127. Ibid., 60–62, 64–65.

128. Ibid., 67–72.

129. Ibid., 39–48.

130. Ibid., 73–74.

131. Ibid., 75–80.

132. Ibid., 104–10.

133. Ibid., 139–49.

134. Ibid., 121–25.

135. Ibid., 33–35.

136. Ibid., 95–104.

137. Collins, *Conflict Sociology*, 373, 377–78.

Notes   363

138. Ibid., 394–95.

139. Habermas is an exception to the charge that conflict theorists fail to take cognizance of this factor. But in discussing Weber on legality, he rejects it as an adequate source of legitimacy of democratic norms. Instead, as already noted, legitimacy is increasingly demanded in the form of a rational consensus formed in the ideal communicative interaction. Habermas, *Legitimation Crisis*, 100–102.

140. See Gabriel A. Almond and Sidney Verba, *The Civic Culture* (Boston: Little, Brown, 1965) for a comparative study of citizens' attitudes toward five democratic states for evidence of the legitimating effect of democratic rules. Americans, for instance, have pride in the Constitution. See especially 204, 313–14 for their conclusions regarding legitimacy.

141. In this context Collins writes: "The state consists of those people who have the guns . . . and are prepared to use them. . . . The state *is*, above all, the army and the police, and if these groups did not have weapons we would not have a state in the classical sense. This is . . . much disputed by those who like to believe that the state is a kind of grade-school assembly in which people get together for the common good. Of course, this is one of the things that a state can do; if its members are organized in such a fashion that there is a stalemate over the use of violence" (Collins, *Conflict Sociology*, 351–52).

The statement is a caricature of contemporary democracies, much of whose effort is directed to welfare.

142. Weber, *Economy and Society*, vol. 1, 37, 50–51, 52–53.

143. See Stanley M. Elkins, *Slavery: A Problem in American Institutional and Intellectual Life* (Chicago: The University of Chicago Press, 1976), 81–89, 115–33; James Calvin Morgan, *Negro Culture in the United States: A Study of Four Models for Interpreting Slavery in the United States* (Ann Arbor, Mich.: University Microfilms International, 1984), 102, 107, 112–13, 126–27.

144. Parsons wrote: "The legitimation subsystem of a highly differentiated polity, therefore, centers around the constitutional system and the judicial agencies that interpret it." Talcott Parsons, "The Political Aspect of Social Structure and Process," repr. *Politics and Social Structure* (New York: The Free Press, 1969), 339. The reader is referred to the more complete summary of the polity in the preceding chapter.

145. Parsons, "Political Aspect of Social Structure," 328.

146. Talcott Parsons, "Religion in Postindustrial America: The Problem of Secularization," repr. *Action Theory and the Human Condition* (New York: The Free Press, 1978), 308–9. See chapter 7 for Parsons on liberalized Protestantism.

147. Talcott Parsons, "Christianity," repr. *Action Theory and the Human Condition*, 203.

148. Robert N. Bellah, "Civil Religion in America," in *The Religious Situation: 1968*, ed. Donald R. Cutler (Boston: Beacon Press, 1968), 337–340, 342–348.

149. Talcott Parsons, Introduction to "Part Four: Culture and the Social System," in *Theories of Society: Foundations of Modern Sociological Theory*, vol. 2, ed. Talcott Parsons et al. (Glencoe, Ill.: The Free Press, 1961), 971.

150. Harvey Wish, *George Fitzhugh: Propagandist of the Old South* (Gloucester, Mass.: Peter Smith, 1962), 38–39, 42–43, 48–49, 50–52.

151. In his analysis of the role of religion in contemporary America, Parsons took into account the historical trend of secularization. Despite the separation of church and state,

364   Notes

denominational pluralism, the loss of religion's monopoly on education, and an autonomous secular sphere of the "good society," Parsons returned to the theme of Calvinism
as the highest level of legitimation. Here is what he wrote: "My main theme in this paper
has been that the religious constitution of American society is fundamentally in line with
the great Western tradition of a society organized about Christian values. . . . Looked at
by comparison with earlier forms, religion seems to have lost much. But it seems to me
that the losses are mainly the consequence of processes of structural differentiation in the
society which correspond to changes in the character of religious orientation but do not
necessarily constitute loss of strength of the religious values themselves" (Talcott Parsons,
"Some Comments on the Pattern of Religious Organization in the United States," repr.
Structure and Process in Modern Societies [New York: The Free Press, 1960], 320).

This was written in 1958, but Parsons basically held to this view. In 1974 he predicted
that the commune movement in the counterculture is a religious movement that has a
"basic continuity with the American civil religion as this has been outlined by Bellah."
He also asserted that the Protestant ethic is not dead. See Parsons, "Religion in
Postindustrial America," 322.

152. Parsons referred to this notion as another example of an ultimate existential belief
system. See Parsons, Introduction to *Theories of Society*, vol. 2, 971.

Chapter 9

1. Rogers Brubaker has written a book with this phrase in the title. He, however,
limits the discussion to the relevant ideas of Weber, especially the latter's concepts of
Wertrationalität and *Zweckrationalität*. The following discussion includes some of the
points Brubaker makes but goes beyond Weber. See Rogers Brubaker, *The Limits of
Rationality: An Essay on the Social and Moral Thought of Max Weber* (London: George
Allen & Unwin, 1984), especially chapter 2.

2. Talcott Parsons, *The Structure of Social Action: A Study in Social Theory with
Special Reference to a Group of Recent European Writers*, 2d ed. (Glencoe, Ill.: The Free
Press, 1949), 7–10.

3. Ibid., 7–9.

4. Ibid., 9.

5. Ibid., 10.

6. See Ralf Dahrendorf, *Class and Class Conflict in Industrial Society* (Stanford,
Calif.: Stanford University Press, 1959), 289–314, passim, for his analysis.

7. It is interesting to note that in the preface to *The Structure of Social Action* Parsons
acknowledged that the delineation of a common theoretical scheme in the thinking of
Marshall, Pareto, Durkheim, and Weber was not his original goal. Rather he set out to
examine how these theorists analyzed capitalism. This study was not only not theoretically
derived in the sense we have been considering, but also underwent a shift in interest as it
proceeded. See Parsons, Preface to *The Structure of Social Action*, vi.

8. I do not argue that the formation of concepts is not at all subject to scientific
criteria. There is always the weight of evidence, at least in principle, some ideal-types,
for example, being better "fits" to empirical facts than others. The point is rather that

Notes 365

concepts shaped by different interests and values are not *directly* comparable in terms of rational criteria. Hence, attempts to demonstrate some scientific superiority of conflict over consensus remain unconvincing. See Thomas J. Bernard, *The Consensus-Conflict Debate: Form and Content in Social Theories* (New York: Columbia University Press, 1983), 198–205 for a summary of such arguments.

9. The following discussion is mainly taken from Emile Durkheim, *The Elementary Forms of the Religious Life*, trans. Joseph Ward Swain (New York: The Free Press, 1965), bk. 2, chap. 7, passim and 462–74, passim. This theory of religion was briefly touched on in relation to the normative order in chapter 5.

10. Ibid., 389.

11. Ibid., 236.

12. Ibid., 465–66.

13. Ibid., 242, 245–48, 250–51, 389–92.

14. Ibid., 236–39.

15. Here are Durkheim's words: "Since it is in spiritual ways that social pressure exercises itself, it would not fail to give men the idea that outside themselves there exist one or several powers, both moral and, at the same time, efficacious, upon which they depend. They must think of these powers, at least in part, as outside themselves, for these address them in a tone of command. . . . It is undoubtedly true that if they were able to see these influences which they feel emanate from society, then the mythological system of intepretations would never be born. But social action follows ways that are too circuitous and obscure, and employs psychical mechanisms that are too complex to allow the ordinary observer to see . . . [whence] it comes" (ibid., 239).

16. Ibid., 257–58.

17. Ibid., 257.

18. Ibid., 258.

19. See ibid., bk. 1, chaps. 2–3 for Durkheim's criticisms.

20. He put it this way: "In fact, it is an essential postulate of sociology that a human institution cannot rest upon an error and a lie, without which it could not exist. If it were not founded on the nature of things, it would have encountered in the facts a resistance over which it could never have triumphed" (Durkheim, *The Elementary Forms of the Religious Life*, 14).

21. Ibid., 474–79.

22. See chapter 1.

23. Reified society also appears in commonsense thinking. Today we hear about institutionalized racism, which is often contrasted with the racism of individuals. Where evidence of racial attitudes is lacking in specific individuals, the view is nevertheless expressed that society as a whole acts in discriminatory ways. Irrespective of their wills or attitudes, individuals are thus caught up in society's collective attitudes and actions. This analysis of racism is often followed by a call to reform society as whole.

24. Habermas cites these examples from Austin. See Jürgen Habermas, *Communication and the Evolution of Society*, trans. Thomas McCarthy (Boston: Beacon Press, 1979), 55–56.

25. See chapter 5 for a summary.

26. Max Weber, "Science as a Vocation," repr. *From Max Weber: Essays in Sociology*, trans and ed. H. H. Gerth and C. Wright Mills (New York: Oxford University Press,

366   Notes

1958), 150–52. Weber's conviction about the irrationality of the world is, of course, compatible with the precept of ethical neutrality for science. The irreconcilability of conflicting ultimate values on scientific grounds according to Weber has been brought up in chapter 5.

27. Alfred Schutz, *The Phenomenology of the Social World*, trans. George Walsh and Frederick Lehnert (Evanston, Ill.: Northwestern University Press, 1967), 98–107.

28. Alfred Schutz, *On Phenomenology and Social Relations*, ed. Helmut R. Wagner (Chicago: The University of Chicago Press, 1970), 135–37; Alfred Schutz, *Collected Papers: The Problem of Social Reality*, vol. 1, ed. Maurice Natanson (The Hague: Martinus Nijhoff, 1962), 27–34.

29. George Herbert Mead, *The Philosophy of the Present*, ed. Arthur E. Murphy (Chicago: Open Court Publishing Company, 1932), 11–12, 21–28. The analysis of Mead in this section overlaps with that given in chapter 6.

30. George Herbert Mead, *The Philosophy of the Act*, ed. Charles W. Morris (Chicago: The University of Chicago Press, 1938), 412–420. These pages set Mead's discussion of emergence within a sociological context.

31. Mead, *Philosophy of the Present*, 31.

32. George H. Mead, *Mind, Self, and Society: From the Standpoint of a Social Behaviorist*, ed. Charles W. Morris (Chicago: The University of Chicago Press, 1934), 214–15.

33. Ibid., 214–18.

34. Harold Garfinkel, *Studies in Ethnomethodology* (Englewood Cliffs, N.J.: Prentice-Hall, 1967), 14–15. Garfinkel expressed the conclusion in cumbersome prose: "An inquiry was apt to be heavily guided by the inquirer's use of imagined settings in which the title will have been 'used' by one or another interested party, including the deceased, and this was done in order to decide, using whatever 'datum' might have been searched out, that *that* 'datum' could be used to mask if masking needed to be done, or to equivocate, or gloss, or lead, or exemplify if they were needed."

35. Mead, *Philosophy of the Present*, 11.

36. See ibid., 27. In this regard Mead wrote: "When one recalls his boyhood days he cannot get into them as he then was, without their relationship to what he has become; and if he could, that is if he could reproduce the experience as it then took place, he would not use it, for this would involve his not being in the present within which that use must take place" (ibid., 30).

37. Schutz, *On Phenomenology and Social Relations*, 139. Also see ibid., 137–40 and *Phenomenology of the Social World*, 59–60, for his analysis of the temporality of action.

38. See chapter 6 for the relevant discussion according to ethnomethodology.

39. The theories I have in mind are symbolic interactionism, phenomenology, and ethnomethodology.

40. See the conclusion of chapter 4.

Index

accounts, 190, 319 (*see also* concepts); indexical, 56–60, 191–93; loose, 191–92, 321; reflexive, 69, 191–93

action (*see also* cultural structures; cultural system; organism; personality; social system; symbolic interactionism): definition of, 132; and exchange theory, 207–11; and habit, 189, 194, 317–18; interpretation of, 330n. 55, 365n. 15; and methodological individualism, 132–33, 139–47; and methodological structuralism, 91–99, 103, 108, 140, 146–47; and motives, 140–44; and normative order, 183–84; novelty of, 186, 188–90, 194, 317–21; and positivism, 24–25, 49–50; reconstruction of, 186–90, 194, 317–21, 366n. 36; unit act, 23–24, 146–48, 181–82; and utilitarianism, 197–98, 200, 206

adaptation, 95–98, 107–8, 112, 150, 202, 318, 337n. 101

alienation: and division of labor, 264–65; 269–70; political, 269–70

analogy, 128, 237, 258–59; and methodological structuralism, 77–78, 113, 337n. 103; and unity of science, 18, 25–26, 29–30, 36–37, 326n. 78, 355n. 31

analytical element, 23–24, 27, 49

analytical laws, 23–24, 43, 49, 308

anomie, 83–84, 113, 127–28, 131, 235, 255

antipositivism, 8, 19 (*see also* concepts; constructs); and causality, 43, 46–47, 70; definition of, 39–40; and ethnomethodology, 40, 56–60, 63, 68–69; and hermeneutics, 60–69; and methodology, 39–56, 60–67; object-

constitution, 61, 64–65; and rationality, 308; and value-relevance, 42–46, 48, 50, 309

Aristotle: on distributive justice, 212–13; on moral restraint, 346n. 22

authority, 155 (*see also under* morality; rules); charismatic, 172; in conflict and functional theory, 221, 236–38, 275, 283–87, 300–305, 309, 363n. 139; definition of, 300–301; legitimacy of, 284–85, 300–302; and power, 236–38, 243–44, 257, 303, 305; rational-legal, 171–74, 322; traditional, 172

behavioral system, 336n. 66

Bellah, Robert, 303–4, 355n. 26, 363n. 151

Bentham, Jeremy: on positivism, 197; on social order, 196–201, 210–11, 214; on utilitarianism, 196–201, 210–11, 214

Bittner, Egon: on ethnomethodology, 57–59

Blau, Peter, 345n. 103

Blumer, Herbert, 350n. 9

Calvinism, 233, 246, 355n. 24, 363n. 151; and instrumental activism, 231–32, 244, 255, 304, 314

capitalism: advanced, 106, 109–12, 283, 288–91, 338n. 121, 339n. 144; and conflict, 135, 265–67, 274, 288–91, 360n. 56; liberal, 289, 338n. 121; and methodological structuralism, 89–91, 106–12

causality: agreement and difference, 17, 21; and antipositivism, 43, 46–47, 70; comparative, 16–17; concomitant variations, 17, 24; definition of, 19; and generalizations, 36; and

368   Index

methodological individualism, 117–18, 132; and methodological structuralism, 78–84, 105, 114–15, 344 n. 92; objective possibility and adequate causation, 20–21, 55, 330 n. 5; and positivism, 7, 9, 16–21; transparent, 134–35

Cicourel, Aaron, 63, 331 n. 68

class (concept), 3, 331 n. 68 (see also concepts); and ideal-type, 43–45, 48–50, 69–72

class (social) (see also under conflict): culture of, 295, 362 n. 119; definition of, 134, 278–79; formation of, 135, 265–67, 286, 300; and methodological structuralism, 88–91, 134–35, 148–49; and organizations, 292, 294–95; and property, 134, 266–67, 269, 272, 275, 279–80, 283–85, 294; quasi and interest groups, 284–85; and status groups, 277–80

class consciousness, 88, 91, 135, 266–67, 276, 279, 284

codification, 33–34

collective representations, 77–79, 224–28, 252, 257

Collins, Randall, on conflict sociology, 258, 292–98, 362 nn. 111, 118, 119, 363 n. 141

communication, 187, 189, 295 (see also ideal-speech situation; see also under consensus); and collective representation, 226–27; and conflict, 221, 315; and genuine intersubjective understanding, 249–50; "significant symbol," 247–49; and sociocultural system, 106–8, 110–12

Comte, Auguste, 2; on classification of science, 147–48, 151; on consensus, 222, 354 n. 2; and functionalism, 8, 157–60, 166; influence on Durkheim, 13–14, 16–19, 160–63, 165; on morality, 157–63, 165–66, 202, 217; on positivism, 3, 8–13, 22–23, 31–32, 70, 157, 354 n. 2; on religion, 156–60, 354 n. 2; on unity of science, 3, 26, 37, 157, 326 n. 76

concepts, 61 (see also accounts; class; constructs); analytical, 22–25, 49, 71; and collective representations, 226–27; formation of, 34–36, 45, 48–56, 364 n. 8; generic, 40–44, 48–49; "historical individuals," 328 n. 4; ideal-type, 8–9, 43–50, 52–56, 59–60, 69–72, 118, 172, 216, 342 n. 60, 348 n. 55, 364 n. 8; and indices, 18, 35; postulate of adequacy, 53–55; postulate of logical consistency, 52–55; postulate of subjective interpretations, 53–55; and rationality, 311, 322; real and implicit, 29–30

conflict, 4; class, 88–89, 134–35, 265–74, 277, 279–80, 282–89, 300, 309–10; and coercion, 262, 281–88, 294; consensual aspects of, 258, 262–63, 294, 301, 303; critique of, 300–302, 305; and division of labor, 263–67, 272–75; dysfunctional, 299–300; and equilibrium, 235, 255; and functionalism, 236, 274–77, 297–305; and historical change, 273–74, 276,

282, 286–88; in Hobbesian state of nature, 177, 258–63, 293; and ideology, 221, 270–72, 275–76, 284; imperatively coordinated association, 283; and individualism, 126–28; intensity and violence, 285–87; of interests, 257, 260, 262, 264, 266–67, 271–74, 277, 283–84, 287, 290–93, 296–97, 301; and legitimation, 288–91; in organizations, 292, 294–97; and pluralism, 285–86; and the polity, 236–37, 239–40; propositions of, 292–94; and social evolution, 246; and social order, 217, 222; and social system, 113, 247, 280–82; and status groups, 277–80, 360 n. 64, 362 n. 119; sudden and radical change, 286–87; superimposition of, 285; and values, 257–58, 278, 280–81, 295–97, 300

conflict sociology, 258, 292–98

consciousness, 187, 248 (see also consensus: and collective conscience); belief and desire, 120–22; and direct relationships, 249, 251–53, 316; and sociation, 123–25

consensus (see also under ideal-speech situation): collective affirmation, 227; and collective conscience, 222–28, 230, 232, 302; and collective representations, 224–28, 253, 257; and communication, 66–67, 180–82, 221–22, 226–29, 247–48, 254–55, 257, 290–91, 294, 314–17, 332 nn. 86, 92, 361 n. 106; -conflict debate, 2–3, 221–22, 242, 257–58, 268, 277, 280, 300, 305, 364 n. 8; and cultural standards, 229–30; cynical realism, 293; of definitions, 228–29, 253–54; and division of labor, 224, 241, 254, 274–75; and duty, 237, 300; ego-alter dyad, 228–30, 233–35; and equilibrium, 224, 233–35, 240, 245, 254–55, 276, 281, 355 n. 31; and influence, 239, 274, 356 n. 49; and instrumental activism, 230–32, 234, 238, 241–44, 246, 255, 280, 304, 314; moral standards, 229, 232–33; and power, 235–40; rational, 66–67, 180–82, 290–91, 314–17, 332 nn. 86, 92, 349 n. 84, 361 n. 106, 363 n. 139; and religion, 231–33, 242, 246, 255, 304, 354 nn. 1, 2; and significant symbol, 247–49; and social evolution, 221, 245–46, 255, 287; and social order, 217, 354 n. 2; and social status, 136–37; and society, 226–28, 230, 253; value-, 106–7, 221, 228–30, 233–35, 239–40, 242, 254, 257, 262, 274–76, 281–82, 313–14, 354 n. 1; and value-relevance, 310–11

constructs: first order (common sense) and second order (scientific), 14, 19, 39, 51–53, 56–60, 63–64, 114–15, 139, 147, 149, 312, 321–22, 365 nn. 15, 23

conventions, 167–68, 171, 177, 289, 346 n. 27

Coser, Lewis: on conflict, 298–300, 362 n. 126

critical theory, 4, 40, 288, 332 n. 92, 349 n. 84

cultural structures, 102–5, 113–14, 338 n. 11

cultural system, 26, 247, 249 (see also sociocultural system); and legitimation, 304–5; and methodological structuralism, 91–95, 102–4, 107; and normative order, 182, 304; and pattern-maintenance, 97–99, 111–12

customs (*see also* rules): 160, 165, 168, 175, 346n. 27

cybernetic hierarchy, 94, 98–99, 150, 175, 239, 276, 336n. 71

Dahrendorf, Ralf: on conflict, 258, 280–88, 294–95, 309–10

Davis, Kingsley, 357n. 66

deductive-nomological model, 28; antipositivism on, 39, 42–43, 45, 47–50, 65; and conflict, 308, 310–11; in positivism, 13, 28–33, 36, 39, 207, 308

democracy: and civil religion, 232, 304; and class conflict, 269–70, 309–10; and consensus, 221, 232, 236–40, 255, 302, 310–11; in functionalism and Marxism, 275–76; and legitimacy, 289, 291, 301, 304

determinism, 87, 114, 235, 247, 280; normative, 178, 183, 185, 188, 190, 195, 229

deviance, 122, 200, 276, 281. *See also under* norms

distributive justice, 212–13, 215, 217, 244, 274, 291, 315

division of labor, 165, 175, 202–3. *See also under* conflict; consensus

domination, 258, 264–66, 269, 274–75, 294; legitimation as, 272, 288–91, 293

Durkheim, Emile, 22, 88; on anomie, 83–84, 127–28, 131; on causality, 16–19, 21, 24, 78, 80–84, 117–18; on consensus, 222–30, 232–34, 241, 246, 253, 255, 257, 293, 298, 302, 304, 354nn. 1, 6; on functionalism, 8, 102–3, 135–36, 204–7, 215, 222, 274, 314; influence on Parsons, 177, 181, 224, 228, 233, 314; and methodological structuralism, 76–85, 91, 93–94, 99, 105, 109, 118, 125, 127–32, 145, 147–50, 311–14, 333n. 15, 334n. 29; on morality, 3, 160–66, 177, 217; on normative order, 156, 160–67, 172–73, 175, 177–78, 181, 184, 200, 216–17, 287–88, 346n. 27, 349n. 67; on positivism, 8, 13–19, 51–52, 77, 333n. 15; on religion, 29, 82, 84, 122, 224, 304, 311–13, 334n. 29, 355n. 26, 365n. 15; on social facts, 14–18, 22, 26, 31, 44, 51–52, 71, 76–84, 117–22, 127, 147–48; on social order, 204–7, 215; study of suicide, 16–17, 29, 31–33, 80–84, 101, 122, 224, 346n. 22; on utilitarianism, 2–3, 160, 204–7

economy: and adaptation, 96, 107, 112; and conflict, 87–88, 268–70, 274; and crisis, 109–12, 289, 291; and integration, 107–8; and purposive rationality, 106–7, 111–12; and social system, 98–99, 238; and societal

community, 240–41; and stratification, 243–44, 255; system interchanges, 108–11, 289, 291, 339n. 129

ego: -alter dyad, 228–30, 233–35; general thesis of the alter ego, 249–54, 316

emergence, 189–90, 317–19

empirical-theoretical system, 24, 26

Engels, Friedrich, 85, 90–91, 268–70, 289, 335n. 50

equilibrium, 18, 326n. 78 (*see also under* consensus); static and dynamic, 233–35

ethical neutrality, 21–22, 37, 39, 67, 328n. 8, 365n. 26

ethics, 268, 270–71, 315, 346n. 33, 365n. 26

ethnomethodology, 4, 40; on accounts, 56–60, 63, 190–93, 366n. 34; definition of, 56–57; on meaning-contexts, 68–69; "occasioned corpus," 191, 351n. 10; on rules, 185, 190–95; and rationality, 319–21, 366n. 39

exchange, 4, 45, 113, 345n. 103, 353n. 73; general propositions of, 207–11; and methodological individualism, 118, 136–38, 345 n. 103; and utilitarianism, 186, 206–14, 353 n. 85

facts, 313 (*see also* social facts); empirical, 26, 35, 37, 40, 364n. 8; social and natural, 10, 14, 18, 36, 39, 41–42; and theory, 28, 33, 61–62, 308–9; and value-relevance, 37, 39, 50, 62, 65, 67, 309, 311

false consciousness, 149, 271, 276, 291, 303

forms (*see also* typification): individuality, 125–32; personality, 124–28; types, 123–24, 143

Frazer, Sir James George, 346n. 36

functionalism, 4, 8, 18 (*see also* action system; social system); and conflict, 236, 297; and consensus, 222–47, 254–55, 258, 274–77, 294, 303; critiques of, 135–36, 195, 258, 277, 284–85, 288, 291, 300–305; and Marxism, 274–77, 282; and methodological structuralism, 76, 85, 102–3, 135–36, 138–39, 337n. 101; and morality, 156–60, 177–78; and normative order, 156, 164, 184, 188; and reification, 344n. 92; and rationality, 313–14; and religion, 312, 355n. 26; and utilitarianism, 204–7

Garfinkel, Harold: on ethnomethodology, 56–60, 64, 68, 190–92, 319, 366n. 34

generalizations, 34, 57, 65, 69–70, 281–82 (*see also* propositions); *a priori*, 34; empirical and higher-order, 32–33, 35–36, 45, 47–48, 207, 292, 295–96; and value-relevance, 42–43, 50, 56, 71, 309–10

generalized other, 187–88, 249, 253

gentile society, 268–69

goal-attainment (*see also under* polity): 95–98, 150, 337n. 101

goals (*see also* norms: means-ends chain): and

370   Index

conflict, 257, 260, 284, 290, 297, 300, 308; and consensus, 95–96, 235–40, 242, 254, 262, 275, 299, 303–5, 308, 310, 354 n. 1
God, 159, 162, 201, 225; in Calvinism, 231–33, 244, 246, 304

Habermas, Jürgen, 71, 339 n. 129; on antipositivism, 60–67; on capitalism, 106–12, 361 n. 106; on conflict, 288–91, 363 n. 139; and methodological structuralism, 106–12; on normative order, 178–82, 288, 314–15, 349 nn. 83, 84
Hegel, George W. F., 270–71, 276
hermeneutics, 60–69
historical materialism, 87–91, 134–35, 149, 263–64, 268–74
Hobbes, Thomas, 7, 293; on conflict, 177, 258–63; on social order, 2–3, 206–7, 258; and utilitarianism, 206–7
Homans, George C.: on exchange theory, 345 n. 103, 353 n. 85; on methodological individualism, 118, 135–39, 343 n. 64; on positivism, 26–32; on social order, 207–15; utilitarianism in, 207–14
Husserl, Edmund, 50, 249
hypothetico-deductive theory. See deductive-nomological model

ideal-speech situation: and consensus, 66–67, 315, 332 nn. 86, 92, 361 n. 106, 363 n. 139; and legitimation of norms, 180, 361 n. 106, 363 n. 139
ideology, 221, 270–73, 275–76, 284, 289–91
imitation, 120–22
individual (see also ego; methodological individualism; organism; personality; reflexive self; self-interest; see also under methodological structuralism): integration of, 96–97, 159–60, 176; and irrationality, 313–14; and law of equal freedom, 201–4; and morality, 161–66, 176–77; and normative order, 157–69, 166, 174–78, 182–84; ontological nature of, 3, 75–80, 82–89, 105, 112–13, 311, 334 nn. 30, 45
individuality, 125–32, 231, 341 n. 26; and freedom, 129–32, 164, 231, 321–22
induction, 16, 19
instrumental activism, 291, 357 n. 61. See also under consensus
integration, 101, 121, 150, 198, 337 n. 101 (see also under normative order; norms; societal community; sociocultural system); conflict, 97, 257, 281–85, 287, 299–300; and consensus, 224–25, 229–30, 235, 238–41, 245–46, 253, 257, 276, 280, 293; and definition of, 95–98; mal-, 104–5; and morality, 176–78, 181; and normative order, 159–60, 181–84, 195, 215; and stratification, 97, 138–39, 313; system, 107–8, 113, 338 n. 123; value, 146–47

interests (see also self-interest; see also under conflict): artificial identification of, 198–201; general, 87, 180, 183–84, 186, 290–91, 302, 315; identity of, 185–86; knowledge-constitutive, 61–62, 67; latent and manifest, 283–84; natural identity of, 198, 200–201, 203, 207; objective and subjective, 88–89; objective class, 86–89, 148–49, 266–67, 284–85, 342 n. 58; and rationality, 364 n. 8; of status groups, 278–79; sympathetic fusion of, 198, 200, 212
irrationality (see also rationality): 169–70, 172, 215–16, 315, 346 n. 36, 347 n. 37, 349 n. 74, 353 n. 96, 365 n. 26

Kant, Immanuel, 8; on morality, 162–63; on nature, 122–23
Kuhn, Thomas S., 1

language, 250–51. See also communication; ideal-speech situation
law (legal) (see also legitimate order; normative order; norms; rules): and equilibrium, 234; and formalism, 165, 175; goal of, 155, 174, 179–80; and morality, 156, 160; and norms, 348 n. 63; and rationality, 155, 183; and utilitarianism, 198–200, 203, 205
law (scientific) (see also deductive-nomological model): abstract and concrete, 11–12, 23, 47; of action, 326 n. 68; of adaptation, 202; analytical, 23–24, 43, 49, 308; and causality, 18, 35, 40–41; of equal freedom, 201–4, 213; of the excluded middle, 36; "law of three stages," 9–11, 13, 157; and morality, 201–2; natural, 75, 179, 196, 206–7, 259–61, 290–91; natural and social, 13–14, 42–43, 196–97, 329 n. 32; nomology, 47–48, 69–70; of proportionality, 16; of rationality, 24, 43, 313; of social process, 233; static and dynamic, 11–12, 156–57; universal, 10, 40–41, 43, 47–48; and utilitarianism, 196–201, 203–5
legitimacy. See under legitimate order; polity; state
legitimate order: and authority, 171–74, 301–2; and conflict, 305; and consensus, 301–3, 321; definition of, 167, 346 n. 27; and ethics, 349 n. 33; and integration, 97, 177; lawmaking and lawfinding, 168–70, 178, 184–85, 302, 346 n. 35; legitimacy of, 167–74, 178–84, 269, 302–3, 349 nn. 83, 84; and methodological individualism, 166; and rationality, 169–73, 178–80, 182–83, 301, 321–22, 346 n. 36, 347 n. 37, 347 n. 42; in social system, 173, 177
Lévi-Strauss, Claude, 332 n. 3
lifeworld (Lebenswelt), 66, 107, 111, 339 n. 133; formation of, 181–82
Locke, John: and utilitarianism, 206

Machiavelli, Niccolo, 293
Marshall, T. H., 241
Marx, Karl, 2, 106, 281; on conflict, 88–89, 258, 263–77, 282–89, 291, 293–94, 300, 360 n. 56; Dahrendorf's revision of, 282–88; and methodological structuralism, 84–91, 109–12, 118, 132, 134–35, 148–49, 344 n. 92; Weber's critique of, 134–35, 258, 277–80, 342 n. 58
Mead, George H., 4; on action, reconstruction of, 186–91, 194, 251, 293–94, 317–21, 366 n. 34; on consensus, 222, 247–49, 253
meaning, 39, 61–63 (see also accounts; constructs: first and second order; lifeworld; understanding); objective and subjective, 45–47, 53–56, 59–60, 70–71, 250–53, 330 n. 55
meaning-complexes, 64
meaning-contexts, 53–54, 60, 67–69, 118, 252, 305, 316, 332 n. 92
Merton, Robert K.: on functionalism, · 8; and methodological structuralism, 102–5; on positivism, 32–35
metaphysics, 16, 37, 135, 207, 330 n. 57; and "law of three stages," 9–10, 13, 157
methodological individualism, 2–3; and action, 132–33, 139–47; and social class, 134–35; and collective conscience, 119–21; and consciousness, 120–25; definition of, 76, 117–18; and forms, 141–43, 341 n. 24; and groups, 128–31; and imitation, 120–22; and individuality, 125–32; and rationality, 146, 322; and reification, 145–51; and social facts, 118–21, 135–36, 148; and social status, 136–39; and sociation, 123–28, 341 n. 24
methodological structuralism: and action, 91–99, 103, 108, 140, 146–47; and anomie, 83–84, 103–5, 113, 127–28, 131; and capitalism, 85–91, 106–12; critique of, 118–21; definition of, 75–76, 332 n. 3; and determinism, 115; and historical materialism, 87–91, 149; and the individual, 2–3, 14–15, 101–9, 113–14, 125–32, 135, 314, 334 nn. 30, 34; and modern medical practice, 99–102; and reification, 145–51, 311–14, 344 nn. 92, 97, 365 n. 23; and religion, 311–13, 334 n. 29, 365 n. 15; and social facts, 14–15, 76–84, 117–19, 127, 135–36, 147–48, 333 n. 15; and the social system, 92–109, 144–48, 344 n. 97; and sociocultural structures, 102–14
methodology (see also antipositivism; ethnomethodology; positivism): of natural vs. social sciences, 36–37, 40–43, 48, 51–52; scientific observation, 15–16, 69–70
Meyer, Eduard, 20
Mill, John Stuart: on causality, 16–17, 21, 24
Moore, Wilbert E., 357 n. 66
morality, 271 (see also rules: and moral duty); and attachment, 160, 162–63; and authority, 161–66, 172–73, 181, 183, 288, 311–12;

autonomy, 163; and consensus, 222, 229, 232–33, 257, 354 n. 1; definition of, 157; and discipline, 161–63, 200; and methodological structuralism, 127, 311–12, 365 n. 15; and normative order, 155, 176–78, 184, 186, 229, 274, 287, 298, 348 n. 66; science of, 157–66, 173, 217; vs. self-interest, 156–62, 164, 166, 183–84, 186, 202, 206; in state of nature, 259–60; and utilitarianism, 3, 160, 196–98, 200–202, 206

natural science, 30–31 (see also science); as model for social science, 1–3, 7–8, 13–15, 18, 21, 35, 37, 52, 57; relationship to social science, 27, 40–42, 46–47, 50, 323 n. 4, 331 n. 72
normative order (see also legitimate order; social order): and coercion, 287–88, 296–98; and collectivities, 174–78; and conflict, 298; and consensus, 229, 234–35, 245–46, 254, 297; critiques of, 185–86, 188, 190–91, 194–95, 200, 204; definition of, 155–56; and duty, 155, 173, 176; and integration, 159–60, 176–78, 181–84, 195, 215; interpretation of, 215–16; and legal system, 241; legitimacy of, 98, 156, 178–83, 214–17, 232–33, 275, 303–4, 321–22; and methodological structuralism, 118; and morality, 156–67, 172–73, 176–78, 181, 183–84, 200, 214–17, 349 n. 67; and rationality, 319; and the reflexive self, 188; and religion, 156–60, 166, 216–17; and role-expectations, 182, 343 n. 76; and social system, 173–78, 181–84; and stratification, 242, 287–88; and values, 156, 173–78, 181, 185, 214–15, 348 n. 55, 349 nn. 67, 70; and utilitarianism, 185, 195, 200, 206–7
norms (see also law [legal]; rules): and action, 93, 97, 139–46, 144–45, 150; as analytical element, 23–24; and anomie, 103–5; and conflict, 274–75, 297, 299–300; and consensus, 228–29, 233, 235, 239–40, 242, 253–54; definition of, 173–74, 348 n. 57; and deviance, 100–101, 104–5, 233–35, 287, 338 n. 111; and domination, 288; and goals, 180, 212, 235, 319; and integration, 97, 103–5, 144–45; interpretation of, 232, 253; legitimacy of, 103, 175, 180–82, 238–39, 288, 301, 307, 314–15, 361 n. 106, 363 n. 139; as legitimation, 288–91; means-ends chain, 139, 173–76, 181–84, 206, 319–20, 349 n. 67; pattern variables, 176–77, 229, 348 n. 66; and rationality, 165; and roles, 248, 253; and self-interest, 212–14; and sociocultural system, 106–8, 110; and values, 241, 253

objectivism, 62, 64–65, 67, 148, 180, 350 n. 84
organism (system), 91–94, 99, 182, 336 n. 66, 355 n. 31

372   Index

paradigms, 33–34, 102, 337 n. 101
Parsons, Talcott, 27, 106, 364 n. 7; on action
  system, 23–26, 49–50, 91–94, 138–40, 144–
  50, 181–82, 248; on conflict, 247, 258, 262,
  298–300, 310, 362 n. 126; on consensus,
  221–22, 228–47, 253–55, 274–77, 280–82,
  291, 302–5, 309–10, 355 n. 31, 356 n. 39,
  357 n. 57, 363 nn. 144, 151; on functionalism, 4, 8, 102–3, 135–36, 195, 204, 206–7,
  221, 274–77, 313–14, 337 n. 101; and methodological structuralism, 76, 91–102, 105,
  118, 145–50, 344 n. 97; on normative order,
  156, 159–60, 173–78, 181–82, 215, 287–88,
  298, 349 n. 74; on positivism, 22–26, 28, 43,
  49–50, 308–9, 323 n. 4; on social order, 2,
  204, 206–7, 215, 298, 300; on social system,
  72, 92–99, 107–8, 112, 144–45, 150, 159–
  60, 224, 257, 280–82, 299–300, 337 n. 101,
  339 n. 129; on utilitarianism, 3, 204, 206–7,
  262
pattern-maintenance (fiduciary subsystem), 150,
  240, 337 n. 101 (see also under cultural system; sociocultural system); and conflict, 257,
  299–300; and consensus, 224, 243–46, 257;
  definition of, 95, 97; and legitimacy, 238,
  303, 363 n. 144
personality, 106, 128, 182 (see also individual;
  see also under forms); and action system, 26,
  91–94, 336 n. 66; and consensus, 229–30,
  235; and methodological individualism, 144,
  149–50; and social system, 93–95; 97–99,
  144, 146, 150, 313
phenomenology, 4, 344 n. 92, 366 n. 39; and
  action, 139–45, 320–21; and antipositivism,
  40, 50–56, 63, 147; and consensus, 249–55;
  and integration, 144–45; and methodological
  individualism, 117–18, 140, 147–49
philosophy, 268, 270–72, 323 n. 5
Plato, 281; on conflict, 221, 258, 357 n. 57;
  doctrine of Ideas, 119; on law, 155–56; on
  moral restraint, 346 n. 22
polity (see also state): and consensus, 235–40,
  262, 268, 310; and goal-attainment, 95–96;
  107–8, 112, 235–40, 244, 275, 291, 302–5,
  310, 321–22; legitimacy of, 303–4, 363 n.
  144; and pattern-maintenance, 363 n. 144;
  political support system, 238–40, 356 n. 49;
  and social system, 98–99, 336 n. 83; and
  stratification, 244–45
Pollner, Melvin, 351 n. 10
positivism, 7–8, 69, 72, 197, 323 n. 5, 354 n. 2;
  and action system, 23–26, 49–50; and analytical realism, 22–25, 49; and causality, 7, 9,
  16–21, 36; deductive-nomological model, 13,
  28–33, 36, 39, 207, 308; and ethical neutrality, 21–22, 37; "law of three stages," 9–11,
  13, 156–57; and propositions, 26–32, 36,
  308; and rationality, 308–11; and social facts,
  11, 14–19, 21–22, 26, 31, 36, 39, 44, 51–

52, 71, 77, 151, 333 n. 15; and social theory,
  28, 31–35; and unity of science, 3, 10–13,
  25–27, 35–37, 157
power: and coercion, 262, 277, 288, 293–94;
  and conflict, 217, 258, 273, 292–98; in conflict and functional theory, 297, 300–305;
  and consensus, 180, 221, 238–40, 254, 274–
  76, 310, 356 n. 49; definition of, 236, 301; in
  division of labor, 264–65; and goals, 257,
  275; and ideology, 272, 276, 294–95, 297;
  and legitimation, 288, 290, 301; in Marxism
  and functional theory, 274–77; and norms,
  274–75, 288–90; organizational, 292, 294–
  97; as rational instrument, 257, 260, 262; and
  the state, 268–71
privatism, civil and familial-vocational, 110–11,
  179, 289–91
property, 264–65, 273–74, 293. See also under
  class (social)
propositions, 27–32, 36, 308. See also generalizations
Protestantism, 280, 291, 304, 363 n. 151
psychology, 207, 248, 259, 327 n. 95. 353 n.
  73; relationship to sociology, 78, 80, 102–3,
  114, 119–22, 125, 136, 333 n. 22

rationality, 340 n. 145 (see also under consensus;
  legitimate order); economic, 146; formal,
  301, 307–8, 346 n. 35; of goals, 319–21; and
  methodological structuralism, 311–14; moral
  and instrumental, 213, 259–61; and normative order, 184, 307, 348 n. 55, 349 n. 67; vs.
  objectivism, 315; purposive (Zweckrationalität), 47–48, 55, 106–7, 110–12, 216, 348 n.
  55; and reconstruction of action, 317–22; and
  reflective intelligence, 189, 194, 317; and
  reification, 308, 311–14; and rules, 165, 212,
  214–17, 319, 322; subjective, 314–15; subjective and objective, 307, 320; substantive, 214,
  217, 301, 303, 307–8, 321, 346 n. 35; and
  utilitarianism, 185, 206, 262; value (Wertrationalität), 215–16, 313–15, 340 n. 145, 348
  n. 55
reflective intelligence, 189, 194, 317
reflexive self, 186–90, 194–95, 249, 251, 253,
  318–20, 350 n. 9
reflexivity, 69, 191–93
religion, 268; civil, 303–4, 363 n. 151; and
  conflict, 87–88, 270–71; constitutive symbolism, 107, 233, 303–5; of humanity, 158–59,
  162–63, 166, 354 n. 2; and integration, 224–
  25; and methodological structuralism, 311–
  13, 334 n. 29, 365 n. 15; and morality, 157–
  59, 162, 166, 231–33, 304; and normative
  order, 156–60, 179, 216–17, 303–4; and rationality, 312–13, 365 n. 15; and reification,
  311–14; and social system, 232–33, 255, 355
  n. 26
revolution, 134, 342 n. 58; conditions of, 272–

Index   373

73, 334n. 44, 360n. 56; and historical change, 272–74, 276; and methodological structuralism, 89–91

Rheinstein, Max, 347nn. 42, 43

ritual: and conflict, 293–94, 296–98; religious, 159, 166, 224, 233, 311–13; and solidarity, 293, 298

role-expectations, 92–94, 182, 284, 343n. 76

roles, 124; of generalized other, 187–89, 248–49; and latent interests, 283–84; and norms, 99–101, 135, 174–78, 215, 233–35, 248, 253, 274; and social system, 93, 97, 99–101, 229, 243–44, 248, 254; and stratification, 243–44, 275

rules (see also conventions; law; norms; see also under social order): authority of, 161–62, 164, 172–73, 178, 181, 183, 215; and conflict, 286, 300; and consensus, 217, 223, 310; ethnomethodological theory of, 190–95; and formalism, 165, 170, 175, 184; goals of, 183, 186, 214–16; ideal-type, 215–16; interpretation of, 350n. 9; legitimacy of, 167–68, 171–72, 214, 216–17; maxims, 189; and moral duty, 3, 155–56, 160–67, 172, 178, 183, 186, 197, 200, 214–17, 222, 257, 312, 349 n. 67; and novelty, 186, 318–19; role of, 188, 190, 193–95, 204–6, 351n. 23; and social order, 2–3, 185–86, 217, 349n. 84; and utilitarianism, 160, 186, 204–6, 213–14

schema: expressive and interpretive, 251–53

Schutz: on antipositivism, 50–56, 59–60; on consensus, 222, 249–54, 294, 314, 316–17, 358n. 83; and methodological individualism, 139–45; and phenomenology, 4, 50–51, 55–56, 63–64, 139, 147, 320–21

science (see also natural science): classification of, 147–48, 151; critical, 60–61, 67, 331n. 72; definition of, 7; empirical-analytical, 60–64; goals of, 26–28, 30–32, 46; historical-hermeneutic, 60–66; as legitimation, 290; materialism, 75, 259; unity of, 3, 10–13, 25–27, 35–36, 157

self-interest, 275; and conflict, 177, 205, 292–94, 297; vs. morality, 156–62, 164, 186, 202, 206; and normative order, 156–64, 180, 182–84, 214, 216–17; and social order, 3, 160, 185–86, 195, 200, 203–7, 211, 213–14, 217

Simmel, Georg, 329n. 32; on conflict, 298, 300, 362n. 126; on forms, 123–28, 143; and methodological individualism, 118, 122–32, 143, 145

Smith, Adam: and utilitarianism, 201–2, 207

social control, 234–35

social evolution, 11–12, 18, 156–67, 221, 291; adaptive upgrading, 245; differentiation, 245–46; integration, 245–46; and utilitarianism, 201–4; value-generalization, 246, 276

social facts, 305 (see also under methodological individualism; methodological structuralism; positivism); and causality, 16–21, 78–84, 117–18; definitions of, 15–16, 80, 120

socialization, 234–35, 253

social order, 242 (see also normative order); and collective conscience, 293; and conflict, 2, 205, 217, 222, 298–300, 362n. 126; contractual relations, 204–7, 214; and distributive justice, 212–13, 215, 217; and ethnomethodology, 58, 60, 68, 190–95; and exchange theory, 207–14; and functionalism, 195, 204–7; in industrial societies, 202–5; nomological, 11, 35–37; and rationality, 260, 319–20; reflexive self, 186–90, 194–95; and revolution, 273–74; and rules, 2–3, 145, 155–56, 185–86, 188, 190–95, 198–200, 203–6, 212–17, 349n. 84; and utilitarianism, 3, 196–214

social relationships (see also ego; reflexive self): associative and communal, 133–34; contractual, 204–7, 214; direct, 150–51, 207, 314, 316–17; direct and indirect, 53–55, 144, 249–53, 358n. 83

social science (see also science; see also under natural science): definition of, 327n. 1; goals of, 19, 30–31, 47, 51, 56, 61–62, 67, 102–5, 165–66, 174–75

social structures, 102–5, 165–66, 174–75; ontological nature of, 75–80, 82–91, 112–15, 117–18, 133, 344n. 92; reification of, 145–51, 312–14

social system, 25–26 (see also adaptation; goal-attainment; integration; pattern-maintenance); and conflict, 299–300; and consensus, 221, 228–47, 254, 302–3; critique of, 72, 280–82; and equilibrium, 233–35, 281, 356n. 39; goals of, 305, 313; latent functions of, 100–102; and methodological individualism, 138–39, 144–45, 150; and methodological structuralism, 91–103, 106, 146–48, 344n. 97; and rationality, 182, 313–14; and roles, 92–94, 243–44, 248; system interchanges, 108, 113, 237–40, 303, 339n. 129, 356n. 39

societal community: and consensus, 236, 238–44; and cybernetic hierarchy, 98–99; democratic association, 238–39; and inclusion, 241–42, 255; and instrumental activism, 241–42, 255; and integration, 98, 238–41, 246, 339n. 129; and stratification, 242–44

society (see also methodological structuralism): definition of, 120–21, 324n. 36; ontological nature of, 2, 122–26, 132, 162, 312, 343n. 74

sociocultural system: and integration, 107–8, 112–13, 339n. 129; and pattern-maintenance, 107–8, 339n. 129; and rationality, 112, 340

374   Index

n. 145; system interchanges, 108–11, 114, 129, 339 n. 129; and values, 106–8, 110–11
sociology (*see also* social science): definitions of, 14, 325 n. 48, 328 n. 31, 330 n. 60; goals of, 19, 35–36, 62, 132, 156–57
Socrates: and morality, 165–66
solidarity, 97, 133; and conflict, 280, 294, 298; and consensus, 230, 244, 254–55, 293, 310; mechanical, 17–18, 223–28, 230, 232, 240–41, 257, 296; organic, 17–18, 230, 241–42, 246; and religion, 233, 304
Sophists, 156, 166
Spencer, Herbert, 2; on social evolution, 201–2, 245; on social order, 201–5, 213, 353 n. 96; on utilitarianism, 201–5, 213
state, the, 338 n. 121 (*see also* polity); and class, 268–73, 275, 289; and coercion, 262–63, 301–2, 346 n. 31, 363 n. 141; and conflict, 87–88, 257–58, 267–71, 276, 309–10; definition of, 346 n. 31; and ideology, 270–72, 301–2; and integration, 107–8; and law of equal freedom, 203–5; legitimacy of, 100–112, 289–91, 180, 301–2, 321–22, 339 n. 129; and legitimate order, 168, 269, 301; Marxist and functional theories of, 275–77, 289; and methodological structuralism, 107–12; and normative order, 155, 216; origin of, 261, 268–70; and power, 261–62, 290; and revolution, 273–74; and state of nature, 259, 261–62; system interchanges, 108–11, 339 n. 129
statistics, 45, 47, 71, 81–82, 121–22, 333 n. 15
status groups, 277–80, 293, 360 n. 64, 362 n. 119
stratification (*see also under* integration): and conflict, 242, 257–58, 287–88, 292–95; and consensus, 221, 254, 275; in functionalism and Marxism, 275–76; organizational, 292, 294–95; and social order, 242–44; and societal community, 242–44, 357 n. 66
suicide: and causality, 16–17, and consensus, 224–25; and deductive-nomological model, 29, 31–33; and methodological structuralism, 80–84, 101, 122; and moral restraint, 82, 346 n. 22; types of, 16, 82–84, 333 n. 24
symbolic interactionism, 4, 71–72, 366 n. 39; and consensus, 247–49, 255; and methodological individualism, 118; and social order, 185–190, 195, 350 n. 9

Tarde, Gabriel, 2, 118–22
theology, 330 n. 57; and "law of three stages," 9–10, 13, 157
typification, 61, 141–45, 253

understanding (*see also* hermeneutics): genuine intersubjective (*Verstehen*), 249–54, 315–17
universal pragmatics, 180, 314, 361 n. 106
utilitarianism, 2, 262; and social order, 3, 160, 186, 195–217
utility, principle of, 196–201, 203, 210–11, 214

value-relevance, 310–11, 328 n. 8; and antipositivism, 42–46, 48, 50; and rationality, 315, 364 n. 8; and stratification, 243–44
values (*see also* ethical neutrality; *see also under* conflict; consensus; rationality): absolute, 216, 348 n. 55; generalized, 246, 313–14; and goals, 235–36, 239, 275; and interests, 214–16, 358 n. 1; and legitimacy, 181, 183, 275–76, 289, 291, 355 n. 26; means-ends chain, 175–79, 314; norms and, 139, 146–47, 150, 175–79, 183, 235, 239, 275, 289, 291, 319; scarce, 287; and status groups, 278, 280; ultimate, 174–78, 185, 206, 315, 348 n. 55, 349 nn. 67, 70, 74, 365 n. 26
value-system, 227, 231, 243, 275, 305
voluntaristic theory, 325 n. 61

Weber, Max, 106, 111, 340 n. 145; on antipositivism, 19, 39–51, 55, 67, 309; on Calvinism, 231, 244; on conflict, 258, 277–80, 283, 288, 293, 296, 315, 360 n. 64, 362 n. 119; on ideal-types, 35–37, 43–49, 52–56, 59–60, 69–71, 112; influence of, 2, 4, 24, 43, 52–55, 174, 178, 231, 258; on legitimate order, 166–74, 178–82, 301–2, 349 nn. 67, 70, 83, 84, 363 n. 139; and methodological individualism, 118, 132–35, 139; and methodological structuralism, 106, 112, 313; on normative order, 185, 216, 307, 348 n. 55; on social action theory, 51, 132–33, 216, 249
Whitehead, Alfred North, 75
Wieder, D. Lawrence: on ethnomethodology, 192–93
world views, 107, 315, 319; and legitimacy, 108, 110–11, 179, 181, 232, 276

Zimmerman, Don H.: on ethnomethodology, 193–95, 351 n. 10